Shakin' All Over

The Birth of British R&B

by

Keith Hunt

The Life And Times Of

Johnny Kidd

Published by

The Magnum Imprint
Magnum House
High Street
Lane End
Buckinghamshire, HP14 3JG
UNITED KINGDOM

Printed in the United Kingdom

ISBN 0 9527961 0 4

Shakin' All Over

by

Keith Hunt

CONTENTS

	Foreword
	Acknowledgements
	Introduction
	Ahoy! Shipmates
Chapter 1	Yes Sir, That's My Baby (1935-55)
Chapter 2	Putting On The Donegan (1955-58)
Chapter 3	Over The Rainbow
Chapter 4	The Five Nutters
Chapter 5	The Fabulous Freddie Heath Band (1958-59)
Chapter 6	The Fred, Mike and Tom Show
Chapter 7	Johnny Kidd and The Pirates (1959)
Chapter 8	The Purple Patch (1960)
Chapter 9	Shakin' All Over (1960)
Chapter 10	Jumps, Giggles and Shouts (1961)
Chapter 11	A Shot Of Rhythm and Blues (1962)
Chapter 12	Ecstasy (High on Life) (1963)
Chapter 13	Right String But the Wrong YoYo (1964)
Chapter 14	Gotta Travel On (1965)
Chapter 15	The Day The World Turned Blue (1966)
Chapter 16	I'll Never Get Over You
Chapter 17	Always and Ever
Chapter 18	Retrospect
	Discography
	Family Tree

Foreword

I am delighted that we have been able to launch The Magnum Imprint with this tribute to the legendary Johnny Kidd.

A clear theme throughout the book is the extent to which the contributing artists and musicians recognise not only the importance of Johnny Kidd in regard to the development of British rhythm and blues but also the influence of him as an individual on them and their careers.

I first saw Johnny Kidd and the Pirates on stage at the Carfax Assembly Rooms in Oxford on 10th April, 1962 followed not long afterwards at Oxford Town Hall on the Bruce Channel tour. Some years later I also caught one of the outstanding package tours of the time at the Slough Adelphi.

During the late-1970's, as the General Manager of Warner Brothers Records, I was fortunate to work with Mick Green, Johnny Spence and Frank Farley in the re-formed Pirates as a power rock trio. The band created an extraordinary following amongst young rock enthusiasts which was not dissimilar to the reaction to Johnny Kidd and the Pirates in the early 1960's.

Johnny Kidd was, without question, one of the most important and influential artists to emerge from the UK. However, until this time, his contribution has largely gone unrecognised. It is that recognition that is provided by this tribute for the first time.

Nigel Molden
May, 1996

As this book was about to go to print we learnt of the death of Keith Hunt. In consultation with his parents it was agreed that the publication of the book should go ahead as a tribute to the life and work of the author.

ACKNOWLEDGEMENTS

Over the years I've read far too many books about rock stars by authors who have never even met their subjects. That's why this book is special because its a true story told through the words of Johnny Kidd himself plus the people who knew and loved him. Although I saw Johnny live on stage, sadly I never had the pleasure of meeting the great man. Since working on this project and meeting various friends and members of his groups, I now feel like I met Johnny. I hope after reading this tribute you will feel the same.

I would like to thank the following people for their assistance and endeavours in helping me with this tribute. Unlike other books I want to acknowledge everyone who helped no matter how little. Mrs J.Y. Moir-Heath, Cilla Heath, Alan Wheeler, Mike and Pat West, Don Toy, Walter J Ridley, Clive Lazell, Frank Rouledge, Johnny Irving, Brian Gregg, Mick Green, Frank Farley, Pete Newman, Clem Cattini, Suzanne Heath, Nick Simper, Brian Saunders, Bert Weedon, John Kerrison, Lord Sutch, Alan Carter, Derek Ron and Yvonne Everard, the late Tubby Rich, Ray Hinton, Brian Jones, Jack Good, Roger Dean, Bobby Elliot, Colin Richards, Mike Rudzinski, Brian Woods, Lez Richards, Peter Wilson, Don Craine, Frank Allen, Pennie Ort, Emily and Danny Rivers, Pepe Rush, Sid Holder, Sandy Regan, Tony Jackson, Tony Dangerfield, Colin Pryce Jones, Wild Bob Burges, Keith Fordyce, Barry Hammett, Raye-Du-Val, Peter Fleerackers, Wally Whyton, Bob Potter O.B.E., John Braley, Phil Guidal, Joe Waite, Stuart Lowes, Rob Bradford, Ron Long, Chas McDevitt, Rick Richards, David J Burgess, Ernst August Cordes, Brian Bowman, Roger Dopson, Roger Arthur, John Firminger, Pete Johnson, Tim Adams, Simon Norris, Graham Self, Harry Sharpe, Paul Smith, Vic Lanza, Peter Bryan, Terry and Sylvia Calloway, Christian Nauwelaers, Bill Taylor, Steve Golly, Bob Rogers, Ivor Knight, the late Kenneth Connor, John Watman, Bruce Welch, Darren Vidler, Brian F Carney, Dave Lilley, Alan Blake, Andy Sztehlo, Rik Berry, Mark Dillman, Fred Philip, Lennart Johansson, Hans Siden, Peter Searles, Mike Bate, Daphne Yardley, Harry Greenway M.P., Barry P Allchin, Dr Ramesh Bart, Mark Newson, Thierry Pannetier (E.M.I.), Maurice Preece, Hugh and Ruth McCallum, Val Bird (Pollytone), Big Del Richardson, Wild Cat Pete, Stuart Coleman, Geoff Barker, Torill Olsen, Alan Taylor and Dave Burke (Pipeline), John Repch (Joe Meek Appreciation Society), Tor Arne Petzold (RnR Society of Scandinavia), Evert Heijnen (Boothill), Dave Peckett (Gandy Dancer), Yann Tear, Russell Newmark, Bert Bossink (Sounds of 60's), Molly Lee, Louise Powell, The Grange Museum, Mick Hill (Rock You Sinners), Now Dig This, special acknowledgements to N.M.E., New Record Mirror, Pop Weekly, Melody Maker, Disc, Willesden Chronicle and my Rockin mates Reg Paine, George Collier, Allan Jarrett (FARX) Jeff Hawkins, Steve Witcher, Arnaud Fontenier (Paris).

A Cannon Salute for Nigel Molden and the Magnum Music Group for being on our wave-length and navigating the final voyage by publishing this tribute for Johnny Kidd for us all to treasure.

© A. S. Lowes

Extra special thanks to my Mum and Dad, brother Dave and my niece Kellie who now knows more about Johnny Kidd's life and music than she should ever need to know.

INTRODUCTION

I'm very proud of the fact that I was born in the same year that Bill Haley and The Comets recorded the first authentic rock 'n' roll (1952). As a young child thanks to my Mother Irene and Father Basil our home was always filled with love plus the sounds of Johnnie Ray, Alma Cogan, Bing Crosby, Connie Francis, Michael Holliday, Dickie Valentine, Bill Haley and Skiffle.

In 1956 at the tender age of 4 I can remember Mum liking Tommy Steele, while my Aunty Iris preferred the American Guy Mitchell 'Singing The Blues'. I, of course, supported my Mum's choice and soon found myself being taken along to the local cinema with my Mum and Nan to see "The Tommy Steele Story".

That was it. 'Cannibal Pot' was my favourite song and Tommy Steele my first idol since Hank the Puppet. For my 5th birthday Nan bought me a red tin guitar, which within a few seconds fell in half (as I grew up I seemed to have the same effect on every musical instrument).

So I've been spinning records since 1958 that's when I bought my very first records "Hound Dog" by Elvis on 78 and Sheb Wooleys "Purple People Eater" on 45. "Ma He's Making Eyes At Me" by Johnny Otis with Marie Adams and "Putting On the Style" by Lonnie Donegan were the most played in our home. I now had my own hero in Lonnie Donegan he was far too frantic for Mum and Dad. 1959 and the rocking decade died with Emile Ford and the Checkmates very original "What Do You Want to Make Those Eyes At Me For" at the top of the charts. This took us from the foot tapping 50's into the swinging 60's. My latest idol was Yogi Bear and yes he did make records. My first LP was entitled "Yogi Bear TV sound tracks on Golden Guinea". Exciting sounds were everywhere Shadows, Elvis, Eddie Cochran, Gene Vincent, Buddy Holly, Billy Fury, Del Shannon, Cliff Richard, Adam Faith, Eden Kane, Johnny Preston and my new idol Joe Brown.

By 1962 Mum found Frank Ifield and I found beat groups and Joe Meek productions. My Brother Dave had just started work so he had the money to buy all the latest 45's. Our home was once again filled with magical sounds Tornados, Spotnicks, Tommy Roe, Chuck Berry, Beatles, Bobby Vee, Searchers, Hollies. Television was also great fun with many Westerns, The Flintstones, 77 Sunset Strip, Route 66, Top Cat, Super Car, Robin Hood and my favourite 'The Buccaneers' which starred Robert Shaw.

Robert Shaw in The Buccaneers
(Always N' Ever Archive)

My greatest school pal Derek Bernard and I would rush home from school and dress up as pirates and try to act like Robert Shaw. After seeing the film 'Pirates of Blood River' starring Christopher Lee and seeing Johnny Kidd on Thank Your Lucky Stars, I would never be the same again.

In 1964 Derek got a copy of "Always 'n' Ever" I was very jealous because I'd spent all my (5/-) pocket money.
I lost contact with Derek during our teenage years. Out of the blue in 1990 Derek got in touch. We met and laughed at our buccaneer antics and his love of The Dave Clark 5, I told him that I was writing a book about the life and career of Johnny Kidd and how I was upset that he had the "Always 'n' Ever" single all those years ago.

He went into the next room and came out with that original 45 which he gladly gave to me after 26 years and then wished me all the best with the book. I now have a complete set of Johnny's singles.

Sadly a few months later Derek died suddenly. This book is dedicated to my best school mate with whom I shared many hours listening to the magical sounds of Johnny Kidd and The Pirates and of course Mum and Dad, Brother David (QPR nut) and my teenage niece Kellie, who when I first started my research was a Bros fanatic now it's Take That. Myself I'm a Johnny Kidd and The Pirates fan for Always n' Ever.

Keith Hunt,
January, 1996

In memory of

Helen Reid
Derek Bernard
Lee Brilleaux
Les Bennett
and
Johnny Kidd

"It has been my hard luck many times to choose between what I thought was the truth and a good pay cheque. That's why I go around so truthfully broke, I reckon".
(Woody Guthrie)

Johnny Kidd

AHOY! SHIPMATES

Welcome onboard land-lubbers and sail through the pioneering days of British rock. Enlist on a voyage through skiffle, rock 'n' roll, R&B, and beat with the Admiral of British Beat - Captain Johnny Kidd and his various crews of Pirates.

Cast anchor and read how Kidd was amongst the very first British rockers to write his own songs. As early as 1959 he wanted to hear his voice under the same acoustic conditions as he sounded on his records, so he started using a tape echo-chamber. The first vocalist in Britain to use echo equipment during live performances. Apart from his very original pirate image he was the first to use lighting effects.

The first to carry around his own stage back drop which consisted of a huge backcloth painted twenty feet high and forty feet long of a big galleon. It was painted with ultra violet paint to give the effect of a galleon in harbour. Three ultra violet lights shone up front to give full impact. The Pirates were the first real powerhouse trio. It looked more symmetrical with a bass and guitar at each side, drums behind and a singer out in front. Swinging a cutless Johnny would chop props in half, he was wild but his vocals superb, as he smashed his rapier to the beat. He had the greatest visual act in 60's pop history.

Throughout my research for this book, hundreds of musicians who have worked on the same bill as Johnny and his Pirates have admitted that it would have been far less constraining walking the plank over the pirates ship side, than to follow Capt Kidd on stage. Even Screaming Lord Sutch who has worked with the very best in over 35 years of rock swears - "Nobody could follow Johnny and his Pirates amazing act not even the Beatles or Rolling Stones. He was an original". The legend of Kidd apart from his priceless recordings has been hidden away buried like treasure for far too many years. Now thanks to his loyal mates and musicians these precious bars of accumulated golden memories have at last been found. You are now holding long lost pirates treasure so weigh anchor,

hoist the Jolly Roger
Yo heave ho
and read on........................

1. YES SIR, THAT'S MY BABY

Johnny Kidd the popular and friendly buccaneer of the ballroom circuit was born plain Frederick Albert Heath in Willesden, London NW10. He was the youngest of three children born to Ernest and Margaret Heath. Lance born 1931, Sister June 1934 and the 'Kidd' of the family 23rd November 1935. Their grandfather used to play bones and was in an amateur version of the Black and White Minstrel show. Grandmother played the piano, but only by ear. In the 1920's Ernest's brother Uncle George formed a band with their brother Uncle Fred and his wife. George played banjo, Fred the violin and his wife piano. Many members of the Heath family lived together in the same house and they used to enjoy lots of parties. The Heath Brothers Ernest, Fred, George, Tom and Jack got on very well and even had a family business 'Heath' Builders in Willesden. They had three sisters Lil, Whin and Florrie.

Ernest and Margaret Heath brought up their three children at 67, Leopold Road, Willesden, London NW10. Young Freddie was a shy Kidd, he never liked having his photo taken, he would often hide behind his mother. Sister June was a very happy child, always joking and making friends. But happiness would soon turn into tears. Freddie was only three years old when the world was at war. London had regular air raids, so along with other local children Freddie and June were evacuated to Edelsborough, which is a little village in Buckinghamshire, just north of St Albans. They lived in the vicarage attached to Edelsborough Church.

67 Leopold Road

Freddie and June were often in trouble for sliding down the vicarage banisters! Their father Ernest was an electrician and worked at that time in a local Willesden factory. The vicarage was about 30 miles away, but every weekend he would cycle there after work on a tradesman's bicycle. He even cycled all the way once through a snowstorm. They stayed there for about 2 years but as the war got worse they were evacuated to Pontrhydygroes in North Wales, where Freddie was encouraged to sing along with the local folk, and soon found himself a member of the Band of Hope choir in the Aberystwyth local church. They enjoyed their stay, but were over the moon to hear that the London bombing was now in decline and they would soon be re-united with mum, dad and older brother Lance in Willesden. Freddie returned to his local Leopold Road School and was still keen to sing.

Freddie Heath
"When I was at school, I took part in a lot of amateur productions, and on one occasion I found to my surprise - that I was cast in the 'Pirates of Penzance' which was quite an experience".

Ray Hinton (School Pal)
"Fred became mates with all of us in the Willesden area in about 1945, we were all about the same age. There was Geoffrey Brierley, Johnny Garrad, Douglas Hendry, Billy Smallwood, Tubby Rich, Alan Carter and the Everards family. We all lived in adjoining streets, Leopold Road, Fortune Gate, Redfern, Glynfields, Brownlow etc. The bomb shelters were still standing from the second world war. Bomb sites were great fun for mucking about and playing on and for finding things. We used the sites for short cuts to other streets. Rationing was still on, so we had to have clothing coupons, so fashion wasn't much. Most of the boys wore air raid warden blouses, they were like army battle dress only they were navy blue.

The majority of us went to Leopold Road, School, if you passed the 11 plus you went onto

Willesden County or Kilburn Polytechnic NW6 or Willesden Tech in Denzil Road NW10. Fred went to Leopold Road and then to Willesden Tech. He was quite good at drawing and sketching, he was witty, funny and great company, he was quite a gentle sort of Kidd.

We used to play a lot in the streets. Pig bins were used as wickets for cricket, for football we used our coats for the goalposts. Fred was not very athletically minded but he didn't mind the odd game of football. He wasn't very good, but tried hard, he always had one sock hanging over his boot and his shirt hanging over his shorts. We used to play other streets up the park or over the recreation ground at Stonebridge. The way Fred and the rest of us were brought up, is a different world far removed from that of today. We played lots of street games, there was no telly or videos then.

In the winter we'd all go to Hampstead Heath with our sledges. Money was very short. For instance if we wanted to go to the pictures we would have to scrounge empty lemonade or beer bottles to take to the shop for the deposit refund 2p or 3p old money, depending on the colour. Brown beer bottles were worth 3p while others were 2p. Cinema seats were 1/-, 1/3d, 1/6d, 1/9d, 2/3d, 2/6d. If we didn't have enough money, two or three of us would go in and save the others seats. Then one of us would go into the toilet and open the back door and let the rest of our mates in. Sometimes you'd open the door and a horde would stampede you.

Now and again you got caught and chucked out. In the summer evenings, Fred and I would go up west, the Edgware Road etc. We were buggers for Yank Baiting. The American Servicemen would hang around Hyde Park and the Serpentine. We would make ourselves a bloody nuisance, while they were chatting up the English girls or trying to make love on the grass under deck chair huts that they used to make. We would throw stones and bits of wood, in fact anything just to annoy them. We were only kids having a bit of fun. Sometimes they would chase us, mostly they would just tell us to F*** off".

Sid Holder (Mate)
"I recall young Fred pinching a pound note from his mums purse so that we could see a snooker match up Leicester Square. We treated ourselves to some packets of crisps. The dirty looks we got as we sat their crunching. Another funny story, our mate Billy Smallwood said he was going to give his girlfriend a sexy phone call. All of a sudden Fred said I'm going home. We all stood outside the phone box as Billy chatted up his girl with a lot of dirty talk. He left the door open, and was telling us the sexy replies this girl was giving. We were all getting very excited by this girls sexy talk until we realised it was Fred on the other end talking like a female. He hadn't gone home just down the street to the nearest public phone."

In 1945, after six years of war, peace descended on a weary world and Johnny came marching home, a demob suit in his kitbag and hope in his heart for the future.

The families welcomed them with tears and laughter, life was tough. Tea was rationed to two ounces a week, milk two pints. Children had never tasted a banana or a grapefruit. The tight weekly food ration, laid down by Lord Woolton included bacon, 4oz, meat to the value of 11/- 2d (roughly a pound in weight), fats 8oz, cheese 3oz.
The ration could be supplemented by tinned food available on a points system which varied from time to time according to the products available. The clothing situation was just as depress-

ing. The annual ration of 48 coupons did not stretch far, a mans suit in utility cloth took 24 coupons, work shirts 5 coupons, flannel shirts 7 coupons, children's gabardine half-lined raincoats 2 coupons. Furniture was rationed, bedding rationed (you could not buy cotton sheets unless you had either just been married or just been bombed out), soap was rationed, cigarettes and cosmetics weren't officially. Tobacconists however, would as a rule, sell cigarettes (2/4d for 20) only to regular customers. Black marketers sold whisky for £5 a time, the official price was 25/-9d.

They were hard times, but young Freddie Heath and his pals had the time of their lives.

Ray Hinton (Mate)
"I seem to remember good summers in 1947, 48, 49 and 50, we had double summertime, so it was still light at 10.30pm. We were not very serious in our teenage years. I think Fred was a bit self conscious about the squint in his right eye, which he always made a joke about.

During the summer evenings we'd go and see the Wembley Lions speedway team at Wembley Stadium. The days were filled with swimming at King Edwards outdoor pool also Kingsbury and Vale Farm outdoor pools. Saturday afternoon about 5 or 6 of us would go to the Genuine Record Shop in High Street Harlesden to get all the latest records.

You could listen in sound proof glass cubicles and even record your own vocals if you wanted. All of us would cram in one cubicle and hear the stars of the era - Nat King Cole, Kay Starr, Frank Sinatra, Les Paul and Mary Ford, Al Martino, Mario Lanza, David Whitfield, Dickie Valentine etc. Sunday nights, we used to go to dancing lessons at the 'Spit and Dribble', as it was known, run by Bob and Ruby.

It was a boarded up shop with a large basement situated at the corner of St. Thomas' Road, Craven Park opposite the Odeon Cinema. All the girls liked Fred because they thought he was cuddly. One girl, Alice, used to do the creep with Fred's head rammed between her boobs because she was that bit taller and a good bit older than Fred (little did I know then that Alice would become my sister-in-law)."

Alan Carter (Mate)
"Fred was an extrovert and extremely advanced for his age. That was the impression he gave me, when we first met. That meeting was in the playground of his school Willesden Poly in Dudden Hill Lane in 1950. We were both fifteen and he was on the verge of quitting school before the proper age of sixteen. Between 1951-54 Fred, Billy Smallwood and I used to hang around together.
Snooker halls were our favourite haunts, 'Ikes' on the corner of Willesden High Road, which used to be an old church converted into a snooker hall, then there was Harlesden Snooker Hall at 'Burtons' in Neasden Lane right opposite the Ritz Cinema, which we used to sneak into regularly.

Fred was a good snooker player and we used to challenge people who we knew Fred could beat after a bit of hustling we used to spend the money on cigarettes and expresso coffee. We'd go to White City Dog Track and increase our income, but we invariably blew it.
Three of four times a week we went to the local youth club where Fred met a girl called Rosie

Knight, she lived locally in Harlesden Road. Like any teenagers at the time, life was always one round of laughs and one some occasions we used to do stupid things. Sometimes we stayed out all night and slept in the parked railway carriages on Old Oak Common Lane at the back of Willesden Junction.

The music at the time was Guy Mitchell, Frankie Lane, Johnny Ray, Joe Stafford and Fred used to sing and hum like the rest of us teenagers. It seemed at the time that Fred wasn't any more musically advanced than the rest of us".

The turning point in Fred's life came on his 16th birthday, when his uncle George impressed by his keenness for music, gave him an old banjo. He never put it down, twanged and strummed it, nearly wore it out. He bought another from a rag and bone mans cart. It was a bit of a mess hidden underneath a load of junk, but he soon repaired it. A few months later he traded it for a guitar.

Johnny Irving (Neighbour and Life Long Pal)
"He only knew about three or four chords, he couldn't play very well, but he never gave up. If he hadn't made it as a singer he would have made it as a rhythm guitarist". On leaving school one of his first jobs was at the 'White Heather Laundry' working with his mate.

Ron Everard (Mate)
"We had some great laughs, sometimes we put all the soap powder in one load of washing and hardly any in another, there were bubbles everywhere".

Derek Everard (Mate)
"Fred and my brother once threw a work mate in a dryer. Another of his jobs was in the Woodyard in Northcote Road, Willesden and as a house painter."

Ray Hinton (Mate)
"Fred got me a job at 'Hewitts Dyers and Cleaners' opposite Colin Road NW10 in the High Road. We were spotters, that is we had special steam guns with a circular brush on the end. It steamed the stains and then removed them with the brush at the same time. The only trouble was if you brushed too vigorously you made a hole in the garments which occurred quite a lot. Fred and I were supposed to work together, but my skip always seemed more full than his. He was always missing pin balling in the nearby 'Rainbow Cafe', he was brilliant at it. We didn't work there that long".

Derek Everard (Mate)
"About six of us fellows and girls went to Richmond. Fred had dyed his hair and had blonde streaks in the sides. Everyone was looking at him because no-one at that time had ever looked like that before. It looked hilarious. We used to go to the outdoor baths every Sunday morning. He used to wear a pair of trunks with braces on. We used to sit around the side of the pool and Fred with his guitar would entertain us. He always used to greet people with "How are you going spot?" He had a double Bobby Kemp who lived near by.

Fred once worked for Taffy Morgan the Bookmaker. He was such a good bookmaker's runner he ran off with the bet money £80 and wasn't seen for a week".

BBC TV started broadcasting the very first pop programme in 1953 entitled 'TeleClub'. It ran until 1955 Freddie was always keen to watch the show and learn the latest songs.

Ray Hinton (Mate)
"One Sunday we, that's Fred, Geoffrey Brierly, Johnny Garrad, Douglas Hendry and myself jumped on the No. 18 bus at Craven Park for a historic tour of London which was all still bomb sites. We posed for a street photographer in Trafalgar Square. We'd often all hang out together dancing, pictures, football, swimming, playing cards down the Six Bells Cafe, Neasden Lane opposite the Granada Cinema in Church Road NW10. Go for a pint in the locals, White Hart or the White Horse pubs.

Ray Hinton, Freddie Heath, Geoffrey Brierly, Johnny Garrad, Douglas Hendry (© R. Hinton)

We all lived in the same street Redfern except for Fred he was on the corner of Leopold Road. He and I would chat to each other across the gardens. I would yell from my upstairs kitchen window to his upstairs back bedroom.

We'd often go to the cinema of which there were six locals, The Ritz, Coliseum, Pickaridy, Odeon, Granada and Metro.

Another favourite haunt was the 'Six Bells Cafe' in Neasden Lane opposite the Granada (the Cafe is now pulled down). There used to be lots of card games being played in the back room, mostly brag or pontoon. The owner was a Mrs Rodwell, Ma to us, an elderly lady.

The White Hart Pub next to the Granada was a popular meeting place. We'd have a few pints, it was always the same crowd Fred, John, Duggie, Geoff, Jimmy Holden, Nobby Newcombe, Keith Cudmore and myself. We were not heavy drinkers any of us.

Harlesden was and still is a hard place to live, even in those days it had its hard men confronting each other for reputation and supremacy. If you were lucky you could survive if you knew who not to antagonise.

Other hang-outs we frequented were the co-op Social Club, Park Parade, NW10, De Marcos Milk Bar and Coffee Bar near the Ritz Cinema at the Neasden Circle as it was then, Newmans Snooker Hall in the High Street NW10. Later the ex-boxer Terry Downes turned it into a club.

During this time there were prefab bungalows still next to Roundwood Park in Long Stone Avenue. The Annual Park Fair for three weeks in the summer was a great meeting place. We usually met outside the boxing booth. There was a local lad called Tommy Murphy, quite a local hero. He could handle himself quite well and earned a few pounds in the ring taking on the fairground pugilists.

I lost contact with Fred from 1952-55. Johnny Garrad and myself joined the army together but they split us up. Johnny got home a lot and mixed with Fred and the lads but sadly he was killed in a car crash. Fred and Johnny were both very nice blokes and I still miss them both".

Sid Holder (Mate)
"Fred was a nice chap, rather quiet, but he loved to wear loud clothes, this was before the Teddy Boys era but he stood out in his flashy jackets. He was always singing Danny Kayes' 'Little Black

Bug' and hanging around 'The Rainbow Cafe'. The last time I ever saw him was in the cafe wearing a very loud 'check drape' playing the pin ball machine. Of course I later saw him on various TV shows. He was a nice bloke who never had an enemy in the world".
In December '54 a tornado whirled its way through Willesden, causing damage to many buildings whilst the roof of Willesden Green Tube Station was blown into the garden of the former Grosvenor Arms and a 15 foot chimney stack collapsed from the roof of Bishop House. The winds were some of the strongest ever recorded in the country. Chiswick, Gunnersbury, Acton had lots of damage; it finally died down in Golders Green." Fred would be hit by another Tornado in 1962.

Unknown to Fred and his mates the very first published photo of Lesley Hornby was taken at the Bonny Baby Show in Roundwood Park in 1950. Lesley won third prize in class two (for girls aged nine to twelve months). Years later as Twiggy, she became the most photographed model of the swinging sixties.

2. PUTTING ON THE DONEGAN

Independent Television first started broadcasting pop shows in 1955. One was hosted by band leader Jack Payne another by disc jockey Jack Jackson. Both preferred family entertainers like Frankie Vaughan, Ruby Murray etc so the new craze, skiffle, was not often included.

ATV's music show was more popular as it featured a rendezvous of popular recording stars from both sides of the Atlantic i.e. Chris Barber Jazz Band, Terry Sisters. It was hosted by Gerry Wilmot and produced by Dicky Leeman.

Skiffle had started out with a real really bad name as something for the Ted's and tearaways. At least that's what the media was saying in the mid fifties. Soho in London was the hub of all skiffle with its vice, Italian grocers, Algerian coffee stores, Greek sweat shops, Hungarian chicken livers, Swiss chocolates and newspapers on sale in a dozen different languages. It was a melting pot of nations, every other doorway seemed to be a coffee bar.

The Mars, The Cat's Whiskers, Orlando's, Skiffle Cellar, the Freight Train and the most famous of them all the legendary Two I's. Everyone wanted music with their drinks so the owners were glad to hire young skiffle groups for a pound or two a night.

No.

The 2-I's COFFEE CLUB, 59, Old Compton Street, W.1

APPLICATION FOR MEMBERSHIP

To the Secretary:

I request you to place my name before the Committee for election as a Member of the above Club and if elected I agree to be bound by the Rules and Regulations in force, or as altered hereafter. I am paying now my membership fee (returnable if not elected) and agree to pay a floor fee on each occasion I visit the Club. I fully understand that until I am elected as a member it is not permissable for me to dance.

Date________ 19

Name (Block Letters)________

Address________

Signature of Candidate________

Name of Proposer________

Name of Seconder________

2-I's Application Form
(Always N' Ever Archive)

The Club originally started out as a snack bar run by three brothers called Ivani (one of whom was Freddy Ivani who later ran a striptease club in Soho). They called the bar the Three I's but as one of the brothers left the business they re-named it the Two I's. Business was bad so they sold the premises to two Australians Ray Hunter and Paul Lincoln in 1955. They were both wrestlers. Paul Lincoln used to be known as Doctor Death and later became one of wrestlings impresarios. 59 Old Compton Street would never be the same again. They served tea, coffee and cakes in the top bar while down in the basement was skiffle and jive. Kids would jive away their lunch break for only six pence a head (2.5p).

Weekends were the post popular. Paul brought in Tom Littlewood who helped him audition new skiffle groups every day in their search for talent. The very first resident group were The Ghouls. Other popular haunts included the Top Ten in Berwick St, the Bridge House in Canning Town (with the boppin' duo Bill Crompton and Thunderclap Jones) Coffee Pot, Churchill's Night Club, Russell Quays Skiffle Club, Chaquitas, The Heaven and Hell, The Breadbasket, The Gyre & Gimbler, Club 51 etc.

On July 13th 1954 Lonnie Donegan along with Chris Barber and Beryl Bryden cut a song that would change the lives of thousands of people including the young Freddie Heath. "Rock Island Line". It was featured on the LP "New Orleans Joys" (Decca LF1198).

Chris Barber
"Lonnie on banjo joined my amateur band in 1952. I played a bit of bass. I had a funny old record called "Home Town Skiffle". We didn't know if skiffle meant rent party or music but we liked the word so we used it. It was more or less black American folk songs, mostly by Leadbelly (Huddie Ledbetter). We had a blues group and we invited Ken Colyer in '53 as he had just

returned from America plus Beryl Bryden on washboard".

Lonnie Donegan
"I had the Tony Donnegans Jazz Band, the first big show we played was at the Festival Hall in '52 with my big hero Lonnie Johnson. The compere introduced Johnson as Tony Johnson and me as Lonnie Donegan. The name just stuck after that".

The Decca staff at the session of Rock Island Line, had no interest in the song and, in fact, went for a cup of tea. The recording was just an LP track but DJ Chris Stone of BBC Radio kept playing it. Requests started pouring in, so Decca released a single in late '55 Rock Island Line/ John Henry (45F10647). Come January '56 the single entered the top charts.

Lonnie Donegan
"Bingo suddenly out of nowhere everyone went mad buying the record. It sold about 2 million in about 6 weeks. Decca never ever bothered to say thank you".

Alan Freeman (Producer PYE Records '54-'65)
"As part of the Chris Barber Skiffle group Lonnie never got any royalties for the hit. He has never got over it to this day. Decca didn't seem to realise what a good talent they had so I helped sign him to PYE".

Lonnie Donegan E.P.

Seemingly over night young skiffle groups shot up all over the country. It was very easy to play just three chords D A7 G on a cheap guitar or banjo plus a tea chest, bass and washboard. It was infectious and rhythmic.

Adam Faith (Terry Nelhams the Worried Man)
"It hit Britain with all the fury of Asian flu. Everyone went down with it. Anyone who could afford to buy a guitar and learn three chords was in business as a skiffler. Skiffle was a bit like mushrooms. It grew in cellars, nice dark cellars, and it shot up over-night like mushrooms".

Donegan was crowned 'The King of Skiffle' his material Rock Island Line, Lost John, Bring A Little Water Sylvie, Don't You Rock Me Daddy-O, Cumberland Gap, Putting On The Style, Gambling Man, Dixie Darling, Jack O'Diamonds plus the Kingston Trio's Tom Dooley, Chas McDevitt and Nancy Whiskey's Freight Train, Johnny Duncan's Last Train to San Fernando. The Vipers 10, 000 Years Ago, Maggie May etc became the repertoire of many young budding skifflers.

Wally Whyton (The Vipers)
"We used to meet up at "The Bread Basket" just off the Euston Road. The lady owner asked us to play a few numbers. We got bowls of spaghetti for our sessions. One night we asked if we could busk at the I's we stayed and became the resident group. Producer George Martin from E.M.I. came one night to see Tommy Steele who was working with us. Decca got Tommy and Martin us as second best".

Brian Silver (Vipers)
"Guitars were very rare in those days. I was going home one night when two policeman said

what's that? They asked where did you take that from? I said nowhere, they said prove it, so in the middle of Charring Cross Road, I had to play 'On Top of Old Smokey'.

Wally Whyton (Vipers)
"The only time we could record was between midnight and 8am in the morning. We had to have a bottle of Scotch before we could record because we were so tired doing day jobs and playing the 2 I's. We cut 'Don't You Rock Me Daddy O'. Lonnie had come down and seen us. I'd rewritten it from an old folk song. We both recorded it, we went to No 5, Lonnie went No 1. Suddenly we had thousands of offers coming in to tour variety. I don't remember Freddie Heath as a skiffler, probably because we turned pro and were out on the road for weeks on end without getting back to Soho. I certainly do remember him as Johnny Kidd the rocker and thought he was the most talented of the whole bunch around at that time".

Skiffle was everywhere - Peter Teague (Cliff Richard), Hound Dogs (Marty Wilde), Spacemen (Joe Brown), Vagabonds (Vince Eager and Brian Locking), Cotton Pickers, Duffy Howard and the Amigos (Duffy Power). Fabulous Five (Eden Kane, Peter Sarstedt), City Ramblers, Sonny Stewart, Rail Roaders, (Hank Marvin, Bruce Welch), Terry Kennedy Group, The Red Sox (Freddie Garrity), The Velfins (Wayne Fontana), Red Mountain Boys (Gerry Marsden), Johnny and The Rainbows (John Lennon), The Crestas (Applejacks), Quarrymen (Lennon, McCartney, Harrison), Black Diamonds (Alan Price), John Henry Group (Chris Farlowe), Swinging Blue Genes (Swinging Blue Jeans), Jewry Rhythm Group (Shane Fenton/Alvin Stardust), Horseshoe Group (Chas Hodges), Gin Mill Group (Spinners), Station Skiffle Group (Joe Meeks first group recording), Paul Russell and the Rebels (Gary Glitter), Rebels (George Harrison), Eddie Clayton (Ringo Starr), Eden Street Group, New Hawleans, Jimmy Jackson Group, Bonny Stewarts Skiffle Kings, Meds Skiffle Group, The Five Nutters (Johnny Kidd) last but one of the best Les Hobeaux.

Adam Faith
"By the time my group The Worried Men got their chance at the I's, the resident band was Les Hobeaux. They were so good that they ended up winning the All Soho Skiffle Contest, and moving on to greater glories. Their win was good for us, because Paul Lincoln put us in as resident band in their place.

Brian Gregg (Bass Les Hobeaux - Future Pirate)
"Terry Dene (Williams) and myself both used to work at 363 Oxford Street, the HMV Record Shop. We both started there on the same day and struck up a friendship. As soon as I heard him singing Heartbreak Hotel, (he used to do a great imitation of Elvis), I took him to the Cat Whiskers in Kingly Street to see Leon Bell and the Bell Cats. There was a pause, the band stopped for a break, Leon Bell asked if there was any requests. Terry and I had had a few drinks, I said to Leon, I've got a request can my mate sing? He said is he any good, I replied he's better than you, Leon tried to ignore me, but the audience took my side and yelled let him sing. Terry got up on stage and tore the roof off the place, and that was the start of Terry going on stage. A while later he sang at the Two I's.

As soon as Terry started to record, I was determined as well. One day while working in the basement at HMV these guys came in and said they were a band and were looking for some blues songs and work songs, where can we find them? I said what type of band are you? They said skiffle/blues. I suggested some that they should listen to. A couple of weeks later the same guys were in the shop and they thanked me. "The songs were great mate". I asked where they played and they said they were just started at the Two I's. I said I'd come along and see them and that I could play bass and harmonica. As luck would have it that night their bass player didn't turn up. Les Bennett said over the microphone "Are you here Brian?" I got up and played bass. After the gig, Les asked me to join the band, Les Hobeaux.

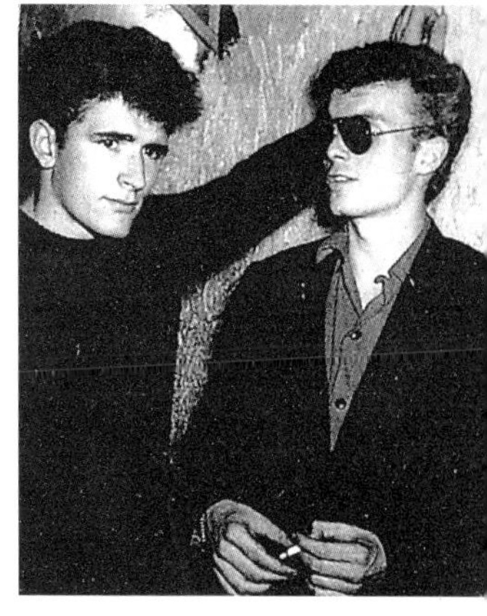

Les Bennett, Brian Gregg (Les Hobeaux) Nucleus Coffee Bar 1957 (© B. Gregg)

Within a couple of weeks of Terry Dene getting a Decca recording contract, I also had one on HMV. One of my first big gigs with Les Hobeaux was at the Commodore Ryel on the Isle of Wight. We met this little guy who used to hang around the Two I's who worked in a film studio in Wardour Street. He asked if he would come with us as our band boy, he humped our gear and stayed backstage. That young guy was Terry Nelhams, later to become Adam Faith.

Chas McDevitt
"My group started in '56, I also played banjo in Ken Colyers' Cranes River Jazz Band. We started skiffle in the interval. As Skiffle got more popular we left the group and recorded 'Freight Train' with Mark Sharratt (Washboard), John Paul (Bass), Dennie Carter (Guitar), Alex White House (Guitar) and Nancy Wiskey (Vocals)".

The Chas McDevitt Skiffle Group featured many first-class drummers i.e. Red Reece who went into The Beat Boys, playing alongside Ray McVay (Sax) and Georgie Fame (Piano). This band later formed the nucleus of the Blue Flames and young Clem Cattini who later kept the beat for the Billy Fury band, (which had Peter Skellern and John Miles in the line up) and, of course, The Pirates.

Wednesday 16 January saw the opening of the Cavern Club in Mathew Street, Liverpool as a jazz venue with The Merseyssippi Jazz Band.

Alan Sytner (Owner of the Cavern 1957-59)
"Skiffle was the roots of the first Mersey Groups. We introduced "The Liverpool Skiffle Championship", this became so popular, we would have 20 groups in one evening."

Mick Groves (Spinners)
"I looked at the 'Echo' one night and it was unbelievable 'cause there were hundreds of Skiffle groups advertised in various parts of Merseyside in one week. It was fantastic."

Stanley Dale (Promoter and Manager)
"I put on the National Skiffle Contest in July '57, it attracted over 800 groups. Among those unknown hopefuls were Adam Faith (as a member of the Worried Man), Hank Marvin and Bruce Welch (then belonging to the Railroaders), Joe Brown, Wee Willie Harris and even Freddie Heath (Johnny Kidd)."

National Skiffle Contest, Metropolitan, Edgware Road (© Always N' Ever Archive)

Entries in the National Contest were amazing, there were family groups, University groups, farm workers, groups from railway depots, in fact from all walks of life. Skiffle took over the British youth, it even spread to Europe. 'The City Ramblers' who's popular Mamma Don't Allow (on Tempo EXA59) became the first British group to play in Russia, in fact in Red Square.

Tom Littlewood (Manager of 2 I's)
"We had autographed, framed photos lining the walls, of the lads who made their debut in the cellar. They hugged their guitars as they climbed down a flight of two dozen stairs.... then everyone stood back as they shot up the ladder to fame.

Tommy Steele had place of honour, there was Larry Page, Terry Dene, Colin Hicks, Johnny Kidd, Dick Shane, Vince Eager, Bachelors, Bill and Brett Landis, Worried Men, Vipers, Chas McDevitt, Cliff Richard, Wee Willie Harris, Les Hobeaux. They all came to the club, the place was jumping. There were queues of people a couple of blocks long, waiting to get in. Skiffle, Big Beat... we had the cream. Naturally, the lads gave up playing at the Two I's when golden contracts were dangled, but they still came back for a coffee and a chat".

Lonnie Donegan EP sleeve

Lonnie Donegan
"The furthest back we traced skiffle was to Chicago in the mid 30's. Skiffle party was the full term as I understand it, or rent house party. The object was that the poverty stricken members of the Chicago Black area would hold parties in order to pass a hat around and raise the rent. The music served at such a party was jazz and folk orientated".

Jack Good (Producer)
"Lonnie always claimed he had nothing to do with Rock obviously there was a strong element that charisma, that violence in his approach, he said he never did bumps and grinds, but if you see his old films the way his hips would move his shoulders went up and down, his eyes flashed, it was quite incredible. He was totally original. Although he said he was singing old American folk songs, nobody in America had heard these songs sung like that before".

3. OVER THE RAINBOW

The White Hart, Willesden on Sunday nights gave Freddie Heath the chance to get up and sing his heart out while putting on the Donegan.

Yvonne Everard (Friend)
"There used to be talent nights, he was always keen to get up and sing a number. He was very keen on Lonnie Donegan, Bill Haley, Johnny Ray, Frankie Lane and Guy Mitchell. I went to Leopold Secondary Modern School and Fred was often to be seen standing at the gates watching the girls playing netball hoping for a flash of navy blue knickers. He used to stand there with a cheeky smile on his face."

Alan Carter (Mate)
"He was very keen and told me he was writing songs and he was going to make it big in show time. Well, I just laughed but as time went on he was gradually getting noticed and was getting bookings at local church halls and other small ventures. He couldn't drive so I used to borrow my brother-in-law's Dormobile van and take him to gigs. His reward for such gigs, I think, was five pounds. On the way home he used to give me ten bob (50p) which made me happy. We'd always stop for our fish n' chips."

Freddies' favourite local haunt 'The Rainbow Cafe' at the bottom of Church Road was the meeting place for all his mates and his now steady girl, Ada Price.

Fred The Ted (© R. Y. Everard)

Ron and Yvonne Everard (Close Friends)
"The cafe was very carefree and an ideal place for us all to meet up and decide the evenings arrangements. Fred was a very likeable fellow. We all would go out together Fred, Ada, Tubby Rich, his girlfriend and us. We often went to Richmond to show off and parade in our Teddy Boy outfits. We'd have a laugh by getting lost in the maize at Hampton Court. A local chap Charlie Wallace would organise outings to places like Southend and various places along the coast.

Fred married Ada Price at the local registrar office in 1956 during a Bank Holiday. In the evening Fred took us all to the London Palladium to see Harry Secombe. He treated us all. It was a lovely evening. Fred and his bride were so happy. They moved in with his parents at Leopold Road where they had the front room. Mr and Mrs E. Heath having the rest of the house.

I recall walking down church road one Sunday afternoon during the time the film 'High Noon' was on release. Fred and his mates were standing on the corner and as I (Yvonne) approached they started singing the theme tune 'Do Not Forsake Me Oh My Darling'. Fred would often stand in the middle of the street, strumming his guitar, singing the latest hits. The six of us always went out together. They were the Three Musketeers and we three girls shared their adventures and laughs. They were happy times. Fred had a fantastic personality."

Freddie with wife Ada
(© R. Y. Everard)

Ray Hinton (Mate)
"Fred's mum worked in the advertising department at Ilfords Films Ltd in Cumberland Avenue NW10 in about 1956. Geoff Brierly was in charge at the dept. I worked in the export dept until they moved to Basildon, Essex."
On August 4th '56 the jazz drummer Tony Crombie informed the music world that he had formed

one of the first R n' R bands in Britain. Bill Haley's film 'Rock Around The Clock' suddenly had British youth going crazy man crazy. Tony and his Rockets with help from entrepreneur agent Jeff Kruger signed for Bernard Delfont. A tour of the Moss Empire dance halls brought them huge success and a recording contract for Columbia.

Film still 'Rock Around The Clock'

During October they made the top thirty with Shortnin' Bread Rock. The Rockets featured many great musicians during its various line-ups i.e. Red Mitchell, Rex Morris, Jet Harris and future Pirate Brian Gregg.

Clem Cattini (Drummer - Future Pirate)
"I went to see 'Blackboard Jungle' with a friend of mine who played guitar. 'Rock Around The Clock' just blew our minds. I started playing drums down the Two I's, I used to back anyone who wanted to play.

I grew up during the war, my father being of Italian descent was on the Isle of Man interned. My mother brought us up. I have two brothers and a sister. Mother used to love Latin American music. She used to have Edmundo Ross on all day long. Maybe that's where I got the drumming thing from. I suppose that was my basic influence. I remember coming home from school trying to do my home work listening to Edmundo Ross.

Clem Cattini at the 2-I's (© Rick Hardy)

I was evacuated to Watford from Haringay, London. We used to go up the A6 to St Albans. There was a hill. We were on a bus it seemed like the end of the world."

Rock and Roll promoter Jeff Kruger hit out about the lack of rocking acts on television and film. "BBC and ITV can't see further than the end of their noses. R n' R has an enormous following over here but neither will give it a showing. They are just a bunch of stuffed shirts. They and the cinema managers who are scared of the name are not giving the music a fair deal".

Apart from all the excitement on the music front Freddie and his wife Ada celebrated the birth of their first child a baby boy. Tony was born on 3rd October 1956.
During the mid fifties both the BBC and ITV agreed not to broadcast between 6 and 7pm in the evening. It was called 'toddlers truce' when parents could put their young children to bed without unruly demands to watch more TV.

ITV broke the truce with the Jack Jackson show followed in December '56 by 'Cool For Cats' originally hosted by Fleet Street journalist Ker Robertson who devised the format. A month later Kent Walton took over and ran the show until it ended four years later. It started as a 15 minute show but it expanded to half an hour. It featured artists miming to their latest releases. Douglas Squires led the resident dancers. The producer was Associated Rediffusion. Walton later found fame at ITV's best wrestling commentator.

January '57 brought great news for guitarists. Gibson introduced Humbucking pick ups to their Les Paul guitars. The twin coil design helped eliminate unwanted electrical hum. But most British lads only had cheapo guitars and were more excited by the news of a new TV show.

The BBC hit back at 5 past 6 with 'Six Five Special' on 16th February '57. It covered topical trends, sport, traditional jazz but most important skiffle.

The opening show featured Kenny Baker and his Dozen, Michael Holliday and the King Brothers. The show was presented by Jo Douglas, Pete Murray and ex boxer Freddie Mills. It was broadcast live from the BBC studios at Shepherds Bush in West London. 10,000,000 viewers tuned in every Saturday.

The show really improved when Jack Good took over as producer. With his single mindedness and visual inventive he brought excitement to the small screen. Good was a newly graduated trainee producer who had passed his producers test by making a rather strange commercial for coffins. He really worked hard to get rock n' roll respected in this country.

Jack Good (Producer)
"The problem in England was that nobody who could play music liked rock. The thing about rock was that it was universally despised by anybody who could play a scale. The jazz people thought it was a joke, a sick joke, that would all be over in a couple of months."

But during the same month Bill Haley and his Comets arrived for a British tour. British Railways printed special tickets for 'The Bill Haley Rock n' Roll Special' which left Waterloo around midday packed with 300 fans, journalists, photographers and the rockin' sounds of Freds favourites Rory Blackwell and his Blackjacks. Skin-tight jeans, badges, banners, sweaters with Haley slogans were the dress and order of the day. Most of the seats were left unoccupied as the fans jived and hand clapped to the sounds of the Blackjacks. On arrival at Southampton station the mass led by The Pied Piper of British Rock Rory Blackwells' outfit headed for the dockside.

As they waited in the rain ships in the solent hooted their welcome and trains blew their whistles. Southampton was just going crazy man crazy. The first sight of Haley's limousine had the crowd going wild. The police got King Haley onto the station platform and to his compartment. The Haley R n' R special now had valuable cargo aboard. The coaches, swaying and rockin all got a visit from the King, who had a kind word and an autograph for them all. If Haley thought Southampton was wild Waterloo Station with over 4, 000 rockers was madness. It took a full 20 minutes to get him through the crowds.

Film still 'Don't Knock The Rock'

Bill Haley
"R n' R is a down to earth simple thing, it is the simplest form of music. We went back to the beginning of music, got the 12 Bar Blues, boogie woogie. We put a solid beat with this, we put four types of different music - dixieland, C/W, R/B and old jazz standards. We kept the lyrics down to easy to remember and, I think, that is the answer to R n' R music - simplicity."

Agent Jeff Kruger organised a film shoot at London's Carlton Vale ballroom in January '57. The whole film took only three weeks to make. February 13th saw its release, the first full length British R 'n' R film 'Rock You Sinners' produced by Small Films. It starred Tony Crombie and his Rockets, Art Baxters Rocking Sinners, Rory Blackwells Blackjacks, Don Sollash and his Rockin Horses, Joan Small, George Brown and Dickie Bennett.
All over the country bands were rockin' round the clock, Leon Bells Bellcats, Rock 'n' Roll All

Stars, House Rockers, Geoff Taylors Rock 'n' Rollers (whose claim to fame was being the first British rock band to go to the States in exchange for Freddie Bell and the Bell Boys), Oscars Hot Icebergs, Bobby Breens Rockers (who included future stand in Beatle drummer Jimmy Nicol), The Kirchins, Don Lang and his Frantic Five, Terry Wayne, Tommy Steele and the Steelemen, Clyde Ray, Wee Willie Harris, Dud Fullers Riot Raisers, Cliff Ball All Stars, Rudy Jones, Lo Don Raving Rockers, Steve Murray, Bluejacks, Billy Sproud, Larry Page, Dean Webb, Ricky James.

Rock n' Roll along with skiffle swept Britain like a tidal wave.

Ted Heath (Big Band leader)
"I don't think the R n' R craze will come to Britain. You see it is primarily for the coloured population, I can't see it becoming a real craze."

Ballad singer Dickie Valentine and various jazz musicians called for the death of R 'n' R, but they couldn't stop the craze. Kids were singing 'Don't Knock the Rock'. Britain's oldest jazz (modern) club, Vi Hyland's Studio 51, had closed and reopened as the 51 Club to feature R 'n' R and Trad. Rory Blackwells R 'n' Rollers got London's first beat club rocking on August 24th '56.

4. THE FIVE NUTTERS

Frank Rouledge (Guitarist)
"I was in Ikes Snooker Hall and got talking to Freddie Heath and Brian England about skiffle. Brian had a banjo, Fred said he could play a few chords on his guitar. So I invited them round my house. I played lead. After hours of thinking of different names we decided on Bats Heath and the Vampires. We got Clive Lazell on washboard to keep the beat."

Clive Lazell (Drums)
"We first rehearsed at my home 150 Villiers Road, in December 1956. We had various names The Vampires, The Frantic Four (because of Don Langs Frantic Five), The Five Nutters. I was now playing drums."

Above, left: Clive Lazell (Drummer) (© C. Lazell)
Above, right: Frank Rouledge and Johnny Gordon (© F. Rouledge)
Below: Skiffle Contest Roudwood Park (© Always N' Ever Archive)

Frank Rouledge (Guitarist)
"When Brian Donalon joined us on washboard he was so zany we named the band The Five Nutters. He did some crazy antics. We found our bass player Johnny Fruit' Gordon playing for The Dusty Bohen Skiffle Group. Fred and I went to the Willesden Working Mans Club to see him play. All of a sudden two yobs started picking on me. I let fly with a great punch and knocked one of them to the floor, I couldn't feel my arm, it was numb. Dusty Bohen stopped his act and jumped off stage, he was trained in first aid. I had dislocated my shoulder. With a quick and very painful pull he corrected my strain. Fred had started writing catchy little tunes. Many a time I found him sitting beneath a tree in Roundwood Park with his banjo on his knee working on new material.

He had some very original ideas. One night he said lets play a song using just one chord. Fruit Gordon and I laughed "that's impossible it will sound tuneless". We decided to give it a go just to please him. It went down a storm. The couples were soon jiving and stamping to this primitive beat."

Clive Lazell (Drummer)
"We used to play Bring A Little Water Sylvie, Cumberland Gap, Don't You Rock Me Daddy O, Butterfly, Shake Rattle Roll, Rock Around The Clock, Blue Suede Shoes, When The Saints Go Marching In, Teddy Bear, Singing The Blues, and our own song Blood Red Beauty."

The Five Skifflers became very busy sometimes working six nights a week. Fred's vocals were really pushed to the limit. "My throat's killing me", he would cry. Brian would say "get another drink down him."

Frank Rouledge (Guitarist)
"On one occasion we were doing a special gig in South London. We couldn't find Brian anywhere. He was in prison in Pentonville. We raced there by motorbike and had to bail him out. He really was The Main Nutter. His brothers had a group The Corncobs. They were at the Roundwood Park Contest in '57."

WE WANT FRED!
Willesden Chronicle reporters Mike Rothwell and Ted Rayner came up with the great idea to

stage a skiffle contest at the Willesden Carnival, Roundwood Park on August Bank Holiday Monday. It was advertised as a 'Mammouth Skiffle Contest' and that's what it proved to be.

Thirteen groups played altogether 56 numbers and at the end they were awarded five prizes totalling £37 10/- instead of the scheduled three. Only 2 1/2 points separated the first four. Principal judge was Roy Heath from the Two I's Coffee Bar. Assisting him were Fraser White known as the skiffle expert for the Sporting Record and reporters Rothwell and Rayner.

Ted Rayner (Reporter)
"Sitting on the stage near the bowling green we had the surprise of our lives when, after the contest had been going for a couple of minutes, we saw the size of the audience. It had been hoped it would be quite a draw but nobody reckoned with such numbers that the fence around the stage had to be strengthened. We soon had a tight-packed swaying 8, 000 strong crowd.

All the groups played three numbers in the first round. 'The Metropolitans' had bad luck when they lost first a guitarist and then a guitar string and were forced to retire. But they came back later to win their way into the second round.

Dress was varied 'The Black Cats' led by Bernard Pistell wore black shirts. The neatest uniform was worn by 'The Corncobs' led by Chris Donalon. They wore bright yellow sweaters and blue jeans, were more or less the same height and being brothers looked alike.

In the second round The Skiffle Cats from Kensal Rise, The Black Cats from Harlesden, The Metropolitans, The Corn Cobs and The Frantic Four led by Freddie Heath from Willesden. They all played two numbers, we couldn't decide on the winners so The Frantic Four, Skiffle Cats, Black Cats and Corn Cobs went into the final. We decided they'd have to play a fresh number each. A good group should be capable of playing more than three tunes well - and the battle commenced. First to play were The Black Cats, as they finished 'Daddy O' the contest had been going for 3 1/2 hours. Then came The Skiffle Cats, The Corn Cobs followed with Wabash Cannon Ball and Chris Donalon who bore a striking resemblance to Lonnie Donegan and even sang like him too drew another burst of applause from the crowd. Young Freddie Heath's group The Frantic Four went into Cumberland Gap' whose asides and jokes kept the crowd laughing. As the song finished there was a burst of applause. We couldn't agree on a decision, and in the end, had to add the marks we had awarded individually.

Roy Heath told a hushed crowd our findings. There was consternation when it was announced that The Frantic Four had been placed third, applause when The Black Cats were adjudged second and near-riot when The Skiffle Cats were classed winners. The Corn Cobs received £5, The Metropolitans £2, but when the Mayor of Willesden Ald W J Hill went to present the first three groups their prize of £15, £10 and £5 10/- a section of the crowd started to shout "WE WANT FRED".

WHO'S FRED?

WHEN 21 stone ROY HEATH, manager of The 2 I's Coffee Bar in Soho, swayed majestically towards the microphone to announce the results of the Willesden Annual Carnival Skiffle Contest, I felt more than slightly nervous, writes WSR columnist and co-judge, Fraser White.

After all, there was a waiting audience of over 3,000 who had stood watching the contest for four hours and it seemed to me that most of them were supporters of a gent called Fred, whose group was called The Frantic Four.

Winners were: First: The Skiffle Cats; second: The Black Cats; third: Fred and His Frantic Four; fourth: The Corn Cobs.

Fred's supporters roared their disapproval and a shower of pennies landed on the judges' platform—but not enough to pay for our trip back to town!

ROY HEATH

Two added attractions as a grand finale to the contest were **Sonny Stewart and His Kings Of Skiffle** who recently waxed their first disc for Philips, and the latest 2 I's singing hope **Mickey The Most.**

'Who's Fred' Press report
(© Always N' Ever Archive)

Derek Everard (Mate)
"Their act was fun and they certainly acted like nutters. We were all proud of Fred and thought he was the best. A few of us started yelling "WE WANT FRED" suddenly others joined the

chant."

Ted Rayner (Reporter)
"Nobody knew who Fred was. Loads of teenagers took up the cry but the mythical Freddie Heath failed to appear. Manager 'Bomber Harris' reprimanded the crowd. He held his hands up for silence. The Mayor announced that the contest had been such a huge success that an even greater one would be held in 1958.

Judge Frazer White was more than slightly nervous when Roy Heath announced the winners. It seemed to me that most of the crowd were supporters of a gent called Fred of The Frantic Four. Fred's supporters roared their disapproval and a show of pennies landed on the judges platform - but not enough to pay for our trip back to town."

Two added attractions as a grand finale to the contest were Sonny Stewart and His Kings of Skiffle, who had just waxed their first disc for the Philips label and the latest Two I's singing hope Mickey the Most (Mickie Most).

METROPOLITAN
AMBassador 2478 6.30 & 8.45
ROCK - SKIFFLE - CALYPSO
THE BUTLIN SKIFFLE GROUP
SKIFFLE CONTEST
JIMMY PARKINSON | HARRIOTT & EVANS
NORMAN VAUGHAN | Vic Gordon & Peter Colville
THE FURTIVE FUNSTER | ACCENT ON LAUGHTER
The Victor Silvester SCHOOLS OF

Skiffle Contest, Metropolitan Edgware Road

The Skiffles were really excited to get another chance of stardom. Mr Star Maker, Carroll Levis, was coming to the London area with his Discoveries show.

Clive Lazell (Drummer)
"We played the 'Met', Edgware Road, during 'Bring A Little Water Sylvie'. Brian came running on stage wearing his long johns and hit Fred on the head with his washboard. It almost knocked Fred out cold, the audience and even Carol Levis laughed their heads off. Cy Grant won first place followed by the Two G's (two brothers who played drums) but we thought we had won."

They got tremendous applause. The whole basis of the show was that at the end each group returned and did a few bars from their number again and the audience clapped like mad for their favourite act. It was the final clap that was registered and the winners decided. The loudest cheer of the evening was for 'The Five Nutters' but alas once again they had failed to win Brian Donalon and his brothers chased after Levis shouting that the show was fixed.

Levis promised The Nutters TV work but alas nothing materialised but under his presentation they did appear at three of london's top variety theatres. The Metropolitan, Edgware Road, Chiswick Empire and Finsbury Park Empire.

2-I's Membership Card

THE 2-I's COFFEE CLUB
59, Old Compton Street, London, W.1
1958 MEMBER'S CARD
This is to certify that
is a Member of the above Club

For the special show at Finsbury Park, Clive Lazells mother went out and bought them four matching pullovers but Zanny Brian preferred to wear his long johns. Mrs Lazell acted like a roadie. She really encouraged the five young nutters.

They carried on entering talent shows and won quite a few, plus working in local working men's clubs and the famous Two I's Coffee Bar. Their finest hour was performing on BBC Radio's Skiffle Club (later Saturday Club). The BBC light programme were very slow to realise the great effect the skiffle craze had had on British youth as Skiffle Club producer Jimmy Grant explains - "It takes time for suggestions to get through. At the time the light programme was not all that interested in 'pop' music. It took a year or so to

get it under way. When it finally got on the air, skiffle was over its peak".
The boys recorded two numbers at Wilkinsons Radio Shop 'Shake Rattle and Roll' and 'Blood Red Beauty' which Fred and the lads wrote because of Ada Heath's long red hair. These priceless recordings still exist featuring - Freddie Heath (vocals), Frank Rouledge (guitar), Johnny Gordon (bass) and Clive Lazell (drums).

Clive Lazell - Puttin' on the style (© C. Lazell)

Skiffle moved on, part of it became a thriving folk scene and the other became rock 'n' roll and ultimately British beat. Thousands of young skifflers were now rocking daddy O.

With the decline of skiffle 'The Five Nutters' hung up their washboard, tea chest and Brian's long johns.

Frank Rouledge (Guitarist)
"I got a job in a car showroom. To be truthful I did skiffle for kicks. Jazz was my love but its nice to know I've done it and was there with Fred and the boys. I still treasure our recordings."

Fred went from job to job. He even worked on a local fair with his good mate Johnny Irving. He would still spend his spare time playing pin-ball over the 'Rainbow Cafe'. "I'll wish upon a star and become a star somewhere over the rainbow" he would think as he dreamed his days away. The evenings was when he really came alive singing solo in local Willesden pubs. With more time alone his interest in song writing really grew.

5. THE FABULOUS FREDDIE HEATH BAND

Don Toy (Agent)
"I first met Fred in early September 1957. I had been running for a few years 'The Don Martin Dance Band and Orchestra'.

I also got caught up in the skiffle craze in '56 playing washboard and drums in the Dusty Bohen Skiffle Group with - Peter (Dusty) Bohen (vocal and guitar) and John Summerhil (bass).

In '57 I had a contract with the C.I.U. Clubs covering all the Working Mens Clubs in North London. I used to supply any size band from a trio to a full orchestra whatever was requested. My pianist lived in Glynfield Road near a young singer called Freddie Heath and he introduced me to Fred. During this period Fred was in The Five Nutters who I saw on one occasion but I didn't think much of them."

Fred occasionally joined his father Ernest for a pint at the local Working Mans Club where his dad was a member. Mr Heath was really proud of his son when he got up to sing with Dons' band for the very first time.

Don Toy (Agent)
"Fred came over to me and asked if he could get up and sing. I thought he sounds quite good. Over the next few gigs I let him sing with my band. His taste in music being rock 'n' roll was not fantastically popular with Working Club members, being mainly older people they still enjoyed ballroom dancing.

I suggested to Fred that we should form a band based on Bill Haley and the Comets. We tried out many budding musicians. I would bring in people to try out and Fred also brought in budding sax players like Pete Cotton, Geoff Wiggins and Pete Newman." Pete was very surprised to be asked to join the band because he was still just learning the sax.

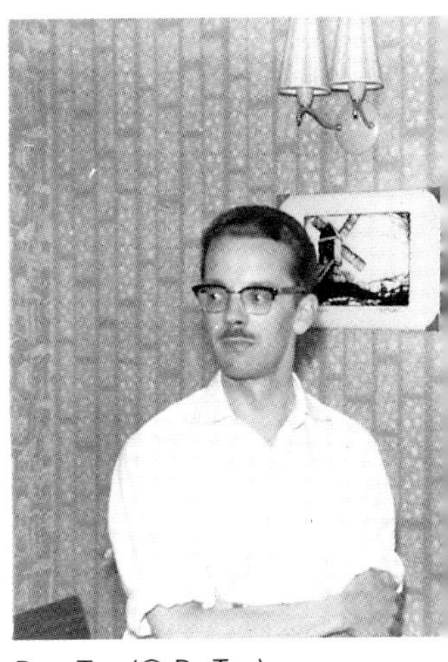
Don Toy (© D. Toy)

Pete Newman (Sax)
"I was playing my sax in my front room. I was blasting away making a lot of noise. I just about heard a knock on the front door which my mum answered. I was amazed to see Freddie Heath, he asked "Who was playing the sax? Well I'm just learning." I replied. "Why don't you come and play with my band he asked?" I replied, "I'm not very good." But he was undeterred. "It doesn't matter it will sound good." So I joined. I first got involved at school with Jet Harris (harmonica/bass), Ray Edmunds (drums), John Welsh (clarinet) and myself on (harmonica/sax). We were only about thirteen or fourteen years old."

Krazy Kurzon Klub Stamp (courtesy Don Toy)

With Don Toy acting as Manager, Agent, Promoter and even drummer, Fred had a man who would help change his career in more ways than he had ever dreamed over 'The Rainbow Cafe'. On Wednesday 2nd October 1957, Don started the Krazy Kurzon Klub at the White Horse Willesden. It was named after a local street, Curzon Crescent. The Fabulous Freddie Heath Band were the resident attraction. Bouncer Duke Carter would greet the clientele with a stamp on the hand bearing K.K.K. which was dipped in raspberry juice so it could be easily washed off. The band varied in size and players depending on who was available to play, size of the venue and how much they were being paid.

The following musicians played in the Fabulous Freddie Heath Band
Johnny "Fruit" Gordon (Bass and Piano)
Frank Rouledge (Guitar)
Pete Newman (Sax)
Pete Cotton (Sax, Clarinet)
Brian Saunders (Drums)
Don Toy (Drums)
The aforementioned musicians were most used.
From time to time the following budding musicians helped out.
Geoff Wiggins (Sax)
Ken Tootle (Sax)
Jimmy Digby (Sax)
John Summerhil (Bass) plus four of five others who's names have been lost in the passing of time.

Brian Saunders (© B. Saunders)

Brian Saunders (Drums)
"I was being taught by Jim Marshall (later to find fame with Marshall Amplifiers). Jim apart from teaching drumming, had a band called 'Wind Noise and the Rhythm'. I took over from him on drums. We were a five piece dance band. I got a phone call from Jim telling me about an audition for the Freddie Heath Band at The White Hart, Willesden. Don Toy had phoned Jim asking if he had any up and coming drummers. I didn't know who they were or what they played. I was told to set up my kit on the floor. Being into dance music I didn't know any of their material. The only r 'n' r I knew was Bill Haley and the Comets. I had his records, so I thought if it is a r 'n' r band I better learn some Bill Haley.

I did my stint Fred and Don came and said that I had passed the audition. I was thrilled but I said what about the other drummers who were waiting? "We want you" came their reply. They wanted me straight away for the coming Saturday but I had another gig.

The White Hart Pub (© Always N' Ever Archive)

I soon found Fred to be a very nice person. He couldn't do enough to help you. If someone was in trouble he would help out the best he could. He wore some unusual clothes. He used to turn up wearing Bed Ticks' trousers. They looked like old fashion mattress covers. They were striped on a white background.

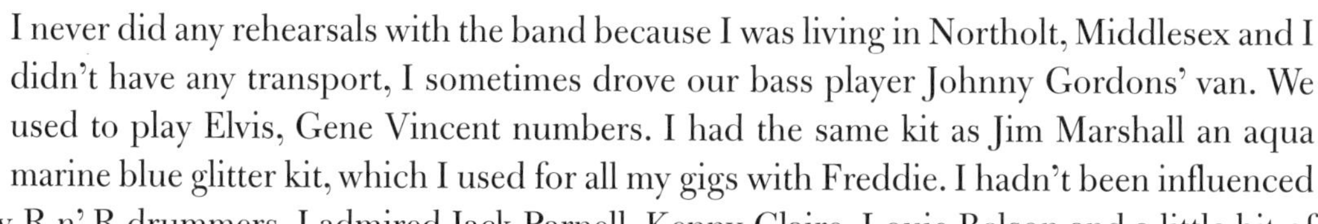
I never did any rehearsals with the band because I was living in Northolt, Middlesex and I didn't have any transport, I sometimes drove our bass player Johnny Gordons' van. We used to play Elvis, Gene Vincent numbers. I had the same kit as Jim Marshall an aqua marine blue glitter kit, which I used for all my gigs with Freddie. I hadn't been influenced by any R n' R drummers, I admired Jack Parnell, Kenny Claire, Louie Belson and a little bit of Buddy Rich. I recall going to a party and playing alongside the then unknown Brian Bennett. Another young lad who played on my kit and wrecked my top hat was Keith Moon who later became a great showman with 'The Who'.

Another time when I thought my kit was going to be destroyed was at Burtons in Uxbridge. We were unaware that there was two rival Teddy Boy gangs standing each side of the stage. All of a sudden a chair chopped down on this blokes head, then a great punch-up. Freddie continued singing, we kept on rocking and rolling. So did the Teds all over the floor. We kept the beat until the boys on the beat (police) came."

Fred was still busy writing new material, one of his best was 'Wow Wow Beat' which he recorded privately. Russell Turner of the 'Six Five Special' TV show heard this test disc, liked it and wanted to play it on the juke box spot in the show but no commercial recording company would take a chance.

Brian Saunders (Drummer)

"Fred was always writing his own songs, which was very unusual at the time. He worked very hard to get on in the music world. I remember going to a small studio to record one of his originals. I think it was Wow Wow. I was put in a box, the number was recorded live. My crash cymbal kept ringing, so Don Toy had to grab it to dampen the sound. I was on top of the world being in a band. It was all new to me especially all the fresh rocking material."

Press advertisement - Granada Willesden

Pete Newman (Sax)

"Freddie wanted a sax player after seeing the Little Richard band in the film 'The Girl Can't Help It'. I auditioned for Freddies' Band at 'The White Horse Pub'. Some of the band members didn't want a sax player but Fred had made up his mind and I was in. Slowly I gradually learnt a few numbers. I even sang harmony duets with him on Everly Brothers and Buddy Holly numbers. We played anywhere i.e. Railway Hotel, The Calypso Club, White Horse in Willesden. We would rehearse at the Altermora Club at Stonebridge Park."

The band were not only getting popular but also thanks to Don Toy looking very smart in black trousers and red cheque blouse type shirts. Don recalls promoter Guy Robinson and his wife coming to the K.K.K. Club in October '57. "We started talking about music, at the time I wanted someone to help finance the band because it was costing me a fortune. Guy was keen and they were able to do this.

One of the first things we did was book Fred with Freddie Winrose for professional singing lessons. He taught Fred voice projection and how to sing from the diaphragm". Unlike his daddy baby Tony Heath didn't need any help to cry from his tiny diaphragm. He would soon form a baby duo with an early xmas present. On the 12th December, Fred cried "Oh Boy!" as his wife gave birth to Russell Terence.

Film still - 'The Girl Can't Help It' with Little Richard

Derek Everard (Mate)

"Fred was really getting into his music. We used to go to the 'Heaven and Hell'. The rock n' roller Rory Blackwell would often come over for a chat. This really pleased Fred because Fred was a keen fan of his. We used to go to various musical spots. I recall at the 'Coffee Pot' when he told me he liked Brook Benton. Fred would wear velvet collar jackets, tight drainpipe trousers and brothel creepers, a real Teddy Boy. He was a bit lazy, he didn't enjoy going to work, he lived for music."

Rory Blackwell (Blackjacks)

"My band had a gig in a London pub. Outside the pub was a young skiffle group. I thought the young singer had got talent so I invited the young man to do a small spot during my act. Young Freddie Heath went down well."

As early as October '55 Rory Blackwell and his rock 'n' rollers had been performing rock. They appeared at Battersea Town Hall on 'The Jazz Band Ball', along with six Trad bands and soon had the crowd jiving.
When they signed for Parlophone they became Rory Blackwell and the Blackjacks. Rory had many first rate musicians in his band - Georgie Fame (Clive Powell), Terry Dene, Brian Gregg etc.

Brian Gregg (Bass - Les Hobeaux)
"Rory saw Terry Dene singing with Leon Bell and offered him a job with the Blackjacks as vocalist. Terry did a few gigs until Rory sacked him for fighting over a girl but Terry soon went on to greater success."

Alan Wheeler
"Rory used to be billed as Rory (Shakes) Blackwell and featured a shake routine that pre-dated Dickie Pride and Johnny Kidd (Freddie Heath). He was certainly an inspiration to John in creating his shake routine."

Blackwell was a superb drummer and a British r 'n' r pioneer. In 1958 Liverpool singer Alan Caldwell became 'Rory' Storm. Rory being an acknowledgement to Blackwell.

On the 3rd March '58, Freddie and his mates were glued to the TV as Buddy Holly, The Crickets and the Fender Stratocaster raved on Sunday Night At The London Palladium.
Buddy also appeared on 'See You In Soho' and 'Off The Record'. Throughout March Buddy toured all over England. The 20th March saw Marvin Rainwater enter the charts with 'Whole Lotta Woman'. Years later in April '64 Freddie would record a superb version himself.

left: The Crickets
centre: Brian Gregg (back centre) in film still from 'The Golden Disc'
right: Clem Cattini (drums) in film still from 'The Golden Disc'

One of the better guitarists at the Two I's Brian Rankin loved Marvins's record and name and became Hank B Marvin. Within a couple of years Hanks' Fender Stratocaster sound would leave most other guitarists standing in the shadows. The Most Brothers recorded 'Whole Lotta Woman' for Decca and performed their cover-version on 6-5 special during May.

Future Pirates Clem Cattini and Brian Gregg both appeared in the Terry Dene film 'The Golden Disc' which was released in March '58 by British Pathe.

Brian Gregg (Bass) Les Hobeaux)
"I appeared in the film with Les Bennett (lead), Keith Lardner (vocals), Roger Smith (vocals), Roy Tobing, Dyral Lyte and Rory Blackwell (drums). Clem (drums) was with Terry Kennedy,

Micky Donehuge, Pete Edelfield (bass), backing Terry Dene. After Terry cam out of the army I joined the 'Dene Aces' with Clem, Eric Kershure (lead) and Tommy (piano).

My first recording band was Les Hobeaux. I left to join Colin Hicks and the Cabin Boys either late '57 or early '58. Colin had sacked members of his band. They had not been together very long. His new band was Tony Eagleton (lead), Don (rhythm), Jimmy Nicol (drums) and myself on double bass. Don left after a week or so and was replaced by Ronnie Mills (piano).

Colin and Cabin Boys
(© B. Gregg)

We had a successful tour of Italy in May '58 with The Platters, The Trio Raigner, Jack Elliott and a compere who's name I can't remember. Because of the tour we were seen by a top Italian film producer and we were offered a spot in a film Europa Di Notta (Europe by Night). It was through this appearance that Colin and his Cabin Boys became very big in Italy.

When we returned home as well as playing for Colin I was doing gigs with Roy Blackwell and the Blackjacks.

Colin decided to leave Larry Parnes management in June '58. I introduced Colin to a friend of mine called Freddy Clifford he was an insurance broker from Croydon who I had first met at the 'Freight Train' coffee bar. He agreed to be our Manager.

Our pianist Ronnie Mills left and went home to Glasgow. He was replaced by Lou Brian (Perry Ford) and we also added a sax player an Irishman called Johnny Stanley.

Freddy Clifford took us over but we auditioned Lou and Johnny. Unfortunately Freddy got decapitated on an autobahn in Germany much later on. I was in the Cabin Boys on three or four different occasions. The last time was with Alan Caddy and Clem Cattini when we left the Pirates."

Another superb line up of Cabin Boys featured David Tick (zom) (lead), Mike O'Neill (piano), Jimmy Nicol (drums), replaced by Laurie Joy and Rod 'Boots' Slade (bass).

Freddie Heath Band
left to right
Pete Newman (sax)
Tony Carlaw (drums)
Freddie (vocals)
Frank Rouledge (rhythm)
Johnny Gordon (lead)

The Freddie Heath Band now had a large local following. A local rival was a lad called Johnny Bowden. His show stopper was 'Cindy'. Some great characters followed the band. Freddie Howard was at most gigs. He was a great jiver. Freddie and his mates called him rubber legs.

On July 26th 1958 Freddie and the lads gave their drummer a surprise musical wedding gift.

Brian Saunders (Drummer) (Freddie Heath Band)
"I asked Don Toy if he could get me a band for my wedding reception. Leave it with me replied Don. During the reception Don turns up. I said have the band arrived yet? Yeah, in a minute he smiled. Next in walks Freddie Heath. I said, What band is it? Freddie says, ours. Who's on drums?, I enquired. Don said 'I am.' He played on a couple of numbers then he announced that

I was going to play drums. I ended up playing all night. My new bride loved seeing me on stage. In fact she has always supported my career as a musician over the years. My wife and Fred's wife would often come along to gigs and have a good chat to each other."

Don Toy (Manager)
"The Krazy Kurzon Klub was now very popular. The pub was selling lots of drinks but the manager became greedy. He told us one Wednesday that we were finished and that he would take over running the club. We took him to court and won the case because we had a so called gentlemen's agreement. We decided not to return due to the bad feeling."

White Horse (K. K. Klub)
(© Always N' Ever archive)

Later that night Fred and the band set up outside the pub and plugged in their gear in a local shop. The protest gig soon had the road really rocking as their fans jived in the middle of the street.

Brian Saunders (Drummer) (Freddie Heath Band)
"I'd just come back from my honeymoon and was shocked to be told to set up on the pavement outside the White Horse pub. In fact this was on a Tuesday night in early August and my very last gig with the band. As far as I can recall I never heard of 'The Freddie Heath Band' again. I was very disappointed that Don and Freddie never contacted me again. Perhaps they lost my phone number or I just wasn't good enough.

Three months after leaving I joined the Greenford group The Chessmen. Once again it was Jim Marshall who told me about the vacant drummers stool."

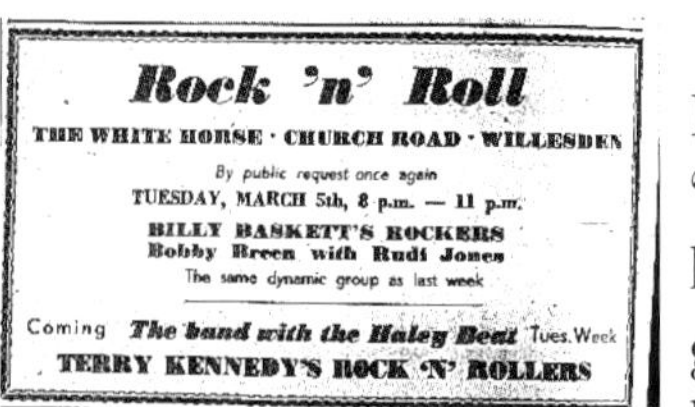

Press advetisement - White Horse Pub (© Always N' Ever Archive)

Pete Newman (Sax)
"We were so angry so Fred had an idea to run a cable across the main road to a shop owner he knew and plugged the power in there. We set up on the pavement outside the pub. The crowd got so large that the Willesden High Road came to a standstill. It took police with truncheons to break up the crowds of dancers in the street."

After losing their favourite venue The Freddie Heath Band, just fell apart. Promoter, Guy Robinson told Don about his successful nights at the Wandsworth Town Hall where the Mike West Group were becoming very popular. The main line-up was Mike West (vocals), Alan Caddy (lead), Tony Doherty (rhythm), Ken McKay (drums) and latest member Tom Brown (vocals).

left: Rockin' N' Rollin' at the KKK
right: The KKK Protest

6. FRED, MIKE AND TOM SHOW

Fred and Don Toy went along to Wandsworth Town Hall to see Mike West's Group.

Mike West recalls that first meeting
"One Wednesday night Guy came up to me and said I've got another singer whose lost his band, they've broken up, would you mind if he came and did a number with you. I said "no problem". In walks Freddie Heath. We said "What number are you going to do?" He replied, "The Only Girl in the World." We had a quick rehearsal in the back room of the Town Hall. From that night Fred was in the line-up. We called ourselves Fred, Mike and Tom Show.

I had first started with an audition with Tommy Steele's manager at the Two I's Coffee Bar when they were looking for a new Tommy Steele. I formed a band. I found Art Caddy playing in a pub in Wandsworth. Other members were Tony Doherty and Ken McKay on drums. Art was originally a violinist in his youth but later took up the guitar. I had a job to get Alan to play. He wouldn't go on stage. He would only play behind the curtain. Our main gig was the Wandsworth Town Hall. We played twice a week Mondays and Wednesdays. It was there that I met Guy Robinson and he soon took an interest in our group."

Fred was thrilled to be in a band again and was keen to get his mate Fruit Gordon in on bass. Fruit had been with Fred right from the early skiffle days and was pleased to join. By day Fruit earned his living as a maintenance engineer for Singer sewing machines in Church Road, Willesden. His wife Tina and Fred were always having a go at each other. Fred called her Horse Face while she would yell 'Dogsbody' back at him.

Having three vocalists was very unusual but they all got on very well as Mike West explains
"Art, Tony, Fruit and Ken would go out and do an instrumental sometimes supported by Pete Newman and Geoff Wiggins on saxes. I would go on and sing Marty Wilde, Cliff Richard, Elvis, Ricky Nelson numbers, then Tom Brown would do his spot. He was a little chap, wore glasses, hair slicked back. He worked by day as a fishmonger but come evening he performed great vocals especially on Buddy Holly material. Then Fred would come on and Tom and I would do backing vocals. Fred always did a lovely version of 'Whose Sorry Now'. Tom loved to sing 'The Three Bells' while Fred and I added the backing. We always mucked about while Tom was putting his heart and soul into it."

Mike West (© M. West)

Don Toy (Agent)
"Tom was a very good singer but he always had a fishy smell. Ha! Ha! Wandsworth Town Hall became one of, if not, the biggest pop venue in London. People would queue for hours to be part of the scene. We charged 1/- (5p) for entrance. Most Saturday nights we had a thousand people. Most of the money was made by selling soft drinks. The canteen was as large as the dance hall. Guy Robinson would spin all the latest records. Sometimes our roadie, Peter Horn, would take over while Guy had a drink.

I once had my own business making sound equipment so I decided to make an Amp for Fruit Gordon. It had a huge speaker cabinet which gave out a hundred watts. It must have been one of the very first british bass amps. You could feel the Town Hall floor vibrate. Real power. It was very heavy. Peter Horn and the group all moaned about the weight.

When we first started at the Town Hall most of the evening was records and the stars were Freddie, Mike and Tom. We later began featuring more live acts. We encouraged young up and coming groups to play".

Guy Robinson also booked the band for the Derby Arms, East Sheen. The ex-boxer Len Harvey was the proprietor. They played there every Sunday.

As time went by their act was getting better and more professional. They soon had record companies knocking on the door.

Mike West (Vocalist)
"Guy Robinson told us that someone from H.M.V. was coming to the Town Hall to watch our act with regards to a contract. Our performance that night was a disaster. Guy was really mad with us, but as luck had it, H.M.V. came again and we were offered a recording contract."

top: Freddie Heath
(© F. Rouledge)
centre: Freddie Heath
(© Jean Heath collection)

Walter Ridley (Producer)
"Peter Sullivan my assistant introduced Freddie and the band to me. I was asked to go out and hear them perform at Elstree. The performance took place in a corrugated sheet hall. I couldn't believe what went on there because I couldn't hear anything. It was just a loud howling metallic noise and this went on for two and a half hours. When I walked out my head was going ga-ga-ga. I thought this can't be true, it's just not on. Anyway I met Freddie Heath who, as it happens, was an absolute lamb. He was a little darling. I became very fond of that boy."

On Saturday 18th April 1959 they arrived at EMI's studios in St. Johns Wood for a recording session.

Mike West (Vocalist)
"Fred had a lot of original material Wow Wow Beat, Mr and Miss, Please Don't Touch etc. We decided to work on Please Don't Touch. Peter Sullivan met us at Abbey Road recording studios. The first person we saw was Don Lang of the Frantic Five. As we entered we were given a piece of paper with the name Johnny Kidd and The Pirates recording session. Fred said to me who the hell is that? A voice spoke out that from now on that's your recording name. We never did find out who's idea it was. Perhaps Guy Robinson or our producer Pete Sullivan."

below: Johnny Kidd (EMI)

Pete Newman (Sax Player)
"I think it was Peter Sullivan's idea to call the group Johnny Kidd and The Pirates."

Freddie took the name from a real Pirate Captain William Kidd (1650-1701). Of all the reckless sea-rovers who flew the Jolly Roger at the mastheads of their pirate ships, made their poor victims walk the plank and buried their ill-gotten treasures on lonely isles, Captain Kidd is the most famous - though one of the least typical. Despite the many legends that have grown upon his name. William Kidd was a Scottish ministers' son and followed the sea from his youth.

In King William's war between the English and French he became known as the bold captain of a privateer in the West Indies. By the end of the 17th Century he had become a successful shipmaster sailing from New York. British commerce then suffered greatly from marauding pirates. So, at the request of the governor of New York, Kidd received two commissions from the King addressed to 'our trusty and well beloved Captain Kidd' - one for suppressing piracy and the other as a privateer against the French.

With his 30 guns and his crew of 155 men the captain jauntily set sail in his ship, 'Adventure', for Madagascar, Malabar and the Red Sea region, the chief haunts of the pirates.

Then his troubles began. No pirates were found. A cholera plague destroyed some of the crew. The ship grew leaky and supplies began to give out. Then, apparently, Captain Kidd followed the advice of his discontented crew and himself turned pirate. He took several small Moorish vessels, was defeated by a Portuguese man of war, and captured a Portuguese and an American vessel.

In 1699 he deserted his leaky old 'Adventure' boarded one of his prizes and headed for America, learning that he had been proclaimed a pirate he sent to the governor a part of his booty. He was arrested in Boston where he landed and sent to London for trial. There he was convicted of murder for killing a mutinous sailor. After a trail in which the evidence was inconclusive and he kept protesting that he was the most innocent person of them all he was pronounced guilty and for piracy. He was hanged at Execution Dock and his body long hung in chains.

Pepe Rush (Recording Engineer)
"I was on the first demo record Freddie ever cut. This was in Regent Sound studios in Denmark Street. He came in with his manager Guy Tyngate-Smith also known as Guy Robinson and accompanied himself on an acoustic guitar. I have to say that at this time I had no idea of how good a singer he was going to turn into or that he was going to become a star. He was a most pleasant and friendly chap."

7. JOHNNY KIDD AND THE PIRATES

Pepe Rush (Recording Engineer)
"I do not remember how long it was before I met him again. By this time he was using the name Johnny Kidd and had formed the Pirates. I don't think it was more than a few months. He had by then become a very good singer though his personality and manners had not changed. I seem to remember seeing him quite regularly and can remember recording him many times in my basement studios called Radio Music Recording Studios in Berwick Street that I ran with my late mother, father and grandfather. It was I remember usually very late at night often after they returned from a gig.

It was always a great pleasure to work with a singer and backing group who were so professional and easy to get on with. In my basement studio I recorded the demo of the first hit the Shadows made 'Apache'.

After I had moved out of recording into design and manufacture of sound equipment. I let another engineer Chris Kerry use the studio to record Rod Stewarts first recordings."

Johnny Kidd (Freddie Heath)
"I always wanted to be a writer not a singer. When I'd saved up enough cash from my work as a house painter I gave myself three months to make the grade. At the end of three months I'd written 30 songs none of which had sold. Then, when I was desperate with despair and quite hungry, I sold the 31st, Please Don't Touch. 'Touch' had quite a bit of capital invested in it from the music publishers but the two singers chosen couldn't punch the song home to the public.

Sheet music - 'Please Don't Touch'
(Always N' Ever Archive)

It was suggested that I take a recording test. I passed, was liked and well you know the rest of the story. Its the most melodic song I've yet written. I played all the chords I knew and then began switching the order to form different combinations. Eventually I stumbled on a pattern of chords that intrigued me and this became the foundation of 'Please Don't Touch'. I thought of a title for the song before I tackled the lyrics. I wanted a well known phrase - something like No Smoking, and I finally settled for Please Don't Touch. Then I built the words around the title."

Johnny was really thrilled to be part of the song written fraternity which was based in Denmark Street, and collectively known as Tin Pan Alley, just off the busy Charing Cross Road, London. The original version of 'Touch' was recorded by the British duo 'The Bachelors' on Parlophone and produced by George Martin. They were two youngsters who met purely by chance in the Two I's Coffee Bar. Their names were Rikki Gabin born Greenock, Scotland and Steve Keen from London. They were managed by Paul Lincoln who soon got them booked on the nation-wide tour Stars of Saturday Club with Ricky Valance and Bert Weedon etc. They also toured with Cliff Richard on the Move It package show and Johnny Kidd and The Pirates. Please Don't Touch /Ding Ding Parlophone 45R4547.

An American rocker Chico Holiday covered the song in the States, a virtually unknown event in those days. It was released in Britain on an EP. CHICO HOLIDAY R.C.A. RCX 171
Please Don't Touch, Young Ideas, Lonesome Stranger, Your Kid Sister.

During this period there were only four leading record companies E.M.I., DECCA, PHILIPS and PYE.

Mike West remembers their very first session for E.M.I. Please Don't Touch took about 28 takes. We played the song all the way through, they edited the tape and joined the best takes. "We didn't have the slightest idea for a B side so we threw a few ideas quickly together and actually wrote Growl in the studio, I got paid £7 10/- for the session. We all thought we were well off."

Don Toy (Agent)
"All the numbers that were written by Guy, Fred and myself were a joint effort. I would write down the music it was composed in a pure Heath Robinson style and that's why we put Freddie Heath and Guy Robinson on the writing credits."

Please Don't Touch/Growl was released on May 8th 1959. Roadie Johnny Irving recalls the excitement of getting on wax. "I remember at the time Johnny was staying with me at my home in Margate. We got a call from Mills Music to come to London so that Johnny could record it himself.

It really took off so I moved back to the London area. Everyone in the business knew that it should go to number one. Sadly there was a national strike, no newspapers etc, which didn't help with promoting it."

Pat Sherlock
PROFESSIONAL MANAGER

MILLS MUSIC LTD.,
20 DENMARK STREET,
LONDON, W.C.2.

PHONE (DAY) COV. 1745
" (NIGHT) COV. 1749

Mills Music business card (Always N' Ever Archive)

Mike West (Vocalist)
"Sadly the very day 'Touch' was released Ken Mackay was sacked. His drumming wasn't that hot. In fact Don played drums on the overdubs for 'Touch' because Ken's timing was out. Sadly Ken left as we turned professional. I remember earning 30/- (£1.50p) and Johnny Kidd was on £2.10/- (£2.50p). Sunday was our pay day. We would meet Guy Robinson in the Derby Arms pub. Guy's wife Pam would pay us and say "Don't spend it all at once." Halfway through the week we'd run out of money. I'd have to walk from Battersea and Johnny from Willesden to Guys' office in Shaftsbury Avenue. We were really dedicated."

To help with promoting 'Please Don't Touch' Manager, Guy Robinson went over to Luxembourg to wine and dine the leading D.J.'s who in return made sure that it suddenly got a lot of air play. During the late 50's Radio Luxembourg was the best radio station for pop music. It was a must for young British teenagers, '208' with shows such as Top Twenty, Tune a Minute, Transatlantic Pops, The International Night Service'. It had a daily listening audience of six million. Like the broadcasting stations in the United States Luxembourg was a commercial channel. Adverts being inserted between programmes.

Radio Luxembourg business card (Always N' Ever Archive)

DAVID SAMPSON
PUBLICITY OFFICER

RADIO LUXEMBOURG,
38, HERTFORD STREET,
LONDON, W.1.

TELEPHONE:
HYDE PARK 5961

The station situated in Luxembourg's Central Park was built in 1930. In September 1939 the Luxembourg Government took over the station, broadcasting special war bulletins daily. By the end of September the station was silent. July 1940 the station was back on the air. The Germans used it for propaganda broadcasts.

William Joyce (Lord Haw-Haw) worked from the station. September 1944 the American forces liberated the city of Luxembourg. The allied forces took control of the station and Radio Luxembourg played an important part in the final defeat

of the Germans.
The station became one of the best information services available to the allied commanders in Europe.

British listeners heard the station on the air again in 1946. By the mid 1950's it was by far the best for rock n' roll and pop music. Although it was hard to obtain a good reception you had to fine twiddle, getting a lot of German and French babble in your search.

Don Toy (Agent)
"Not long after the recording of 'Touch' we decided to sack Ken Mackay. We decided to hold auditions for a new drummer so I booked the White Hart, Willesden the following morning."

(© Jean Heath Collection)

The group were always encouraged to rehearse, Don was friendly with the vicar at St. Matthew's Church and for 5/- (25p) a night they practised in the Church Hall. They also used the Hall at the back of St Mary's Church, Willesden. Even the downstairs back room at Johnny's home in Leopold Road was used at times.

During this period Johnny had not yet developed his out and out Pirate image. He usually wore a suit. In fact on the first hand out postcard photos produced by E.M.I. Records. Johnny wore a plain shirt thin striped trousers, black shoes and no eye patch.

Pat Newman (Mike West's Wife)
"During the summer we all went to a promotion at Ruislip Lido. Rory Blackwell and actor Stanley Baker were there. The following week at a fete near Wandsworth a young fellow went up to Fred and said "Oh you're Johnny Kidd, can I have your autograph? I've got your record." Fred said "You're the first person I've ever met who's bought my record." We all went back to this guy's house and Fred signed his record. The lad was over the moon, and so was Johnny Kidd. Johnny loved to look different. He once joined two shirts together. He cut them right up the back and joined them with safety pins. Under his jacket it looked great. He also had a green suit made up of tailors patterns."

Mike West recalls the first time he wore that unusual suit.
"We were doing the radio show at Olympia. Guy Robinson told us that from now on in public I don't want to hear anyone call him Fred. It's Johnny Kidd from now on. Anyway we went on and performed 'Please Don't Touch'. Afterwards we stayed around to give out autographs. Of course, I completely forgot, I yelled out, "Fred where are we going next?". All the girls were yelling his real name is Fred. He's going 'Mike you twit', I said sorry John. It took us a long time to get used to his new name."

(Johnny could never forget his real name. He had a tattoo on his arm with 'Fred' clearly readable).
Johnny started using a tape echo chamber for his live shows. He wanted the public to hear his voice under the same acoustic conditions as he sounded on his single. He was, in fact, one of the very first vocalists in Britain to use echo equipment during a live performance.

Mike West (Vocalist)
"We had the first echo chamber which Don Toy made. He even devised a stereo type effect for Johnnys' vocals. We first used it at Battersea Town Hall. The Kidd had two leather suits made. One black the other white. Both had chains hanging from the jackets. On stage in Norfolk, he was teasing the girls in the front row. As he leaned forward they all grabbed his chains and ripped them off. After the show Johnny was on his hands and knees trying to find his chains crying, "The bastards, I've lost my chains and we're starting a tour tomorrow."

The first real big tour for the group was all the American bases across Britain. A Tito Burns Promotion. They hired a rehearsal room in the Charing Cross Road to really get the act together for this special tour. The young unknown Jimmy Tarbuck was the compere. Other acts included Lisa Noble who was pushing her latest release on Decca, Maggie Yes Ma/Whose Sorry Now, The Carson Twins who were an all-girl close harmony trio also on Decca, The Bear/My Christmas Dream, and Bill n' Brett Landis (England's answer to the Everly Bros), Bill (William Hobbs) and Brett Landis (Stuart Freedman). Stuart had been the choreographer for the Six-Five-Special film. They cut their musical teeth at the Lyceum Ballroom and had appeared on early Benny Hill shows during the 50's. For the whole of the tour they had the luxury of a coach but they had to return home every night sometimes as late as 5am.

MELODY MAKER June 20, 1959

Melody Maker TOP 20 POPS

WEEK ENDED JUNE 13, 1959

		Title	Artist	Label
1	(4)	ROULETTE	Russ Conway	Columbia
2	(1)	A FOOL SUCH AS I/I NEED YOUR LOVE TONIGHT	Elvis Presley	RCA
3	(5)	DREAM LOVER	Bobby Darin	London
4	(3)	IT'S LATE/THERE'LL NEVER BE ANYONE ELSE BUT YOU	Ricky Nelson	London
5	(2)	IT DOESN'T MATTER ANY MORE	Buddy Holly	Vogue-Coral
6	(14)	A TEENAGER IN LOVE	Marty Wilde	Philips
7	(6)	I'VE WAITED SO LONG	Anthony Newley	Decca
8	(—)	PETER GUNN/YEP!	Duane Eddy	London
9	(11)	THREE STARS	Ruby Wright	Parlophone
10	(8)	NEVER MIND/MEAN STREAK	Cliff Richard	Columbia
11	(7)	I GO APE	Neil Sedaka	RCA
12	(12)	SIDE SADDLE	Russ Conway	Columbia
13	(10)	COME SOFTLY TO ME	Frankie Vaughan	Philips
14	(9)	GUITAR BOOGIE SHUFFLE	Bert Weedon	Top Rank
15	(—)	PERSONALITY	Lloyd Price	HMV
16	(13)	DONNA	Marty Wilde	Philips
17	(—)	GOODBYE, JIMMY, GOODBYE	Ruby Murray	Columbia
18	(18)	MAY YOU ALWAYS	Joan Regan	HMV
19	(20)	POOR JENNY/TAKE A MESSAGE TO MARY	Everly Brothers	London
20	(—)	PLEASE DON'T TOUCH	Johnny Kidd	HMV

MICHAEL RISPOLI

HYDE PARK 8751
(10 LINES)

TITO BURNS PRODUCTIONS LTD
3 VERE STREET, LONDON, W1

top: Top Twenty - Melody Maker, June 13, 1959

bottom: Tito Burns International business card
(© Always N' Ever Archive)

Mike West looks back to the era with sincere feelings.
"They were magic years. Nobody thought of the future. It wasn't a business. It was like a little clan, we enjoyed each others company. It was incredible. It was just the crazy days of rock 'n' roll. Johnny really felt his music, Guy Robinson would suggest various styles of music, but Johnny wouldn't do any material that he didn't like which was very unusual in those days as most artists were dictated to by their management. Guy always wanted us to look A1 whenever we were in the public eye. He used to do his nut at John because Johnny was a scruffy sod. Guy even wrote a song about the Kidds appearance - "There is a cute little guy in this town and he always runs Johnny Kidd down." Never does any work, all he does is just shirk."

Guy was different from the other managers of the period. Stanley Dale, Reg Calvert, George Cooper etc, were all very shrewd. Guy did it for the love of it. He really enjoyed the scene. I honestly don't think he gained anything out of us. He was fanatical about the band especially Johnny's image. Guy was very creative. He used to take me and Johnny and give us elocution lessons and stage presentation. We used to go to his office in Shaftsbury Avenue. At the top of the building he used to have three lights on. He made up look up, down etc, he gave us presentation, how to move, walk etc. He even bought our first pirate gear. We had striped jeans, bright orange shirts, with Johnny wearing dark red. We were very colourful. Johnny also wore a lime green suit while us pirates wore orange.

I remember Guy telling Johnny when the curtains open on the first number you will hold your audience, your second number you've got to start to do a production and gradually increase it until you get to the climax. He groomed Johnny for stardom. If we did a gig and it wasn't up to scratch, Guy would soon have a few words with us. If Johnny performed better than me or I better than Johnny he'd had a real go at us. He used to keep everybody on their toes. He had a rostrum built for our drummer. I remember Kenny hitting the drums a bit too hard and his kit fell off. Guy was concerned about Johnny's weight, he wanted Johnny to look macho, a real buccaneer. So Johnny decided to stuff newspaper under his shirt. He was halfway into a number when suddenly the papers started falling out around the stage. We were in tears, we couldn't stop laughing and had to stop and leave the stage."

An appearance on BBC radio's Saturday Club, brought the act to a far bigger audience. Saturday Club had started in 1958. It featured records and recorded sessions. A mixture of pop, trad-jazz, C/W, skiffle and rock 'n' roll.

DJ Brian Matthew presented the show and confirms just how important the show was.
"Enormously, I think partly for its variety value in so far as there were not pop music programmes all day, everyday to be received. There was no pirate radio. Of course the BBC certainly didn't put on anything like the amount of pop music it does now on Radio One.

So for the kids and pop fans there was one highlight of the week. Every Saturday morning so that made it special, made it important. It had an audience which by today's measurement because of the proliferation of choice is unthinkable. It was sometimes as much as twenty five, thirty five million people. Obviously a preponderance of young people so it was a very powerful market indeed."

Jimmy Grant (Producer)
"I went along to Wandsworth to hear them perform and immediately realised that they were an extremely good group making the right sort of sound and were well worthy of encouragement."

Co-Producer Bernie Andrews was responsible for guest artists recording sessions for the programme. Johnny and The Pirates arrived at the Playhouse in London to record their spot for the show.

Bernie Andrews
"The sessions usually lasted three and a half hours normally booked for Tuesday afternoon and Tuesday evening at the Playhouse where we pre-recorded four or five numbers to play in the programme the following Saturday. That was the day of straight mono recording. When the recordings were done they were done for transmission. They weren't mixed later or anything. They went straight from there and were played on the programme from another tape machine on the Saturday morning."

EYE PATCH!
The lads were very excited about their radio debut but hardly had time to be nervous because they kept laughing at Mike West.

Mike West (Vocalist)
"I had a very bad sty so I wore an eye patch. Compere Brian Matthew asked me if it was part of our act but I'd only worn it because all the lads were taking the mickey out of my eye. Our session went well. I recall Johnny singing, Yes Sir That's My Baby and I took lead vocals on 'Here Comes Summer'. Jimmy Grant very kindly gave me a recording of the session. Cliff Richard, The

Springfields and Bert Weedon were also on the programme. Bert was then having great success with Guitar Boogie Shuffle. Alan Caddy played his version to Bert who sat there gob smacked because Alan's fingering was so fast."

Saturday Club was bombarded with mail, leading to a re-booking. The lads were thrilled.

Derek Everard (Mate)
"Guy Robinson had lots of cards printed. Johnny's mates posted them to Saturday Club requesting Fred's latest release. It must have impressed the producers."

FAN CLUB
A fan club was started by a teenage fan Miss Josephine Pacey of 508 Osmaston Road, Derby Johnny was proud to inform the music press.

Johnny Kidd
"After my first appearance on Saturday Club, Josephine wrote immediately afterwards and said she would like to start a fan club. She was my first fan and the first girl to believe in me. I've met her several times and she really is something special."

Johnny (© F. Rouledge)

Saturday July 4th may have been a big day in the States but for Johnny it was to be the start of a magical month. His very first single 'Please Don't Touch/Growl' was released on the 8th and he was also pleased to hear that fellow ole skiffler Adam Faith from Acton was to star on BBC Television in a new programme called 'Drumbeat'. The show was broadcast from the BBC's Riverside Studios. Producer Stuart Morris worked very hard. He used to have about 70 changes of lighting and the music demanded a good 20 arrangements. Most shows featured Adam Faith, John Barry Seven, Bob Miller and his Millermen, Gus Goodwin and Trevor Peacock were comperes, Barry Sisters, Roy Young, Sylvia Sands, King Pins, Raindrops and Vince Eager.

As Johnny sat on the edge of his seat enjoying the show, he almost fell on the floor as Vince Eager and the John Barry Seven broke into 'Please Don't Touch'. A few days later on Wednesday July 8th Johnny and The Pirates made their TV debut on Jack Parnells 'Record Round Up'. They were proud to appear along with Eddie Calvert, Tony Brent, Acker Bilk and Petula Clark.

Tony Doherty (Pirates Rhythm Guitarist)
"The studio set was so small only Johnny, Art Caddy and myself could get on it to mime the record. We had no rehearsal and the show went out live."

They celebrated later that night with a great booze up. Johnny was keen to tell the media that apart from r 'n' r he loved Frank Sinatra and Sammy Davis Jnr. The following day Guy Robinson booked the Abbey Road Studios to record their stage favourite 'Yes Sir That's My Baby'.

Mike West (Pirates Backing Vocalist)
"On the day of our second recording sessions Guy said be there on time because Walter Ridley and Peter Sullivan are busy producers. We all turn up except the 'Kidd'. 2 o'clock no sign, 3 o'clock. By this time Guy was tearing his hair out. He was so worried he hired a private detective. Johnny was found sunbathing with a girl on Bournemouth beach. A shocked Johnny was rushed back to Abbey Road, but the session was not up to standard."

E.M.I. RECORDS LIMITED
(CONTROLLED BY ELECTRIC & MUSICAL INDUSTRIES LIMITED)

TELEPHONE: LANGHAM 3544

8-11 GREAT CASTLE STREET,
LONDON. W.1.

TELEGRAMS & CABLES: EMIRECORD, WESDO, LONDON

WJR/BJ

6th August, 1959

Mr.F. Heath,
67, Leopold Road,
London. N.W.10.

Registered

Dear Mr.Heath:

I am sending you herewith counterpart of the Agreement between yourself and this Company, duly signed by the Secretary and witnessed. This is for your retention.

Yours faithfully,

Blanche Jones

Secretary to Walter J.Ridley
Artist & Repertoire Manager

Encl.

"HIS MASTER'S VOICE" · CAPITOL · COLUMBIA · PARLOPHONE · REGAL-ZONOPHONE · M-G-M RECORDS
REPRODUCERS AND ACCESSORIES

Contract with E.M.I.
(courtesy of Don Toy)

Mike West's parents were not very keen on him entering the wild world of rock 'n' roll.
"I had passed my city and guilds and was working for Queens Printers. My governor had a word - its got to stop. I saw you at the Playhouse Theatre, Charing Cross. You were all dressed in black, a red guitar under your arm, with a lead singer acting like Captain Kidd.

To get his parents off his back Mike had a scheme. "I got Jerry Kellers record 'Here Comes Summer' washed off the label, struck on a white piece of paper and wrote demo Mike West. Suddenly my mother was really proud of her 'pop' star son."
The red cut out guitars that the Pirates used were designed by their bass player Johnny 'Fruit' Gordon. The Shadows and The Pirates had a friendly rivalry. When the shads got the first fenders imported into England they were proud to show The Pirates. But Johnny and the lads were just as proud of their 'Gordon' cut outs.

Don Toy (Pirate)
"We were playing this theatre with a huge stage. We built up two huge platforms both sides of the stage. I was playing drums on one tower while we had another drummer on the other side of the stage."

A few weeks later Kent Walton came to see the show and offered them a spot on his TV series. They also appeared on the popular mid-day TV show Lunch Box and performed 'Please Don't Touch'. Another show was recorded at the ABC studios. Johnny went with Guy Robinson without his Pirates and mimed to the record. ATV's Disc Break also gave them TV exposure.

Johnny with Johnny Irving
(Roadie)
(courtesy of J. Braley)

SEXY IMAGE

Mike West (Vocalist)
"Guy said to Johnny, 'you've got to look sexy for TV'". He gave him two golf balls and said put them in your trouser pockets. The Kidd certainly looked well built that night. Ha! ha!"

Guy's Grandmother Tynegate Smith owned a dance hall in Baker Street, London. It was very popular and always full of ballet dancers. The place was full or mirrors so it was the ideal place for us to go through the entire act and be able to watch it for ourselves.

Not every gig was successful. We did a big variety show at Portsmouth and hardly any crowd turned up. We ended up in the audience Johnny and all The Pirates. The tours we used to do the management used to come along and we used to moan to them that we were shattered. We would pass the time on the coach playing cards. We'd start in London, next Edinburgh then back to Southampton. We hardly got any sleep so when we arrived for the gigs we were not fit to perform. We were given 'speed' to keep us awake but we got to the stage when we started to rely on the tablets to help get us through those demanding tours."

No one was happy with the 'Yes Sir That's My Baby' session. So on Monday 2nd November they decided to work on another Heath-Robinson number 'Feelin' and a ballad 'Steady Date'. The sessions were booked under producer Walter Ridley. Walter who was one of four artists and repertoire managers at E.M.I. The other three were George Martin, Norrie Paramor and Norman Newell. Every Tuesday morning a supplement meeting was held at E.M.I. House in Manchester Square, London to determine the records that would be released some time ahead. Whenever possible Walter would try and have a completed record with him so that everyone could hear what he was offering. He would have until the following Monday to complete a recording for this issue and this schedule would be kept pretty rigidly.

Walter had been in the music world for many years. He was born in St. Pancras, London on 28th February 1913 and from an early age he just loved music. He started playing piano, which his Father had bought. After a few lessons he was playing very well. On leaving school he joined a publisher, his job playing the latest songs on a piano for the customers. He developed a great talent for writing songs. One of his very first compositions was recorded by Gracie Fields ' The One Little Hair on his Head'. Walter's writing talent got around and soon most of the leading vocalists were knocking on his door for help with arrangements and hopefully a new hit song.

Apart form publishing and writing he went onto become recording manager at H.M.V. His first real pop chart success came with Max Bygraves and Malcolm Vaughans' Every Day of My Life' which reached number 5 in July '55. Another early hit artist was the late Alma Cogan. Many, many sessions followed - Ronnie Hilton, Frankie Vaughan, Harry Secombe, Joe Loss, Donald Peers, Bert Weedon and more recently Iris Williams in the 1980's.

The strangest period of his career was Johnny Kidd. He is the first to admit that he was out of his depth. In fact he let Peter Sullivan and later Norman Smith have complete control of most sessions.

Walter Ridley (Producer)
"Technically I am a load of rubbish. I'm so grateful to so many people who helped. You know you can't make a record on your own, not even the artist can, you have to have a lot of people around you. A lot of talent and the better the talents and I owe so much to so many people at E.M.I. The engineers etc, incredible people and I'm so grateful to them all. Throughout my career I stuck with the things I knew how to do but of course like everything there's always the exception and the exception in this case was Johnny Kidd."

Peter Sullivan was in control at most sessions. Sometimes they reached a master in one take - other times it took longer and had to be edited. This musical surgery which involved the splicing together of the best pieces was the job of balance engineer Norman Smith. Norman had always been keen on music, as young as seven he played drums, went onto trumpet and other brass instruments then took up vibes.

Norman Smith (Balance Engineer)
"I came out of the R.A.F. in 1947, did the usual round of auditions, got nowhere. Most of the plum big band jobs had gone. I eventually took a job in production for music programmes on the BBC. In 1959 I joined E.M.I. as a balance engineer. I was always disappointed about the general balance of music programmes. I felt not enough was made of rhythm sections."

He got his chance to use his ideas with Johnny Kidd and later The Beatles.

'Feelin' was chosen for release but 'Steady Date' remained unreleased until 1983. They decided that Johnnys stage favourite 'If You Were The Only Girl In The World' would make an unusual single. A session was booked for Thursday November 12th. Bert Weedon played lead while Ivor Raymonde conducted the chorus and orchestra.

above: (both © F. Rouledge)

'If You Were The Only Girl In The World/Feelin' was released on December 4th 1959. Although 'If You Were The Only Girl In The World' was a very popular live number it didn't set the charts alight. It was also available at the same time by a vast selection of artists i.e. Russ Conway, Ivor Emmanuel, Gene Krupa, Mitch Miller Gang, Sony Rollins Trio, Victor Silvester Orch, Malcolm Vaughan and George Robey. This strange choice for a follow-up single didn't make much headway, but it aroused agent Stanley Dale interest in the Kidds' style and potential.

Dale was a former flight lieutenant in the R.A.F. during World War Two who rejoiced in the nickname of 'Scruffy' and had won the D.F.C. for sitting on an incendiary shell which had penetrated his aeroplane. In 1955 Dale formed Associated London Scripts with Eric Sykes. They soon had Frankie Howerd, Spike Milligan, Tony Hancock and script writers Galton and Simpson on the payroll. Their offices were above a greengrocer's shop in the Uxbridge Road, Shepherds Bush, London. During the skiffle craze Dale signed up various groups and budding rock n' rollers such as The Vipers skiffle group, Jim Dale, Dean Shannon, Rory Wilde and the Wild Cats. One of his first big pop promotions was The National Skiffle Contest which toured all over Britain.

Jim Dale was top of the bill. The Vipers, then the biggest group in the country closed the first half. Dale never really promoted his rock n' roll acts. He would often only place a small advert in the N.M.E. music paper. He owned various dance halls, The Teenage Ballroom at Ramsgate, Aylesbury etc etc.

Johnny Kidd decided to sign for Stanley Dale's Associated London Scripts. The contract was for one year. Terry Anton also from Willesden had signed with Dale two week previous for a reported £50,000 for a five year contract. One of the first bookings for Johnny and his crew was for Dale's Rock Show at the Coronation Hall, Kingston-upon-Thames along with the other new signing Terry Anton and his Rhythm Rockers.

Press advertisement

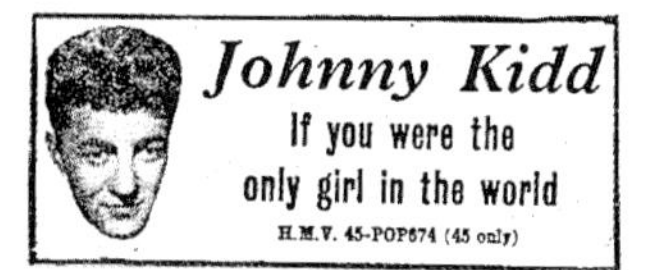

Mike West (Vocalist)
"When we weren't fully booked we played Dale's venues, The Top Ten Club, Peckham, Hatfield, Borehamwood, Aylesbury, Ramsgate. Johnny always like to do 'If You Were The Only Girl In The World', Feelin, Baby That's All You Gotta Do. I remember at Hatfield this yob tried to get in

for nothing and Dale told him to go home. The bloke lost him temper and the next second Stanley Dale has got the bloke on the floor. Dale said "I forgot to mention I'm very handy at judo and I told you son, you don't get in here for nothing - go home."

Don Toy (Agent)
"Everytime we went to Dale's house he was always in bed wearing an old dressing gown which must have been forty years old. He always had a box of Players cigarettes by his side, a fag hanging on his lip, he'd chat and it would be hanging there - it would never fall off."

Mike West (Vocalist)
"For one gig at Aylesbury we all went in our Bass players 'Fruit' Gordon's taxi. It was a freezing cold night so we decided to cover up the engine with a blanket. After the gig we had forgotten all about it, started up the engine and it caught fire. The taxi got completely burnt out. Our main driver during this period was Peter Horn. He was also in charge of setting up the groups gear which consisted of Leak amps and Goodmans speakers. We used a Dormobile which had added windows, thank God, as the main activity that took place was farting competitions. It used to be a real scream and smell travelling up and down the country.
The Busy Bee Cafe with its egg and chips in thick greasy fat was always a popular place with us half starved musicians. To help with the release of 'If You Were The Only Girl In The World' I took a pressing demo to Luxembourg (Radio) and Cologne (Family Favourites Show).

Press advertisement

Guy Robinson had booked some work for Johnny in Germany, but the 'Kidd' was very busy at home in England so I took his place. During my visit I had to speak slow and clear to get the Germans to understand a rocker from Battersea. On my return to England I was speaking with a completely different voice. Johnny couldn't stop laughing. 'Why are you talking like that, all nice and posh?"

1959 had been a tremendous year for Johnny Kidd he had achieved far greater success than he could have ever dreamed of over the 'Rainbow Cafe'. His greatest Christmas present was seeing his idol Gene Vincent on TV. Gene had landed at London Airport on December 5th. Promoter Larry Parnes signed Vincent to an exclusive 30 week contract. Gene appeared on three editions of the 'Boy Meets Girl' TV Show, December 12th, 19th and a special Boxing Day edition.

It gave Johnny and many other British fans a real chance to see Gene. Having made only one live show at Tooting, his tour was not planned until the new year. Little did Johnny realise he would not only meet his idol but they would become good mates in the near future.

8. THE PURPLE PATCH

The new decade started with a new Fan Club at 75 Swinburne, Roehampton, London SW15. Monday January 4th saw them back in the studios at Abbey Road, St Johns Wood, London. The result of the session was a fine cover of Marv Johnson's recent hit 'You Got What It Takes'. The B side was another written by Johnny and Guy Robinson 'Longin Lips'. Some sad news reached Johnny - Wandsworth Town Hall was stopping all live music.

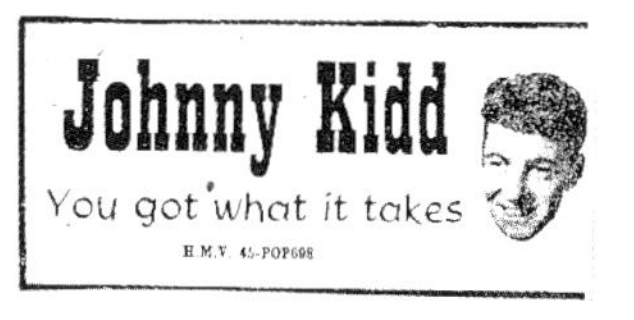

Press advertisement

Don Toy (Agent)
"We were forced to close down at the Town Hall. We just couldn't believe it. They decided to redecorate the place and put up thousands of pounds worth of chandeliers and it became only available for private functions. I started running another venue at the Limelight Ballroom, St Mary's Hall, Putney. It was very popular but never in the same league as the Town Hall."

Over the years Don auditioned many unknown bands. He turned down Manfred Mann and Georgie Fame and The Blue Flames thus proving not everything he touched turned to Pirates Gold.

CHANGE OF CREW
Dony Toy (Agent)
"We decided to change the line-up of the group. We wanted musicians who could read music. Art Caddy was the only one to remain. He had been to the Royal College of Music as a violinist and was now becoming a great guitarist."

Mike West (Vocalist)
"In all the years I knew Johnny we never had a row. He was easy going, never selfish, he lived for the day. There was no rivalry, only friendly, like John would try and get more screams than me. It was healthy competition. Eventually the day came when the group broke up. I wanted to go solo. There were no harsh words. I didn't mind John leading The Pirates. Tony Doherty (rhythm guitar) left with me, I got Micky Cottle on drums. Micky, in fact, played a few gigs with The Pirates plus Carl Hasden who had the very first five finger bass in England. Fruit Gordon made this unique instrument. I also signed for Stanley Dale and later became Robbie Hood and his Merry Men and often toured around the country with Johnny Kidd and The Pirates."

The Pirates became a three piece Alan Caddy (lead) remained and was joined by Clem Cattini (drums) and Brian Gregg (bass).

Clem Cattini (Drums)
"I started with Terry Dene and the Deneaces that would be the beginning of it all, with Brian Gregg on bass. Then I went with Larry Parnes as part of 'The Beat Boys' backing all his artists, Duffy Power, Dickie Pride, Vince Eager, Billy Fury etc. When I left, I played in a pub next door to the Two I's Coffee Bar where a guy said Johnny Kidd needed a drummer so I went for it and got it."

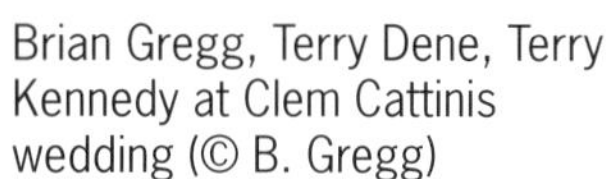
Brian Gregg, Terry Dene, Terry Kennedy at Clem Cattinis wedding (© B. Gregg)

Johnny Kidd
"It is partly for economic reasons and additionally because I've adopted a new approach to mu-

sic. Art Caddy has been with me from the very beginning and I wouldn't swap him for all the tea in China."

Brian and Clem at Aylesbury. Brian's big bold bass plus bleached blond image influenced many, especially future Tornado Heinz (© B. Gregg)

Brian Gregg (Bass)

"Clem and myself had been working for Larry Parnes. We'd been touring Ireland with Billy Fury. We were called the Blue Flames. During the tour we played the Theatre Royal, Dublin. Billy was asked to change his act, they said it was too sexy. Billy wouldn't, so we came back to England. On returning Clem and I insisted we stayed together, we had got used to each others playing, apart from being good friends. We had a row with Larry Parnes. Probably over lack of money and we told him to stuff it. A short while later Clem was in the Swiss Pub just along from the Two I's. This guy told him that Freddie Heath was looking for a bass player and drummer. Clem rang me up and told me, I said OK, I've got nothing else. It will be something to tide us over for now, until we get something good. It was arranged that we would meet Johnny along with his manager. They hired a room near Denmark Street, we waited for Alan Caddy to arrive. When Alan turned up I nearly had heart failure. In he walks wearing a 'Robin Hood' hat with a feather and a long overcoat. He looked more like a country squire than a rock 'n' roll guitarist. I turned to Clem and said look at the state of this guy I hope he plays better than he looks. We set up and ran through a few things, mostly rock 'n' roll standards. We were surprised Alan was good, he was tight, his timing was good and he seemed a nice guy. He wasn't your typical rock merchant, he was sort of middle class. He worked in an estate agents. He was a wee bit refined, Alan was fine. We said we would join but Clem and I both decided that this would just be a stop gap in between bands. Johnny said we could rehearse at his mothers house in Leopold Road, Willesden.

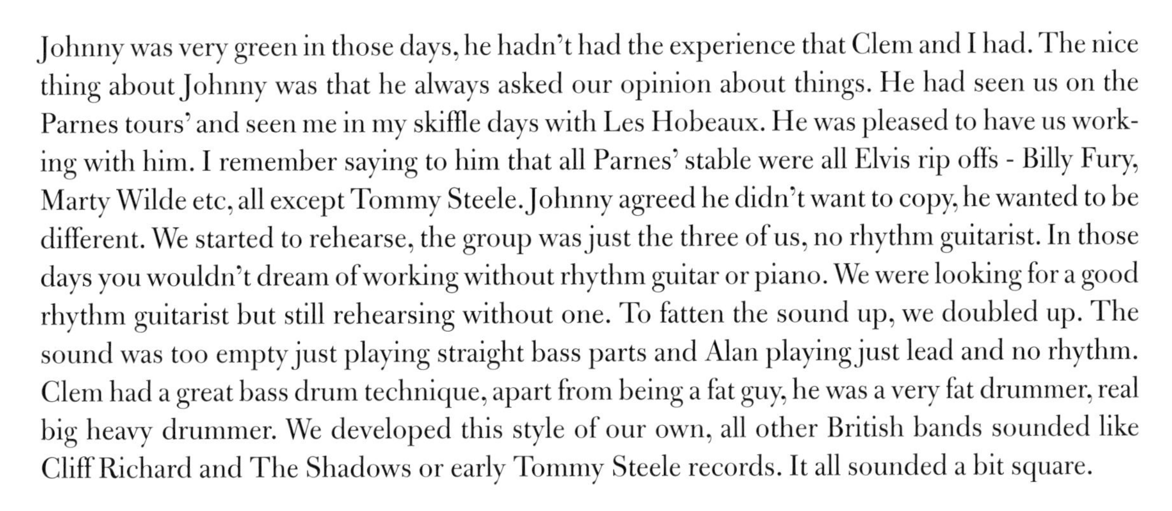

Johnny was very green in those days, he hadn't had the experience that Clem and I had. The nice thing about Johnny was that he always asked our opinion about things. He had seen us on the Parnes tours' and seen me in my skiffle days with Les Hobeaux. He was pleased to have us working with him. I remember saying to him that all Parnes' stable were all Elvis rip offs - Billy Fury, Marty Wilde etc, all except Tommy Steele. Johnny agreed he didn't want to copy, he wanted to be different. We started to rehearse, the group was just the three of us, no rhythm guitarist. In those days you wouldn't dream of working without rhythm guitar or piano. We were looking for a good rhythm guitarist but still rehearsing without one. To fatten the sound up, we doubled up. The sound was too empty just playing straight bass parts and Alan playing just lead and no rhythm. Clem had a great bass drum technique, apart from being a fat guy, he was a very fat drummer, real big heavy drummer. We developed this style of our own, all other British bands sounded like Cliff Richard and The Shadows or early Tommy Steele records. It all sounded a bit square.

One day during rehearsals Johnny brought along ex Five Nutter, Frank Rouledge. Frank was a good player, nothing wrong with Franks playing at all. We put him in the band but, because we had been rehearsing for a while without rhythm guitar, we didn't really leave any gaps in the music for Frank. It seemed a bit out of place, too much sound. After Frank left we had a chat amongst ourselves and we decided that the sound was better without a rhythm guitar. We decided to be just a trio. We worked very hard working out this sound. It was a big fat sound, a fat bass and drum sound. The thing that let us get away with being a trio, I had this big bass amp. In those days you couldn't buy a bass amp. I kept blowing speakers. As soon as I put a lot of bass on the speakers would blow. A few years earlier I was in the Freight Train coffee bar and I met Pepe Rush. He was one of those electronic boffins. I explained to him about my amp problem. This was years before I became a Pirate. He made me one with the speakers in a separate cabinet to the amp. It was huge but it had tremendous bass and volume. I feel sure I was the first on the London

below (1st): Gene Vincent & Eddie Cochran
below (2nd):Johnny (© F. Rouledge)

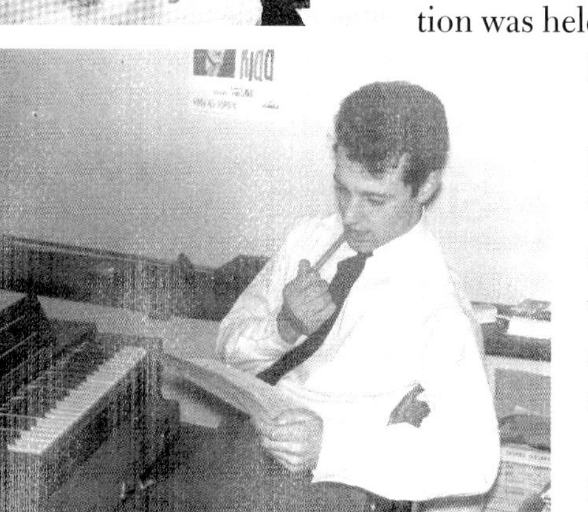

rock scene to have a really powerful bass amp. People like the Shadows were using Vox AC30. I think their bass amp was an AC50 or something but it was still just a guitar amp.

Alan decided to play chunky chords and then put a bit of lead in as well because if he just played lead it would be too empty. A good example is 'Weep No More My Baby'. Alan created the chunky guitar sound of The Pirates. We used to try out songs from the hit parade. If they came off well we'd stick them in our act. If we got a good audience reaction we'd leave it in the act, if not we'd boot it out. We didn't try and copy the sounds of the records. In fact we couldn't with just three musicians. We did our own versions of other peoples songs. Often people would say that they preferred our versions better than the originals. Johnny would go on, halfway through the act he would go off and change his clothes. The Pirates would carry on. I used to sing 'Rip It Up' Gene Vincent, Buddy Holly numbers, plus instrumentals Peter Gunn, Forty Miles of Bad Road and some 12 bar instrumentals of our own."

January 9th saw the arrival from America of Eddie Cochran. The following day an official reception was held for Eddie at the Albert Embankment headquarters of Decca Records. Johnny and Mike West went along to the special reception party.

Mike West (Vocalist)
"Johnny was crazy on Eddie. Along with a crowd of about a hundred we waited for the American rocker. Johnny kept saying "Where's Eddie? Come on Cochran". He was getting very excited and started to talk very loud. I suddenly noticed Eddie was standing right behind us. Johnny was now talking very loud. I tried to tell him. He suddenly spotted his idol and was more than slightly embarrassed."

Brian Gregg was amongst the first to have sound equipment made by the multi-talented Pepe Rush.

below: Robby Hood (Mike West)

A GREAT NEW ARTIST
ROBBY HOOD
Watch for his first disc
Personal Management :
REG CALVERT GER 6202–3111

Pete Rush (Recording Engineer and Music Equipment Designer)
"I also built a P/A system for Joe Brown and an amplifier for his bass player Pete Oakman. Also Marty Wilde who bass player Vince Cooze had the first bass amp I ever built. Billy Fury's bass player also had one of my amps. Emile Ford, Pete Townsend, Raye Du-Val and many others I can't remember after all these years. I also designed and built two sound mixing desks for the London Palladium. The first in 1968 and the last one in 1980. The latter is still in use. I also built Pete Townsend's first home studio on which he recorded some of the Tommy album and the first Thunderclap Newman hit single."

By February 1960 other artists were beginning to take an interest in Johnny's song writing talent. Italian rocker Little Tony recorded Magic of Love and former Pirate Robbie Hood (Mike West) lined up another of his ex-leaders songs, 'Tell Me When', for his debut single. Johnny was increasing his popularity with frequent guest spots on Saturday Club.

Both producer Jimmy Grant and compere Brian Matthew were most impressed with Johnny as a performer and his accompanying group of Pirates. They now had a well balanced stage show which included rock, ballads and even comedy routines. Johnny had always enjoyed a laugh on stage ever since his early skiffle days with the 'Five Nutters'.

Manager Stanley Dale's right hand man was Tony Secunda. Dale had first met Secunda when he was promoting dances putting on acts like Joe Brown. Secunda became a unique and creative force in the music world. A few years after leaving Dale he created outrageous publicity stunts for The 'Move. His best was a scandalous cartoon postcard of British Prime Minister Harold Wilson naked in the bath which he used to promote The Moves 'Flowers in the Rain'. He also signed the Moody Blues with his partner Alex Murray. He later worked for the Beatles merchandising company Seltaeb.

A new look EYE PATCH.

ABC TV started 'Wham' on Saturday April 23rd 1960 as direct competition to the BBC, Juke Box Jury. Both shows were transmitted from 6 to 6.30pm. It was another excellent show devised by Jack Good. Johnny and the Pirates recorded their spot on April 10th along with Davy Jones, Wee Willie Harris, The Four Jays, Peter Wynne, Vince Taylor, Richard Allen. It was broadcast on Saturday April 30th. The show attracted over 5, 000, 000 viewers. Apart from a star line-up of solo singers, producer Good had a big gun to aim at the tele viewers. It was an 18 piece, hand picked band led by Syd Dale, former pianist and arranger with Ronnie Aldrich and the Squadronaires, entitled 'Jack Goods Fat Noise'. It featured some first class musicians Red Price (sax), Andy White (drums), Eric Ford (guitar), Reg Guest (piano) etc.

left: Eye, Eye! Trying out the new gimmick
right: Yeah, I like it
(both © Jean Heath Collection)

Brian Greg (Bass)
"For the 'Wham' TV Show we wore suits. The Pirates wore lime green while Johnny was in bright orange. It's a shame it was on black and white television."

Johnny Kidd
"I was on Jack Good's 'Wham'. He suggested I wear the eye patch for effect. Unlike a lot of people suggest I do not get any medical trouble with it. In fact it helps me out at times. I look completely different without the patch, nobody recognizes me. There are sometimes five hundred kids there and I pass without a murmur!"

There are many stories concerning how Johnny got his trademark, Brian Gregg's true story doesn't see eye to eye with Johnnys tale.

Brian Gregg (Bass)
"Johnny had a bad cast in his eye which only showed at night when he was tired. His eye used to really turn in and we thought it would be a good idea to hide the eye with a patch. There was a story that a guitar string broke and hit him in the eye but there is no truth in that."

Johnny started to take his Pirate image seriously. The patch was criticised by some critics as being in bad taste. In fact it didn't do his eyesight any good - he had great trouble focusing after a long spell on stage. Johnny really worked hard to build up the image of piracy. He started to fill his wardrobe with pirate costumes and he'd spend a lot of spare time searching for antiquities connected with the robbers of the seas.

Mike West (Vocalist)
"Johnny had a bad squint. Jack Good said, 'for camera angles we've got to do something about the eye', so Jack suggested an eye patch. Johnny first wore an elastic one but the fans would pull on it and it would spring back and hurt his eye. He eventually got a tie on one and was out of pain. He used many different types - plain black, green and square pattern one. He was always pleased to pull it off after a performance."

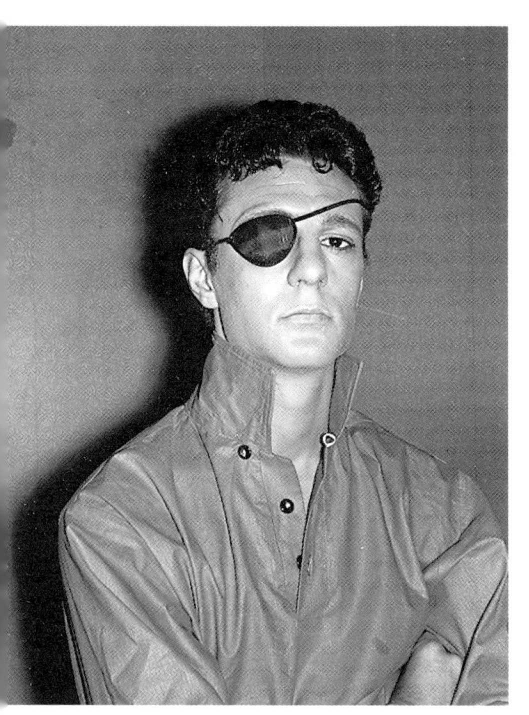
'The Legendary Photo' (taken by F. Rouledge ©)

When visiting a new town Johnny would regard himself as a raider not just a mere visitor. He loved to tell the press the following Ole Pirates Tale about how he became the Buccaneer of the Ballroom Circuit.
"I strode on stage wearing an eye patch after being struck in the eye by a guitar string in the dressing room, and a girl shouted that I looked like Captain Kidd. So I adopted the name and never looked back." I look mysterious and sinister, like Captain Kidd, you know by sticking a trademark on my face its made me big. I'll admit I can't see very well for about an hour after I take it off. I looks horribly red and sore. But I'm sure its not dangerous even though it makes me tired. If my eye became so sore and had to be operated on, I'd stop it... then I'd turn to a peg leg or something. Ugh!"

Brian and Johnny (© B. Gregg)

Spinning Disc reporter, Mike Nevard, criticised the image and wrote the following under the headline
"SCRAP THIS NEW LOW IN GIMMICKS"
"A little man is sitting in an office in Shepherds Bush, London today wondering if he's gone too far and no wonder because Stanley Dale, Manager and agent, is currently peddling the sickest gimmick yet in this gimmick-ridden business. I don't mind a gimmick that's stupid, adolescent, banal, ridiculous, wacky or just plain daft. But when the gimmick goes sick I draw the line. The puppet Mr Dale is peddling around the entertainment world is a 21 year old Londoner named Johnny Kidd. The gimmick : make the boy blind in one eye. For Johnny who sang 'Please Don't Touch' into the best sellers with two eyes is now swaggering on stage to plug his records wearing a black eye patch. All his old pictures are being scrapped to make way for what are described as the new, sinister ones. The origin of the 'sinister' approach is obvious when Johnny says one of his favourite singers is Sammy Davis. Sammy Davis wore a patch after he lost an eye in a car crash. Kidds' is just a gimmick. An acquaintance of his told me "There is nothing wrong with Johnny's eyes except that he may wink at the girls too much. I phoned manager Stanley Dale to arrange a meeting with Kidd. I wanted to meet this swash buckler who trades on one eye. But though this sick stuff is apparently all right for the fans and for business. Mr Dale seems to have a guilt complex about it.
"What do you want to talk to my boy for?" he asked, and then finally, "No we don't want any publicity pictures! No."

Mr Dale doesn't like the public to know too much about his artists. Maybe Johnny hasn't considered that he's on to a rather tasteless line. I suggest he thinks about it now. Throws the patches, all six of them, on the waste heap or gives them to an eye clinic which would make better use of them. Mr Dale - he's old enough to know better. I suggest he too drops the idea or goes the whole hog and give his boy a white stick and a tray of matches."

Another tale Johnny told was that the patch happened by accident when he got a bit of grit in his eye which proved very painful and made his eye puff up. He was due on stage that evening so he popped into a chemist asked him to dab something on it and get the grit out. The chemist told him to wear an eye patch to keep out the cold and prevent infection. "I felt a bit of a Charlie with this gear on." "I thought the kids would yell their heads off at me and make me take it off." They yelled all right, but after a minute or two, I realised to my surprise that the roar was of approval. So, the eye patch was IN, every night from then on, but only on stage."
The fans really loved his new look and Johnny was pleased to read the following poem from a young fan printed in a leading pop mag.

"I've really gone and flipped my lid,
For that dreamboat, Johnny Kidd!
I'd like some info, tell me why,
He wears that black patch on one eye?"

Susan Taylor
(Brighton)

(© Jean Heath Collection)

9. SHAKIN ALL OVER

Brian Gregg recalls the events leading up to the writing and recording of the classic 'Shakin All Over'.

"In those days you had no say in what you recorded. The A&R man told you what your next single was going to be. It didn't matter if it was your image or not. Terry Dene is a good example. They kept giving him ballads while he was going out on the road doing rock 'n' roll. Peter Sullivan our A&R man he was Walter Ridleys' assistant, said we could have the B side of our next record. The A side was going to be the old trad song 'Yes Sir That's My Baby'. We'd got to the day before the recording session and we hadn't come up with any idea for the B side. That evening at the Freight Train coffee bar in Berwick St, Soho we'd decided that we had a session in the morning. We couldn't walk into E.M.I. and say that we hadn't got any songs so we decided to write any old rubbish so at least they would see we had made some effort. The three of us, Kidd, Alan and myself, we didn't have any instrument, we sang the parts to Shakin All Over sitting downstairs on some coke crates."

Brian and Johnny (© B. Gregg)

Johnny Kidd

"When I was going around with a bunch of lads and we happened to see a girl who was a real sizzler we used to say that she gave us quivers down the membranes. It was a standard saying with us referring to any attractive girl. Well that phrase stuck with me because I saw it in a new angle on the old familiar shakes routine. I can honestly say that it was this more than anything that inspired me to write 'Shakin All Over'."

Frank Rouledge (Five Nutters Skiffle Group)

"Fred told me that it was because of my saying - she gives me quivers down the membranes that he wrote 'Shakin All Over' I'm very proud of that fact plus I mimed on second guitar for the WHAM TV performance."

On Friday 13th May they got up early and met round Brian's house.

"We had a quick run through in my front room not plugged in. We went to the studio and recorded it. In fact we were a bit ashamed of it."

Even drummer Clem Cattini didn't think much of the song.

"I think I got £5 15/- for the session. That's what the current rate was at the time. We thought 'Oh God' we can't release a thing called Shakin All Over quivers down my backbone. We wanted to be musicians. Musicians didn't play things like Shakin. I'm so pleased now that I was on it. It is a classic and its nice to be part of that record."

'Shakin All Over' turned out to be one of the best rock and roll records ever made in a British studio. From the opening guitar riff (courtesy of Joe Moretti, which must still be the best known guitar break in British rock 'n' roll), Johnny's vocals at their very best, Brian laying down a superb bass line, Clems great fat' drum roll and Alan on haunting second guitar. The raw excitement captured that day has stood the test of time.

Joe Moretti (© Rick Hardy)

Joe Moretti who played that magic timeless riff hailed from Scotland. On leaving school he began playing guitar in various skiffle outfits. His big break came in 1956 when he entered a competition to find the Scottish Tommy Steele. He never won but the winning artist Alex Harvey asked

Joe to join his band 'The Clyde City Skiffle Group'. They soon changed their name to 'The Kansas City Counts' joining up with a rival band the 'Rick Barnes All Stars'. In 1959 they became the legendary Alex Harvey Soul Band. The 'soul' wasn't taken from Motown, it was found in the mag 'Crescendo' which meant Jazz New Wave. The band played in their own right and also backed rock legends Eddie Cochran and Gene Vincent on their UK tours.

Brian Gregg (Bass)
"Joe wasn't a session man. The session men in those days were people like Bert Weedon, Roy Plumber, Eric Kershaw. They were older guys left over from the era before. When we asked Joe to play on 'Shakin' we rang him at home. He certainly wasn't signed to any of the studios as a session man. I had first met Joe in Glasgow when I was working on the Larry Parnes tours. I suggested to him to come to London and get into rock 'n' roll. When it was arranged to do the session for 'Shakin' we thought we better have another guitarist. We decided lets get Joe, he is a great player. Alan said let Joe play the lead and I'll do the high pitch. It was nothing to do with E.M.I., we got Joe in, we wanted to earn him a session fee."

Clems' amazing rolling crisp snare complete with his fat thumping bass drum set the perfect beat along with Brians' nice pounding bass. Their timing was faultless. Superb musicianship.

Clem Cattini (Drums)
"My drum sound on 'Shakin' was all down to Peter Sullivan our producer. Peter miked my bass drum, this was unknown in those days. Joe Meek was the only other guy to do this."

This close-microphone technique was only used by Meek and Sullivan. Most engineers would use only one microphone suspended above the kit. Clems heavy bass drum 'thunderfoot style' would later in the 60's be featured on countless sessions. He really was the man who put the beat in British Beat. A rock 'n' roll pioneer who created and learned as he went along because he had no other drummer to copy.

Clem Cattini (Drums)
"I came in the era when most of the drummers about were jazz men. People like Eric Delaney, Kenny Claire etc. I came on the scene as a rock 'n' roller. I had no idol. There wasn't any rock 'n' roll drummer that I could look up to."

(Eric Delaney's Big Band were very original in the fact that they carried around their own backdrop and special lighting. Johnny and the boys copied this idea).

Chas McDevitt - Proud that 'Shakin'' was written in his coffee bar (© Chas McDevitt)

Chas McDevitt
"I was a big fan of Johnny Kidd and The Pirates, and I was aware that he, with Brian Gregg and Alan Caddy wrote 'Shakin' in the basement of the Freight Train coffee bar. It was intended as a B side and the night before the session they realised they had nothing ready. Apparently they didn't even have a guitar - it must have been very uncomfortable for them in the basement, it was really just a damp cellar full of coke crates and broken furniture. I have a vision of them sitting on a broken door over some old crates!

If I remember correctly I also introduced Joe Moretti to the group. Joe had come down from Scotland and was looking for work. So in a way I was instrumental (ha!ha!) for that classic intro to

'Shakin' as well! Clem Cattini had played in my group for a while after he left Terry Dene. He recorded with Shirley Douglas and I on a couple of tracks which were released on a Columbia EP 'Naughty But Nice'.

Red Reece was also with me for quite a while before going in the end to Georgie Fames Blue Flames. They were both great drummers and among the most respected of their time. Many of the groups in those days used the Freight Train as a pick-up and set down point for their gigs. Their girlfriends used to wait in the coffee bar for them to return late at night. In fact I believe Hank Marvin met his wife there."

The Freight Train Coffee Bar (© Chas McDevitt)

Brian Gregg (Bass)
"We used to go to the Freight Train a lot because we got sick of the Two I's. It had become very commercial and was full of tourists, especially after the 6 5 Special TV show had been filmed there. It became a pain, no peace, so we preferred Chas McDevitts place."

Johnny Kidd
"The boys are always trying for new musical sounds. That weird sound on 'Shakin' was a brainwave of Brian's. He took his cigarette lighter and pressed it on the strings of Art's guitar, and that's how it was recorded. I am very sound conscious. If I hear anything which makes my ear twitch I'm with it. The sound is very important these days. The kids like to listen to music, they won't listen to rubbish. I'll tell you what makes our stuff different. Most groups playing this sort of music are four in number, including a rhythm guitar, and they use a lot of stuff left over from skiffle. My three boys Art Caddy (guitar), Brian Gregg (bass) and Clem Cattini (drums) produce far better effects by playing real notes behind me. For 'Shakin' we did bring the number up to four. Joe Moretti came in on guitar and he's the one who makes the ear catching sound on this disc."

SHAKIN' ALL OVER
JOHNNY KIDD
Recorded by JOHNNY KIDD on H.M.V. Pop. 753.
MILLS MUSIC LTD · MILLS HOUSE · DENMARK STREET W.C.2 2/-

Sheet music 'Shakin' (Always N' Ever Archive)

Joe Moretti was now living in London and at various times worked with Colin Hicks (Tommy Steele's Brother), Johnny Duncan, Eddie Calvert, Georgie Fame, Nero and The Gladiators and Vince Taylor. In March 1959 Isleworth rocker Vince Taylor and his Playboys released Brand New Cadillac/Pledging my Love on Parlophone R4539. Vince dressed from head to toe in black leather, he really was a tremendous showman. His playboys featured some of the finest musicians in the country. Brand New Cadillac along with Shakin All Over and Cliffs' Move It, ranks as one of the best British rock 'n' roll records and Joe played on two of them. The Brand New Cadillac session featured Vince Taylor (vocals), Lou Brian (piano), Brian Locking (bass), Brian Bennett (drums) and the amazing guitar of Joe Moretti.

'Shakin All Over/Yes Sir That's My Baby' was released on the 10th June 1960. A few days earlier Peter Sullivan had rung Johnny and said everyone is knocked out with Shakin' including Jack Good. 'Shakin' is going to be the A side. Jack Good plugged it on his TV show 'Wham' and it went straight into the charts the following week. The resident 'Wham' attractions were Billy Fury, Joe Brown along with compere Keith Fordyce.

Keith has some funny memories of the show.
"I remember Johnny on the series and years later on my radio show 'The Pop Inn' and 'Ready Steady Go' (ITV). My fondest memory of 'Wham' was of the several occasions when during an

interval in rehearsal we played a game of cricket in the middle of the studio floor. It was a totally imaginary game as we had no bat, ball or stumps and we simply imitated the actions of bowling, batting and fielding. This amazing performance was quite hilarious and there were various arguments about whether anybody had been bowled, caught, stumped etc. Joe Brown and Jess Conrad were amongst the regular players and probably even Oliver Reed joined in as at the time he made a pop disc and appeared on the show."

left: (taken by © F. Rouledge)

The first time airing of 'Shakin' was shown on 'Wham'. Johnny looked very sinister dressed in jet black leather and new image eye patch. He made great use of the cameras slowly turning round after singing 'Tremors down the thigh bone' to face the camera for the title line 'Shakin All Over'. A real powerful performance. His old manager Guy Robinson must have been pleased. It was Guys' training in his office with those three lights they had groomed Johnny for his magic TV performance. Johnny was now a star.

below (left): Poster 'Royal Daffodil'

below (right): Frank Ifield, Jess Conrad, Mark Wynter, Johnny and Michael Cox 'Come Aboard'

Sunday 12th June was going to be a gig with a difference. For one full day they could really act like Pirates, well nearly, they would be all at sea aboard the 'Royal Daffodil'. Ballroom owner Ed Waller had this great idea of a trip down the Thames from London to Margate. He billed it as 'Rockin' Down The River' and had a host of stars - Johnny Dankworth Band, Jess Conrad, Mark Wynter, Michael Cox, Ron and The Couriers and Frank Ifield. Over 1,000 fans made the 12 1/2 hour trip at only 35/- head. There was music and jiving on every deck. The fans had a good chance to mingle with their idols. Johnny was only too happy to please his many fans with autographs.

Come Aboard THE "ROYAL DAFFODIL"
with
JOHNNY DANKWORTH BAND, JESS CONRAD, JOHNNY KIDD & THE PIRATES, MICHAEL COX, RON & THE COURIERS, MARK WYNTER
and a host of others on
SUNDAY, JUNE 12th
for a Fabulous Day's Outing to
MARGATE and BACK
TICKETS still Available at 35/- each
Write, Call or Phone for Tickets, or Free Brochure to:— The Secretary, 16 Park Lane, Croydon. Phone 9453

Life on the road was very hard work. The band and their instruments would be piled on the band wagon a Ford Thames 15cwt Van. They were packing dance halls up and down the country. Attendance records were smashed during stage and ballroom performances. Popular venues were the Rank Ballrooms, the Majestic Finsbury Park, the Orchid Purley, State Kilburn, the Majestic Reading etc etc.

Johnny would set himself behaviour rules while on tour.
"I never tread on the toes of people who are looking after me such as clippies, waitresses, chambermaids. They have plenty to put up with. Boys like myself should do all they can to help and not take the mickey which happens too often."

While on tour in Hampshire Johnny wanted to see Nelsons Victory ship docked at Portsmouth. He was lucky to get away with a spectacular act of Piracy whilst on board.
"I was pretty bold. I hosted the Jolly Roger from the Victory ship. I don't know how I got away with it."

'Shakin' was placed with AM PAR records in the States. Stanley Dale was convinced the disc would sell well in the USA. He made hectic transatlantic cabling to various firms wanting the American rights and plans were made for Johnny to record 'Shakin' in German especially for the German market. As well as fixing the American release. Dale was busy trying to line-up big dates for a personal appearance tour of America. Sadly no tour materialised but 'Shakin' was released in the USA on APT 25040. Johnny and The Pirates were now being played on radio stations all over the globe. It was even released in Portugal on A VOZ DODONO 45-EQ5030.

above (top): Reg Calvert and Johnny - Torquay June '60 (© B. Gregg)

above (bottom): Alan, Johnny, Brian - Reg Calvert Tour June '60 (© B. Gregg)

Lez Richards (of New Zealand Group 'The La De-Das')
"As a child I listened to a lot of radio, one of my brightest memories is hearing 'Yes Sir That's My Baby, Shakin All Over, If You Were The Only Girl In The World and You've Got What It Takes'. I cannot ascertain whether these records were ever released in New Zealand as our NZBC, similar to the British BBC, often played imports.

'Shakin' was played on BBC TV's Juke Box Jury as Brian Gregg recalls.
"We were there live and the panel voted it a miss, which choked us off, but I'm glad to say they were wrong."

'Juke Box Jury' had first started on June 1st 1959. BBC TV decided to try out the show on a temporary basis once a week. It was an adaption of the American show devised by American disc jockey Peter Potter. The original function for the programme was for reviewing the latest record releases.

D.J. David Jacobs was the chairman and a panel of celebrities would give a hit or miss after hearing the new recordings. The very first panel, consisted of Alma Cogan, Pete Murray, Gary Miller and Susan Stranks. The show was an instant hit and not to be missed. 12 million viewers watched every Saturday as cameras often trained on the audience moving in to large close ups. This, in itself, was very original. Three teenagers would sit in the front row and give their opinions if the panel were undecided. With their round record like cards bearing the words 'Hit' and 'Miss' on opposite sides, ready to vote on their pop idols if called upon by chairman, David Jacobs.

Just two days before Shakin' was recorded at Abbey Road Johnny's idol, Gene Vincent, cut two classic tracks with Billy Fury's group, The Beat Boys, Colin Green (lead), Vince Cooze (bass), Georgie Fame (piano), Billy McVay (tenor sax), Red Reece (drums). 'Pistol Packin Mama', the song recorded less than one month after Eddie Cochran had been killed, was arranged for Gene by his mate Eddie. They sang it as a duet during their UK tour in early '60. Also recorded that Wednesday 11th May, 'Weeping Willow' with the Norrie Paramor Orchestra.

above: Johnny plugging 'Shakin' on 'Cool for Cats' - taken by B. Gregg off screen (© B. Gregg)

At the beginning of July Johnny and his manager Stanley Dale visited the Record and Show Mirror offices and were interviewed by Ian Dove. Johnny dressed in blue suit, black eye patch and flamboyant cowboy boots - sipped a cup of tea and talked about his latest hit 'Shakin All Over' and his career.

MELODY MAKER June 25, 1960

Melody Maker charts service

TOP TWENTY

Week ended June 18, 1960.

1.	(1)	CATHY'S CLOWN	Everly Brothers. Warner Bros.
2.	(3)	THREE STEPS TO HEAVEN	Eddie Cochran. London
3.	(4)	MAMA/ROBOT MAN	Connie Francis. MGM
4.	(11)	GOOD TIMIN'	Jimmy Jones. MGM
5.	(2)	CRADLE OF LOVE	Johnny Preston. Mercury
6.	(5)	HANDY MAN	Jimmy Jones. MGM
7.	(12)	AIN'T MISBEHAVIN'	Tommy Bruce. Columbia
8.	(7)	I WANNA GO HOME	Lonnie Donegan. Pye
9.	(6)	SWEET NUTHIN'S	Brenda Lee. Brunswick
10.	(9)	DOWN YONDER	Johnny and the Hurricanes. London
11.	(10)	SIXTEEN REASONS ..	Connie Stevens. Warner Bros.
12.	(13)	ANGELA JONES	Michael Cox. Triumph
13.	(14)	HE'LL HAVE TO GO	Jim Reeves. RCA
14.	(8)	SHAZAM	Duane Eddy. London
15.	(—)	FOOTSTEPS	Steve Lawrence. HMV
16.	(19)	RIVER STAY 'WAY FROM MY DOOR	Frank Sinatra. Capitol
17.	(16)	STAIRWAY TO HEAVEN	Neil Sedaka. RCA
18.	(—)	PISTOL PACKIN' MAMA	Gene Vincent. Capitol
19.	(—)	JOHNNY COMES MARCHING HOME/MADE YOU	Adam Faith. Parlophone
20.	(—)	SHAKIN' ALL OVER	Johnny Kidd. HMV

left: Top Twenty chart - Melody Maker, June 18, 1960

Ian Dove - "What are you doing now?"
Johnny - "Frankly I don't know. We are just waiting to see what happens, just exploiting the record. We've had offers for concerts and tours and all that but we don't know which ones to take. I s'pose were just waiting to see which way the wind blows."
Ian Dove - "The patch and the pirates image gimmick."
Johnny - "Of course it's a gimmick, an identification tag is an important thing in this business. I'm never seen without my patch over my right eye although the fans do pinch it occasionally. That's why I've got about six of em' all black. Another thing, I can take it off and not be recognised, not like Wee Willie Harris and his red hair. Joe Brown said that Jack Good made me put it on to stop me winking at the Vernons Girls on the TV Show 'Wham' but that's not true. This sinister approach is a good gimmick. I act sinister on stage. A TV hero pirate type approach. The name Kidd, Pirates, the patch it all swings into place. I don't like singing other peoples songs, songs should be written with certain artists in mind. I write with me in mind and I know that when I sing other peoples music I have to change my style. I'm not interested in rock, I'm interested in Johnny Kidd, in being an artist. Last December I recorded, 'If You Were The Only Girl In The World', it didn't catch on but I'm glad I did it. I don't want to limit myself, not at all, I want to move with whatever comes along, I really want to start a new trend."

Johnny and Stanley Dale

Ian Dove - "Why have you reduced the pirates from six to three?"
Johnny - "It's much more musical. When I had two guitars behind me it was a bit of a jangley sound, now with three instruments its much more musical. Each instrument plays a separate note. I defy anybody to say it isn't the best backing group in the country.

Alan Caddy lead guitar, Clem Cattini drums and Brian Gregg bass guitar. They don't wear patches but they do act sinister. Art Caddy is 20 and comes from Chelsea in London. Beside guitar playing he has two great crazes, fast motor bikes and jive dancing. For him the two things go together. No matter where we are or what we're doing, as soon as a break comes, off shoots Art on his bike like a rocket.. to the nearest dance hall. Sometimes in the middle of a mad jiving session he loses all sense of time and tears back to the theatre just ready to go on stage. When a break isn't long

JOHNNY
KIDD
and the Pirates
with his fabulous hit
SHAKIN' ALL OVER
and
Yes sir, that's my baby
45-POP758

above: 'Shakin' All Over'

enough for going out he asks one of the girls in the show to jive with him backstage. A real crazy cat.

Brian Gregg from Kilburn, London is 21. He is very good looking with blond hair and big blue eyes. He played with Billy Fury, Chas McDevitt and Vince Eager before joining me. Practical joking is his speciality. I remember once in Scotland we put up at a very expensive hotel meaning to live it up for once. I asked to be called at 8am but I was called instead at 6am. I knew straight away that Brian must have changed my call. I went back to sleep happily thinking I'd have the laugh on him later on since he hadn't got me up. Then blow me I overslept and missed breakfast anyway. When I rushed down the boys were just finishing the last of four fabulous courses. Was I mad!

Clem Cattini is the safe, solid, dependable one of the group. He is 22 and comes from Wood Green, London. Clem's parents are Italian. Just recently Brian, the joker, had a smash on his bike and got concussion. Luckily it wasn't too serious but when he came back to work he had no bike. Careful Clem offered to take him on the pilion of his bike. Just as they were setting off Art and I started to take the mickey. "Watch It Clem, don't got into orbit, keep both hands on the wheel, mind you don't get a tick for flying too low." As we expected Clem took the bait. "Look, if you were all as steady and safe as I am there would be no trouble." he said. "I'm the most careful driver among the lot of you." He drove off and only twenty yards or so away, at the first bend, he hit a patch of oil. The back wheel slid and Brian and he fell off. They weren't even scratched so the four of us just stood by the roadside and laughed. Passers-by must have thought we were nuts."

below (top): Brian and Johnny (© Brian Gregg)

below (bottom): Brian vocal backing 'Please Don't Touch' (© Brian Gregg)

Brian Gregg (Bass)

"Although Chas McDevitt was a good mate I'd don't think I actually played for him but Johnny was right about Billy Fury and Vince Eager. I did a lot of shows where Chas was on the same bill, remember Shirley Douglas played bass for Chas. I played for Billy Fury on numerous occasions and line-ups with The Beat Boys, Blue Flames and Tornados. I played for Vince Eager with the Parnes package tours although later Vince had his own band The Quiet Three. I also played for Tony Crombie and The Rockets backing Wee Willie Harris. We did a lot of playing abroad entertaining the troops and cabaret."

A popular gig was the Windsor Horse Hall. It was the major venue in Windsor. Colin Richards then a young budding musician and fan had never forgotten the very first time he saw the Kidd live on stage. "This was the very first time I had seen a name band play live at such a venue. It used to be quite a lofty building with a four foot stage, plus a balcony. What knocked me sideways was the volume produced even though Alan Caddy (lead) had only a 15 watt Selma or Vox Amp. Clem Cattini (drums) was very loud but quite brilliant. When he used accents on his snare drum Johnny would move to this, or something in his tight red trousers would, causing the girls in the audience to scream. Yes its the old hose pipe story again. Brian Gregg the bass player had what looked like bleached blond hair. Alan played every solo note for note correct to the recordings. In fact he sounded more like Joe Moretti especially on their current hit 'Shakin All Over'. He used a Fender Stratocaster through an echo unit and was fond of tweaking the tremolo arm. He was very good but sounded too much like Hank Harvin for my taste. I seem to remember Red suits, but Johnny had the frilly open white shirt and tight red slacks. Their stage act was quite polished. They were quite famous for their 'leg kicks' in

'Please Don't Touch'. This was copied all over the British Isles by many lesser known groups including my group The Avalons. There used to be a lot of wrestling on TV in those days and Jackie Pallo was the star on Saturday afternoons and a lot of his antics reminded me of Johnny Kidd."

Johnny was over the moon with the success of 'Shakin' and told the press of his initial shock. "Success as a singer! That's something I've always dreamed about, and now it's reality I can hardly believe my good fortune. But success as a songwriter, too! Well, honestly I'm just knocked

Contact strip showing rare stage shots (taken by F. Rouledge ©)

out its all just too good to be true! My career had been progressing by leaps and bounds over the past few weeks - thanks entirely to the success of my composition 'Shakin All Over'. Its uncanny that one song should ring so many changes in my life. Already I've had people ask which I'm going to concentrate on most singing or songwriting. Personally I see no reason why I can't do both and I'm going to try not to emphasise one more than the other. Singing is my profession, composing happens to be a side line that I enjoy and as long as I go on getting ideas for songs, I'll put them on paper. Lets face it, I've got nothing to lose. Apart from 'You Got What It Takes', I've written all the major songs I've recorded - Please Don't Touch, Feelin, Growl and of course Shakin'. I place a lot of importance on originality and I'd much rather record a new untried song than do a cover version of an American hit. And I'll be perfectly honest about this - financially its much better for me this way. I'm quite certain that British songs stand as much chance of success as those that reach us from America. First and foremost I simply can't write to order I have to wait for an idea to come to me. Sometimes the inspiration comes when I'm sitting on a train listening to the rhythm of the wheels. Or perhaps I'll be sitting at home thinking about a particular girlfriend. Right now, I've got a lot of ideas buzzing around my head but, as yet, I haven't been able to find time to put them together on paper. One outcome of the success of 'Shakin' All Over' and 'Please Don't Touch' is that other artists have approached me with a view to writing songs for them. This, I might add, has flattered me beyond words. Can you imagine it? Me, Johnny Kidd being asked to write songs for stars! I haven't yet got over the initial shock but, when I do, I'm going to sit down and see what I can turn out. I've been asked who writes the arrangements which I feature with the Pirates on my discs. In the main we work them out among ourselves but I would like to stress here the importance of our H.M.V. recording manager Peter Sullivan who frequently helps out with the scores. Peter's advice and assistance has, at all times, been quite invaluable.

Now that I've got going I intend to do everything possible to maintain my popularity. At the moment my fans seem to go for the earthy, basic rock 'n' roll sound which I've strived to produce so there are no immediate plans for a change in my style. But if the fans change their tune and demand something different I'll certainly give it to them. For the purposes of my stage act I want very much to broaden my scope and I'm keen to try my hand at ballads. One of my aims for the future is to record a set of ballads with string backing. Another ambition, which you might already know about, is to go to America. 'Shakin' All Over' was released there a few weeks back on the Am Par Label and if it clicks in a biggish way then I'll be off there like a shot for a promotional tour. Looking back over my career (which though short, is very satisfying from my own point of view) I can readily call to mind the names of many wonderful people who have helped to put me on the musical map. Peter Sullivan I've already mentioned. Another fellow to whom I'll be eternally grateful is Jack Good who has produced such wonderful TV beat shows as Six-Five Special, Oh Boy!, Boys Meets Girl, and Wham!! Jack influenced me in so many ways.
For example, before I met him, I was purely and simply a singer and had little or no idea of presentation. Now however I'm more of a visual performer. Jack Good possesses a strange knack of being able to bring all the latest talent in an artist to the surface. To my way of thinking it's essential for every new beat singer to get to know him, because Jack knows just about every trick in the rock 'n' roll trade. The popularity of 'Shakin' All Over' has meant a lot to me both as an artist and as a person. For example when the royalties start arriving I hope to be able to get down to the job of buying a big house for the family. Mum and Dad, my married brother and sister and their children. I want to buy a lovely house on the Thames, overlooking the water, with a huge garden. I want very low furniture, possibly Swedish design, parquet flooring throughout and the house and garden floodlit by night. This I tell you will please me no end! But I fully realise that I've still got a long way to go in this hectic show business world and the real test is going to be my next record which will be released in a few weeks time. I'll be keeping a watchful eye on the charts to see how it fares and all I can say at this stage is that if it proves as popular with you the fans as my last record I'll be 'Shakin' All Over' with excitement."

Press notice

Melody Maker advertisement

Achievement!
E.M.I. Records are proud to have gained—for the first time in the history of any record company—
The first six places in this week's 'Melody Maker' Chart

Melody Maker charts service
TOP TWENTY
Continue to watch E.M.I. group releases for
still more hits from

EMI
The greatest recording organisation in the world

During the time when Shakin' was zooming up the charts Johnny was asked his opinion on the staying power of beat music and who was the greatest influence on his music and career.
"Rock is here to stay mind you, there are two or three distinct types of rock today as opposed to the one blatant kind when Bill Haley was King. We consider ourselves rockers today but were very different from Haley. You know I'm not really influenced by anyone. I just open my mouth and sing! After all there are so many people in the business these days you've got to have originality. Maybe you think it strange that I should ever have written a piece called 'Shakin' All Over'. Several people have said to me that it seems rather dated, titles like this, they say went out in the

very early days of rock 'n' roll. Perhaps they're right and I agree that it was taking something of a gamble to come up with a tune of this name. After all I think the secret of the records success is to be found primarily in the lyric. You see its very simply constructed and easily memorised from the point of view it has a sort of nursery rhyme appeal. I have to admit that I am extremely surprised at what has happened. It never occurred to me that it would catch onto this extent.

below (left): Charts

Below (right): Melody Maker charts - Aug, 1960

MELODY MAKER. August 6, 1960

Melody Maker charts service

Data supplied by over 100 record dealers

TOP TWENTY

1. (1) PLEASE DON'T TEASE .... Cliff Richard. Columbia
2. (3) SHAKIN' ALL OVER .... Johnny Kidd. HMV
3. (8) MESS OF BLUES .... Elvis Presley. RCA
4. (2) GOOD TIMIN' .... Jimmy Jones. MGM
5. (5) WHEN WILL I BE LOVED? ..Everly Brothers. London
6. (15) APACHE .... Shadows. Columbia
7. (4) MAMA/ROBOT MAN .... Connie Francis. MGM
8. (10) ITSY BITSY TEENIE WEENIE YELLOW POLKA DOT BIKINI .... Brian Hyland. London
9. (12) BECAUSE THEY'RE YOUNG .. Duane Eddy. London
10. (7) IF SHE SHOULD COME TO YOU Anthony Newley. Decca
11. (11) LOOK FOR A STAR .... Garry Mills. Top Rank
12. (8) AIN'T MISBEHAVIN' ...... Tommy Bruce. Columbia
13. (9) JOHNNY COMES MARCHING HOME/MADE YOU Adam Faith. Parlophone
14. (18) LOVE IS LIKE A VIOLIN .... Ken Dodd. Decca
15. (13) WHAT A MOUTH .... Tommy Steele. Decca
16. (14) ANGELA JONES .... Michael Cox. Triumph
17. (—) PAPER ROSES .... Kaye Sisters. Philips
18. (—) I'M SORRY .... Brenda Lee. Brunswick
19. (—) TIE ME KANGAROO DOWN SPORT Rolf Harris. Columbia
20. (17) HE'LL HAVE TO GO .... Jim Reeves. RCA

JUKE BOX TOP 20

1. (2) PLEASE DON'T TEASE .... Cliff Richard. Columbia
2. (1) GOOD TIMIN' .... Jimmy Jones. MGM
3. (5) SHAKIN' ALL OVER .... Johnny Kidd. HMV
4. (11) LOOK FOR A STAR .... Garry Mills. Top Rank
5. (3) AIN'T MISBEHAVIN' .... Tommy Bruce. Columbia
6. (8) MADE YOU .... Adam Faith. Parlophone
7. (4) ROBOT MAN .... Connie Francis. MGM
8. (10) WHEN WILL I BE LOVED? .... Everly Brothers. London
9. (—) MESS OF BLUES .... Elvis Presley. RCA
10. (6) ANGELA JONES .... Michael Cox. Triumph
11. (7) WHAT A MOUTH .... Tommy Steele. Decca
12. (20) IF SHE SHOULD COME TO YOU .... Anthony Newley. Decca
13. (15) ITSY BITSY TEENIE WEENIE YELLOW POLKA DOT BIKINI Brian Hyland. London
14. (—) APACHE .... Shadows. Columbia
15. (17) BECAUSE THEY'RE YOUNG .... Duane Eddy. London
16. (9) THREE STEPS TO HEAVEN .... Eddie Cochran. London
17. (—) PISTOL PACKIN' MAMA .... Gene Vincent. Capitol
18. (14) CATHY'S CLOWN .... Everly Brothers. Warner Bros.
19. (12) I WANNA GO HOME .... Lonnie Donegan. Pye
20. (—) DOWN YONDER .... Johnny and the Hurricanes. London

Supplied by the makers of the Music Maker Phonograph.

TWENTY TOP TUNES

1. (1) LOVE IS LIKE A VIOLIN (F/B) (2/-) .... Keith Prowse
2. (2) PAPER ROSES (A) (2/-) .... Leeds
3. (4) A SUMMER PLACE (A) (2/-) .... Blossom
4. (3) PLEASE DON'T TEASE (B) (2/-) .... Belinda
5. (6) ITSY BITSY TEENIE WEENIE YELLOW POLKA DOT BIKINI (A) (2/-) .... Feldman
6. (7) THE SINGING PIANO (B) (2/6) .... Hit Songs
7. (5) ANGELA JONES (A) (2/-) .... Southern
8. (11) SHAKIN' ALL OVER (B) (2/-) .... Mills
9. (8) HE'LL HAVE TO GO (A) (2/-) .... Campbell Connelly
10. (9) I WANNA GO HOME (A) (2/-) .... Essex
11. (10) MAMA (F) (2/-) .... Macmelodies
12. (14) WHAT A MOUTH (B) (2/-) .... Francis Day
13. (13) ROBOT MAN (A) (2/-) .... Joy
(17) LOOK FOR A STAR (B) (2/-) .... Filmusic
15. (18) GOOD TIMIN' (A) (2/-) .... Sheldon
16. (—) LUCKY FIVE (B) (2/-) .... Clover-Conway
17. (12) STANDING ON THE CORNER (A) (2/6) .... Frank
18. (16) CRADLE OF LOVE (A) (2/-) .... Good
19. (19) SIXTEEN REASONS (A) (2/-) .... Campbell Connelly
20. (—) IF SHE SHOULD COME TO YOU (F) (2/-) .... Essex

Supplied by the Popular Publishers' Committee of the Music Publishers' Association, Ltd. A—American; B—British; F—Others. (All rights reserved.)

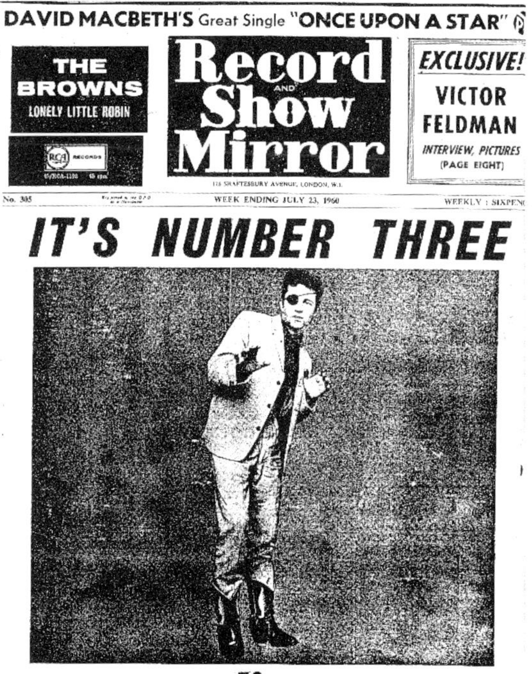

DAVID MACBETH'S Great Single "ONCE UPON A STAR"

THE BROWNS
LONELY LITTLE ROBIN

Record and Show Mirror

116 SHAFTESBURY AVENUE, LONDON, W.1

EXCLUSIVE!
VICTOR FELDMAN
INTERVIEW, PICTURES (PAGE EIGHT)

No. 385 — WEEK ENDING JULY 23, 1960 — WEEKLY : SIXPEN[CE]

IT'S NUMBER THREE

I'm Shakin' All Over

I've just arrived back from a seven day Scottish tour and I find that the disc is still in the top five. How about that? Fantastic isn't it? You see if I am to be honest I must tell you that in my opinion there's nothing worthwhile musically in the number, no chords even. In fact I don't really consider it is a song, I regard it as a piece of material. But its certainly been very lucky for me and I only hope that I can produce more like it. I shall be rehearsing next week for my new record. I can't give you any indication of what it will be like because I haven't written it yet! I'm thinking like mad. Trying to work up an original idea is the most important in my estimation. This new disc will have to have an unusual sound. This I can promise you. It will be quite different from Shakin' although it will still have a pronounced beat."

For his third single of 1960 'Restless' Johnny had a new song writing partner Teddy Wadmore, the bass player with the very respected Ted Taylor Four Johnny had first met the 'Four' on his early TV debut. In the early days of TV all transmissions were broadcast live so musicians had to be able to sight read and ad-lib. Ted Taylor (piano), Bob Rogers (guitar) and Teddy Wadmore (bass) were very talented and in demand for many TV shows i.e. Six-Five Special, Time for Tich, Studio E etc.

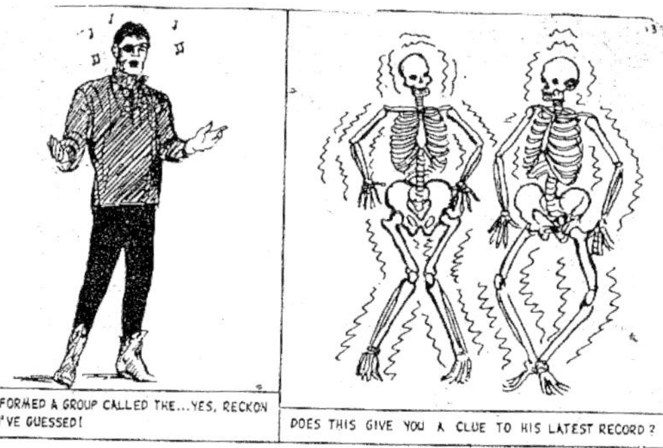

HE BOUGHT HIS BANJO FROM AN OLD RAG-AND-BONE MAN!
HE FORMED A GROUP CALLED THE...YES, RECKON YOU'VE GUESSED!
DOES THIS GIVE YOU A CLUE TO HIS LATEST RECORD?
The Star : Johnny Kidd. The Disc : Shakin' All Over

Cartoon strip

Johnny liked the group and was especially impressed with Teddy Wadmores bass. Teddy, in fact, had one of the very first electric basses in England. One evening while playing at an American base, this GI showed him a Fender electric bass. During the 1950's American instruments were almost impossible to buy so Teddy asked to borrow it, took it to Jimmy Burns who quickly carved out a copy. Within a few weeks 'The Ted Taylor Four' had the most original sound. Ted with his clavioline, along with Teddy's pounding bass. Johnny really liked this group and enjoyed their company. The late Ted Taylor once described Johnny as a frustrated Frank Sinatra who occasionally asked if he could come along on some of their gigs.

October 8, 1960. MELODY MAKER

Adam Faith · Johnny Worth · John Barry
have done it again—
HOW ABOUT THAT! (Parlo)
Orchs. available shortly
Johnny Kidd's latest and greatest
RESTLESS (HMV)
David Macbeth's Gay Parce Song
PIGTAILS IN PARIS (Pye)
MILLS MUSIC

Bob Rogers (Guitarist with Ted Taylor Four)
"I remember Johnny singing standards such as 'The Lady is a Tramp' on stage with us. Regarding 'Restless' Teddy Wadmore and I put down the melody on a Italian two-track reel-to-reel through a copy-cat echo. We were asked to write a melody within a couple of days for Johnny Kidd. In those days there was a tremendous amount of 'ghosting'. The whole thing centered around Denmark Street(Tin Pan Alley) and the music publishers. They would come up with the material, get in a dozen or so of us players and make a demo which was then farmed out for the popular stars to learn."

Restless and Magic of Love were both recorded on Monday 5th September 1960. For the first time he used the name Kidd on the writing credits and once again he wrote the B side with Guy Robinson and even new manager Stanley Dale got himself on the credits. The 30th September was the day of release. They must have been expecting it to shoot up the charts because Teddy Wadmore decided to leave The Ted Taylor Four so he could devote more time to his newly discovered talent song writing. Alas it was a modest hit by the standards of 'Shakin'. Johnny was quite shocked, he thought he had another big hit on the cards."

above: Press advertisements

Johnny Kidd
"Naturally I was very excited about the success of Shakin' and I expected 'Restless' to do even better because it was the immediate follow up and I thought it was a stronger number. But it didn't mean very much and that for me was the real let down."

Magic of Love was one of the very first songs that Johnny had written. He had been playing around with it for over 18 months. Its original title was Mr and Miss. Once again Radio Luxembourg gave Johnny a lot of air play. DJ's Ted King, Ernie Williams and Barry Alldis all made 'Restless' their record of the week.

Chas McDevitt
"I recorded Johnny's song ' Magic of Love' (Mr and Miss). However Top Rank went bust before the record saw the light of day."

MELODY MAKER. October 15, 1960

TOP TWENTY
Melody Maker charts service
Data supplied by over 100 selected record dealers

		Title	Artist	Label
1.	(2)	ONLY THE LONELY	Roy Orbison.	London
2.	(1)	TELL LAURA I LOVE HER	Ricky Valance.	Columbia
3.	(3)	NINE TIMES OUT OF TEN	Cliff Richard.	Columbia
4.	(5)	SO SAD/LUCILLE	Everly Brothers.	Warner Bros.
5.	(4)	HOW ABOUT THAT	Adam Faith.	Parlophone
6.	(10)	AS LONG AS HE NEEDS ME	Shirley Bassey.	Columbia
7.	(8)	WALK DON'T RUN	John Barry.	Columbia
8.	(6)	MESS OF BLUES/GIRL OF MY BEST FRIEND	Elvis Presley.	RCA
9.	(7)	APACHE	Shadows.	Columbia
10.	(12)	PLEASE HELP ME I'M FALLING	Hank Locklin.	RCA
11.	(11)	WALK DON'T RUN	Ventures.	Top Rank
12.	(13)	EVERYBODY'S SOMEBODY'S FOOL	Connie Francis.	MGM
13.	(14)	LET'S THINK ABOUT LIVING	Bob Luman.	Warner Bros.
14.	(9)	BECAUSE THEY'RE YOUNG	Duane Eddy.	London
15.	(18)	CHAIN GANG	Sam Cooke.	RCA
16.	(—)	TELL LAURA I LOVE HER	Ray Peterson.	RCA
17.	(15)	PAPER ROSES	Kaye Sisters.	Philips
18.	(—)	TOP TEEN BABY	Garry Mills.	Top Rank
19.	(—)	McDONALD'S CAVE	Piltdown Men.	Capitol
20.	(—)	RESTLESS	Johnny Kidd.	HMV

Top Twenty - Melody Maker
Oct, 1960

On September 15th Johnny flew out to Holland to represent Britain in a special E.M.I. convention of record dealers in Amsterdam. He also appeared in a Hilversum TV presentation. 'Shakin All Over' was voted No 1 in Holland.

The record company invited Johnny, Tommy Bruce, Tony Brent and Vera Lynn to a celebrity weekend. Johnny was really thrilled.
"They put on a 12 course luncheon for us to which the Mayor and everyone important in Dutch society came. A terrifying experience but Tommy Bruce was even more scared than I was! Just imagine all those knives and forks laid out not knowing which to take up first!"

On his return to England Stanley Dale lined up the following gigs.

SEPTEMBER
Aylesbury 18th, Newbury 20th, Northwick 23rd, Aylesbury 24th, Barrow-in-Furness 29th,

Whitehaven 30th.

OCTOBER
Crewe 1st, Central Pier Morecombe 14th, Aylesbury 15th, Rawthenstall 20th, Leeds 21st, Barnoldswick 22nd, Bury St Edmunds 29th.

They had a short break from the tour on the 6th and 7th October to record 'Lets Talk About Us', 'Linda Lu', 'Big Blon Baby', Weep No More My Baby'.

Johnny Kidd
"At our disc sessions we largely depend upon the ideas and suggestions of our recording manager Peter Sullivan. I've been fortunate enough to be teamed up with him right from the start, and there's no doubt that he's brilliant at his job. It is impossible to over-estimate the important part he had played in helping to boost my career. I hope to go to America in the near future. Originally, the visit was to be purely speculative and Stanley Dale and I were to finance it between us. But now things are happening and it begins to look as though there might be some financial return when I arrive therefore the GAC Organisation have started to take an interest in me - and you can bet that I am anxiously awaiting the result of their efforts. There is a strong possibility that if everything goes according to plan, I shall be able to take my group with me so that we can work there on a few dates, which of course would be wonderful, not only for the satisfaction of working in America but also from the financial point of view. Meanwhile, I'm going along very nicely with a lengthy string of one night stands which takes me up to September 16th and after that, all being well, off to America. Though let me make one thing perfectly clear this American trip is for one brief visit only. I've far too many ties in Britain to stay there for very long whatever happens. Besides I'm anxious to establish myself fully and effectively here at home."

left: (taken by F. Rouledge ©)

Below: contact strip containing rare stage shots (taken by F. Rouledge ©)

Once again the American trip fell through so it was back on the road.

NOVEMBER
Grimsby 4th, Wisbech 5th, Middlesbrough 7th, Hull 8th, Bradford 9th, Scarborough 10, Friday 11th a five day tour of Scotland, York 16th, Warrington 17th, Shrewsbury 19th, Spennymoor 20th.

Brian Gregg (Bass)
"We used to travel in a Ford Thames van and an Austin which Johnny and Johnny Irving (roadie) painted bright pink with horns all over it. They made it very comfortable in the back. They converted it with a sofa in there. It was very nice. Johnny was a bit of a scruff. There were times when he would do the journey to the gig and he would come straight out of the van and go on stage without changing. He'd have a quick wash and stick his patch on and grab his sword and on he'd go. We were starting to get big, been on television, had a hit record, we pulled him aside one

day and said "look John, you've got to start looking like a star. You look like Joe Bloggs from down the road." We decided to get some sharp suits for him. He didn't want to know. In the end we convinced him and dragged him along to a tailor, and he had these two suits made. Both shiney mohair material, well tailored, made to measure. One grey and one dark blue. We thought if we went to a press conference or an E.M.I. party we'd have Johnny looking smart. One day after a reception we got in the van to go home and I felt something soft under my feet. It was pouring with rain outside. I put my hand down and picked up this material. When we put the light on it was one of Johnny's suits. He had slung them in the back of the van and they had landed in the wet. He hated them so much he wanted to ruin them. We all laughed and thought what's the bloody point. That's when it was decided let him wear what the hell he wants but we did insist that he wouldn't wear the same gear that he travelled in on stage. So that's where the Pirates gear came in.

We had red cowboy boots which we wore under tight black trousers made of satin material. We liked cowboy boots because they had high heels. We couldn't get pirate boots, they came later

Contact strip containing rare stage shots
(taken by F. Rouledge ©)

on. Bright red shirts with the collars turned up and a leather pull over. Johnny had various outfits, black and white stripes, a leather top with a short jacket with silver chains hanging off it. He used to tear off the chains and throw them to the girls in the audience. He had a large collection of cowboy boots. The day we bought those first red boots in Shepherds Bush by a strange coincidence these two guys were watching us. I thought they look like a couple of heavy dudes. I learned years later that those heavy characters were in fact future pirates Frank Farley and Mick Green."

CUTLESS

Johnny was now using a real sword in the act and the throwing of it into various stage boards meant he had to obtain a public liability insurance policy as cover. He would sometimes take his cutless to private parties. Mr and Mrs C H Hill Junior often allowed their daughter Sandy Hill (now Regan) to hold parties at the family home Woodhouse Place, Mansfield. It was a beautiful mansion house around 700 years old. Sandy has many fond memories of Johnny and his crew.
"Johnny and the guys loved the place. Johnny had a thing about swords and knives. At one party a lot of well known people were there. I felt very confident in my new black dress, stockings and suspenders. Johnny got me down on the floor in front of everybody snatched up my shirt and cut all my suspenders off one by one with a big curved sword. I nearly died of embarrassment. I could have killed him. Needless to say it was the highlight of the evening. Johnny just collapsed with laughing. This was his sense of humour, bless him."
During the swinging sixties many other legends of rock attended Sandy's parties and stayed at

the family home. The Tornados, Freddie and The Dreamers, The Hollies, Rod Stewart even The Beatles after a Granada show. They piled into a coach with Tommy Roe, Chris Montez and The Viscounts to travel to her home (March 26th, 1963). As usually happens at good parties things tend to get rather high spirited and one of The Beatles certainly upheld this tradition when he emptied a bottle over poor ole Chris Montez. Who wasn't having some kinda fun.

Sandy Hill
"I first met Johnny and the boys in about '60-'61. It was at Alfreton Drill Hall in Derbyshire. Johnny Irving was the roadie. They drove me home and it all started from there. My home became their base. We had photos taken Johnny Irving, Alan Caddy, a friend and myself sitting on top of the Pirates van. I think Johnny Kidd was sleeping it off inside the van. We had so many happy times on my dads farm. We had photos taken on the tractor, what a laugh that used to be. Johnny Kidd always used to call in the local village shop and buy a cream sponge cake and eat it all in one go, just like a biscuit. He loved fresh cream cakes. He used to turn up at my house with all sorts of cars I remember he had an American Rambler. We had to push it everywhere. When we were on the road one of our favourite haunts was Tony's Cafe on the A1. All the boys used to meet there. That's where I first met Screaming Lord Sutch. There was a three legged table in there and we always seemed to get it. When you sat down with your plate it slid on to the floor. Wherever we sat it always seemed to be there. I had an old banger van. Johnny used to drive us to some gigs in it. Once we got lost in Lincolnshire coming home from a show, ending up sleeping in a farm yard. We didn't realise until we woke up and found ourselves surrounded by cows. That was a shock I can tell you. He really did enjoy the country side, and the quiet side of life sometimes. We spent some really wonderful moments on my dads farm which has since been bulldozed away and now its a big housing estate. Such a shame but I suppose that's progress isn't it?"

top: Johnny Irving, Sandy Regan, Alan Caddy and friend Delia (© Sandy Regan)

bottom: Johnny has his cake and eats it (© Jean Heath Collection)

Brian Gregg (Bass)
"When we weren't working we used to knock around together socially. We'd go bowling, west end clubs, coffee bars etc. I remember we used to go out on my motor bike to the country and go sailing on the river. Johnny Irving was the Kidds best mate. The three of us would go out together. I remember going to the Ace cafe where all the rockers used to hang out. Johnny Kidd would play on the machines. He'd stand there in amongst the lads, no big time crap. He was a great guy. Anybody who knew Johnny would tell you the same. When my wife had just given birth to our son, there was a knock on the door. Johnny was standing there. He had a load of toys with him, used toys from his kids. I laughed because they were all for little boys of 3 and 4. Our baby was only two days old but you know he had a heart of gold bringing that stuff over for our child. After a night out going around the coffee bars, we'd often end up at my place and we'd sit there half the night listening to music I'd get a guitar out, we'd write some tunes and eat bacon sandwiches."

Alan Wheeler
"It was late 1960 early '61. I was working for pop promoter/manager Larry Parnes in Oxford St, running the World Fan Club for Marty Wilde when I was offered a job by Stanley Dale. He invited me down to meet him at his dance hall in Peckham, South London. Now this was a really tatty dive and you would certainly never have got any of Parnes lesser star names such as Duffy Power or Dickie Pride there in those days let alone the likes of Marty Wilde, Billy Fury or Vince Eager. Imagine my surprise and disbelief to see the name Johnny Kidd and the Pirates appearing

tonight scribed up outside the grubby doorway. As it turned out Dale owned the hall so it was easy to put Johnny in there as an alteration! But how ridiculous! He was a man who had four hit records including a No 2, which had sold over 200, 000 singles and here he was performing in a dingy club without any publicity whatsoever! Actually a good crowd of regulars to this club turned up, strengthened by those who had heard on the grapevine. My interview with Dale who tried to entice me away from Larry Parnes was conducted over the bar before the crowd was let it Drummer Clem Cattini, as I recall, came behind the bar and helped himself to a pint!

I recall Johnny Irving pulling back the curtain behind the rostrum to let Johnny emerge in a full leather outfit complete with chains hanging from the wrists of the jacket! He got a warm welcome with his opening number 'Please Don't Touch'. After 'Touch' with its leg kicks Johnny went into 'You Got What It Takes' and introduced the members of The Pirates. Alan, Brian and Clem then featured his second disc, 'If You Were The Only Girl In The World'. A great stage number especially the second part which pounded out like Gene Vincents' Baby Blue. This was followed by most of the songs Johnny had recorded to date, Restless, Magic of Love, Big Blon Baby, Lets Talk About Us, Weep No More My Baby.

A special mention for his next single 'Linda Lu', followed by a fast 'Yes Sir That's My Baby' and into 'Shakin All Over' (knockout). A really great show which deserved to be seen by a wider audience in more spacious surroundings. This of course in fact happened later when Johnny worked a number of theatres and concert halls supporting the likes of Jerry Lee Lewis and Gene Vincent."

December saw the release of 'Big Blon Baby' and 'Weep No More My Baby' on the Saturday Club compilation album (Parlophone PMC1130) and back on the airwaves of Saturday Club. During their live session of 'Restless', 'My Babe', 'Magic of Love', 'Weep No More My Baby' and 'Baby That's All You Gotta Do' they proved that they were one if not the finest live act in the country. Johnny was so keen on recording 'Baby That's All You Gotta Do' that it was tried out at an E.M.I. session but considered not strong enough material so it was scrapped. An EP featuring 'Please Don't Touch', 'Shakin' All Over', 'You Got What It Takes' and 'Restless' was released - HMV 7EG8628 - and sold very well.

left: EP sleeve

right: Press advertisement

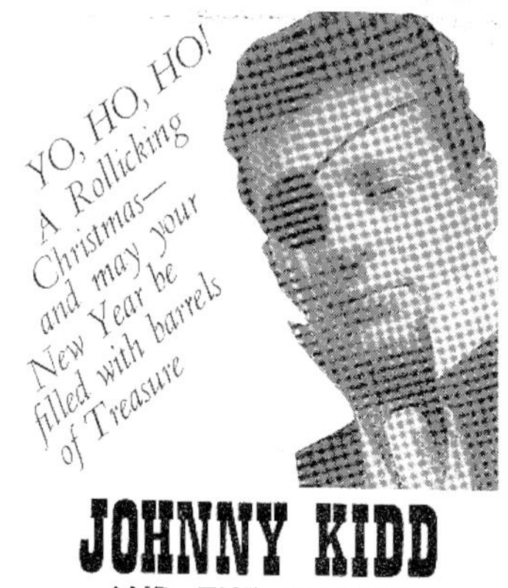

1960 had been a great year. In the New Musical Express poll station 'Shakin' All Over' was voted 7th best British disc of the year. Johnny was the 4th most requested artist for the poll concert, 9th most popular British male singer and 11th British vocal personality. Shaking All Over reached number 5 in the best selling sheet music chart.

Johnny was really thrilled to learn that Stanley Dale had got him booked on a tour with his idol Gene Vincent for early in the New Year. He just couldn't wait for 1961.

10. JUMPS, GIGGLES AND SHOUTS

A new year and a fresh voyage they cast anchor on January 9th at The Central Pier, Morecambe. For just 5/6 (27 1/2p) at the door you could jive to Johnny and the lads from 8.00pm to 2.00am.

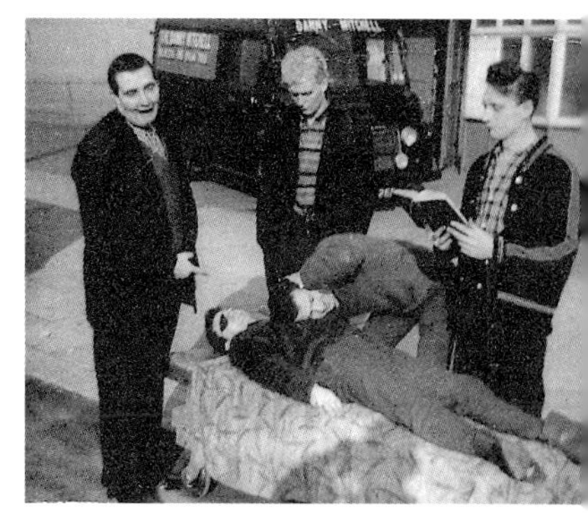

Morecambe Pier - The Crew with Johnny Irving acting like loonies (© B. Gregg)

To prepare himself for the forthcoming Gene Vincent tour Johnny took a short holiday. "I took myself to a remote, craggy island in the North of Scotland, stayed on a farm, fished for salmon and trout, rode around, ate like the horse I was riding and didn't meet another soul except the farmer and his wife. Wonderful."

Brian Gregg (Bass)
"The records we made although some of them were successful they didn't really capture the sound Johnny Kidd and The Pirates had on stage. With the big heavy sound we had, Clems heavy drum sound, we couldn't play at that volume in the studio. We played much more orchestrated and controlled in the studio. Even 'Shakin All Over', the version we did on stage although the same notation was a much more heavier sound altogether. In fact all our tunes were on stage. In those days the A&R man and the record company told you how you had to play it. Well not quite, we played it, they would control it with their equipment. They would bring you down or they'd say you'd have to play quietly on your bass, we will bring up the volume. You can't have that type of volume in a studio. So really it was a totally different feel on the records as to the feel we had on stage. The excitement we generated in halls with our sound was nothing like the sound on our records. Over the years I've had lots of letters from various people who saw our band live and they insist that we Alan Caddy, Clem Cattini and myself were the definitive Pirates. Lots of people have said to me, Clem and Alan, that the bands that Johnny had after us had nothing like the excitement and they certainly didn't work as much as we did because when we were with Johnny he had 'You Got What It Takes', 'Shakin All Over' which was the biggest record he ever had. Johnny was at his peak. We worked every night of the week and did more work in those two years than Johnny ever did afterwards."

below (top): Johnny and Crew before sailing off for Sunday Concert with Cliff and the Shadows (© B. Gregg)

below (bottom): Brian and Alan support Captain Kidd (© B. Gregg)

Bobby Elliott, drummer with the Hollies, recalls his semi-pro days as a member of Ricky Shaw and The Dolphins.
"We did quite a few Johnny Kidd songs, 'Please Don't Touch', with the kicks, 'Linda Lu', etc. We first supported The Pirates at the Majestic in Barnoldswick, Lancashire. There was Clem, Alan and Brian, we were impressed that it was only a three piece band. We didn't realise that it was a money saving exercise.

Dear Joe Moretti obviously wasn't there. The three piece line-up inspired The Dolphins to later have bass, lead and drums and later the Hollies."

Mike West (Original Pirate backing vocalist)
"Brian was a very good showman, he looked the part on stage, a good player. Both Brian and Alan Caddy looked tall guys each side of the 'Kidd'. Although they looked big it was Johnny who really shone."

Throughout February and March Johnny was thrilled to be on tour with his idol Gene Vincent and his mate, Screaming Lord Sutch and The Savages plus Johnny Duncan and his Blue Grass Boys, Mark Wynter, Michael Cox, Terry Dene, Danny Rivers, Chris Wayne and The Echoes, Rory Blackwell, Vince Taylor and The Playboys plus comperes Mike and Bernie Winters.

Brian in Kidd's car
(© B. Gregg)

The tour went all over the British Isles

eg.	Eastham	Feb 12th	
	Kingston	Feb 27th	
	Dartford	Feb 28th	
	Greenford	March 1st	
	Woolwich	March 2nd	
	Sutton	March 3rd	} Terry Dene replaced
	Rugby	March 5th	} Mark Wynter

"Mike Winters is the finest person I've worked with on-stage. He is so natural, smart, clean and intelligent and will aways help and advise anyone. He's also one of the very few in the profession who never talks about himself."

Like many people in show business Johnny was superstitious, he never went anywhere without his lucky charm, a silver three penny piece.

Johnny Kidd
"I found it in a Christmas pud about seven years ago. It's in my pocket whenever I go on stage and whenever I make a new recording too... just for luck! And of course there is my eye patch too! I wouldn't move an inch without it. Both boys and girls like it now its part of me. I always carry one in my pocket and I have to have a lot of them because the kids grab them from me as souvenirs. On-stage or in shows I feel lost without one now. The heat on stage and the perspiration when we are going all out soon crumples them up so I have to use one every night. I reckon to buy three dozen every week or so. I always go into the same chemist shop for them, have done for a while now. The same old chap always serves me, he has never once asked me why I want them! I must be his only customer for eye shades in that quantity yet he has never said a word, just wraps them up and hands them over. Funny. You'd think he'd say, son, that must be a very bad eye you have? Maybe he hopes it will never get better?"
The longer the tour went on the more time Johnny spent with Gene Vincent. Clem recalls a very strange event.

Gene Vincent, Johnny Irving and Johnny
(© N. Simper)

Clem Cattini (Drummer)
"Gene was a great entertainer on stage but a very weird person. One night he went berserk and attacked Johnny with a knife. He would down a couple of bottles of scotch each day of the tour. I remember these two girls who always seemed to be at every show. Billie Davis (Jean) and her mate Blond Sue. They were Johnny Kidd freaks and everywhere we went they went too. We actually auditioned the then unknown Billie Davis through the window of the dressing room. We were getting her at it outside the dressing room, singing, but she wasn't known as Billie Davis then, and years later, producer Joe Meek said you've got a rehearsal up at Holloway Road at some hall towards Archway and we were backing the singer Billie Davis. I walk in there and when she walked in I fell about laughing cause suddenly from the 'Kidd' days this girl appears.

Bobby Elliott the drummer with The Hollies would travel hundreds of miles just to see our act. I didn't realise how important Johnny and The Pirates were are that time."

The Granada tour had kicked off at East Ham on Feb 12th. The fans were in for a treat of top class rock 'n' roll. Johnnys' mate Screaming Lord Sutch and the Savages soon had the fans laughing and screaming. His Lordship with his long wild hair, horned head dress and leopard skin savages got the show off to a frantic start. Jess Conrad making his very first live stage performance was backed by the superb Flee-Rekkers with vocal backing by the Four Jays. Jess opened with his latest release 'Mystery Girl'.

Liverpool born Michael Cox hit the crowd with his Joe Meek productions 'Angela Jones' and 'Along Came Caroline'. Surprisingly Johnny Duncan performed more country than skiffle. Johnny and The Pirates were as usual polished and very appealing. Johnny ending the performance by throwing his cutless into the stage floor. Top of the bill was Gene Vincent. British group The Echoes built up a tremendous beat as the curtains drew back to show Gene in a classic pose, dressed from head to toe in jet black leather. Johnny watched from the side of the stage as his idol turned into a wild, uninhibited frantic rocker, the highlights of his performance were 'Blue Jean Bop', 'Summertime' and of course his classic 'Be Bop A Lula'.

Future Pirate Frank Farley remembers the tour.
"My first memories of Johnny was when he played the Kingston Granada on Feb 27th '61. Mick Green, Johnny Spence, Jimmy Page (he was then unknown playing with Dean Shannon and the Crusaders, he later of course found fame and fortune with Led Zepplin) and myself bunked in for free. Mick, John and myself were then in an outfit called The Ramrods. John played lead, Mick rhythm guitar, Bill Darling (he later joined the Wild Angels) piano and yours truly on drums. Shortly after this John and myself along with Johnny Patto (lead) became The Redcaps featuring Red E. Lewis on vocals plus we became backing band for Cuddly Dudley. We recorded a single with Cuddly 'Sitting in a Train', 'One Thing I Like', Ember Label (EMB5136)."

The Granada tour was a great success, but sadly The Echoes lead guitarist got injured in a car smash so the very respected Big Jim Sullivan took his place. Backstage all the stars got on well and had a few laughs. Gene Vincent asked a reporter to deliver a surprise gift to Lord Sutch's dressing room. His Lordship was thrilled and held out his hand for the gift but he soon jumped, giggled and shouted as a large toy spider landed in his grasp. Gene was a wild cat on stage but behind the scenes Johnny saw many sides. A young blind girl fan had been give permission to visit Gene before a show. Gene presented to her a beautiful bunch of flowers. She was so happy.

Pirate Alan Caddy couldn't wait to try out his new VOX AC15 amp which he had got for his 21st birthday on February 2nd. Alan later made history by owning the second Gibson guitar in this country a Gibson ES 355 TD Blond.

Joe Brown had the very first A Sunburst.

Joe Brown
"When I formed Home Brew I sold my 335 and got a Les Paul. I went down Selmers and got a Les Paul. It was the worse thing I ever did. I let them have my original Gibson. Roy Wood (Move/Wizzard) bought it and has still got it I've tried to get it back but he won't let it go."

top: Johnny, Jean and Gene photographed by S. Terry (© Jean Heath Collection)

bottom: Johnny and Gene photographed by S. Terry (© Jean Heath Collection)

Vince Taylor (Brian Holden) and his Playboys were so impressed working alongside the pop buccaneers that they recorded a version of 'Shakin All Over/Don't Let Me Go' for the French Barclay label 60955.

top: Business card King's Agency (© Always N' Ever Archive)

centre: Sheet music 'Linda Lu' (© Always N' Ever Archive)

bottom: Record review - Melody Maker, March '61

Brian Gregg (Pirates Bass)
"I'd worked with Vince Taylor along with Clem during late '58 early '59. We did some touring on the south coast for promoter Reg Calvert as Vince and The Playboys. I was never really part of the outfit, it was only for a short period."

Taylor became a phenomenal sensation in France. He recorded performances of 'Twenty Flight Rock', 'Too Much', 'What'd I Say' and 'Shakin All Over' for French Scopitones juke boxes. Vince and his boys were filmed in the studio of Tele Monte Carlo under the production of Mrs Davis Boyer. (Scopitones made juke box movie shorts).

LICENSED ANNUALLY BY THE L.C.C.

KING'S AGENCY

DIRECTION: Terry King, Reg Calvert, & Kenny Bell

7 DENMARK STREET
LONDON, W.C.2.
TEMPLE BAR 6303/4

Presented By

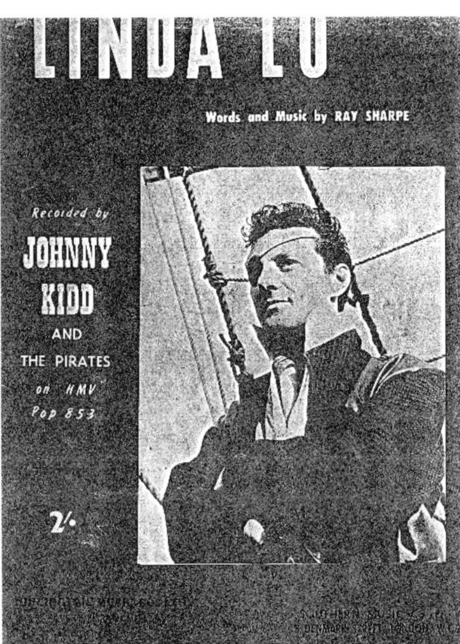

Alan Wheeler
"Johnny, Johnny Irving (roadie) and myself saw Shakin' on a cine juke box. It was in Dirty Dicks pub opposite Liverpool Street Station late at night after a Kidd gig. It was obviously ahead of its day and Johnny remarked that he would like some of that. I know that we also watched Screaming Lord Sutch - 'Jack The Ripper' which was quite effective and I seem to remember the French rocker Johnny Hallyday."

The crews first release of '61 was 'Linda Lu', 'Lets Talk About Us' on Friday 24th March. That evening they played the Central Pier, Morecambe. 'Linda Lu' had originally been recorded by American Ray Sharpe. Sharpe like Johnny dressed up for his stage shows usually in cowboy gear and sang like an Arkansas hill billy which was very strange as he was black. Sharpe is credited as composer for 'Linda Lu' but in 1973 the late guitarist Roy Buchanan told writer Bill Millar the following.
"I've made several things with Jerry Hawkins, Dale's brother. We took one song, 'Linda Lu' to LA and got 30 bucks for it. They promised they were gonna release it but two or three weeks later it came out by Ray Sharpe. Now that was a stolen song Ray copied the arrangement, Jerry's voice, the way he sang, everything." Sharpe's version made the American top fifty in '59 and inspired many covers - Johnny Rivers, Bobby Vee, the Flying Burrito Brothers, T-Bone Burnette and Doug Sahm. It was the unique stammer-like phrasing that was so unusual and caught the ear of Johnny. He was always searching for something different. Years later in April 1966 Sharpe re recorded the classic with a super line up featuring King Curtis (tenor sax), Chuck Rainey (bass), Cornell Dupree and the then unknown guitarist Jimi Hendrix (it remained unissued)."

★ Johnny Kidd and the Pirates

LINDA LU/Let's Talk About Us.—Linda opens with a snatch of monologue reminiscent of Donegan's famous "Rock Island Line"—but this one is the story about a cute chick, Linda Lu.

Johnny Kidd sings with potent rhythmical feeling to a finger-snapping backing from the Pirates. No need to be press-ganged into buying this one—just go in and get it. Definitely a hit by our rating.

Flip also rides along, though in less arresting fashion. (HMV.)

Johnny and the lads guested on BBC TV's Juke Box Jury to help promote 'Linda Lu.' They were invisible to the panel but in full view of the audience and could be seen either smiling or wincing as the panel gave their verdict a MISS.

Throughout April they started playing more and more gigs up North travelling 1,000 miles a week.
Johnny told the music press.
"I've got fed up with London. Down here the fans are spoiled. They wouldn't go much further

than their own door step to see anybody. Up North they'll travel to see you by the coach load. In fact the further North you go the more the old rock 'n' roll scene is alive. If you get off the stand now I'll punch your head. That was the kind of enthusiasm I got from a bloke in Scotland. They're more responsive than the kids down south particularly around London. I've had a ball working rather than just promoting myself but, now I've got 'Linda Lu' as my new disc, I've decided to do some promoting. I shall probably be going out on tour on one nighters with a comedian Terry Thomas. I think, it will be sometime in April."

TV's 'Thank Your Lucky Stars' gets raided

April 22nd saw the opening of Les Fous Hiboux 'The Mad Owls' in Streatham High Road. Johnny couldn't make the opening night with Michael Cox, Gerry Temple, Danny Rivers etc but he topped the bill the next night with Nero and The Gladiators and Keith Kelly and the semi-tones. Keith was trying hard to find fame as a solo act. He had previously played rhythm guitar for the John Barry Seven. He could have passed for the late Buddy Holly. Nero and the Gladiators were so impressed with Joe Morettis' solo's on 'Shakin' and 'Restless' they asked him to play lead on their instrumental release, 'In The Hall Of The Mountain King'/'Trek to Rome', Decca F11367. It became a classic instrumental. Joe had once again played on a legendary British session. Nero and The Gladiators wore authentic Roman dress complete with togas and gladiator helmets. Whenever they stood too near the front of the stage girl fans would look up their skirts and scream at the sight of their flowing togas.

If they ever had a spare night Stanley Dale would book Johnny and the boys for his own clubs in Aylesbury, Buckinghamshire or South London. Some of his clubs were real dives but, when bookings are falling off, any old port in a storm will do for a crew of Pirates.

The Gladiators and The Pirates

Pete Newman (Sax)
"Johnny heard about my break up with my girlfriend and telephoned me to ask me to come out on a gig with The Pirates to cheer me up. Roadie Irvo picked me up and took me to Aylesbury. It was a great night. Alan, Brian and Clem had a great sound."

Roadie Johnnie Irving recalls a spooky night on tour up North.
"We'd spent the evening talking to the medium who lived at promoter Reg Calverts' mansion. He told us various ghostly tales and strange facts such as dripping water being a sign of a lost spirit trying to make contact. Later that night at our hotel The Seven Stars in Rugby we all climbed into our bunk beds and turned out the lights. Next minute Johnnys jumped in bed with me yelling, "There's water dripping from the ceiling. Its a GHOST!" The water tapped all through the longest night of our lives. Come morning Brian Gregg had a shoe missing and one of Johnny's socks had gone. We never found these missing items. Very strange. Perhaps they had gone for a walk to the spirit world.

Brian Gregg (Bass)
"During this tour we met up with Screaming Lord Sutch who was a good mate of ours and especially the Kidd. We all went for a walk around the town, and ended up in Woolworths. Dave Sutch had very long hair then, when it wasn't accepted in our country. It wasn't the thing that a bloke did, it looked very freaky. He had his pair pushed up under his hat all of a sudden Dave wiped off his hat. He looked like an Apache Indian. He was running around the shop like a loony.

He cleared the shop. All the old dears were screaming. It was really funny."
His Lordship would often ride in The Pirates band wagon complete with his strange gear which included a coffin, swords, dead bodies (plastic of course) and his minge pole! His group The Savages featured many first class musicians and now included ex Freddie Heath sax man, Pete Newman, who Johnny was always pleased to see.

Screaming Lord Sutch
"Johnny gave me a Vortexion Amp. He really was a nice guy. He was always calling at my South Harrow home and chatting to my Ma."
Johnny had used this 4 channel Vortexion Mixer on stage. He bought the amp direct from Vortexion Ltd at 257/264 The Broadway, Wimbledon for £40 8s.6d. It featured balanced line, heavy mu-metal shielded transformers, hermetically sealed controls. Outputs 1/2v on more than 20,000 ohms or 600 ohms, 1m W, screened power pack for AC mains, size 18 1/4" x 11 1/4" x 6 1/4".

Since the start of his career Johnny liked to use an echo chamber on stage. This is a device for producing simulated echo or delay reverb effect. Echo chambers in the 60's fell into three categories. The actual studio chamber where a microphone at one end of a room picks up signals from a speaker at the other end making use of the rooms known 'live' characteristics. Tape echo where tape loop utilises distance between single recording head and several spaced playback heads to give adjustable effects. Pure electronic, normally "echo-plates", where the signal is delayed electronically with almost infinite adjustment reverberation systems - not strictly speaking echo effect without an actual repeat signal.

Some of the younger fans were starting to turn-up to gigs dressed as Pirates. It was an amazing sight when Lord Sutch was on the same bill because some of his followers would don top hats, thus creating a happy crowd of 'Raving Loonies'.

Photo by Leslie Barry
(© Jean Heath Collection)

During May Johnny helped out at the NME charity gala with other stars, The Avons and Paul Hanford. On the 25th they recorded 'Please Don't Bring Me Down' but were not happy with the session. For the months of June and July manager Stanley Dale organised 'The Beat Contest Tour'. This took place in 60 major cities in Britain including Northern Ireland. The show also starred Nero and The Gladiators and Terry Anton and his Rhythm Rockers. Local talent had the chance to win cash prizes of £100, £50 and £25 in the London finals.

Stanley Dale (Manager)
"The idea for a 'Big Beat Contest' grew out of the success of my National Skiffle Contest. The last one attracted more than 800 groups." Entry forms were obtainable from Dales' office at 12 Holland Villas Road, London W14.
Johnny was always pleased to get back home to his family in Willesden and the Rainbow Cafe. He also used two cafes in Park Royal owned by the Buxbaun family.

Daphne Yardley (Fan)
"The Go-To-It Cafe was next to the Central Middlesex Hospital and the other was opposite next to the Nat West Bank. Francis Buxbaun was a friend of Johnny and on occasions lent him his car (a Ford Consul). I did attend a party in Golders Green to which Johnny also attended and he did

wear his patch. I also saw him at the Boat House Kew and Fulham Town Hall where he actually mentioned my girlfriend and I from the stage and dedicated a song to us."

Peter Meers was a member of Willesden group 'The Hotrods' was playing with a group from around Curzon Crescent at a private party in a large house in Paddington.
"All of a sudden there was an excited din I looked around and saw a pair of shiny black boots walking into the party. Inside those boots was Johnny Kidd. The Kidds hair was unusually long for the times and of, course, he was dressed in his stage gear, frilly shirt, eye patch etc. He was asked to perform a couple of songs. We did 'Please Don't Touch', although I wasn't sure of the chords and 'Shakin All Over'. I couldn't believe his vocals much better than on his records."

Brian Gregg (Bass)
"The people Johnny knew in Willesden were the lads. We'd be driving through and they'd all yell "Alright John, How you're doing?" The boys on the corner all knew him. We used to love playing snooker. Often we'd get to a town in the afternoon and there was always a snooker hall above Burtons clothes shop. Alan Caddy was an excellent snooker player. We always said if he wasn't a guitar player he would have made it as a snooker player. In fact Alan used to make money. He'd go around the halls, play people and win. Near Willesden, open all night was a right shady place. It was supposed to be a snooker hall. We'd group there about 2.00am. There was a lot of gambling going on, guys throwing dice. They covered the snooker table with canvas. A big guy on the door keeping a look out in case the law came and we'd all go back to playing snooker. Nothing really heavy, it was all friendly, no booze just tea and sandwiches. Johnny wasn't one for posh restaurants or putting suits on for trendy night clubs' and posing. That's what we all loved about him, he was a smashing guy."

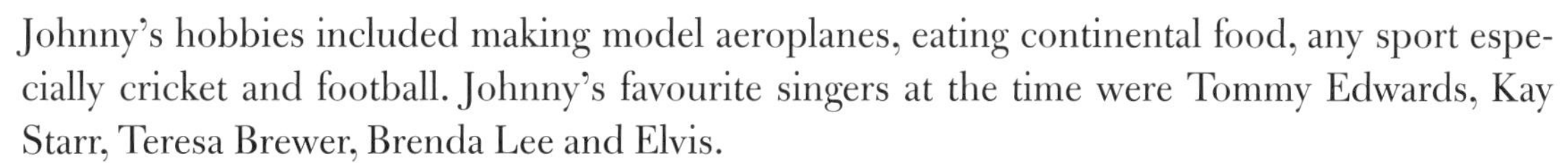

Johnny's hobbies included making model aeroplanes, eating continental food, any sport especially cricket and football. Johnny's favourite singers at the time were Tommy Edwards, Kay Starr, Teresa Brewer, Brenda Lee and Elvis.
"We do a couple of Brenda's numbers in our act, 'Weep No More' and 'All You Got To Do'. I type the words of the songs inside my eyeshield because my memory is so poor".
Most of the Pirates agree that his main addiction was pin ball machines. Driving up and down the country, they stopped at many a greasy cafe and most had machines and juke boxes. Once he became the pin ball wizzard the buccaneers always had a job to persuade their Admiral of the Beat to get off and get back in the van.

Brian Gregg (Bass)
"We did this gig and the audience was full of Teddy Boy nasties. Funny thing was we usually got on well with the Teds and the Rockers. In fact a lot of them looked on us as their band. We were honorary members of the '59 club which was the Big Bikers Club in London and we used to play there. This particular night there was a few drunken Teds and they were giving us a bit of stick. They kept interrupting our performance. We left the show and got in the van and were driving away from the place. Some of the Teds were standing about in groups in the streets leading away from the venue. We stopped the van and bought some fish n' chips, got back in the van and drove off. We saw this group of Teds standing on the corner. I was sitting on the left hand side, Johnny was in the middle, while Johnny Irving was driving. I was enjoying my chips and I saw these

Teds. I thought swines, for the stick they gave us so I slid the door open and I screwed the fish and chips into a ball and I threw it and hit one of the Teds right on his DA at the back of his head thinking we would just drive past, lean out the window and give them a lot of lip. What I hadn't noticed was just ahead was some traffic lights - the rest of the lads 'yelled you 'silly sod, what did you do that for?' These Teds went mad and started to chase after the van. As we got up to the bloody lights they went red. We looked out the back and these Teds were getting closer and closer. We're all panicking yelling to Johnny Irving quick! quick!, go Johnny go, go, go, they're coming. Just as they got to the van they started to bash on the windows and doors. Thank god the lights changed and we shot off. Of course as soon as we got to the safe side of the lights we're all leaning out of the windows giving lip again and shouting as we drove off. We were dreading playing that town again. We did but nothing happened."

Friday June 9th saw the boys back at Morecambe's Central Pier rocking from 8pm to 2am. On the 17th August they returned to Abbey Road to re-record 'Please Don't Bring Me Down'. This was a far better performance and featured Big Jim Sullivan on lead guitar.

Johnny - photo by Ken Palmer (© Jean Heath Collection)

Big Jim (Wildcats)
"I'd first met Kidd when I was a member of The Soho Skiffle Group. We all went down the Two I's, the Kidd, Brian Bennett, Joe Moretti, Tony Sheridan, Bobby Woodman, Vince Taylor, Red Reece etc, were all around and we would just sit in and play. As a result one of the regulars Tex Maikins invited me to join Marty Wildes' Wildcats."

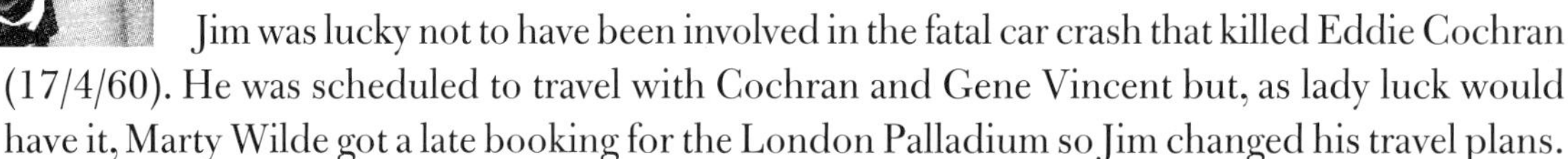

Jim was lucky not to have been involved in the fatal car crash that killed Eddie Cochran (17/4/60). He was scheduled to travel with Cochran and Gene Vincent but, as lady luck would have it, Marty Wilde got a late booking for the London Palladium so Jim changed his travel plans.

For the B side they put down a real raving rocker, 'So What', written by Crompton and Jones. Thunderclap Jones and Bill Crompton had in fact both started out as regulars at the Bridge House and Two I's where they rubbed shoulders with many young would be rock 'n' rollers including Freddie Heath.

Rick Richards (Worried Men/Jets)
"I knew Crompton and Jones well as I had worked The Bridge House once with Meehan, Marvin and Welch. Crompton was a songwriter and used to buy songs from would be singers and adapt them and publish them."

Jones had first recorded in 1957 when he cut an amazing piano instrumental for Oriole entitled 'Hurrican Boogie'. Jones and Crompton first duo release also for Oriole was 'Parisian Rhapsody'/'Stumbling' CBI 378.

The pounding piano solo on 'So What' was provided by Jones along with Brians' amazing bass runs, Alan's frantic guitar and Clems' fat drums. This was the Pirates finest hour and sadly to be their farewell voyage. September 15th was the release date Johnny should have been happy but mutiny faced the Admiral of The Beat. He met his crew for a nosh at the popular Lotus House restaurant in the Edgware Road but was shocked to hear the Brian, Alan and Clem were on another wave-length. His entire crew were to be shanghaied by Colin Hicks.

It was yo-heave-ho as the pirates enlisted as cabin boys. Johnny just couldn't take it in.

Brian Gregg (Bass)
"When we left Johnny he said he was sick of being on the road. He wanted to cut down and be with his wife and family. Thousands of people saw us throughout the country, we toured Scotland, we went up and down Britain doing one night stands, radio, television etc."

(both © B. Gregg)

Clem Cattini (Drums)
"I left Johnny which is one of the biggest mistakes of my life. I loved working with Johnny. It was one of those situations. The guys in The Pirates had been offered a gig with Colin Hicks (Tommy Steeles Brother) in Italy. We told Johnny at the last minute and he was in tears. Colin was enormous over there. A star. We either all went or none of us went. It was the bit where if you don't come we can't get the job, so I thought of security, which I still regret to this very day."

Brian Gregg (Bass)
"When we decided to leave we had been doing a lot of one night stands. A hell of a work load we were getting a bit stale. We were fed up with it and we thought we were sounding a bit old hat. It seems daft now because when I hear it now I realise Johnny's material was a wee bit ahead of its time. Also we hadn't had a big hit since 'Shakin All Over', our other releases hadn't really made it. So we thought we were finished, it was all over, water under the bridge, and we needed a change, fed up with the one night stands. Clem, Alan and myself went to Italy and backed Colin Hicks. Colin had recently appeared in a film called 'Europa Di Notte' (Europe By Night) which was a huge success. We got a fantastic reaction over there, it was really good, although Colin wasn't anything like the singer that Johnny was. When we went on stage our opening gig was in Rome, our sound was there, exactly the same. Colin did 'Shakin All Over' and a few other Kidd things but when the intro would come in and then Colins' vocals but, I'm sorry, it just didn't happen the same as with Johnny. We thought oh my God it sounds dreadful. We stayed with Colin for about six weeks.

On returning to England I answered an advert in Melody Maker for the Rhett Stoller Band. I passed the audition. While on tour we met Eden Kane and Eden asked us if we would like to back him because he had plenty of work. Clem and Alan went to work for Joe Meek doing sessions and then formed The Tornados. I also did sessions for Joe and later became a Tornado.

When we left Johnny he played the new line-up our records. The sound that we had created was handed onto the next band, they copied our sound. I'm sorry to say that Mick Green did not start this chunky guitar style of lead and rhythm - Alan Caddy did. I'd like to end with a funny story from my days as a Pirate.

I got a car off Frank Rouledge the ole Five Nutter. I swapped a record player for an Austin 7. I was going to a rehearsal at Leopold Road. I drove from Kilburn where I lived which wasn't a long drive. Suddenly I'm halfway there and had no brakes. On that make they had cable brakes. When I got to Johnnys home, there's Johnny Irving, Alan, Clem and Johnny all sitting on the wall outside I came round the corner, they were all looking at this little car, when I got level with them, I couldn't stop. I went sailing past them and mounted the curb, hit a wall and ended up in a garden. They were all falling about laughing. Johnny Irving came over and said for Chrissake let me have a look. Underneath the cables had broken, Johnny Irving bodged it up for me and I drove it home."

A complete change of crew. In came The Redcaps. Johnny Patto (guitar), Johnny Spence (bass), and Frank Farley (drums) plus a five year contract with the George Cooper Organisation. Johnny also signed a contract with E.M.I. for another ten years.

Frank Farley (Drummer)
"We backed Cuddly Dudley who was managed by Guy Robinson who also used to manage Kidd. When Clem and the boys left to join Colin Hicks, Johnny asked us to be The Pirates."

Contact strip with rare stage shots of lead guitarist Johnny Patto (taken by F. Rouledge ©)

Johnny Kidd
"Alan, Brian and Clem left me to better themselves. How could I possibly begrudge them their opportunity?"

Johnny had first heard his new crew playing in a ballroom and discovered that they had previously been backing Cuddly Dudly and Red E. Lewis. Dudley used to advertise himself as Bristols' answer to the Big Bopper.

Johnny Spence, Red E. Lewis, Johnny Patto (© F. Farley)

Bobby Elliott (Drummer Hollies)
"Our band The Dolphins worked with Heath in the Manchester area but the band had changed to Frank on drums but not yet Mick Green. Tony Hicks and I are from a small town, Nelson in Lancs. The local ballroom the IMP (Imperial) was very famous. Johnny and The Pirates played there, but we were on the road and unable to catch them during their many visits. I think the Hollies were influenced by Clem, Caddy, Gregg more than the Green, Spence and Farley band. Our lead guitarist Tony Hicks was impressed by the stark line-up, just drums, bass and guitar. The 60's Hollies backing sound was just lead/rhythm, Tony played both at the same time. Eric Haydock (bass) myself on drums. Graham Nash was never allowed to plug in although he was a good rhythm player. We felt that it cluttered the distinctive sound. So you see Heath and the boys were instrumental in influencing The Hollies one way or another.

Apart from the Dolphins another popular Manchester group were the Deltas, Alan Clarke (vocals), Graham Nash (guitar/vocals), Eric Haydock (bass) and Don Rathbone (drums). In 1963 Tony Hicks joined and with a change of name the Evergreen Hollies were born. Bobby Elliot joined towards the end of '63 followed by Bernie Calvert another ex Dolphin in 1965.

During Sept-October promoter George Cooper lined up a series of concerts staring Eden Kane, Johnny Kidd and his latest Pirates, Nero and The Gladiators, Flee-Rekkers, Joe Brown and his

Bruvvers, Michael Cox, Vince Eager and Danny Rivers.

i.e.	Sept	17th De Montfort Hall, Leicester
	Oct	2nd Granada, Eastham
		14th Royal Lido, Prestatyn
		15th Hippodrome, Birmingham

Throughout the long cold months of November and December the crew were Shakin' up a storm with Gene Vincent, Jess Conrad and Johnny Duncan and the Blue Grass Boys.

(Photos taken by F. Rouledge ©)

Nov	6th Kilmarnock
	7th Arbroath
	8th Ardrassan and Elkin
	11th Luntley
	12th Rosewall
	13th Perth
	14th Sunderland
	15th Astoria, Middlesborough
	16th Crewe
	17th Southampton
	18th Leytonstone
	20th Adelphi, Slough
	21st State Kilburn
	24th Imperial, Nelson
	25th Grimsby
	26th Southall
	27th West Bromwich
	28th Ebbisham Hall, Epsom
	29th Corn Exchange, Bedford

On Thursday 30th November Gene Vincent along with Sounds Incorporated spent the day at Abbey Road recording 'Space Ship to Mars' and 'There I Go Again'.

Dec	1st Fairfield Hall, Croydon
	2nd Lido, Prestatyn
	3rd Oasis, Manchester

Farley, Patto, Kidd and Spence
(Photo by F. Rouledge ©)

During the day of December 1st Johnny entered the recording studios alone to record 'Hurry On Back to Love/I Want That'. A real powerhouse performance, his vocals at their very best. The superb backing was supplied by the Michael Sammes Singers and Orchestra. Both were very original productions and years ahead of their time.

Johnny Kidd
"Well yes, I quite like it, I suppose, I'd like to do more like it. The thing that worries me is that every time the reviews say they go for a record it doesn't seem to mean a thing as far as sales are concerned. The records

they have been more enthusiastic about in the past have been 'The Only Girl In The World' and 'Linda Lu' and they fell flat! When I recorded this number I'd never seen session men so enthusiastic. Not many of them can play R'n'R but with R&B all they've had to do is read the dots and after one or two play throughs they can really begin to feel the music. I've switched to R&B because to be frank I couldn't find the right rock material. But I'm glad about 'Hurry On Back To Love' because its something different and I'd really like to have a crack at everything.

I envy Elvis because that's exactly what he can do. So can Cliff Richard and the other top artists. I can't think why they don't have a try at R&B. I have never found the right pattern. In the past my records have sold well but nothing really sensational. Shakin' was the only big hit I ever had but the follow-up which was exactly the same type of number didn't mean a light."

Richard Adams wrote at the time.
"I've known Johnny before he even recorded his first disc. He's been extremely unassuming perhaps so much so as not to fit cleanly into the showbusiness world. He certainly raves less about his work than most singers. But if Johnny makes it with 'Hurry On Back To Love' I've a feeling an awful lot of our top pops are going to follow him into the R&B field."

Picture story
(© Always N' Ever Archive)

(Photos by F. Rouledge ©)

11. A SHOT OF RHYTHM & BLUES

At the start of 1962 Stanley Dale sold Johnnys contract to the George Cooper Organisation under a new management and agency contract. Cooper was in partnership with Harry Dawson and together they managed many artists. Their main office was in the heart of Soho at Alderman House, 37 Soho Square, London, W1. Later they were based at 107-111 New Oxford Street, London.

Harry Dawson (Agent)
"George and I managed many artists Joe Brown, Tornados, Marty Wilde, Bert Weedon, Heinz, Johnny Kidd etc etc. We used to arrange all the bookings TV and radio work. We even helped them with their clothes and to invest their money the right way. George and I used to spend a lot time listening to songs. We used to receive about two hundred songs every week from publishers and song writers. We would listen to them all hoping a new number would suit one of our artists."

(Photos by F. Rouledge ©)

Johnny and The Pirates soon found themselves on a huge Cooper Tour of Granada Cinemas. One show at the Granada, East Ham on Sunday Feb 11th with Joe Brown, his Bruvvers, Vince Eager, Danny Rivers, Tommy Bruce, Nero and The Gladiators, Johnny Gentle, Shane Fenton and The Fentones, Nelson Keene and compere Freddie Earle is well remembered by Alan Wheeler.

"Back in those days Joe Brown was not the easiest of performers to follow and only a handful of people could do it. Gene Vincent, Billy Fury, Marty Wilde, King of Skiffle Lonnie Donegan and of course Johnny Kidd and The Pirates are the only names that spring to mind. Two packed houses responded to Joe Brown's energetic act with The Bruvvers that included the preview of 'A Picture Of You' - later to become a No 2 hit. The guitar behind the head routine produced an ovation at the end of his act which Johnny and The Pirates had to follow. But as soon as they opened up with 'Please Don't Touch' complete with chunky guitar, thumping drums, heavy bass and leg kicks, the audience soon settled down to enjoy Johnny's great stage act.

Granada East Ham poster (courtesy Danny Rivers)

Johnny and The Pirates looked really moody in their all black leather outfits, and although the act looked basically the same as I'd seen before, the sound had changed to become more powerful and slightly R&B influenced by this new line up. After touch came 'You Got What It Takes' followed by 'Lets Talk About Us' then into a very moody version of a less successful single called 'Hurry On Back To Love' (with Johnny Spence doing a great bass run on the intro). This went down well and the applause greeted 'Linda Lu' which sounded great. Johnny then introduced his new line-up and went into 'If You Were The Only Girl In The World' which Johnny described as a small salad ballad. A knockout rendition with a great build up by The Pirates that really went down big at both houses as did the final number the classic 'Shakin All Over'. Plenty of girls screaming at Johnny during his 'Shake' routine in the guitar break, which Mick Green really belted out, lots of applause and shouts of more as the curtains closed on the final bars of this R 'n' R standard. A relatively short act but the most impressive (looking back at this stage show, I can still vividly remember Johnny dropped the microphone during the guitar break in 'Shakin' only to see the cable come away from the mike. I did wonder at the time if he would realise this by the time he picked it up again. He did of course, but only just in time!)."

GEORGE COOPER ORGANISATION LTD.
37 SOHO SQUARE, LONDON, W.1 Telephone: GERrard 4894
SOLELY REPRESENTING TOP STAR ATTRACTIONS

JOE BROWN AND HIS BRUVVERS
BERT WEEDON
MARTY WILDE AND THE WILDCATS
DANNY RIVERS
LINDA DOLL
THE PUPPETS
NEIL CHRISTIAN'S CRUSADERS
THE FOUR MACS

JOHNNY KIDD AND THE PIRATES
THE TORNADOS
FLEEREKKERS
MICHAEL COX
BOBBY SHAFTO
DUFFY POWER
THE ECHOES
BRIAN HOWARD AND THE SILHOUETTES
THE OUTCASTS

HEINZ AND THE SAINTS By arrangement with JOE MEEK
JESS CONRAD By arrangement with AL PARKER
VINCE EAGER
MIKE PRESTON
THE SUNDOWNERS
THE VICTORS
PAT BURNS
THE CYCLONES

THE GEORGE COOPER ORGANISATION ARE PLEASED TO ANNOUNCE THAT
BIG DEE IRWIN IS AVAILABLE FOR CONCERTS, BALLROOMS, FUNCTIONS, etc. FROM JUNE 12th UNTIL SEPTEMBER 18th

Johnny Patto had just recently left the band due to bad ulcers. He was replaced by an old school mate of both Frank and Johnny Spence. His name Mick Green. Spence recalls their very first meeting.

Johnny, Frank and Mick

"This little kid in short trousers turned up on my doorstep one day, we were both fourteen, holding a guitar and said I'm told you know the opening bit to 'Cumberland Gap.' Can you teach me? That was Mick Green."

Mick made a big impression on Frank the first time they met by falling out of a tree and hitting Frank on top of his head. Mick reckons he was only about 10 or 11 when they all first met.
"We'd played in various bands together over the years. The Pirates guitarist Johnny Patto had been taken ill so they rang me and asked if I wanted to sit in. So I went along had a bit of a rehearsal and that was it."

The Pirates were now Mick Green (lead), Johnny Spence (bass) and Frank Farley (drums). The three had first met in the skiffle era and soon formed a group along with another pal. They played washboard, tea chest bass and Spanish guitar in an outfit called The Wayfaring Strangers. They entered all the local talent shows.

Frank Farley (Drums)
"We reached the finals of a competition at the Tottenham Royal Ballroom. We came 2nd. The winners were a band from Liverpool called The Quarrymen (later to become the legendary Beatles)."

Mick Green (Guitarist)
"Johnny Kidd was a very ordinary bloke, very down to earth and a happy go lucky chap. He didn't have airs and graces like some of them. He was just a nice bloke who'd be in the back of the van with the rest of us. Johnny liked the trio set-up because of its presentation on stage. It wasn't so much the sound which was pretty rotten in those days. He was considering what it looked like on stage. It looked more symmetrical with a bass and a guitar at each side, drums behind and a singer out in front. Johnny was an innovator. His whole thing and everything we did was visual. The Pirates were one of the first groups in Britain to carry their own lights around. Johnny was

always thinking of new things to do on stage. If he saw anyone doing anything good he'd adapt it. I remember Jerry Lee Lewis used to shake his trousers up and down and straighten the creases. Kidd saw the idea and knew how to use it for his own benefit, he was very quick."

Although the three piece line up was still very rare and unusual The Pirates weren't alone in this field. Vince Eager had without really realising, one of the first real super group trios. His backing group The Quiet Three featured first rate and very respected musicians Colin Green, ex Nero and The Gladiators on lead, Tex Maikins, ex Blue Flames on bass and ex Cabin Boy, Jimmy Nicol drums (future stand in Beatle).

Another superb mainly instrumental trio were The Scorpions. They had supported Johnny and the lads a few times at the Wandsworth Town Hall. The late Dickie Pride and Ricky Valance both used the Scorpions as backing, alas only on live gigs, never on recordings.

'Hurry On Back To Love'/'I Want That' had been released on 19th January and Johnny's first appearance on television to promote it was on the very popular 'Thank Your Lucky Stars'. The show had been running since April 1961. The programme was pre-recorded at A.T.V. Studios in Aston, Birmingham on Sundays and transmitted the following Saturday. During this time the show was only regionally shown (not networked) and hosted by another ex-Stanley Dale artist Jim Dale prior to Brian Matthew taking over. Other TV appearances to promote the new disc included Juke Box Jury, Disc-A-Go-Go and a special E.M.I. spectacular on Radio Luxembourg. A tremendous set was broadcast on Border Television's 'Beat The Border' - 'Please Don't Touch', 'If You Were The Only Girl In The World', 'A Shot of Rhythm And Blues, 'A Little Bit of Soap, Linda Lu', 'I Can Tell', 'You Got What It Takes', 'Shakin All Over' and 'Feel So Fine'.

On Sunday March 4th '62, Johnny and his crew played at the Dudley Hippodrome on the 'Rock A Long Show' along with Vince Eager, The Echoes, Nelson Keene, Roly Daniels, Tommy Bruce, Bert Weedon and compere John Smith. Johnny was thrilled to be touring with Tommy Bruce.
"Tommy did his first big show with me at Hereford and I've never seen such a big lump of shivering jelly. My poor pal, Tommy, could hardly speak let alone sing. Before he went on I said to him, "Tommy, just act like they were a bunch of peasants out there and don't give a damn what they think of you!" Not really my attitude at all but it worked wonders."

Your programme for tonight

THE ECHOES
VINCE EAGER
NELSON KEENE
JOHNNY KIDD
and THE PIRATES

interval

ROLLY DANIELS
TOMMY BRUCE
BERT WEEDON

God Save The Queen

This programme is subject to alteration at the discretion of the management

'Rock A Long' Programme 4/3/62 (© Always N' Ever Archive)

Bert Weedon (Mr Guitar)
"I have lots of very happy memories of the tour. I had the great pleasure of touring quite a lot with Gene Vincent who I got on very well with, Marty Wilde, The Wildcats, Joe Brown, Lord Rockinghams XI, Russ Conway, Brenda Lee and Johnny Kidd and The Pirates, so I had some very good times. I only wish those times would come back because these days the tours that go on are by very big superstars with perhaps one supporting band whereas in the 60's you got 6 or 7 artists on the same bill all contributing their varied styles of rock 'n' roll which made for a very entertaining show where I think the public certainly got their money's worth. I worked with Johnny on several shows and found him a really nice man and a fine and original performer. I did

play on some of his early sessions but I'm afraid I cannot remember which ones. You see I played on literally thousands of records when I was a session player and it is impossible to remember them all."

Johnny and Pirates (© Jean Heath Collection)

Pete Searles (Mark Shelley and The Deans)
"We used to support the big boys when they came down to Essex such as Joe Brown, Vince Eager, Sounds Inc., Lord Sutch, Johnny Kidd etc. I remember Johnny came down to Rayleigh near Southend to play at the Crown Hotel and we were lucky to be support. Talking to Johnny back stage I rambled on about the girls making a grab for his eye-patch (I still can't believe I said that). Johnny just laughed and said no worry mate I've got these and produced an old battered shoe box full of eye patches. Our act changed a great deal after appearing with Johnny. From a Cliff and Shadows Fender line up we went to a four piece tight Gibson sound. Kicking off with 'I Can Tell'. Like Johnny I used an old Vortexion as a PA with a 50 watt output. Gosh."

twist 'n' shout
at the
CROWN
Hotel Rayleigh
every Fri' and Sat'
to top bands
THE FOUR JUST MEN.
THE COSSACKS. THE NITERIDERS.
RIP and THE VAN WINKLES.
MARK SHELLY and THE DEANS.

Crown Hotel advertisement (courtesy of P. Searles)

John Lodge (Bass Moody Blues)
"There used to be a lot of gigs around the Birmingham area, where they would bring the stars up from London. Johnny Kidd and Nero and The Gladiators were very popular. Johnny was one of the favourites, they used to do this part in their act especially on 'Please Don't Touch' they used to stamp their feet and The Pirates would kick their legs up. We worked with Johnny quite a few times back in the late 50's and early 60's. Well we were playing in Worcester alongside Johnny and they did this kick routine. We had a band at the time called Earl Riot and The Rebels which featured Ray Thomas, Mike Pinder who along with myself went on to form The Moody Blues. Anyway we saw Johnny do his wild kick so we copied and put it in our stage show. On returning to Birmingham we entered a local rock 'n' roll competition called The Tulip and featured the kicking routine. We brought the house down, everybody loved it. Up to then of course especially in Birmingham the bands had no action. The best act by far in Birmingham was Danny King, his voice was superb, he should have been a huge star, with his group The Mayfair Set. Another was Jimmy Powell who was the first Birmingham artist to cut a record. He was produced by Jack Good. There was about 20, 000 bands in the Midlands during the early 60's all fighting for a gig, sadly they never made any inroads in Liverpool or London. Birmingham was a different type of music."

Johnny always enjoyed working for the Stringfellow brothers at 47 Kingston Street, Sheffield.

Peter Stringfellow (is now owner of the successful Stringfellows nightclub)
"The first bands we ever booked were Johnny Kidd and The Pirates and Nero and The Gladiators. I remember paying a £100 for Johnny and booking the unknown Beatles for £80. Luck was on my side because when the Beatles played our venue they had just hit the big time. One of my early venues was a church hall. I certainly had a lot of explaining to do to the Vicar after Johnny's cutlass had left deep marks in his cherished church floor."

Keith Grant (Downliners Sect)
"While with my pre-Sect band The Vigilantes we supported JK at a hall in Hillingdon. I thought the Kidd and Co. were great and felt it was wonderful that a local hero had become a national pop star."

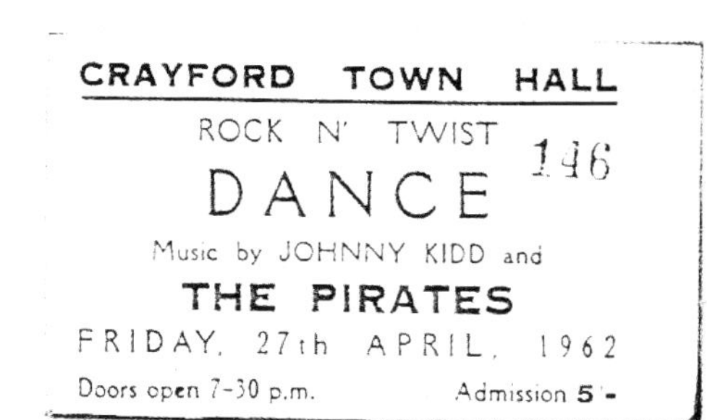
CRAYFORD TOWN HALL
ROCK N' TWIST
DANCE 146
Music by JOHNNY KIDD and
THE PIRATES
FRIDAY, 27th APRIL, 1962
Doors open 7-30 p.m. Admission 5/-

On April 29th Jerry Lee Lewis returned to the UK for the first time since his disastrous tour of '58 when it became known that he was married to his 2nd cousin who was only 13 years old.

TOWN HALL, BIRMINGHAM
JERRY LEE LEWIS
TUESDAY, 1st MAY, 1962,
at 8-45 p.m.
UPPER GALLERY 8/6
B18
PLEASE RETAIN
Tickets will not be exchanged or money refunded

above Jerry Lee Lewis tour ticket
above Crayford Town Hall ticket
(both © Always N' Ever Archive)

April couldn't come quickly enough for Johnny. Agent Don Arden by arrangement with John Gordon and Hopelevy Productions had lined up a huge tour for 'Mr Great Balls Of Fire' along with Johnny Kidd and The Pirates, Vince Eager, The Viscounts, The Echoes, Mark Eden, The Bachelors, Danny Storm, Buddy Britten and Stuart Gaston.

Newcastle City Hall	Sun April 29th
Leicester, De Montford	Mon April 30th
Birmingham Town Hall	Tues May 1st
Cardiff Sophia Gardens	Wed May 2nd
Blackburn King Georges Hall	Thursday May 3rd
Grimsby Gaiety	Friday May 4th (J L Lewis only with Echoes)
Portsmouth Guildhall	Sat May 5th
Cannock Danillo	Sun May 6th
Brighton Essoldo	Mon May 7th
Bristol Colston Hall	Tues May 8th
Sheffield City Hall	Wed May 9th
Bradford St. Georges Hall	Thurs May 10th
Norwich Theatre Royal	Sat May 12th
Hull Cecil Cinema	Sun May 13th
Mitcham Majestic Cinema	Mon May 14th
Tunbridge Wells Essoldo	Tues May 15th
Glasgow St Andrews Hall	Fri May 18th

below: Jerry Lee Lewis tour programme
(Always N' Ever Archive)

The killer hit the crowd with 'Down The Line', 'You Win Again', 'Breathless', 'High School Confidential', 'Great Balls of Fire', 'What I'd Say', 'Whole Lotta Shakin', and 'Good Golly Miss Molly'. His shake routine during Whole Lotta Shakin received wild ovations, the whole audience stamping and clapping. Johnny's spot had closed the first half. He went down very well with 'Please Don't Touch', 'Shakin All Over', 'Feel So Fine' and a new number 'Hey Baby', Bruce Channels No 3 hit. The crowd went wild.

Many people recall that Lewis wasn't happy as Johnny and The Pirates were able to give him a run for his money in terms of audience reaction prior to The Killers' entry as top of the bill. After his wild act he was whisked away by bodyguards as he came off stage but Lewis must have been in mourning because just before he left for the UK on the 24th April his three year old son Steve had drowned in the family swimming pool.

Cliff Bennett and The Rebel Rousers played some of the dates. Cliff recalls.
"Johnny and I went to Lewis's room. Johnny was asking about the shake routine in 'Whole Lotta Shakin.' Jerry Lee just looked Johnny up and down and never even answered."

(© Always N' Ever Archive)

During '62 the press was claiming that rock 'n' roll was on the way out and that Trad jazz was now the major force. The likes of Johnny, Lord Sutch and Cliff Bennett stuck rigidly to their roots.

Cliff Bennett
"The kids still wanted real rock. Many new trends the watering down bits, had been pushed on groups by record companies. Trad, some Trad, sure was good to hear but not much. For every one Trad club in the London area within a few miles radius there were five which concentrated on rock and beat Music. Johnny and I toured with our idol Jerry Lee Lewis. Lewis stuck to the old rock, good old rock. If Lewis hadn't had such bad publicity when he first came here. He'd have torn the country apart - he was great."

On Wednesday 14th May Johnny broke from the tour and played the first of four consecutive appearances at the Cavern in Liverpool. Ray McFall used to book the groups for the worlds most famous Beat Cellar.

Ray McFall
"I wasn't too sure that strangers would be readily accepted by our club members but the reaction to Pete Maclaine and the Clan from Manchester convinced me that we should broaden our horizons and fetch in artists from much further afield. On the jazz side I'd booked scores of London bands but the occasions when we'd featured non jazz, non Liverpool people were few and rather special. At the height of his pop fame in 1960 we'd used Emile Ford and we'd had the John Barry Seven on Dec 14th 1960 too. At the beginning of 1961 we had a Wednesday evening appearance of The Shadows (Jan 1st) but I considered their popularity to be extraordinary enough to break the general rule. By the middle of '62 I was satisfied that Cavern members would like to see current hit parade stars more frequently. I fixed dates for Johnny and The Pirates for the 14th May (first Southern beat group to visit) followed by Mike Berry and The Outlaws (21st May). Then in June we welcomed our first American star attraction Bruce Channel."

Cavern advertisement
(© Always N' Ever Archive)

The Cavern had almost stopped Trad bands, and was now featuring mostly local groups. As special attractions national stars such as Shane Fenton and The Fentones and from London Johnny and Joe Brown were becoming very popular. One evening as Johnny and the crew took to the stage they looked into the crowd and were shocked to see many members of various leading Liverpool groups watching them. They quickly proved that these buccaneers from London were a very serious threat to Mersey Beat and soon had the crowd of musicians cheering them on.

Mike Pender (Vocalist/Guitarist Searchers)
"In those days when very few groups wrote their own material, we copied a lot from American rock 'n' rollers. Johnny Kidd really impressed me that night at the Cavern."

Frank Farley (Drummer)

"We used to go and play the Cavern. We would be up there for a week playing a lunch time session and an evening session. At each session there would be about three or four local bands i.e. The Beatles, Gerry and The Pacemakers, Pete McLaine and The Dakotas, The Big Three and another great band King Size Taylor and The Dominoes. They played a lot of R&B numbers from America that most of the bands and general public down south in London had never heard. The Pirates, in fact, got off on it and nicked quite a bit of these Liverpool bands material. They were very, very talented and leading the field in their own area. We were influenced partly by them before they made it. Later in Oct '62 we recorded 'A Shot Of Rhythm And Blues.' It was a change of style, actually people thought it was heavy for us, it highlighted the chopping guitar style of Mick Green. I recall a quote that Kidd made at the Cavern to Mike Green and I we often used to bring it up at later dates to annoy Johnny. Each day there were different scouse bands as support. The Beatles were our support. Mick and I said to Johnny that The Beatles were very good and perhaps it would be a good idea to book them for the dance halls in London and make some money. During this time Joe Brown was high in the charts with 'A Picture Of You'. Johnny's famous quote "They'll never be as big as Joe Brown."

above: Johnny
(both photos © Jean Heath Collection)

While appearing at the Cavern thieves broke into the band wagon and stole four suits. The van was parked at the rear of their hotel. The thieves gained admission to the van by breaking the rear window. This was the third time in '62 that gear and equipment had been stolen from their van or dressing room.

Johnny and Crew
(© Jean Heath Collection)

During this period Johnny Hutchinson was regarded as one of the top drummers on Merseyside. Maltese born Johnny was a member of Cass and The Casanovas who became The Big Three when Brian Casser left the group. When the group became The Big Three Johnny turned down a two year contract with Johnnys' Pirates to remain with them. According to Cilla Black when Pete Best was dismissed from The Beatles Hutchinson was first choice as his replacement but Ringo got the job. Popular Liverpool singer Beryl Marsden was a keen fan of Johnny and the boys. She followed the act around at various times. Forty miles north-east of Liverpool stands Blackburn. The biggest group from this town were The Four Pennies. Their drummer Allan Buck played the odd gig for Johnnys' Pirates and Joe Browns' Bruvvers.

Freda Kelly (Norris)(Secretary of The Beatles Original Fan Club)

"The Cavern was a full house that night, hot and sweaty. Johnny was in a riotous mood and really had the crowd screaming for more."

Brian Jones (Sax - The Undertakers)

"Having seen Cass and The Casanovas and later The Big Three working on Merseyside they were very similar to The Pirates. I think they were very influenced by Johnny and the lads. If you listen to some of their recordings you can hear that Pirates sound. It's great that The Big Three's

old bassist, Johnny Gustafson, joined Mick Green's Pirates in 1990."
Mick Green (Lead)"We were working the Cavern for the first time and, while we were on stage, there was a part of the act where Johnny would take out a cutless while I was doing a heavy blues solo. At the crescendo of the solo he would throw the cutless at my feet and it would stick in the wooden stage as part of the act. However, when Johnny had the cutless raised above his head. I looked down at the stage and realised that where the lino had been worn away it was not wood but concrete. While playing I tried to tell him not to throw the sword because it would not stick in but he didn't take any notice. He threw it and it landed inches from my foot and bounced into the audience. At this point a member of the audience grabbed it and ran out of the Cavern with it. Johnny Irving our road manager had to chase him halfway round Liverpool before he got the sword back."

Photos by Philip Gotlop
(© Jean Heath Collection)

During a quick trip to Scotland (May 18th) for a special Glasgow gig they stayed close to a so called haunted castle. For a laugh they made an Ouija board to try and make contact with the spirit world. They put towels over the light bulbs to darken the room, placed their hands on a tumbler, and it started moving around to various words and numbers. The room felt very eerie as the seance took off. All of a sudden the towels burst into flames, panic and shock took over. They never ever dared to mess with the supernatural again.

A great tour was lined up for June supporting the American star Bruce Channel who had just had a top ten hit with 'Hey Baby'. The bill also included Cliff Bennett and The Rebel Rousers, Frank Ifield, Dick Charlesworth, Jackie Lynn, The Barons, Jack and Tommy Scott, Bobby Shafto, Beryl Bryden and Dis Disley (compere). The four week tour kicked off with the Granada Theatres followed by two weeks of dance hall dates.

June 4th Maidstone, 5th Aylesbury, 6th Bedford, 7th Mansfield, 8th Grantham, 9th Tooting, 10th Walthamstow, 11th Dartford, 12the Kettering, 13th Woolwich, 14th Kingston, 15th Harrow, 16th Slough, 17th Rugby, 18th Cheltenham Town Hall, 19th Imperial Hall, Waltham Cross, 20th Town Hall Oxford, 22nd Plaza Ballroom Norwich, 23rd Corn Exchange Wisbech, 24th Colston Hall Bristol, 25th Majestic Ballroom Reading, 26th Public Hall Wallington, 29th Cooperative Hall Gravesend, 30th Wilton Hall Bletchley.

The tour was a very busy time for all especially Bruce Channel. Bruce arrived early on the morning of June 4th with his manager, Marvin Montgomery, direct from the States. He was then rushed straight off to rehearsals and later that night was on stage at the Granada, Maidstone.

The first house audience of only 300 soon realised that Channel had a more powerful rhythm n' blues oriented voice than on record but there wasn't a lot of enthusiasm from the audience. The rest of the bill varied Jack and Tommy Scott were quite slick, Frank Ifield was very professional, Bobby Shafto earned mild applause, Beryl Bryden did well considering it wasn't her kind of audience, Dick Charlesworth showed that trad and pop audiences just don't mix, Dis Disley (compere) worked hard to be bright and cheerful but the best applause of the entire night went to Johnny and The Pirates who were by far the best act. As the tour went on Channel got better and the tour was a resounding success.

On Thursday 21st June Channel and The Barons broke from the tour and did a one night stand at the Tower Ballroom, Liverpool along with the North's No 1 group making their first tour appearance since their return from The Star Club in Hamburg, The Beatles. Many musicians followed 'The Channel Tour' including The Beatles, Rolling Stones and Yardbirds. They all became fans of Delbert McClinton who played harmonica for Channel. John Lennon became good friends with McClinton who between shows spent time teaching Lennon how to play the harmonica properly. The Beatles were so impressed with his original sound on Channel's 'Hey Baby,' as can be heard on 'Love Me Do'.

Frank Farley (Drummer)
"I remember for the performance at the Colston Hall, Bristol on the 24th June my drums were on a rostrum consisting of four sections pushed together. Midway through the show during 'My Babe' Kidd would throw his sword into the stage but as he did this my rostrum came apart so that my drum stool slipped between the four sections resulting in me going arse over backward, kicking my drums completely off the rostrums. To make it worse the audience were seated behind the stage as well so it was very embarrassing.

I'll always remember Bruce Channel being so thrilled when he came over to England because he had never seen the sea before."

George Cooper tried hard to obtain insurance cover for Johnnys' use of swords and daggers in his act but was unable to get any suitable cover. After a vast amount of protests from various venue managers and council officials Johnny had to drop this side of his act.

Manager George Cooper wasn't that popular with The Pirates. They felt he could have made Kidd a far bigger star.

Mick Green (Guitarist)
"I don't think George knew what he was doing. He was not particularly good compared to Brian Epstein and people of that character. He was interested in getting you out and doing gigs, taking the money and going home. Epstein had more of an idea. George handled Joe Brown at the time and really paid more attention to him than he did to Johnny Kidd. The Pirates didn't like him and never signed a management contract. He advised Kidd to get rid of us which Kidd didn't do because he knew we were important for his stage act. But there were never any hassles. The boss

just said you should get rid of that unruly mob! In those days it wasn't as important as it is today, there were no big stars except Cliff and The Shadows. We were just having fun doing something we always wanted to do getting on TV, travelling around Europe and having a ball and, if we got paid for doing it, that was a bonus."

(Photo by Philip Gotlop)

Alan Wheeler
"Like Larry Parnes who I once worked for George Cooper was an accessible manager. In some ways he emulated Parnes by assembling a list of several artists under his banner but unlike Parnes he made few discoveries and tended to sign up established acts and in the case of Johnny, bought up the remaining portion of his contract with Stanley Dale. In my opinion Dale was a far greater rock 'n' roll fan, though he lacked the managerial motivation and financial backing of Cooper who at one time, attempted to separate John from The Pirates. Fortunately John resisted it. Dale would not have been one for considering such a move."
Coopers two sons Ken and Cliff were also involved in sixties beat as lead vocalists with The Millionaires. He helped them get bookings. They were one of the last groups to record for producer Joe Meek at his Holloway Road Studio 'Wishing Well' came out in August '66 on Decca F12468. Cliff is now a highly successful manager and publisher and also owns a studio. Ken runs his own business.

Alan Wheeler was the secretary of the fan club back in the heydays of the sixties and even formed the Appreciation Society in the late '70's. Sadly it no longer exists but his loyalty to Johnny Kidd had never died.

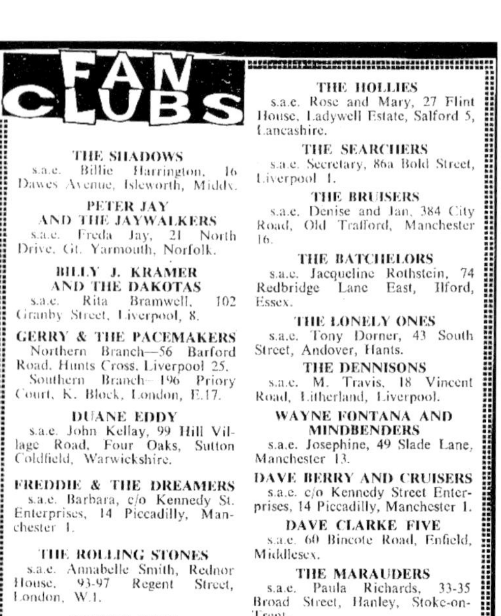
FAN CLUBS

THE SHADOWS
s.a.e. Billie Harrington, 16 Dawes Avenue, Isleworth, Middx.

PETER JAY AND THE JAYWALKERS
s.a.e. Freda Jay, 21 North Drive, Gt. Yarmouth, Norfolk.

BILLY J. KRAMER AND THE DAKOTAS
s.a.e. Rita Bramwell, 102 Granby Street, Liverpool, 8.

GERRY & THE PACEMAKERS
Northern Branch—56 Barford Road, Hunts Cross, Liverpool 25.
Southern Branch—196 Priory Court, K. Block, London, E.17.

DUANE EDDY
s.a.e. John Kellay, 99 Hill Village Road, Four Oaks, Sutton Coldfield, Warwickshire.

FREDDIE & THE DREAMERS
s.a.e. Barbara, c/o Kennedy St. Enterprises, 14 Piccadilly, Manchester 1.

THE ROLLING STONES
s.a.e. Annabelle Smith, Rednor House, 93-97 Regent Street, London, W.1.

JOHNNY KIDD AND THE PIRATES
s.a.e. Al Young, 114 High Holborn, London, E.C.1.

THE HOLLIES
s.a.e. Rose and Mary, 27 Flint House, Ladywell Estate, Salford 5, Lancashire.

THE SEARCHERS
s.a.e. Secretary, 86a Bold Street, Liverpool 1.

THE BRUISERS
s.a.e. Denise and Jan, 384 City Road, Old Trafford, Manchester 16.

THE BATCHELORS
s.a.e. Jacqueline Rothstein, 74 Redbridge Lane East, Ilford, Essex.

THE LONELY ONES
s.a.e. Tony Dorner, 43 South Street, Andover, Hants.

THE DENNISONS
s.a.e. M. Travis, 18 Vincent Road, Litherland, Liverpool.

WAYNE FONTANA AND MINDBENDERS
s.a.e. Josephine, 49 Slade Lane, Manchester 13.

DAVE BERRY AND CRUISERS
s.a.e. c/o Kennedy Street Enterprises, 14 Piccadilly, Manchester 1.

DAVE CLARKE FIVE
s.a.e. 60 Bincote Road, Enfield, Middlesex.

THE MARAUDERS
s.a.e. Paula Richards, 33-35 Broad Street, Hanley, Stoke-on-Trent.

THE FEDERALS
s.a.e. Maureen Harrison, 19 Southmoor Road, Oxford.

Fan Club
(© Always N' Ever Archive)

Alan Wheeler
"I first met the great man in '62 I was running a British fan club for Chuck Berry at the time. Being a big fan of Johnny Kidd I made him an Honorary Member of the Berry Club and had included a short article on him and The Pirates in the newsletter. Imagine my surprise when after sending Johnny a copy I received a very nice letter from the man himself saying how knocked out he was by being made an Hon. Member and getting mentioned in the Berry Newsletter. He went on to say he did not have a fan club (which I found surprising) and that he would be pleased if I would run one for him and The Pirates. If I was interested I was to phone him at home to arrange a meeting. Like I said I was a big fan of Johnny's and so I was more than delighted to start a club under the name of Al Young giving up the Chuck Berry in preference. Having duly phoned Johnny it was arranged that I would meet him at his parents home where he lived at the time in Perivale, Middlesex. The arrangement being that his road manager, Johnny Irving, would pick me up in town and drive me over to Perivale. I well remember the old BC bandwagon trundling up Old Compton Street, Soho suitably adorned with hand painted inscription such as Capt' Johnny Kidd and Ye Olde Pirates on the back door.

On arriving at his home I was met at the front door by Johnny in his dressing gown who, after having a hurried few words with Johnny Irving on the door stop explained that he had arrived back late from a gig the previous night. In contrast to the sinister image I was immediately struck by his friendly manner, not at all big headed, and a real down to earth person. We had a long chat and I can remember Johnny going on about his friend, Gene Vincent. He showed me a couple of photos taken with Gene back stage at a show in Greenford, Middlesex. One showed Gene in his famous leather outfit shaking hands with Johnny wearing an eye patch looking slightly unfamiliar in a pullover. The other showed Gene with Johnny and his second wife, Jean. Johnny was very pleased to show me these pics and also talk about his stage shows with Gene who he held in high esteem.

Whilst Johnny went off to dress, his mother Mrs Heath made some tea and I could hear Johnny strumming away on guitar in the bedroom above. When he came down he asked me if I would like to meet The Pirates as he was going over to rehearse a radio spot with the boys. After a bit of lunch we went off in Johnnys' car, a Ford Zodiac (with JK on the hub caps) to where he was going to rehearse with the boys. On the way we pulled into a tatty transport cafe and I was amazed to see Johnny get out and stroll casually in and buy some cigarettes. Few people if any recognised him without his eye patch which Johnny said was a great advantage in getting in and out of theatre stage doors. Eventually we arrived at a tiny cafe, behind which was a small hall, from which would be heard a powerful group thumping away. As we walked in The Pirates were just finishing a number but there was sufficient music to tell that this was an ace band that backed Johnny.

After talking to Johnny Irving, who was in fact a close friend of Johnnys from years back, Johnny took me over and introduced me to The Pirates, Mick Green, Johnny Spence and Frank Farley. They seemed genuinely interested and pleased that a fan club was being started. They talked a fair amount about Chuck Berry and his more obscure discs at that time with Mick also mentioning that he had worked with Vince Taylor and the Sheik of Shake, Dickie Pride, prior to his days with Johnny Kidd.
Johnny and The Pirates then went into two numbers they were going to perform for their radio spot 'The Fool' and 'Some Other Guy'. I was privileged to witness the great man in fine form. Johnny had a very good voice, more bluesy than his records suggest, and quite powerful. After the rehearsal we all went through to the cafe for a coffee and it was here that I was to see another side of Johnny - generosity! For he just handed over the cash I thought I needed to start the fan club off. Right there and then that proved to me how genuine this man was. A few days later I was in the audience when Johnny and The Pirates performed 'Some Other Guy' and 'The Fool' on a radio show with The Springfields and Bert Weedon. This was recorded at the BBC Paris Theatre in Lower Regent Street, W1. It was to be the start of many recording sessions and stage appearances I was to be present at with Johnny and the boys. I must confess to the pseudonym used by Dickie Bishop on 'Waterloo'/'Washbash Cannonball' by the Kenny Ball's Jazzmen. It had vocals by Al Young (Dickie Bishop) and The Bandboys. I needed another name at the time to separate the JK Fan Club from the Chuck Berry one and so picked up on that name which had a link."

Johnny Kidd and The Pirates
C/O Al Young
114 High Holborn
London EC1

Johnny and the boys were really thrilled to have such an enthusiast running their fan club.

Johnny Irving (Roadie)
"Alan Wheeler (Al Young) was a nice guy. He is a great fellow and a really dedicated sort of

person. A real ardent fan of Johnny and his various Pirates. It doesn't surprise me that he still remembers many facts and gigs. He was that kind of guy, really dedicated."

Hamburg

Johnny was hearing tales of a wild rock scene in Hamburg, Germany where sex was always available, bars open 24 hours a day, stimulants such as Preludin could be bought in any chemist shop but most important rock 'n' roll was still alive and loud. It was arranged that in July they would do a short tour. Johnny and the lads couldn't believe their eyes as they walked along the Reeperbahn the main street in Hamburg's Soho. This street has more strip clubs than any other street in the world. The St Pauli area must have seemed like heaven with its bright lights and girls on every corner. They were entering a world where some British teenage musicians away from mum's cooking for the first time were now on a new diet of sex, drugs and rock 'n' roll. This wild place really was where the seeds of British beat were sown in more ways than one. It was, in fact, club manager Bruno Koschmider who got the rock n' roll scene first rolling in 1960. The American GI's who attended his clubs wanted English speaking rockers not the German imitations. The cost of American rockers would have been expensive so he looked to the UK. He made for the Two I's coffee bar in Soho, London. There he met pianist Ian Hines who told him that he was leader of a popular rock 'n' roll band. Koschminder was impressed and booked him for the Kaiser Keller in Hamburg. Hines didn't have a band at all but soon got some mates together and called themselves The Jets with Del Ward (drums), Rick Richards (vocals/guitar), Colin Milander (guitar), Pete Wharton (bass), Tony Sheridan (guitar and vocals). The Jets became the very first British rock band to go to Hamburg.

Koschminder, with the help of Mersey club owner Allan Williams, started booking many Liverpool groups to play both his clubs, the tatty Indra Club and the Kaiserkeller. Williams kidded Koschminder that all the best British groups came from Liverpool. Derry and The Seniors were the first with the Mersey Beat.

This really was the wildest and greatest training ground for British Beat. Two of the best clubs were the Top Ten and the Star Club both situated in the Reeperbahn the round the clock entertainment street where nobody ever slept. The Top Ten was owned by Peter Eckhorn who hit on the idea of employing young British musicians.

Peter Eckhorn

"I was only 21 years old. My father was running a circus type club. It was very old fashioned German entertainment and it was no longer popular. My father was very sick, dying of cancer, and he didn't know what to do with the club. We were badly in debt. I persuaded him to let me try a modern club using the best rock musicians from Britain. It nearly broke his heart to see us painting his white walls black and putting strips of red light in the ceiling but we went ahead and I opened with Tony Sheridan.

From that night we did great business and my father lived long enough to see it was a success. I used only British musicians and paid them fair money. If the union had forced me to employ only Germans nobody would have come to the club and I would have closed. The British bands and

top: Alan Wheeler in the guise of failed pop singer 'Bobby Shore' (© A. Wheeler)
bottom: Press advertisement for Hamburg's 'Star Club' (© Always N' Ever Archive)
right: British rock pioneers 'The Jets' - Tony Sheridan, Rick Richards (Hardy), plus 'Niggor' Tony (drums) on stage Top Ten 1960. They were the first and set a very high standard (© Rick Hardy)

singers had a great reputation in Germany. The audiences were mostly young people but those under 18 had to leave by 11pm to comply with German law. The bands used to start at 8pm every night and play through till 4am. On Sundays things started rocking at 4pm and rolled right through to 4am Monday morning."

Usually there were three house bands but when Eckhorn opened another Top Ten in neighbouring Hanover one of the bands were diverted there. The house band were called the Top Ten All Stars and were led by pianist Ian Hines.

Here are just a few of the bands who cut their musical teeth in this exciting venue, The Beatles, Dave Sampson, The Flinstones, The Checkmates, Blackjacks, Dave Berry, Tony Sheridan, Rick Richards. Tony loved the wild city and decided to stay and become the resident vocalist at the Top Ten.

Geoff Nugent (The Undertakers)
"Tony Sheridan was a great guitarist. He taught a lot of budding guitarists chords they'd never heard of. John Lennon and Gerry Marsden both copied the way he held his guitar."

Brian Gregg (Ex-Pirate)
"Tony was very original, a great player, he should have been a bigger star in England. Another great talent was Jackie Lynton. He was a great vocalist."

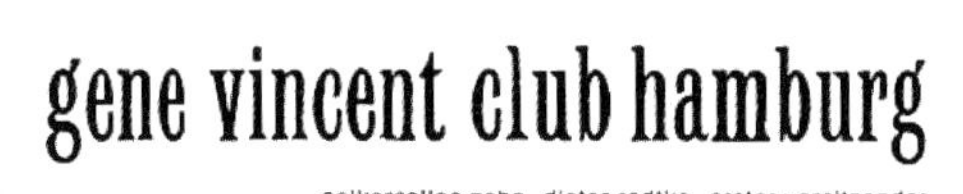

Vincent's Club, Hamburg
(© Always N' Ever Archive)

Tony Jackson (Ex Searcher) (The Vibrations)
"Tony Sheridan was managed by the Star Club and one night played a gig in Kiel. The manager refused to pay him so the bouncers at the Star Club drove to Kiel and destroyed the venue with hand grenades!"

Johnny Hutchinson (Drums, Big Three)
"The Beatles owe everything to Sheridan because they copied him to a T. He was a fantastic guitarist, the governor, and they copied his finger style.

Johnny Gustafson (Bass, Big Three/Pirates 1990)
"My memories of Hamburg drunken insanity'. I was reduced to a physical wreck after four days but it was enjoyable to be a physical wreck. It was wonderful to be lying in the gutter in a whisky sodden head in rain water. I'll never do it again.

Mit freundlicher Empfehlung
Star-Club
HAMBURG-ST. PAULI
Große Freiheit 39

Star Club, Hamburg
(© Always N' Ever Archive)

Johnny and the bands exciting swashbuckling stage act was full of energy and along with Tony Sheridan they inspired many future Star Club stars.

In April of '62 an enterprising club owner called Manfred Weissleder decided to open a club for rock 'n' roll fans only. Calling it the Star Club it soon gained a reputation as he offered more money and looked after the groups booking them into hotels etc. Weissleder had made his money running a string of strip clubs in the St Pauli district so he had the money to book the biggest names in rock 'n' roll, Bill Haley, Gene Vincent, Jerry Lee Lewis, Chuck Berry along with British beat groups.
In July Johnny and the band played their very first gig at this raving club. Their four week top of

the bill spot proved very successful breaking all attendance records with crowds of over 4,000 on some nights. Hamburg really was a wild place as roadie Johnny Irving recalls.
"Manfred Weissleder gave us special badges to wear. These passes allowed us to go about our adventures in and around the St Pauli district without getting any trouble. It really was a bizarre place."

Mick Green (Guitarist)
"Hamburg is not the place for the squeamish. I was 19 and a babe in arms when I went there. It was seven nights a week in one place and we were competing every night even though we were top of the bill. Every band wanted to blow us off the stage. And when those bands included King Size Taylor and the Dominoes, The Undertakers and The Big Three we couldn't afford to be slack. It certainly sharpened us up."

Johnny Hutchinson (Drums, The Big Three)
" We were doing an hour on and an hour off for three months and so we played every song we knew about five million times. We used to make up songs like 'The Gas Stove Twist' and 'The Bucket Mop Song' and we'd even get requests for them. They were a load of rubbish but Tony Sheridan was the governor in Germany. One night we were doing 'The Gas Stove Twist' when this big ladder was brought on-stage. Soon we had Tony Sheridan, Johnny Kidd and The Pirates and Cliff Bennett and the Rebel Rousers all climbing up the ladder and jumping into the curtain. Owner Wiessleder didn't seem to mind us wrecking his stage because the audience was loving it. They saw us fellows jumping over one another and kicking drums in and throwing guitars about. It was fantastic."

above and below:
Johnny at the Starclub, Hamburg.
Photo by Gunter Grzesik
(© Jean Heath Collection)

Alvin Stardust (Shane Fenton and The Fentones)
"The Big Three had a real earthy sound, real dirty guitar playing, good drumming and good bass playing. It was raw and simple and that's what rock 'n' roll was all about. The only other band that got in their league was Johnny Kidd and The Pirates."

Cliff Bennett and The Rebel Rousers along with Johnny and the boys were amongst the most popular British acts.

Cliff Bennett
"I worked the Star Club with Johnny Kidd, Davy Jones, The Bachelors (duo), Tony Sheridan, Roy Young etc. The club opened from 6pm to 3am and weekends from 4pm to 6am. Sometimes we played half an hour, even as long as three hours. They really like out and out rock. Funny thing was the fans didn't seem wild about Elvis or our Cliff Richard, they really liked Little Richard, Chubby Checker, Fats Domino. Chuck Berry was the biggest rave among the young fans."

Frank Allen (Searchers)
"I was there with Cliff and the Rebel Rousers and clearly remember Johnny Kidd at the Star Club. His act was dramatic, exciting, he used lights effectively before most other, and, of course, the ship back cloth that the Star Club gave to him."

Mick Green (Lead)
"They gave us a huge painted back cloth twenty feet high and forty feet long, of a big galleon. It was painted with ultra violet paint to give the effect of the galleon in harbour and we'd have three ultra violet lights up for full impact. Kidd would come on-stage with a huge sword and he'd chop props in half and wave and smash his sword into the stage. Other groups came on in suits and just stood there ... and Kidd was a great singer too. Nobody could follow us. Johnny was one of the greatest showmen to come out of this country. He was certainly ahead of his time and its sad to think what he might have been capable of today with a musical ability to back up his sense of image. He had the image, the patch, the back drop and he wrote songs like 'Please Don't Touch', 'Shakin All Over' etc. He really was tremendous, leaping around cutting things us. A great live performer."

Frank Farley (Drummer)
"When we first went to Hamburg we were just what people called a typical beat group and then we heard all these scouse bands playing rave stuff like 'Castin' My Spell', 'A Shot of Rhythm And Blues'. When we came back to England we were a different band entirely. In fact our own 15 minute set which we used to play before Kidd came on stage, was always far more Rhythm And Blues slanted than his part of the show. Johnny Spence would take the vocal spot."

both above: At the Starclub (© Jean Heath Collection) (above bottom: Photo by Gunter Grzesik)

Johnny Spence (Bass)
"The three of us would play together, everything seemed to come across quite natural and I believe that to be the secret. Mick could do whatever he wanted in the knowledge that Frank and I were always there right behind him."

Johnny Irving (Roadie)
"I got our lights idea from the Star Club. The stage had all these lovely lights so I worked out a beautiful lighting plot. I spent a lot of time working out new images for the act. On some numbers that Johnny had double tracked in the studio I would stand backstage with a mike and join in on the vocals."
The St Pauli area was full of porn shows (cinemas), prostitutes, bars, clubs and of course rock 'n' roll. You could be rocking twenty four hours a day if you could keep it up. Most of the British groups would meet at Alphons and Gretels Cafe and chat over frikadella and chips or the Mambo Schanke Cafe where Tony Sheridans wife Rosie worked. The Star Club owner Manfred Weissleder was a typical looking German, big, blond who stood out in a crowd dressed in his snake skin coat.

His right hand man Horst Fascher (top bouncer) would look after the groups by arranging badges, hotels (The Pacific and Germania) even tear gas pistols in case the badges weren't good enough protection. When the tired Buccaneers left Germany 'Shakin All Over' was at the top of their hit parade. Johnny was well pleased and proud to see a large photo of himself and the crew on the Star Club wall along with photos of other visiting British stars such as Tony Sheridan, Screaming Lord Sutch, Roy Young, Earl Sheridan, Emile Ford, Lee Curtis, Cliff Bennett and The Beatles.

below: Starclub entrance (© Always N' Ever archive)

Back home in England throughout August-September the New Record Mirror held a prolonged debate about who was the first rocker to wear all leather gear.

Johnny sent in the following letter which captures a glimpse of his harmless humour.
"I have watched the recent controversy raging over who wore black leathers first. The claims made by both Vince Taylor and Manager Don Arden (for Gene Vincent) have been a joy to watch. I should imagine you are quickly reaching the point where you are thinking of closing the correspondence on this matter so that there shall be no further complications from me. For I notice my name had crept into it. Might I add a confession that whoever it was wore them first, IT WASN'T ME! But I have written this letter sitting in a leather covered armchair. Please don't let start another topic "Who sat in black leather covered arm chairs first?"
It was, in fact, super fan Alan Wheeler who wrote the letter bringing Johnny into this funny controversy.

top: 'Comp' - Floral Hall, Morecambe
(© Always N' Ever Archive)
centre: Southall poster
(© Colin Richards)
bottom: Terry Franks - Avalons
(© Colin Richards)

During August it was all happening in Liverpool. Ringo Starr replaced Pete Best, John Lennon married Cynthia Powell and Granada Television filmed The Beatles live at The Cavern. On the 10th The Cavern organised a special Liverpool Riverboat Shuffle aboard MV Royal Iris. Johnny and The Pirates were supported by The Beatles and The Dakotas (then working without Billy J Kramer who was still with The Coasters). This was to be one of Pete Bests last ever gigs as a Beatle. By the 16th he had been kicked out.

FLORAL HALL — MORECAMBE
THE RENDEZVOUS OF THE YOUNG AT HEART
OFFICIAL COMPLIMENTARY PASS
Admit one holder
for the season/year/week/day
valid until a.m. p.m.
Issued by: ALAN BIRDSALL, Manager

Friday 29th September they played the very popular Floral Hall, Morecambe supported by local band The Alan Taylor Orchestra. 3/- (15p) on the door from 7pm - 11.45pm

Joe Waite (Dolly Blues)
"The Floral Hall had a wild reputation. When you were younger you went in the place with some trepidation but there was some brilliant acts played there, Johnny and The Pirates, Screaming Lord Sutch and The Savages, Beatles etc. and for a while the music scene in that area was unbelievable. Apart from the Floral, there was the Pier and Tivoli. Many times I saw local bands upstaging the main acts (not Johnny or Lord Sutch). There were some phenomenal local musicians around then The Doodlebugs, The Leaders, Phythagoras and The Squares, The Petermen, The Milestones, Dolly Blues etc. The Leaders guitarist Bill Parkinson went on to work with megastar Tom Jones, PJ Proby, The Fourmost and The Savages. The Kinks, The Yardbirds, The Who, Four Pennies, Honeycombs, Hollies are just a few of the great bands who played there. My band supported many chart acts eg Moody Blues."

T.V. AND RECORDING STARS - THE SENSATIONAL
JOHNNY KIDD
AND THE PIRATES
TERRY FRANKS AND THE AVALONS
SUNDAY, 7TH OCT.
SOUTHALL COMMUNITY CENTRE
ADMISSION 5/- MEMBERS ★ DOORS OPEN 7.30

They had returned to England a far tighter unit. The marathon session at the Star Club had turned The Pirates into a solid hard edge R&B anchor behind Kidd. With their sound so together they decided to capture this new found vigour on wax. On the 26th October Bo Diddley's classic 'I Can Tell' was given new life and beat blood by the sea rovers.

Sunday 7th October along with Terry Franks and The Avalons they played the very popular Southall Community Centre. This great venue was run by Pete Lynsey.

Colin Richards (Rhythm Guitarist, The Avalons)
"We arrived about 6.30pm and started carting our gear up to the front of the stage. We could see the galleon back drop being hoisted up by two roadies. The new roadie was an old mate of ours who used to work for our agent, Ron King. We used to call him Bill Stickers because he was

always getting nicked for sticking up posters all over London and its suburbs. Some of these posters were still up years later. He used to stick them everywhere, bridges, telephone boxes. In fact there was one poster of Lord Sutch under the Viaduct in Windsor that was still there during the early 70's. As we were setting up our gear, Kidd and The Pirates were rehearsing 'A Shot Of Rhythm And Blues'. They kept running through it time and time again. Bill Stickers told us its gonna be the next single. They are recording it soon that's why they keep going through it. It saves a lot of time in the studio. After about the fifth run through a jobbie appears "Come on, how many more times, the doors open in half an hour? I've got to get the support group set up and ready to start at 7.30pm on the dot." Mick Green replied, What's this then Sunday Night at the London Palladium." He then goes into shuffling movement as though he was on the famous Palladium roundabout and starts shouting out the theme tune "La, La, La La La La La. The jobbie was furious but we made it on stage for our first set as the doors opened at 7.30pm.

Johnny - The Boys
(© Jean Heath Collection)

Nick Simper (Future Pirate)
"I went to the Southall Community Centre, loads of young musicians were there including Mitch Mitchell. They were all fans of Mick Green. He was very respected and had a large following. The Savages drummer, Carlo Little, also had a cult following."

Ten days later on the 17th October Arthur Alexander's 'A Shot Of Rhythm and Blues' was given a shot of Kidd's magnificent charisma and The Pirates power. Johnny was a keen fan of Alexander because apart from being a good singer he was a fine songwriter. 'You Better Move On' (1961), 'Anna' (1962), 'Go Home Girl' (1962), and he also recorded the following classics, 'A Shot Of Rhythm And Blues', 'Pretty Girls Everywhere', 'Soldiers of Love', 'Where Have You Been', etc. etc. Johnny and Gene Vincent and later a generation of British Rhythm And Blues bands were raised on Alexander's original feel. The Rolling Stones, The Beatles, Bee Gees, Dusty Springfield, Tina Turner, The Drifters the list is endless.

'A Shot Of Rhythm And Blues'/'I Can Tell' was released on November 9th. To help with its promotion they recorded a live Rhythm And Blues set for BBC radio and on Saturday November 16th appeared on ITV's Thank Your Lucky Stars. A short Granada tour was set up with The Tornados, Joe Brown and The Bruvvers, The Echoes, Chris Wayne, Bobby Shafto, Vince Eager and top of the bill the American Nut Rockers' Bee Bumble and the Stingers.

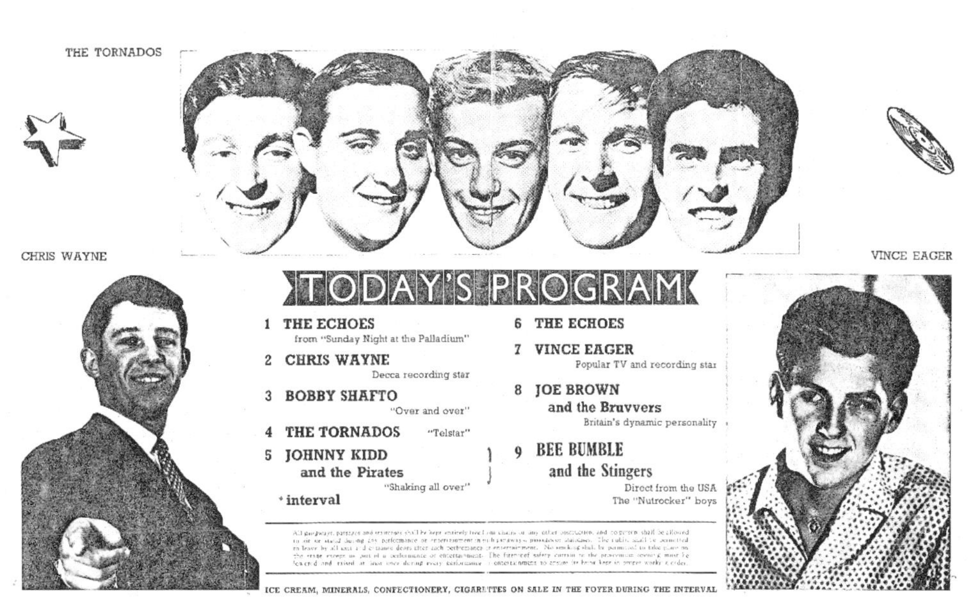

THE TORNADOS

CHRIS WAYNE

VINCE EAGER

TODAY'S PROGRAM

1 THE ECHOES
from "Sunday Night at the Palladium"

2 CHRIS WAYNE
Decca recording star

3 BOBBY SHAFTO
"Over and over"

4 THE TORNADOS "Telstar"

5 JOHNNY KIDD
and the Pirates
"Shaking all over"

* interval

6 THE ECHOES

7 VINCE EAGER
Popular TV and recording star

8 JOE BROWN
and the Bruvvers
Britain's dynamic personality

9 BEE BUMBLE
and the Stingers
Direct from the USA
The "Nutrocker" boys

ICE CREAM, MINERALS, CONFECTIONERY, CIGARETTES ON SALE IN THE FOYER DURING THE INTERVAL

Tour Line-up
(© Always N' Ever Archive)

Alan Caddy and Clem Cattini were having great success with The Tornados and 'Telstar'. Brian Gregg had formed a group called The Pack with Rob Grodway (vocals/guitar), Andy Rickell (harmonica/guitar), Roger Hartley (guitar) and Bob Duck (drums). They were formed in Wiltshire and were very popular in the West Country. Although The Tornadoes were having great chart success, their live act wasn't as polished as Johnny Kidd and The Pirates. Clem admits the Kidd was in a difference class.

'The Tornados' (© Always N' Ever Archive)

Clem Cattini (Drums, Tornados)
"I'd been with such good musical acts like Johnny and Terry Dene and people like that. Johnny Kidd, musically, spoilt me for everything because he was so good."

Friday 14th December Floral Hall, Morecambe supported by Danny Davis' Dynamos, Sunday 16th December. Promoter Bernard Hinchcliffe booked the following Big Top Acts, Joe Brown, Kenny Ball's Jazzmen, The Tornados, Jimmy Justice and Johnny and the boys. The show was presented in a circus ring with the group set up on a revolving stage. This fun event was held at The Queens Leeds, a really smashing early Christmas treat for the fans. As its title suggested it really was a mammoth Jazz 'n' Pop Show. Johnny and the crew went on stage during the afternoon. Later in the evening they did yet another gig at a night-club. The previous day on ABC Thank Your Lucky Stars The Tornados were presented with a gold disc for over a million sales of Telstar.

below top: Raye Du-Val (© R. Du-Val)
below bottom: A note from Johnny to Raye (© R. Du-Val)

below right: Business card 'Gardenia Club'

Clem Cattini (Drummer Tornados)
"We were working the circus in Leeds and I said to Johnny I must show you our old gold disc. He thought I was having a go, trying to put the knife in. I wasn't. It always upset me that Johnny thought that I done that on purpose to say well we left you and made a bigger success. I wanted John to share in the success. I still had then a great respect for John."

Thank Your Lucky Stars was a huge success but in '62 many unsuccessful pop shows came and went. Disc-A-Go-Go, Needlematch, The 625 Show (which was presented by Jimmy Young), even the young David Frost hosted a couple of twist competition programmes.

If Frank Farley was ever unwell Raye Du-Val would be the first choice as a replacement.

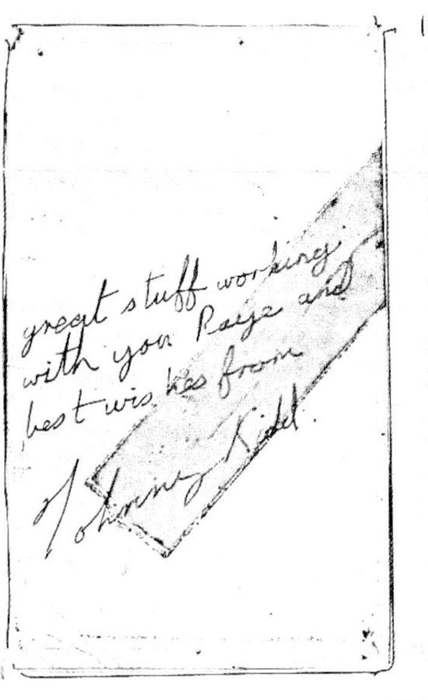
great stuff working
with you Raye and
best wishes from
Johnny Kidd.

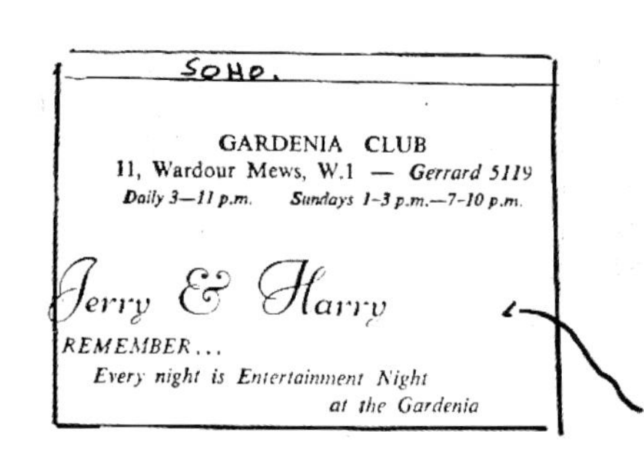
SOHO.
GARDENIA CLUB
11, Wardour Mews, W.1 — Gerrard 5119
Daily 3—11 p.m. Sundays 1-3 p.m.—7-10 p.m.
Jerry & Harry
REMEMBER...
Every night is Entertainment Night at the Gardenia

Raye Du-Val (Drummer, Checkmates)
"My first Pirates gig was at the Gardenia Club in '62. I was lucky to have been born in Soho and was there at the birth of skiffle and rock 'n' roll. I worked with Johnny on the Soho circuit, the Two I's, Top Ten, the Guildhall, Portsmouth and the Granada Circuit. I didn't become a permanent Pirate but we spent quite a lot of time together. I played the odd gig between '62-'64. I used to take him around a few jazz clubs and night spots. The guy was a gem, he was superior to a lot of rockers that were on the scene. He was quiet and had knowledge of many things. We were friends for 5 years, you know I never once saw him lose his temper. He used to kip down at my flat in Soho. We would have a ball. Johnny came and witnessed me dubbing drums on to a Johnny Burnette rock and roll Trio recording. When I played on one of my drumming marathons in 1959 Johnny came and cheered me on. In fact Pirate Brian Gregg sat in on my '59 marathon."

Raye is the only drummer in the world to hold the title of triple winner of The Worlds Non Stop Drumming Marathon Record Contest verified by the Guinness Book of Records and The National Jazz Federation. He once turned down both The Shadows and The Beatles when their own drummers were indisposed as circumstances did not permit Raye to accept their offer. Raye formed the original Rock 'n' Roll Preservation Society in Soho in 1959 when he was known as the Drum Crazy Kid from Soho."

Johnny was always pleased to play the California Ballroom in Whipsnade Road, Dunstable. The resident band were Russ Sainty and The Nu-Notes. They in fact played this venue well over 200 times.

Roger Dean (Lead Guitarist, Nu-Notes)

"The place was owned by a Mr Green. He opened a bloody great big hanger of a ballroom in the middle of nowhere. It served the whole area, Bedford, Luton, Dunstable etc. The place used to be jumping, we were there most Saturdays with some great bands, The Outlaws, The Quite Five, Mike Cotton Sound, Graham Bond and of course Johnny and The Pirates. Mick Green had a unique guitar style, he still is a tremendous rock guitarist, he was completely on his own. I'd never heard anyone play like him. Johnny and The Pirates were great."

1962 had been a hard year of touring, sadly they weren't rewarded with good chart success but Johnny was very proud to see Alan Caddy and Clem Cattini top of the American charts on December 22nd with 'Telstar'. The Tornados had pushed the Four Seasons 'Big Girls Don't Cry' from the No 1 spot to become the very first UK group to top the US charts. The Tornados had started life as The Charles Blackwell Orchestra. Blackwell played keyboards and was Music Director. Other members were ex Pirates Clem Cattini (drums), Alan Caddy (lead guitar), ex Freddie Heath band members Pete Newman (sax) and Pete Cotton (tenor) plus Heinz Burt (bass) and George Bellamy (rhythm guitar).

(© Jean Heath Collection)

12. ECSTASY (HIGH ON LIFE)

During January 1963 a fan presented to Johnny a small souvenir to remind him of the town he had played in. He thought that from then on it would be a good idea to collect such souvenirs from every town he visited thus building up quite a selection of memories. He bought himself a trunk and re-named it the Treasure Chest. The souvenirs he collected were known as booty and were cast into the chest just like real pirates treasure.

Their year had begun with mainly local gigs. On Tuesday 29th they played the Ex Servicemen's Club in Windsor. For just 4/- (20p) entrance you could see the Friendly Buccaneers of the Ballroom Circuit. Johnny was now living at 36 Devon Close, Perivale, Middlesex with his mum and dad and two sons. His father Ernest worked near home in Wandsworth Road but he never walked. He always went by motorbike. Johnny always found this funny and often took the mickey out of his dad. His mother Margaret took good care of the children. She was a very down to earth person. No. 36 was a very ordinary semi, a regular working class home. Apart from a couple of small cannons outside the front door the house showed no happenings of success. A close neighbour was Pennie Ort. Although then just a child Pennie has some lovely memories of her pop star neighbour.

top: Poster 29/1/63
(© C. Richards)

centre (from left)
Russell Heath - Yes Sir, That's My Baby
(Photo F. Rouledge ©)
Kidd keeps an eye on the kids
(Photo F. Rouledge ©)
Big blonde baby
(Photo F. Rouledge ©)
Russell and Tony Heath with Paul Rouledge
(Photo F. Rouledge ©)

right: Paul Rouledge is Shanghaied
(Photo F. Rouledge ©)

"I used to ask Fred (Johnny) for autographs which I used to sell at school. My father Bill used to own the local Ort Bakery in Bilton Road. Fred, his sister and parents were our customers for sometime. I got to know Fred quite well. I even taught his kids to ride their bikes. I don't think his sons Tony and Russell ever saw his stage shows but they certainly knew his songs. I remember asking Russell what 'Growl' sounded like. He stood in the middle of the Close and gave me this loud rendition of a song which began 'Well I go to bed and take off my head, then I get up and go out and shout and growl, just growl. Russell was an extrovert, always into mischief, while Tony was the quiet one, well behaved. I remember Fred, Frank Farley, Johnny Spence and Mick Green having a kick about in the street. Frank was well liked by the children, he often played with them. Years later I was given the skull and crossbones scenery I had it stuck on my garage doors for years. I guess I just left them behind when I grew up and left home."

Johnny and The Pirates cut a pounding version of Ritchie Barretts 'Some Other Guy' on January

31st but it was inexplicably withheld until 1990. They were very disappointed especially when The Big Three released a version on the 29th March (Decca F11614) which entered the top 50 in April.

John McNally (The Searchers)
"The Beatles did 'Some Other Guy', as did The Searchers, The Big Three etc. Everybody did it but they always did it their own way. If you listen to all the recorded versions you'll find that no two versions are the same. That was the good thing about Liverpool. All the bands had their individual styles and that set them apart from each other."

Freddie Garrity (Freddie and The Dreamers)
"If I were to choose just one record from the Merseybeat era it would be 'Some Other Guy' by The Big Three. The noise really typified the Mersey Sound. We did the song ourselves but their version was much better than ours."

Johnny Gustafson (Bass, Big Three/Pirates)
"Some Other Guy' was actually a demo tape for Decca. Brian Epstein told us that they were releasing this version. He wouldn't let us do it again and we went berserk. It was awful. The bass was non existent and the drum sound was awful. My voice was completely gone. We'd just got back from Hamburg that morning. It was horrible, the only good thing was Brian Griffiths strong guitar line."

Johnny's 'Some Other Guy' in contrast to The Big Three's version was perfectly produced and really puts all the other versions in the shade. Johnny's vocals at their very best while Mick Green's guitar solo is years ahead of its time. It would have been the perfect follow up to 'A Shot of Rhythm And Blues' but was shelved until 1990. This became a cult number especially on Merseyside. The Beatles very first TV appearance shot at the Cavern captured them performing the classic.

During the 'Some Other Guy' session on 31st January, The Pirates also recorded two instrumentals 'Spanish Armada' and 'Popeye' both written by Mick Green. These numbers were mostly featured on sound checks and not normally in the set. They have never been released.

At Christies Rock Memorabilia in August '93 The Beatles version of 1962 acetate of 'Some Other Guy'/'Kansas City' recorded at the Cavern sold for £15, 000

Future Pirate, Nick Simper, even named his semi-pro group 'The Some Other Guys' and featured Rhythm And Blues after being blown away during a Johnny Kidd show.

On the 1st February Johnny and his crew were filmed sailing down the Manchester ship canal for Granada TV's new current affairs and light entertainment show 'People and Places'. Producer Johnny Hamp, and Director Philip Casson, went out getting appropriate settings for the stars. Poor Little Eva was filmed surrounded by hissing locomotives.

Johnny joined other celebrities Marty Wilde, Bert Weedon, Vince Eager, The Flee-Rekkers, Mike Preston, The Echoes and American vocalist Ronald Rogers on Sunday 4th February at the christening of Bernice Ann Cooper the nine month old daughter of his agent George Cooper. The happy event took place at All Saints Church, Woodford Green. Mr and Mrs G Cooper of 19 Farm Way, Buckhurst Hill, asked Joe Brown to be godfather. Following the christening the 30 guests crowded into the Roding Valley Hall, Buckhurst Hill for the evening reception. They entertained themselves with various artists getting up and giving a song including Johnny.

A weird letter was sent to the press. Could you please tell me if Johnny Kidd is blind? My cousin says he is, and she also says she heard that John Lennon is going blind. Is this true? - Jane Hibben, Sittingbourne, Kent.

Thursday March 21st at the Scunthorpe Baths supported by Terry Franks and The Avalons.

'Shakin' All Over'
(© Jean Heath Collection)

Colin Richards (Rhythm Guitarist, Avalons)
"After finishing our first set we rushed off stage and up into the balcony to watch Johnny and The Pirates first set. The Pirates were kitted out in striped T Shirts, black leather waistcoats, belt buckles and pirate boots. Frank Farley looked massive as he took up his position behind the drum kit. The bass player looked a bit frail with a pink precision bass hanging from his neck. Mick Green came on stage and plugged in his Les Paul Jnr. into a little Fender amp. Kidd came on, white shirt, black slacks, boots, six inch wide belt with a huge buckle. The sound that Mick Green got from such a small amp was amazing. He must have had it on full volume with lots of treble. He played what sounded like finger style, playing lead and rhythm all at the same time. I don't think he used a plectrum. The only other guitarist I'd seen during this period playing in the same style would have been Micky King the ex Rebel Rouser who now played in a trio called The Hawks fronted by Jimmy Royal. King used a Fender Strat. Frank Farley was an excellent drummer and John on bass was spot on. This all added up to a very tight sound. They played their hits and misses but not as originally recorded, plus their latest single 'A Shot Of Rhythm And Blues with 'I Can Tell'. Johnny had a very good voice and was very professional. Even the old standard 'If You Were The Only Girl In The World' sounded great. During this number Johnny did a walk about and sat on the edge of the low stage towards the middle part. 'Feel So Fine' was another song that got some extra treatment. An old Johnny Preston standard followed and Johnny gave each member of the Pirates a verse to sing. Each doing a funny voice. I think Frank did Donald Duck. There was still some leg kicks but not as many as the ole '59-'60 Pirates. Later on we got talking to Johnny and the band and found them to be very friendly and not at all big headed. Johnny Kidd especially went out of his way to talk to us and said he liked Terry Franks voice. They had a roadie and he was helpful too. We had a long trek back to London through freezing pea-souper fog. Johnny and the lads also had to make the same journey and as they knew the way it was decided we would follow their van. The journey back home was an absolute nightmare at times the visibility was about five metres and our speed down to a crawl. Kidds van was a pinkish buff colour except the back door. This was black with a skull and crossbones so we followed this J.2 galleon to our first transport cafe stop. I don't know where it was but they had the biggest mugs I have ever seen in my life. Our drummer being a bit of a cheeky bastard, pointed to Frank Farley and said better give him the big un."

Frank replied, "I'll see you outside and I'll hang you upside down." Terry Franks looked at our drummer, Mick, and said "You've had it now Mick." He nearly did too. When we got up to resume or journey Frank chased Mick round the cafe but he got away and we carried on through the fog.

Some of the time we led the way with Capt Kidd and his crew following us. We stopped at another cafe for another break. Frank must have fallen asleep so our drummer Mick was safe. We sat down with Mick Green and he told us about life on the road in Ireland and Germany. Of Ireland he said "It's so rough they have a wire mesh in front of the stage to stop the bottles hitting you. Half the crowd are pissed and the other half are fighting." His comments on Germany "There was a big fire there one night in Hamburg. It was just like world war three, the police and firemen had the same helmets as storm troopers but these were painted white. There must have been a load left over from the last war." All the time he was telling us these stories he kept playing with the mustard pot on the table. He kept stirring the mustard and chuckling to himself. Mick was either on something or just winding us up. We made one more stop on the A1 at the Baldock Cafe. This time we chatted to the road manager then we headed home. We got to Slough about 9.30am. It had taken ten hours from Scunthorpe."

On the 27th the Captain and his crew were pleased to play a Cardiff concert with their ole mates Nero and The Gladiators. Nero and his men had just recently signed with H.M.V. and were celebrating the release of 'Bleak House'/'Tovarich' released (March 15th) on POP1134 (as The Gladiators).

The Rubery Social Club presented 'A Super Rock, Jive and Twist Night' on Monday April 29th. Johnny and the band were supported by the Rockin' Corvettes and The Cimmarons.

Maurice Preece (The Cimmarons)
"The discipline seemed to have gone with one or other of the Pirates leaving the stage at odd intervals during the performance to visit the bar. On balance though the over all show was good and it was an honour to appear on the same bill. The Cimmarons were on home territory being based in Rubery and we'd played this club many times. Our main claim to fame being our lead guitarist, one Rick Price who later found fame with 'the Move' and Roy Wood's 'Wizzard'."

Nick Simper (Future Pirate)
"I remember getting Johnny's autograph and him looking at me as if we were spiritual brothers. There was some sort of strange feeling between us. About a year later I was playing for Buddy Britten and the Regents. I went backstage at the Starlight Ballroom, Sudbury to have a chat with Johnny while The Pirates were doing their solo set. We chatted away so easily, as if we had known each other all our lives. It was uncanny. When I was semi-pro it was always a joke with my mum and dad. Whenever I came home they would say Johnny Kidd has been on the phone asking for you to play in the Pirates. It was a joke like if Elvis rings. It was just a crazy joke because it could never happen. My mum knew that I rated him so highly I had his pictures on my wall, all his records, he was my idol."

RUBERY SOCIAL CLUB
Presents a
Super Rock, Jive & Twist Night
MONDAY, APRIL 29th. 1963. 8-11 p.m.
Featuring the Fabulous H.M.V. Recording Star
JOHNNY KIDD and the PIRATES
Supported by
The Rockin' Corvettes - The Cimmarons
SIX SHILLINGS
ADMISSION BY TICKET ONLY. (STRICTLY LIMITED)

Ticket - Rubery Social Club (courtesy M. Preece)

This shipmates played St Joseph's Youth Club Dance at Reddish, Stockport 11th May. After the gig they posed for photos with Carol Kay and the drummer out of the Dynachords.
Ex Pirates Alan Caddy and Clem Cattini were joined in The Tornados by Brian Gregg. The original bassist Heinz had left for a solo career. Chas Hodges - Tab Martin had stood in while Heinz was filming 'Farewell Performance' but Brian became the official replacement. Brian was

still keen on writing. His instrumental 'Flycatcher' was recorded by the group plus Alan Caddy's 'Earthy', Alan's tune, 'Popeye Twist' (arr Caddy) and Clem Cattini's 'Blackpool Rock' and 'Lullaby' for Giula which he dedicated to one of his daughters.

Johnny was the only member of the crew with a contract with E.M.I. The Pirates were always employed as session men getting paid the sum of £6- 10/ - (£6.50p) per session. The lads regarded this as a bonus to their weekly wage of £25 each. The sessions were not usually very long and often took place late at night after a gig in town such as a radio spot. Most of the demos were cut in a small basement studio in Berwick Street, Soho not far from the Freight Train coffee bar."

Alan Wheeler

"At E.M.I. everyone was being recorded on four track tape machines. The groups themselves never had the mass of sound equipment being carted around today. The Pirates were using 100 watt Fender amps which were powerful enough for any engagement being worked in those days. All the great rockers, such as Gene Vincent, Jerry Lee Lewis, Marty Wilde could really whip a storm with just a couple of 100 watt amps behind them!

top:
St. Joseph's Youth Club, Reddish, Stockport 11/5/63 with Carol Kay and Dynachords drummer
(© Jean Heath Collection)

above left:
Billy Fury, Brian, Clem, Tiny (fan), and Alan
(© B. Gregg)

above right:
Clem, Brian, Alan (Tornados) at Billy Fury's Fan Club Party, 1963
(© B. Gregg)

Johnny would usually arrive at Abbey Road in the BMC band wagon with this road manager, Johnny Irving, and the Pirates. Occasionally he would come by taxi or minibus. Mostly he wore a plain suit for these recording dates over which he nearly always wore a black leather overcoat which he also liked to wear for most of his travelling around to gigs. The Pirates would usually be set up in the studio. So Frank and his drum kit were partly hidden behind a screen to cut down the sound to the other mikes. Away from Frank and a fair way apart would be Mick and Johnny Spence. Somewhere in the middle would be the man himself also screened off but not out of sight of the guitarists. Being such good pros they rarely did more than 2 or 3 takes of any one number but sometimes the arrangement would be changed at the request of Walter Ridley or Johnny himself.

One number that springs to mind is 'I'll Never Get Over You'. The first time I heard this at a session it was either as a run through for sound balance or may have been the first take. Anyway it didn't sound quite right. It was much faster than the version which eventually came out. A slightly slower treatment was given to the song by the Pirates which sounded much more commercial. But even this had a different ending! To get a more pronounced ending the Pirates taped a separate piece which was used on the actual single after everybody had agreed that the rest of the track was OK. Johnny was always recorded live with the Pirates, as opposed to laying down the backing track first and then doing the vocals separately. Thus it was possible to cut both sides of a single in either a morning or afternoon. Unbelievable when you think how long some people take to make a 45 today. What you hear on disc from Johnny and The Pirates is exactly how they sounded live on-stage. A really tight sound that still stands up today. The only thing that was added to some A sides was some over dubbing by Johnny to get a much fuller vocal sound in keeping with the group scene of the day."

'I'll Never Get Over You'/'Then I Got Everything' was recorded on the 16th May and released 14th June. The B side was a Kidd/Green collaboration. Gordon Mills of The Viscounts supplied the A side. Lionel Conway of Leeds music really believed in the number and through taking it around Tin Pan Alley it eventually came to the attention of Johnny and the lads. Gordon Mills had always been interested in music and at 18 became the harmonica champion of Wales. He soon joined The Morton Fraser Gang, but by the fifties rock 'n' roll had him under its spell and so along with Don Paul and Ronnie Wells they left the Frazer Gang and formed the close harmony group The Viscounts. They played all the major package tours and on the Jerry Lee Lewis tour of '62 they became good mates with Johnny.

After various singles they made the charts with the skiffle infected 'Shortnin Bread' (1960) and Barry Manns' 'Who Put The Bomp" (1961). They all had a go at songwriting but it was Mills who had the success. He left to spend more time on his new found talent. His replacement was Johnny Gentle. Mills was also keen on the management side and went onto manage Tom Jones, Engelbert Humperdinck, Gilbert O'Sullivan, Soloman King and Leapy Lee. He headed the enormously successful MAM organisation. Mills, in fact, sang lead on the original version of 'I'll Never Get Over You' produced by Tony Hatch.

John Irving (Roadie)
"Tom Jones was a keen fan of the Kidd. During the early part of his career he featured many of Kidds numbers. On one occasion I had to give Tom permission for which songs he could perform. Johnny said I'll do 'Shakin' and 'Touch' and Tom can do them in the second half of the show. I must admit Tom did and went down very well."

The night that Mills first saw Tom at the Top Hat in Marthyr Tydfil billed as 'The Twisting Vocalist From Pontypridd' Tom included, 'I'll Never Get Over You' in his act.

Gordon Mills
"The first few bars were all I needed to hear from Tom Scott (Jones) and The Senators to convince me that here was a voice which would make him the greatest singer in the world."

Mills with arranger Les Reed wrote a song that would alter the course of Tom's life. 'It's Not Unusual' would transform unknown Scott to a cigar wielding singer star. Scott changed his name and image to a sexual swashbuckling character complete with lucky rabbits foot. Mills later released an LP in 1965 entitled 'Do It Yourself' featuring his greatest compositions i.e. 'I'll Never Get Over You' and 'Hungry For Love' etc. Decca ACL 1191.

A short two week tour of the North was arranged. Johnny stayed at the home of Liverpool vocalist Lee Curtis lead singer of The Allstars who featured Pete Best on drums.
Johnny Kidd
"I'm looking forward to playing the Cavern on the 26th May it should be the greatest, I've just

top:
Sheet Music
(© Always N' Ever Archive)

centre:
Record advertisement
(© A. Wheeler)

bottom:
Record advertisement

GET WITH IT!

STAY WITH IT!

AT THE NORTH'S FIRST AND FOREMOST STOMPING SCENE

THE CAVERN

10 MATHEW STREET (off North John Street)
LIVERPOOL

(Right in the heart of Britain's Top Teenbeat Town)

Proprietor: RAY McFALL — Telephone: CENtral 1591 — Resident Dee-Jay/Compere: BOB WOOLER

EVENING SESSIONS : 7-15 to 11-15 p.m.
SUNDAYS, TUESDAYS, WEDNESDAYS, FRIDAYS AND SATURDAYS

SWINGING LUNCHTIME SESSIONS : NOON to 2-15 p.m.
MONDAYS TO FRIDAYS

NEW MEMBERS AND VISITORS ARE ALWAYS WELCOME AT

THE CAVERN CLUB

ANNUAL MEMBERSHIP FEE: JUST ONE SHILLING
JOIN NOW AT ANY SESSION

COMING SOON IN PERSON

SUNDAY 19th MAY — *GENE VINCENT*
SUNDAY 26th MAY — *JOHNNY KIDD and The Pirates*
SATURDAY 3rd AUGUST — *THE BEATLES*

"Remember all you Cave Dwellers. The Cavern is the Best of Cellars"

top:
Cavern advertisement
(Always N' Ever Archive)

bottom:
Oasis programme
(© Always N' Ever Archive)

recorded a new single entitled 'I'll Never Get Over You'.

These groups up North especially The Beatles they're the ones who've helped me most. They've helped a lot of people in this business. They've brought down South the music that I've always loved. I've been giving fans this kind of music for years now but those Liverpool groups have been a big help. They tell me that quite a few of them use my numbers in their acts and I couldn't be more delighted because its a great compliment."

Johnny formed a limited company Johnny Kidd Ltd. It was one of a number of registered companies operating from 115 Piccadilly, London, W1.

On Sunday 30th June they played the Oasis Club. This popular night spot was a tremendous venue where youngsters loved to dwell situated at 45-47 Lloyd Street, Manchester. The London Marauders with their musical act of piracy soon had the crowd going wild. One very keen Oasis member was the young Peter Noone.
"It was my local club, I went to see Johnny and the Pirates and I was so knocked out by their power and unique act I decided on that night I wanted to be a singer in a rock 'n' roll Band."

Peter did form a group, a very popular pop group and went on to have huge hits on both sides of the Atlantic as leader of Hermans Hermits.

The Oasis was the North's largest coffee bar and rhythm club. It was open most lunch times from mid-day till 2 o'clock with non stop records and dancing. Most evenings featured live groups. The Beatles, Hollies, Joe Brown, Shane Fenton, The Fourmost etc. The clubs excellent programme always boasted 'The Best of The Best' and they certainly booked the best of British beat. Membership was only 2/6d (12 1/2p) a year. With two resident disc jockeys, live groups and the excellent management of Graham and Pauline Clegg, it really was a great place to see and mix with your idols.

Bobby Elliott (Hollies, Drummer)
"We played the Oasis many times as The Dolphins but never with Johnny Kidd. Joe Brown and his Bruvvers were with us once, a good band, they had the best rock drummer of the 60's, Bobby Graham."

Many young musicians were coming along to gigs to witness the Kidd's magic performances. Peter Wilson recalls the profound effect Johnny and the Pirates had on himself and his mate Pete Townsend.

Peter Wilson (The Hustlers)
"I went to Acton County School and together with Mick Brown (drums), John Entwistle and Pete Townsend formed a band called The Confederates When John and later Pete left to join Roger Daltrey we all remained friends. The first time we'd seen Kidd was at St Marys Ballroom, Putney. Pete, John and myself had dropped into see the venue a few days before as The Detours (High Numbers) were due to play there. Anyway on shuffled three Pirates. Where was the 4th

man? No rhythm guitarist! Pete and I looked at each other. This should be fun, only one guitar and that was a Gibson Melody Maker (single P/U + 3/4 scale). They plugged in - Johnny Spence had a Wallace custom built bass combo (a real pro-job) and Frank Farley looked very large. 'Please Don't Touch' intro a la Mick Green. Our first reaction was not bad. Kidd came on clad in leather with cutless. He sang no more than one verse and on the second high kick split his trousers about nine inches around the crutch. The song ended both quick and professional. Kidd said he would be gone off a while to get stitched up. Pete and I laughed. What would they do now? The answer was stunning and changed the direction of my band The Hustlers and The Who. Mick Green started slowly playing a Chet Atkins number. Then he did 'Peter Gunn' and more for about twenty minutes until Kidd re-emerged for the rest of the set which was so different to what we were doing at the time. The next time I saw Pete he said The Detours had changed to Rhythm And Blues and sacked half the band. We, The Hustlers changed our numbers too and so both bands had taken the Mick Green and Kidd style on board. We both later bought Fender pro amps to match Greens. I saw Kidd many times after that."

DANCES
SOCIALS
WEDDING RECEPTIONS
MEETINGS
REHEARSALS

PUTNEY BALLROOM
St MARYS HALL
HOTHAM ROAD, PUTNEY, S.W.15
Large & Small Halls Available
PUT 3220
Resident Manager.
H. G. HESMAN

Business card - Putney Ballroom
(Always N' Ever Archive)

The Hustlers lead vocalist Malcolm Fox was a frequent visitor to the Kidds household. Johnny bought a Klemot Echolette from him and used it on stage for a short while but he didn't like it.

Alan Wheeler remembers why!
"The trouble with the Echolette was that the tape would keep breaking. John used it in some dance halls because he thought it would be nice to try to recreate the Echo edge on his discs but he soon got fed up with it and it was dropped (out of the van I think)."

Pete Wilson (The Hustlers)
"My original school band with Pete Townsend, John Entwistle and Mick Brown The Confederates broke up after doing an audition at the Hermitage club at Hitchin which had Peter Jay and The Jaywalkers as the main act. Pete's mum took us all up there in her big Wolseley, four guys, guitars, three vox 15 amps and drums. We had no singer, we only played instrumentals. Although we were the best band there we couldn't compete with The Jaywalkers. They were great. After that we slowly fell apart. We were only 15/16 and after we left school the band soon split. Mick and I formed The Hustlers in 1962 and recorded for the BBC. Pete, John and Roger Daltry formed The Detours. Pete phoned me and said that he and John were soon to go as support to Johnny Kidd and The Pirates. So we went to St Marys because we had heard how good an act he had."

above top:
Johnny and the Crew
(© Jean Heath Collection)

above bottom:
Advertisement Ludwig Drums

Roger Daltry (Vocalist, The Who)
"This was 62-63, we went through this Johnny Kidd and The Pirates scene, copied everybody, you know. That was The Detours, then we became The Who, kicked our drummer out and Keith Moon came along."

A couple of years later The Who appeared on 'Ready, Steady, Go' performing 'Please Don't

Touch' complete with Pirate leg kicks.

top:
Publicity photograph (© Jean Heath Collection)

centre:
Tornado Rock E.P.

bottom:
Johnny and the Pirates

Mick Green (Lead Pirate)
"We didn't have a rhythm guitarist and our sound needed filling out. You can only play that way with a trio you can't play like that with another guitar or a piano. It's achieved by bashing out the chords loudly and twiddling around with the strings. It's quite an easy thing to do, there's nothing magical about it. My main influence, I suppose, was James Burton. He wasn't the first guy I listened to but he came along after I'd been learning to play guitar at the age of 13 or 14. The first guys I listened to were Leadbelly and Big Bill Broonzy then I got Burton and never looked back."
To promote the release of 'I'll Never Get Over You' Johnny and The Pirates mimed on ITV's Thank Your Lucky Stars. The show also featured Acker Bilk and Rolf Harris.

JOHNNY KIDD AND THE PIRATES
H.M.V. RECORDS

Johnny Kidd
"When I first heard 'I'll Never Get Over You' on a demo in Wally Ridley's office I wasn't too keen. But the boys in the band played around with it and once we'd recorded it I felt happier."

July saw the release of the first vocals from The Tornados on 'Tornado Rock' E.P. Decca DFE8533.

Brian Gregg and George Bellamy shared vocals on 'Blue Moon', 'My Babe', 'Ready Teady', and Clem Cattini on 'Long Tall Sally'. Two other tracks 'Rip It Up' and 'Blue Suede Shoes' remained in Joe Meeks studio. Producer Meek speeded up everything and sadly lost the real feel of rock 'n' roll.
The following interview with Johnny by Bruce Charlton of the N.M.E. took place on the telephone during the August Bank Holiday of '63 while Johnny, Mick, Frank and John were appearing in Torquay. Johnny explains how his career carried on after a string of chart success within a short space of time, then no hits for three years. One might have forgiven him for becoming disillusioned and bitter, had he reacted that way, but he didn't he kept working hard performing all over the country.

Johnny Kidd
"When my subsequent discs flopped I didn't feel nearly so disappointed as I did immediately after 'Restless' because once I got over my initial gloom, I realised that I had really got to get stuck in and fight my way back no matter how long it might take. Mind you during this time, we had been working pretty consistently. The reaction hasn't been quite as fantastic as the 'Shakin' days, but its been quite good considering we didn't have a hit record. Financially The Pirates and I have been perfectly OK and I reckon we could have gone on this way for a few more years. 'I'll Never Get over You' won't make much change to my way of life, we shall just continue touring as before, but of course it will mean an improvement in conditions. Until now, we have been travelling every night from A to point B irrespective of how many miles separate them and what were going to find when we get there. Now that we are back in the charts promoters will give a little more thought to our welfare. The standard of bookings will be better and the money will be more. Yes the future

certainly looks brighter now! My band Mick (lead), Johnny (bass) and Frank (drums) they're a down to earth group playing real hard stuff. I'm very happy with them! Our material is basically Rhythm And Blues. To my way of thinking rock 'n' roll belongs to Bill Haley and company. I've always dabbled in Rhythm And Blues in fact I think I was one of the first in this country to do so. I believe that my first record 'Please Don't Touch' was similar in vein to today's Liverpool sound through not strong enough to be a hit."

BRITAIN'S TOP 50

COMPILED BY THE RECORD RETAILER

AND there's some pretty fast-risers this week. Buddy moves up eighteen with his newie "Wishing" — more in the usual run things for him after such rockers as "Brown Eyed Handsome Man" an "Bo Diddley". This time last year by the way he was having anoth top twenty hit with "Reminiscing". Brian Poole and the Tremeloes sho up to thirty-three with their version of the fabulous "Do You Love Me — this one could even be bigger than their "Twist And Shout". An they're staving off all competitors so far.

Merseyside still holds the big share with "She Loves You" etc., all doi very well. Fast-riser is "Searchin'" by the Hollies. New boy Tri Lopez clicks with his live performance on "If I Had A Hammer". It good, but we can't help feeling the Peter, Paul and Mary performanc was better one year back.

1 SHE LOVES YOU — 3 (3) The Beatles (Parlophone)
2 IT'S ALL IN THE GAME — 4 (4) Cliff Richard (Columbia)
3 BAD TO ME — 1 (7) Billy J. Kramer with the Dakotas (Parlophone)
4 I'LL NEVER GET OVER YOU — 5 (8) Johnny Kidd & The Pirates (H.M.V.)
5 I'M TELLING YOU NOW — 2 (6) Freddie & The Dreamers (Columbia)
6 YOU DON'T HAVE TO BE A BABY TO CRY — 7 (6) The Caravelles (Decca)
7 I WANT TO STAY HERE — 10 (4) Steve Lawrence/Eydie Gorme (C.B.S.)
8 WIPE OUT — 8 (8) The Surfaris (London)
9 JUST LIKE EDDIE — 9 (6) Heinz (Decca)
10 THEME FROM THE LEGION'S LAST PATROL — 11 (9) Ken Thorne & His Orchestra (H.M.V.)
11 DANCE ON — 14 (5) Kathy Kirby (Decca)
12 SWEETS FOR MY SWEET — 6 (12) The Searchers (Pye)
13 STILL — 17 (4) Karl Denver (Decca)
14 IN SUMMER — 13 (8) Billy Fury (Decca)
15 CONFESSIN' — 12 (12) Frank Ifield (Columbia)
16 APPLEJACK — 49 (2) Jet Harris & Tony Meehan (Decca)
17 TWIST AND SHOUT — 15 (11) Brian Poole & The Tremeloes (Decca)
18 WISHING — 35 (2) Buddy Holly (Coral)
19 THE CRUEL SEA — 18 (10) The Dakotas (Parlophone)
20 DA DOO RON RON — 16 (13) The Crystals (London)
21 WHISPERING — 29 (3) The Bachelors (Decca)
22 COME ON — 24 (8) The Rolling Stones (Decca)
23 ONLY THE HEARTACHES — 22 (7) Houston Wells (Parlophone)
24 I WANNA STAY HERE — 23 (4) Miki and Griff (Pye)
25 SUKIYAKI — 19 (12) Kyu Sakamato (H.M.V.)
26 SURF CITY — 26 (5) Jan and Dean (Liberty)
27 TWO SILHOUETTES — 33 (4) Del Shannon (London)
28 ACAPULCO 1922 — 27 (4) Kenny Ball and His Jazzmen (Pye)
29 WELCOME TO MY WORLD — 21 (14) Jim Reeves (R.C.A.-Victor)
30 DEVIL IN DISGUISE — 20 (11) Elvis Presley (R.C.A.-Victor)
31 THE GOOD LIFE — 31 (9) Tony Bennett (C.B.S.)
32 SEARCHIN' — 38 (3) The Hollies (Parlophone)
33 DO YOU LOVE ME? — — (1) Brian Poole and The Tremeloes (Decca)
34 FRANKIE AND JOHNNY — 46 (2) Sam Cooke (R.C.A.-Victor)
35 ATLANTIS — 25 (13) The Shadows (Columbia)
36 IF I HAD A HAMMER — — (1) Trini Lopez (Reprise)
37 STILL — 40 (3) Ken Dodd (Columbia)
38 SURFIN' U.S.A. — 36 (7) The Beach Boys (Capitol)
39 YOU CAN NEVER STOP ME LOVING YOU — 28 (13) Kenny Lynch (H.M.V.)
40 BY THE WAY — 30 (10) The Big Three (Decca)
41 BLUE GIRL — 43 (6) The Bruisers (Parlophone)
42 I WONDER — 32 (9) Brenda Lee (Brunswick)
43 SO MUCH IN LOVE — 37 (8) The Tymes (Cameo-Parkway)
44 IT'S LOVE THAT REALLY COUNTS — — (1) The Merseybeats (Fontana)
45 TAKE THESE CHAINS FROM MY HEART — 34 (18) Ray Charles (H.M.V.)
46 HELLO HEARTACHE GOODBYE LOVE — — (1) Little Peggy March (RCA-Victor)
47 NO ONE — — (1) Ray Charles (H.M.V.)
48 BE MY GIRL — 48 (3) The Dennisons (Decca)
49 HELLO MUDDAH, HELLO FADDAH — — (1) Allan Sherman (Warner Bros.)
50 HELLO LITTLE GIRL — — (1) The Fourmost (Parlophone)

(First figure denotes position last week; figure in parentheses denotes weeks in chart)

'Top Fifty'

Norman Smith (Balance and Control Engineer)
"I worked with Johnny and later The Beatles. I suppose I had a bit to do with the birth of the Mersey sound. For a start we kept the recordings fairly dry. I was fed up with the sound of echo chambers. John Lennon used to call me Normal Smith. Paul McCartney always called me 'Two DB's Smith'. It means decibels, a technical term.

Later on I did engineering for Manfred Mann, Billy J Kramer, Freddie and The Dreamers, Cliff Bennett and the Rebel Rousers and so on. I was also keen on song writing. The B side of Freddie Garrity's 'Things I'd Like To Say' was one of mine. Over the years I've written many others. In 1971 I recorded a big hit myself under the name of Hurricane Smith entitled 'Don't Let It Die' which I also produced."

In 1973 Smith recorded an LP entitled 'Razzmatazz Shall Inherit The Earth' EMI EMA 761.

By August '63 electric rhythm and blues was at its commercial height. The Rolling Stones had led rhythm and blues out of the clubs and into the charts. Clubs that had refused R n' B bands suddenly wanted live Rockin Blues six nights a week. Cyril Davis, Alexis Korner, Graham Bond Organisation, John Mayall's Bluesbreakers, Dave Berry, Yardbirds, Pretty Things, Downliner Sect etc., have all been given well deserved credit for developing this raw exciting ethnic music but Johnny had been one of the first to perform his own unique style of blues. He had been featuring material by Bo Diddley, Arthur Alexander, Dr Feelgood, Soloman Burke, Willie Dixon, Ivory Joe Hunter, Bobby Parker, Ritchie Barrett etc. years before the Rhythm And Blues craze. Sadly he has hardly been given any praise for playing a very big part towards the popularity of British Rhythm And Blues. H.M.V. were very slow in capturing his superb blues expressing vocals on disc. He had enough American Rhythm And Blues material in his repertoire to record a first-class Rhythm And Blues LP but alas it all fell on deaf ears at E.M.I.

Brian Gregg
"Johnny was performing great blues before most others. He was just brilliant on Willie Dixons' 'I Just Want To Make Love To You'."

Don Craine (Guitarist, Downliners Sect)
"Sadly, I don't recall actually meeting the Kidd but during my school days my favourite groups were Johnny and the Pirates and Neil Christian and The Crusaders. They showed me that British rock could compare favourable with the original American versions."
Dave Berry (The Cruisers Vocalist)
"Like my fellow 60's artists I spent my late school days listening to Little Richard, Fats Domino, Gene Vincent and, of course, Chuck Berry. It was at this time the most of us formed our first

groups only to find that the rock 'n' roll dream had faded. It was the start of a musical wasteland. Here in Britain apart from isolated cases like Vince Taylor and Johnny Kidd no-one had much idea performance wise."

Johnny was always pleased to tell about the time when a young Mick Jagger came up to him and said 'I wish I could sing as well as you Johnny."

Clem Cattini
"John in my view was one of the best blues singers that was ever about even to this day. If John was around today he would be hailed as one of the ALL TIME GREATS!"

Terry Earl (Flying Saucers/Avengers)
"Apart from being a great rock 'n' roll vocalist he had a tremendous soul feel, a great blues singer. I'll never forget seeing him live on stage. I always enjoyed performing his material while I was with The Rapiers."

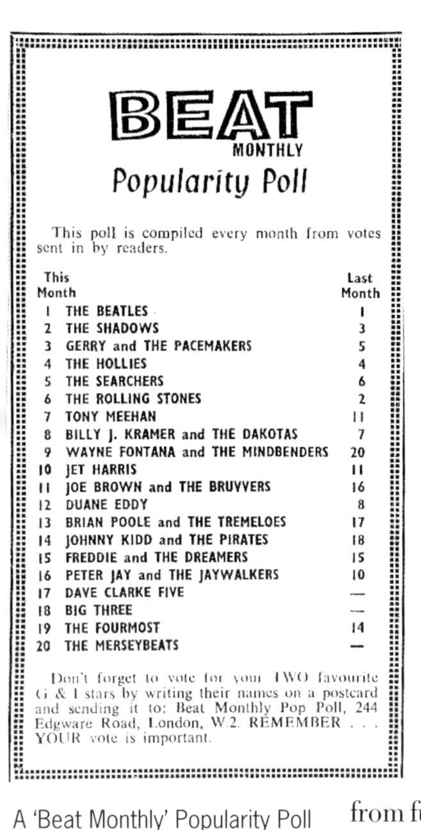

BEAT MONTHLY

Popularity Poll

This poll is compiled every month from votes sent in by readers.

This Month		Last Month
1	THE BEATLES	1
2	THE SHADOWS	3
3	GERRY and THE PACEMAKERS	5
4	THE HOLLIES	4
5	THE SEARCHERS	6
6	THE ROLLING STONES	2
7	TONY MEEHAN	11
8	BILLY J. KRAMER and THE DAKOTAS	7
9	WAYNE FONTANA and THE MINDBENDERS	20
10	JET HARRIS	11
11	JOE BROWN and THE BRUVVERS	16
12	DUANE EDDY	8
13	BRIAN POOLE and THE TREMELOES	17
14	JOHNNY KIDD and THE PIRATES	18
15	FREDDIE and THE DREAMERS	15
16	PETER JAY and THE JAYWALKERS	10
17	DAVE CLARKE FIVE	—
18	BIG THREE	—
19	THE FOURMOST	14
20	THE MERSEYBEATS	—

Don't forget to vote for your TWO favourite G & I stars by writing their names on a postcard and sending it to: Beat Monthly Pop Poll, 244 Edgware Road, London, W.2. REMEMBER . . . YOUR vote is important.

A 'Beat Monthly' Popularity Poll

On August 9th they left for 'the Star Club in Hamburg for a two week tour. They were shocked to find so many changes. The Kaiserkeller had stopped all live music and only had a juke box. Even the tatty Indra Club had been changed into a small cabaret club. The Top Ten was still rocking but the Mersey beat groups took second choice to bands from further up North - Scotland. The Star Club was by far the best venue with its large stage and famous back drop (a Kind of New York tenement scene). Johnny and his Pirates soon had the beer drinking, pill popping crowd going wild. It was the norm to see a drunken guy or sailor being thrown bodily from the excitement by Horst Fascher and his bouncers for causing trouble.

Frank Farley (Drummer Pirates)
"Our famous galleon backdrop was, I believe, painted by art students in Hamburg."

Starclub, August, 1963
(courtesy T. Scott, © A Wheeler)

The hand painted luminous backdrop of a galleon was valued in 1963 at £200. It measured 30ft by 20ft and was painted with ultra violet paint. Three ultra violet lights up front near the stage gave the effect of the galleon being in a harbour. Johnny was really keen on building the stage act into a real powerful production. They even carried their own scenery around including the back drop.

Johnny Kidd
"I've found that promoters won't bother to do anything which will improve presentation so I've decided to do it myself."

Brian Jones (Sax - The Undertakers/Y-Kikamoocow)
"While with The Undertakers I worked the Star Club alongside Johnny and the Pirates. The trio would come on first and play an instrumental then go into stuff like 'My Babe', 'Castin', 'My Spell' etc. Johnny would come on with his cutless. I remember him standing on top of a piano and throwing the sword into the stage. During The Undertakers act we used to take the mickey out of other groups. I used to stand on the same piano with a little toy plastic sword and put a patch over my eye but unlike Johnnys cutless my toy sword would smash as it hit the floor into a thousand pieces. The crowd would love it. We got very friendly with the band, they were always top of the bill. I got

on well with Mick Green, he was a very original guitarist. We were knocked out when we first went to Hamburg seeing stars like Ray Charles, Gene Vincent, Brenda Lee. We stayed at the same hotel (The Pacific) about a fifteen minute walk from the Star Club. We had some great laughs. I rolled up the carpet from one end of the corridor to the other. I knocked on their door and fell into their room on this giant roll of carpet. Johnny's room was on the floor below us. We used to knock on his windows with a long stick. As he opened it we would pour buckets of water all over him. We had a great time."

Their latest release 'I'll Never Get Over You' was recorded for Associated Rediffusion's 'Tuesday Rendezvous' (Five O'clock Club) and broadcast on Tuesday August 13th. On their return to England they appeared on the new weekend starts here show. Ready Steady Go had just started on August 9th. Elkan Allen was Entertainment Dept Head and the driving force behind its creation.

Elkan Allen
"In New York, as head of programme entertainment for Associated-Rediffusion I saw American Bandstand which was a rather sedate disc and dance show. In Montreal, at the festival of light entertainment, I met the BBC head of the sound gramophone department. She said we are doing a swinging radio show called 'Pop In' every week. Why don't you pop in? So the General Manager and I did just that. We saw Keith Fordyce compering and interviewing and playing records and everyone having a good time. On the way back to the office I said why don't we put 'Pop In' and 'American Bandstand' together and add a lot of new ingredients of our own. The GM said "Right". When I heard what time we were on I said lets call it 'Ready Steady Go, The Weekend Starts Here'. The programme didn't just feature beat groups it also dealt with the latest dance crazes. Patrick Kerr and Theresa Confrey used to demonstrate the steps, Mashed Potato, Hully Gully etc. Keith Fordyce, Cathy McGowan and Michael Aldred were joint compere but it was the experienced Fordyce who held this fast moving live show together."

Keith Fordyce (Compere)
"When they hired me as compere they told me to keep it moving faster than any show there had ever been and wow they meant it. Before starting on this programme I think the shortest interview with a star I had ever done was two minutes and many went on for three or even four minutes. But this show they hardly ever lasted longer than a minute. By the time you'd take off a few seconds for applause and for the announcement at the other end they were often only 45 seconds. During the afternoons before the shows I used to chat over with the stars the sort of topics we were going to cover in the interview. Some of the stars - Billy Fury, Heinz, Brian Poole for instance liked to have everything cut and dried before we went out live. Then there were people like Joe Brown, Adam Faith who hated anything prepared. They reckoned they answered best if I just fired questions. When you had someone like Joe Brown it wouldn't be worth rehearsing as it would be bound to come out differently and more madly on the air!"

The whole point of the show was to recreate a club scene. The audience would dance throughout the whole show. Stars were interviewed in quiet corners of the studio while their latest record was clearly audible in the background. During the promotion of 'I'll Never Get Over You' Keith gave Johnny the following speedy interview.

K.F. Hello Johnny,
J.K. Hi Keith,

above: Johnny with Cathy McGowan on R.S.G (© Always N' Ever Archive)

K.F. Something I've been wanting to ask you in ages, What is behind that black patch? A black eye!

J.K. No, it's a real eye, its a perfectly normal eye.

K.F. Why do you wear the patch all the time.?

J.K. Well, it's purely a gimmick which we struck on a couple of years ago and we found it works, it's a trademark.

K.F. Will you be glad to get rid of it?

J.K. Not really because it gives me the opportunity to walk down the street unrecognised.

K.F. You mean with it off. Will you take it off now?

J.K. Yeah! (For the first time on TV Johnny removed his trademark).

K.F. Johnny will you please go over to our autograph table and sign a few.

Johnny was over the moon with the success of 'I'll Never Get Over You' and very proud to learn that it was being released in the States on Capital 5065. His mother just couldn't take it in. She was a very down to earth lady and just carried on as normal.

Johnny was very respected by French superstar Johnny Hallyday who in fact recorded two versions of 'I Want That' for the Vogue label. One of which was a live version cut at a rock 'n' roll package show in Paris at the Palais des Sports in 1961. The French Shadows, Les Fantones recorded a fine version of 'Shakin All Over' for Vogue in 1962 released on EP7918. Also later in 1974 on 'A La Mode' Retro LPCLD899 Brussels band Burt Blanca and the King Creoles often featured 'Shakin', 'Big Blon Baby', 'Dr Feelgood' etc. in their act.

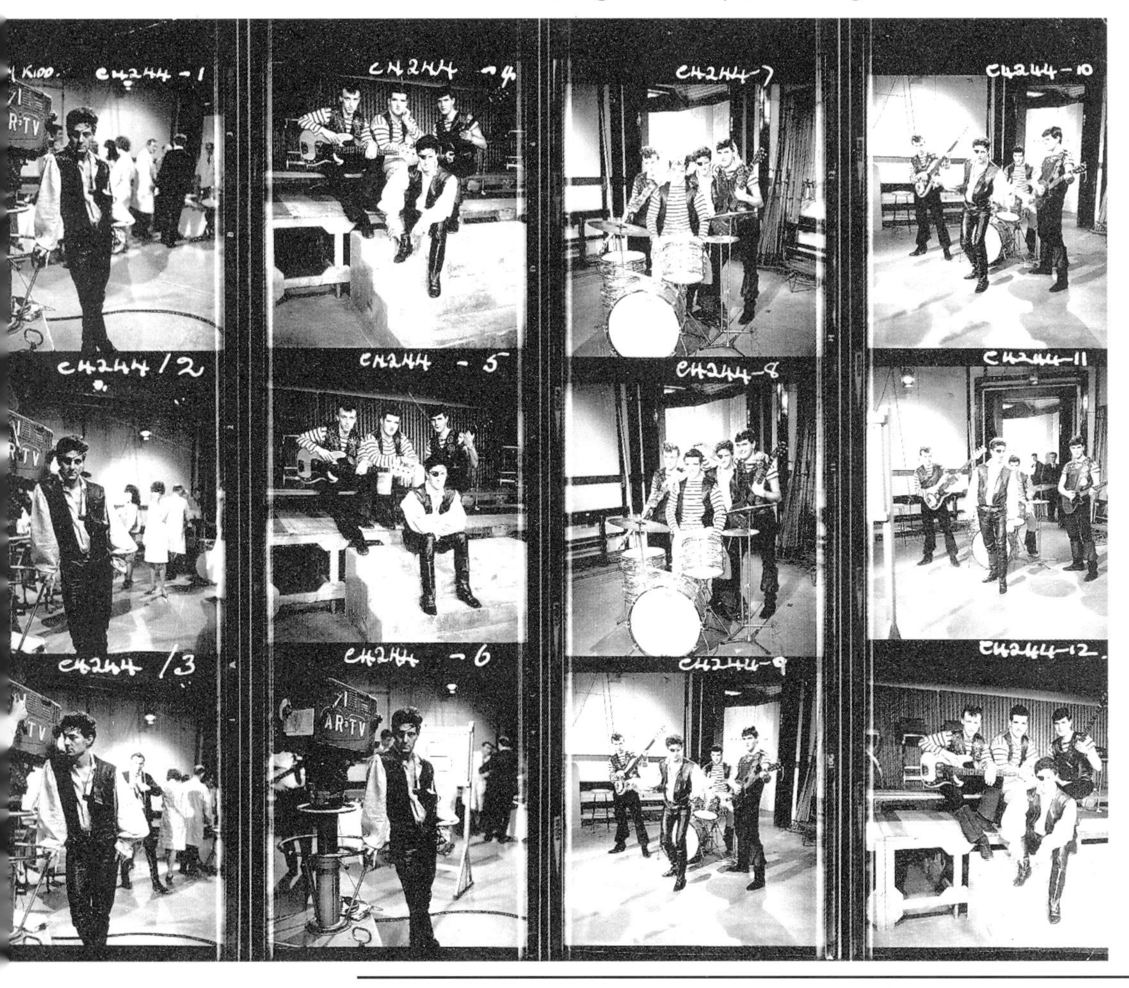

Below: On the set of 'R.S.G.' Photos by Philip Gotlop (© Jean Heath Collection)

For exposure and promotion TV and radio bookings were the icing on the cake but you couldn't live off what was then being paid in appearance fees. The BBC paid 7 guineas (£7.35p) for radio spots on Saturday Club, Easy Beat, Parade of The Pops and such shows on the Light Programme. BBC Television paid about 21 guineas (£21.05p) for a slot on Crackerjack, Rolf Harris Show, Top of The Pops etc. ITV paid a few bob more 30 guineas (£31.50p) for a one number slot on Thank Your Lucky Stars, Riverboat Shuffle, Ready Steady Go etc. Not the earth but then money was not Johnny's motivation. He did enjoy the brief encounter with comfortable dressing rooms and hospitality which the TV and radio studios afforded.

The Easybeat radio show was recorded at the Paris Theatre in Piccadilly in front of a live audience. An amusing incident is recalled by Alan Wheeler.
"When it was mentioned that Bert Weedon, The Springfields, Karl Denver Trio were likely to be the other acts taking part John decided to drop the menacing image' for his two numbers on the first booking. As he and The Pirates strode on in 'civvies' John in a suit and the eye patch as the only Pirates link only to be greeted by an audience full of screaming teenagers. Quickly deciding he had made a genuine error he resolved to correct this for his second booking on the programme a little later. When this time came John and The Pirates confidently strode out in full Pirate garb complete with cutless only to face an audience of mums and dads and O.A.P.s! It was like Screaming Lord Sutch calling out the numbers at a bingo session. Anyway it gave John and the boys many a chuckle for quite a while (taunts of how shall we dress tonight if they played an unfamiliar venue)."

Easy Beat was presented on Sunday mornings between 10.30am - 11.30am by Brian Matthew and produced by Ron Belchier.

Johnny Kidd
"The only place to touch the Star Club in Hamburg in Britain for atmosphere is Liverpool's Cavern. I've played there, but its a lot different in many ways. The Star Club is a converted cinema and has a capacity of 4,000 and, believe me, it really gets packed at weekends. I did two half-hour spots and, having a visual act, I was able to hold their attention when I did ballads as well as the hot rhythm numbers. Most of the supporting groups belt out the beat right through the night. You know there were some really fine groups appearing with me at the Star Club this time. One group from Merseyside, incidentally is, King-Size Taylor and The Dominoes and they could be really big when they get back to Britain. Tony Sheridan and The Beat Brothers. Do you remember Tony? He was backed by The Beatles on a disc recorded in Hamburg two or three years ago. Talking about The Beatles they spent a lot of time in Germany a few years ago and built up quite a following before they really hit it big here. Quite a few hit parade names in fact, have appeared there in the past - The Big Three, The Searchers, Swinging Blue Jeans, Lee Curtis and the All Stars. You know I think The Beatles are the best thing that has happened to the scene for a long time. They've really given the music business the shot in the arm we were all waiting for. For me they can do no wrong. I'd like to see a few more groups with talent break through to success. Too much talent has been suppressed in the past. I'm convinced that there are a lot more talented groups all over the country in places like Birmingham, Newcastle and in Scotland. All over the place. In fact, I'd like to see a lot more people hit the top.
Finally I'd like to thank everyone who has helped to get me back at the top. Its great and I really appreciate it. I've just got back from my third trip to Germany and the Star Club and, believe me, the place is an absolute knockout."

Johnny was amongst the first to be booked for 'The Pop Ball'. This was held at London's Lyceum ballroom on Monday 2nd September. After the show Johnny and the boys chatted and posed for photos along with Freddie and The Dreamers.

Johnny was lucky to escape serious injury when a car in which he was a passenger somersaulted

(© Always N' Ever Archive)

on the London-Dover Road on Sunday 8th September.

Frank Farley (Pirates, Drummer)
"Johnny was a very fast driver when he was behind the wheel. In those days you didn't have an MOT certificate for your car or anything. Bald tyres were the norm. Johnny was fated I believe in some way. Whichever vehicle he went in, whether he was driving or whatever, it had a mishap. I can recall one incident when Johnny was driving. We were, in fact, in the car with him. We weren't going fast as there was thick snow covering the Yorkshire Moors. It was the early hours of the morning. All of a sudden we hit a lamp post. It was the only lamp post for about fifty miles. That's got to be unlucky."

The crew sailed into the BBC studios at Maida Vale on September 10th to guest on The Beatles radio show 'Pop Go The Beatles'. The series ran from 4th June till 24th Sept '63 a total of fifteen programmes. Each week the Fab Four played hosts to a leading group of the day - The Searchers, Swinging Blue Jeans, Brian Poole and The Tremeloes, The Hollies, Countrymen, Lorne Gibson Trio, The Bachelors, Carter Lewis and The Southerners, Duffy Power and The Graham Bond Quartet, Russ Sainty and The Nu-Notes, Cyril Davies Rhythm And Blues All Stars and Long John Baldry, The Marauders, Tony Rivers and The Castaways all performed on this excellent series which was produced by Terry Henebery (except for three produced by Ian Grant). The first four shows were presented by Lee Peters and the rest by Rodney Burke.

Johnny was in fine voice as they rolled through their latest hit 'I'll Never Get Over You' and The Pirates were tight and superb behind their Captain on 'Then I Got Everything'. Their session had been recorded down at the Paris Theatre in Lower Regent Street during the afternoon. The show went on air between 5.00 and 5.30pm that Tuesday. The Beatles adaptation of 'Pop Goes The Weasel' was heard at the beginning and end of each programme. This series allowed the Beatles to perform some of their favourite songs which due to their prolific writing talents would never find their way on wax. i.e. A Shot Of Rhythm And Blues, Carol, Clarabella, Lucille, Some Other Guy etc.

Lifelines of Johnny Kidd from the N.M.E. Friday September 13th 1963.

Height - 5' 10"
Weight - 10 Stone
Colour of Eyes - Brown
Hair - Black
Musical Education - Self Taught
Musical Director - Self
Biggest Influence On Career - My own enthusiasm plus the encouragement of my friends.
Favourite Colour - Blue
Favourite Singers - Brenda Lee and Bo Diddley
Favourite Musicians - Eric Delaney
Favourite Group And Instrumentalist - James Burton and The Beatles
Favourite Actor - Burt Lancaster
Miscellaneous Dislikes - Show Business veterans with chips on their shoulders, finger nail biters, dangerous drivers.
Miscellaneous Likes - Cowboy boots, jewelled tie-clips and cliff links, midnight swims and horse

riding.
Tastes in Music - Very varied, likes distinctive out of the rut sounds and styles.
Personal Ambition - To become a millionaire.

On Saturday 14th September they met up again with Terry Franks and The Avalons in Bletchley for a Ron King Promotion.

Colin Richards (The Avalons)
"We arrived in good time and they're rehearsing again. Mick Green was smartly dressed in a black suit. The roadie told us "Oh he's been to a wedding". We noticed that something else was different. One of us asks "Hello where's the old Gibson then?" he replied, "I like the Tele better." "This is a good one, just got it from Marshalls." Ron King's brother appeared from the back of the hall, "OK girls, you've had your rehearsal let Terry and his band set up."
There was no piss taking from Mick Green this time, you didn't mess with Ron King or his brother Freddy. Johnny Kidd as usual was very polite and friendly and was genuinely interested in how we were getting along. After we finished our first set I climbed up amongst the lighting platform to get a good look at the Pirates. They didn't use their backdrop this time. Bill Stickers must have taken the night off. The Pirates did a few numbers before Johnny came on. Two of these were instrumentals in the Chet Atkins style. Mick's new Fender Telecaster sounded great. It had a lot more treble than his old Gibson. Much more punchy or should I say choppy. I can't describe his sound, you have to hear it for yourself. After their set we returned to the stage to finish off the night. DISASTER STRIKES. Our bass played can't find his bass, it's disappeared from the back of the stage. The Pirates offered to lend our bass player their own bass guitar while they searched the building but our bass player would have none of it. He was too upset. So I had to play bass instead on John Spences' pink Precision but only for a few numbers until we got our own bass player back on stage. Johnny and his crew really went out of their way to help us. They even went to the cop shop to report what had happened. We never got that bass back. It was bad luck that only the bass was taken and not our two Stratts. The guitars were paid for but the bass was behind in payments. That was the last gig we supported Johnny and The Pirates but we used to bump into them from time to time when our vans would pass each other in the streets of London. We'd toot at each other The Pirates van was equipped with an extra horn an old rubber bulb type with the horn part sticking out of the roof.

(© Jean Heath Collection)

We often met Johnny's road manager, Johnny Irving, in a cafe on the North Circular Road. He must have been promoted. He was the driver of the van on the Scunthorpe gig. He told us that the Kidd had his own car and used his own driver. Sometimes we would see a Zepher Six outside the cafe with Johnny Kidd a kip in the back."

Ron King was in partnership with Barry Clayman they went under the name of Clayman Entertainments. They had a regular string of halls which they hired each week. Most were inadequate, often devoid of dressing rooms, backstage area, proper lighting etc.

Alan Wheeler recalls one such venue Wykeham Hall Road.
"The likes of Johnny, Gene Vincent, Adam Faith, Vince Taylor, Dickie Pride, Duffy Power, Vince Eager etc would have to change in the caretakers cottage and walk through the hall (and audience to gain access to the small stage). It was very primitive and the acts often fought against incredible odds to present their show. The lighting was a bit hit and miss and the sound was only as good as

the amps used by the backing groups."

An example of how hard Johnny Irving had to work and how far apart the venues were is well described by Alan Wheeler.
"We all met at Johnnys home in Devon Close early in the day Johnny decided to make up his own mixture in a Pirate Jug which had been presented to him by a fan. He poured just about everything alcoholic he had into the jug and shook it up so that it was well mixed. We all took it in turns to swig out of the jug and by the time we reached a stop at the transport cafe we were all quite merry. Fortunately the quantity was not that great otherwise the outcome might well have marred the performance that night. It certainly had a kick to it!

There was only one motorway open then, the M1, so Cardiff was something of an endurance test to do a one night stand and then come all the way back to play somewhere like Waltham Cross or Romford the next night. I remember that we arrived late in Cardiff. The bouncers were pacing up and down outside the dance hall wondering if we were going to turn up or not! But a very quick change and a hastily arranged set-up of the equipment behind a local band playing an extended set. Soon got the performance underway. John went down a bomb and his late arrival was soon forgotten."

Johnny and the lads, plus girl vocal duo The Caravelles guested on Lance Percival's radio show 'You're Joking Of Course' on the 15th. During September Johnny and his girlfriend Jean moved into a new detached house at 74, South Hill Avenue, South Harrow, Middlesex. He bought the home with the proceeds from 'I'll Never Get Over You'. The house was situated mid-way along the road on a corner with a close running to the left side. It really was a nice quiet area, quite expensive. Johnny and Jean were very happy.

Jean and Johnny outside No. 74
(© Jean Heath Collection)

Jean Heath
"Johnny liked Harrow, it was a very central place, and he did like his home life. He loved to comeback and relax with his family. When he was working he was obviously away a lot. We got on well with our neighbours but I think they found us a bit noisy. They probably thought that having bought a house like that they didn't want to have a pop star living next door - they'd have preferred a bank manager or someone like that. Johnny was often away all night, but we had very nice neighbours and I often stayed with them."

Johnny Kidd
"It's quiet while at the same time I am very near to London for the recording studios and also only half an hour from London Airport."

Because of his success as the Captain of the Beat their home was festooned with mementos of those thieves of the sea who ruled the south coast of England over a century and half ago. Knives and guns lined the walls while on the shelves of his bar were tiny Pirate dolls.
A close neighbour was Carry On star Kenneth Connor, but Johnny never met the actor. Lord Sutch was really pleased to have his mate so close.

"Johnny had got to like the area during his many visits to my house. Now we were very near to each other which was just magic."

During this period Johnny was using a Commer van for the group's gigs. It was a bad runner and on odd occasions the local milkman helped to get it started by pushing the really anxious rocker. Not a very elegant sight seeing a rock 'n' roll star setting off in this style. Living in this pleasing area was really too expensive for Johnny and his family, just the heating bill alone was taking a vast amount of money.

(© Jean Heath Collection)

Wally Whyton
"We'd see each other around when he lived near Harrow on the Hill I lived up the road in Pinner but musicians really don't ever meet up except at weddings and funerals (and the rare TV show). They're usually out putting in 70, 000 miles a year under their belts."

On September 19th in Grays, Essex the crew were supported by The Sundowners who recall the performance of the Kidd.
"His show, as can be imagined, was that of a seasoned performer and The Pirates, two guitarists and drummer, provided a solid backing. Johnny on stage with his pirate gear and sexy gyrations, was a complete contrast to the Johnny off stage. He told us he was knocked out by his record 'I'll Never Get Over You' getting into the Top Ten. He said he and the boys had made several European tours since turning professional and lead guitarist Mick Green added they had been playing eight nights a week and remarked, wiping the sweat from his face, "still its better than working." Our vocalist Tony Shane and Johnny Kidd seemed to find much in common to converse about. As midnight chimed late passers-by saw us bidding bon voyage to each other and packing our respective transports ready for the next days engagements. Johnny Kidd and The Pirates to Coventry and us The Sundowners to nearby Tilbury."

The Boathouse at Q (Kew Bridge) was a wild venue. Screaming Lord Sutch and Cliff Bennett were amongst the most popular acts.

Pete Wilson (The Hustlers)
"One night a perfectly innocent guy crossing Kew Bridge was picked up by a group of Teds and thrown over. He landed on the mud breaking both legs. The local council revoked The Boathouse's music licence and it closed. Pity it was a great place, just ask Lord Sutch. I saw Johnny and The Pirates 3 or 4 times before I saw Mick's Tele, that was at Harlesden and on 'Please Don't Touch'. Kidd used to kick high on 'Please Don't Touch', boof, I shake so much (on the boof from Frank), Kidd almost kicked my girlfriend (now wife) in the teeth."

Johnny was really looking forward to September 29th. He was one of 52 guests invited to Peter Flee-Rekker's wedding at Woodford, Essex. He hired a top hat (Lord Sutch would have been impressed) and tails Johnny looked immaculate, a real posh land-lubber, but he just couldn't resist wearing his buccaneer eye patch.

Other famous celebrities included entrepreneur George Cooper who was the best man plus the Tornados. Johnny was really pleased to meet up with ex-Pirates Clem Cattini and Alan Caddy. The two Tornados were hoping for another 'Telstar' with their latest Joe Meek Production 'Hymn for Teenagers'/'Dragonfly'. Johnny was really proud about his new single 'I'll Never Get Over You' which had entered the charts on the 10th August and was to remain there for a total of ten weeks. Peter Flee-Rekker and his bride were pleased with all their wedding gifts especially Johnny's dozen cut-glasses which Peter has kept polished and shinning to this very day. He regards them as priceless pirate treasure.

Between October 7th-9th they set sail for Belfast, Northern Ireland and cast anchor at The Boom Boom Boom Club. Another popular venue during this period was Wellington Public Halls just outside Croydon, Surrey. Freddie Bannister was the promoter. He booked bands there every Tuesday night. They'd cram about 750 people into the hall. It should have only held about 500.

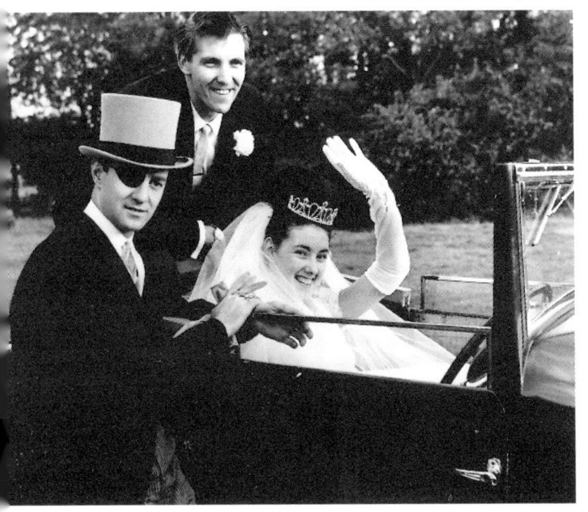

above left:
Johnny with Peter Flee-Rakkers and Bride
(© P. Flee-Rakkers)
above right:
The Tornados join in the celebration
(© P. Flee-Rakkers)
below:
Poster - Granada Mansfield 21/10/63
(© Always N' Ever Archive)

They were keen to work on another Gordon Mills composition 'Hungry For Love'. The Pirates were also allowed studio time to cut two solo gems 'Castin My Spell' and 'My Babe'. These recordings were to be this crews greatest and finest testimony.

Keith Hunt
"Friday, October 25th couldn't come quick enough for me. I'd bought tickets for the Greenford Granada to see Joe Brown and the Bruvvers, Johnny Kidd and The Pirates, Dee Dee Sharp, Heinz, The Saints, The Sundowners and compere Ted King. During the afternoon while I was stuck at school (I was only ten years old) Johnny and the boys played on the BBC Light Programmes' Friday lunch time radio show 'Go Man Go'. The show was recorded at the Playhouse Theatre in the Haymarket. The regular band was 'The David Ede Band' which featured many respected musicians including top session guitarist Eric Ford. My main memories of the Granada show that evening were 'The White Tornado', Heinz, backed by The Saints. He was wild, leaping onto amplifiers and jumping on the piano during the guitar solo on 'Just Like Eddie'.

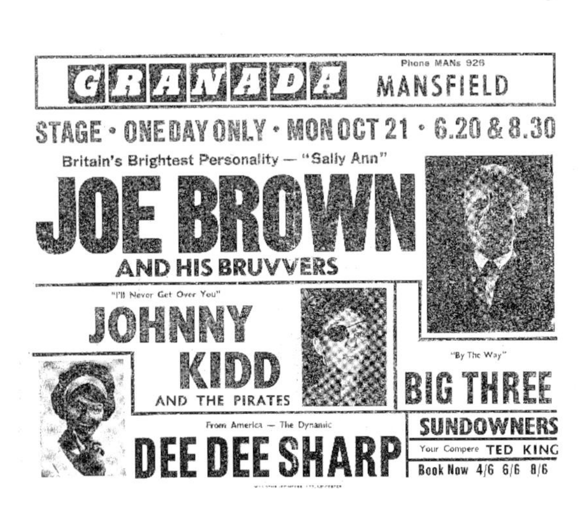

Heinz
"I used to climax my act with a leap on the top of a piano. Of course I always insisted it was protected with some covering. I was on stage one night and noticed the covering was in place. I leapt up on the cover to find the top of the piano hadn't been put on. Just the cover. Down I went with twanging piano wires all around me, a terrible noise and horrible sight. Was my face red, I'll say! I also used to leap on to amps (specially strengthened of course). A few times when I did this my guitar strap broke clean through and the guitar, being a heavy one, swung down with the result that the strings chopped into my hand. I once had blood pouring down from my wrist onto my powder blue stage suit which embarrassed me all right particularly as I hadn't noticed."
Three days running at (Greenford, Dartford and Edmonton) Heinz split his trousers on stage,

three different pairs!

Johnny with Heinz
(© Jean Heath Collection)

Joe Brown and The Bruvvers, Pete Oakman (bass), Brian Dunn (rhythm) and Bobby Graham (drums). Joe was the greatest guitar instrumentalist I'd ever seen and still it. This 6ft 2ins giggling, jiggling, blonde, bopping, neurotic floor mop of spiked hair soon had the crowd going wild. Joes performance was just tremendous with his guitar behind the head routine. Being the star no one had the hard task of following this very polished cockney from Lincolnshire. But Joe had to follow Johnny and the crew whose stage act was so powerful and superb that even to this very day, in '94, various vocalists and musicians have told me that it would have been far less constraining walking the plank over a pirate's ship than to follow Capt. Kidd on stage.

My fondest memory of that magical night is Johnny standing arms folded in his buccaneer stance telling us about his new record 'Hungry For Love' which was not on release yet. I was so excited I was seeing and hearing a live performance of a record that was not yet on sale by a pop star who I'd only seen before on television. I was seated towards the back of the theatre and in the very back row I could see a chap just like Joe Brown watching the other artists. Too this very day I've aways wondered if this was my spiked haired idol. Mind you even boys in my class used to boast about their Joe Brown spiked hair styles, a full year before Beatle mop tops and scruffy Stones styles caught on. So perhaps it was just one of Joes bold fans. I just couldn't leave the theatre without autographs. My cousin, Alan Ashton, and I stood in the pouring rain for over an hour waiting for a glimpse of our idols. Sadly they all escaped us. Perhaps Johnny had sailed straight past us without his eye patch. We just wouldn't have noticed we were so excited.

Johnny
(© R. S. Lowes)

I returned home on cloud nine I looked and felt like I'd been in a cloud. Sadly this drenching made me ill. I was bed-ridden for the next six months with rheumatic fever. Now free from boring school as if decreed by fate I could now listen, watch, collect every release and music publication. If there had been an 11 plus on Johnny and Merseybeat I would have passed with flying Jolly Roger Colours."

Joe Brown
"Johnny and the band played great rock 'n' roll, I know because I worked with them very often live. You could always tell a good band when they were live. You could never really judge on a record in those days."

Alan Wheeler
"Johnny double-tracked five A sides in a row including 'I'll Never Get Over You', 'Hungry For Love', 'Jealous Girl' (64) and 'The Birds and The Bees' (65). Johnny Spence and Mick did backing vocals on 'A Shot Of Rhythm And Blues' and although I remember Johnny Spence singing when 'I'll Never Get Over You' and 'Hungry For Love' were recorded I don't think he was actually picked up on the tape. However he can be heard throughout 'Always 'n' Ever' (64) and also on 'Got To Travel On' (65). On some occasions when Studio 2 was otherwise engaged they would move over to be recorded in Studio No 1. This was a more spacious studio where among lots of other things live albums of Oh Boy, Drumbeat, 6.5 Special and Cliff and The Shadows were cut before a specially invited audience. In contrast to the control room in Studio 2, which was on the same level as the studio floor, the control room in Studio 1 was above the entrance door. Things were generally resembled that of a small television studio and with Johnny and The Pirates being slightly lost in the bareness. Soundwise thought I always thought the Pirates came

through sounding more chunky on the session in Studio 1. Listen to 'Hungry For Love', 'Ecstasy', 'My Babe' and 'Castin My Spell' for instance."

"I have to say that not all the best recordings of some numbers were captured at Abbey Road. John's try out demos with the '63 trio in a tiny basement studio in Berwick Street, Soho of 'The Fool' and 'Some Other Guy' were far, far superior to what has emerged from the E.M.I. vaults, really picking up the atmosphere of his stage work at the time. Also the original, rough demo cut of 'Always 'n' Ever' which I recall as being cut somewhere else, was in blue beat style with a much stronger riff and far better than the commercialised out of all recognition 45 produced at St Johns Wood."

A different version of 'Magic Of Love' in a Buddy Holly style and another cut of 'If You Were The Only Girl In The World' with the original Pirates plus 'Baby Blue' and 'Tricky Dicky' were recorded at E.M.I. but have remained undiscovered in their vaults.
'Hungry For Love'/'Ecstasy' was released on November 8th and quickly made its TV debut on Ready Steady Go. Another show featured The Pirates performing a pounding version of 'My Babe'. Although television was by far the best way to reach his audience, Johnny was never allowed to recreate his wild dramatic free-booter ballroom antics for the cameras.

'Shakin All Over' guitarist Joe Moretti did not play lead for the Jet Blacks, the backing band for Jet Harris and Tony Meehan but he was featured on some of their hits i.e. Applejack. Joe later played for the Cyril Stapleton's Orchestra at Streatham Locarno. Session work for Tom Jones, Petula Clark, Lulu, etc kept him busy until the end of the 60's.

Billy J. Kramer Programme, Nov '63 (© Always N' Ever Archive)

Johnny was pleased to join 'The Billy J Kramer Pop Parade'. The tour kicked off in November at Luton.

Johnny Kidd
"We all had a great time with Billy and The Dakotas, The Fourmost, Houston Wells, Tommy Quickly, The Marauders and Ted King who did a fine job of compering. I've especially enjoyed watching The Caravelles working on stage. It's marvellous how they have done so well in such a short time. That Lois is a great little guitar player too. I can tell you a funny story about 'You Don't Have To Be A Baby To Cry' their big hit. About five years ago I wrote a number called 'Blood Red Beauty'. Frankly, it was a load of old rubbish, but I took it along to Lois's dad who did a spot of recording. While I was there - we knew him as Wilkie, because he kept a radio shop called Wilkinsons he played me a tape of Lois. Guess what she was singing? 'You Don't Have To Be A Baby To Cry'. Of course, it was a lot different from the version that has become a big hit today. Even so I never thought it would turn out to be such a smash. I'm really glad the girls have made it big."

Frank Rouledge (Five Nutters)
"The day our skiffle group recorded 'Blood Red Beauty' at Wilkies he asked me if I would teach his young daughter Lois to play the guitar. I was pleased to teach her and proud she became successful."

By the time Lois left school she was a frequent guest guitar player at London's most famous folk clubs. She soon found an equally attractive partner in Andrea Simpson and signed for the Decca Label.

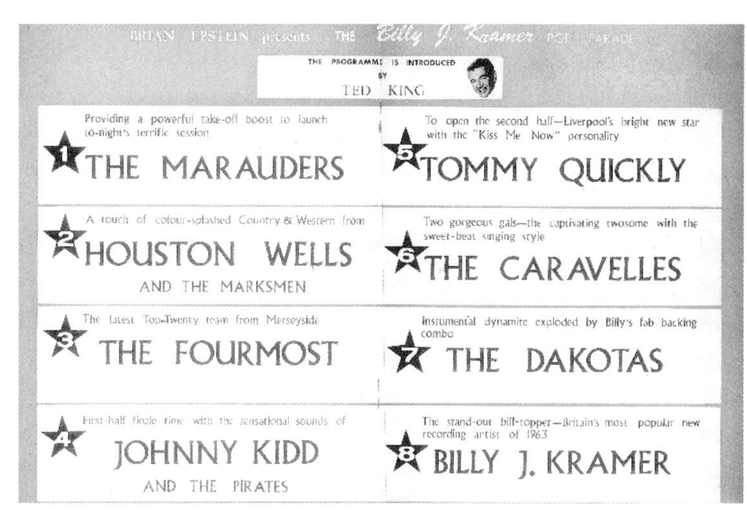

above: The Line-Up

Johnny Kidd

"I've just finished touring with Billy J Kramer and I reckon I've done some of my best ever performances. At Kettering I did my best yet. I couldn't sing a note though because I had terrible flu and I was dosed up with aspirins but I managed to get a good visual impact. The boys were great too. They play the best Rhythm and Blues I've heard in this country, and they make the Liverpool groups sound tame! In fact they're making a single themselves for H.M.V. Me I'm cutting an LP soon and my record company is letting me have a free hand on the material. Before my choice of singles for myself had been appallingly bad. I haven't got a commercial ear. I like off beat Rhythm and Blues stuff as you can tell from quite a few of my discs. Single wise I'm not cutting anything for a newie yet. I have to be very careful about my records. For instance other singers like Cliff and The Beatles sell fantastically well on advance orders. Their fans don't even hear the disc. With me its different I haven't a huge multitude of fans who'll rush out and order my record as soon as they've heard I've got a new one coming out. I do have a sizeable following though but they have to listen to my disc before they buy it. Often it has to grow on them but to get into the charts I simply have to make a good commercial disc.

For the first three years of my career I was on the ups and downs. I had some hits - 'Please Don't Touch', 'Shakin All Over', 'Restless' but it was the songs that did it. Meantime Jack Good - I was on his 'Wham' show - suggested I wear an eye patch for effect. I may be getting rid of the patch next year. I didn't think 'I'll Never Get Over You' would be a hit. It was written by Gordon Mills of The Viscounts. It was a sleeper but I feel that one reason why it clicked was the title. It's an old music hall expression and when people see a title like that I reckon they tend to think 'I must go out and hear that disc'. I've just had an EP released with 'I'll Never Get Over You' and 'Hungry For Love' on it. I don't really like the idea as I'd sooner record new stuff but then my only other EP which contained four of my earlier hits is now selling better than it did when it was issued."

NME TOP 30 11-12-1963
"HUNGRY FOR LOVE" op 24.

1	1	I WANT TO HOLD YOUR HAND	Beatles (Parlophone)
2	2	SHE LOVES YOU	Beatles (Parlophone)
4	3	SECRET LOVE	Kathy Kirby (Decca)
4	4	YOU WERE MADE FOR ME	Freddie and the Dreamers (Columbia)
9	5	GLAD ALL OVER	Dave Clark Five (Columbia)
3	6	DON'T TALK TO HIM	Cliff Richard (Columbia)
10	7	I ONLY WANT TO BE WITH YOU	Dusty Springfield (Philips)
7	8	MARIA ELENA	Los Indios Tabajaras (RCA)
13	9	DOMINIQUE	Singing Nun (Philips)
18	10	TWENTY - FOUR HOURS FROM TULSA	Gene Pitney (United Artists)
7	11	I'LL KEEP YOU SATISFIED	Billy J. Kramer (Parlophone)
20	12	GERONIMO	Shadows (Columbia)
15	12	TWIST AND SHOUT (EP)	Beatles (Parlophone)
11	14	WITH THE BEATLES (LP)	Beatles (Parlophone)
6	15	YOU'LL NEVER WALK ALONE	Gerry and the Pacemakers (Columbia)
—	16	SWINGING ON A STAR	Big Dee Irwin (Colpix)
14	17	IT'S ALMOST TOMORROW	Mark Wynter (Pye)
19	17	BEATLES HITS (EP)	Beatles (Parlophone)
28	19	ALL I WANT FOR CHRISTMAS	Dora Bryan (Fontana)
25	20	I WANNA BE YOUR MAN	Rolling Stones (Decca)
25	21	COUNTRY BOY	Heinz (Decca)
16	22	MONEY	Bern Elliott and the Fenmen (Decca)
23	23	DEEP PURPLE	Nino Tempo and April Stevens (London)
24	24	HUNGRY FOR LOVE	Johnny Kidd (HMV)
21	25	STAY	Hollies (Parlophone)
12	26	BE MY BABY	Ronettes (London)
30	27	NOT TOO LITTLE	Chris Sandford (Decca)
—	28	WE ARE IN LOVE	Adam Faith (Parlophone)
—	29	BEATLES VOL. 1 (EP)	Beatles (Parlophone)
—	30	FROM RUSSIA WITH LOVE	Matt Monro (Parlophone)

December 21st found our wanderers all at sea on Hastings Pier with plenty of sea beat breeze. Johnny was asked to name his top ten of rock stars.

"Jerry Lee Lewis has the most fantastic visual act - I have not seen anyone else to touch him.

Gene Vincent apart from being a personal friend of mine Gene is a great artist - one of the original rockers.

The Beatles. I know everybody says they like them but the boys have so much viability you can't help admiring them.

Original Checkmates. Considering how good they are this group is not known widely enough. They are superb.

Brenda Lee. This little lady really has got what it takes.

Chuck Berry. Every beat artist must have been influenced at some time or other by Chuck who is the tops.

Pirates. For a backing group I could not wish for a finer bunch of musicians or better guys.

Brook Benton. A smooth polished performer who knows what singing is all about.
Dr Feelgood. This guy though I don't know much about him is a raver. I hear he goes mad on stage.
Coasters. They have a great sound. I have always been keen on them.

During December the Star Club told Johnny that they wanted to record his amazing act for a live LP.

Johnny Kidd
"It will be my first LP though I do have an EP just out on HMV, 'I'll Never Get Over You', 'Then I Got Everything', 'Hungry For Love' and 'A Shot Of Rhythm and Blues'.

E.P. Sleeve

Hamburg will give me a chance to do something I've wanted to do for years to record some real toe tapping rhythm and blues stuff. It's a funny thing, you know. All my real fans really dig Rhythm and Blues things, the type of numbers that make up the B sides of my records. I really go for the true Rhythm and Blues things by artists like Sonny Terry and Big Bill Broonzy. I'm also going to record 'I'll Never Get Over You' in German. Then it will be back to London where I'm hoping to do an album in the studio for H.M.V. There's also talk of a film in the New Year so at the moment you could say that I'm a very happy person. I promise you one thing I'll never get big headed I've seen too many come and go ever to do that. Besides, I'm too appreciative of the support you've all given me ever to get an out-size in hats."

On the 24th December the band left for Hamburg to appear at the Star Club on Boxing Day. The booking was for two weeks.

Johnny Kidd
"We must be keen to spend the festive season away from home. I'm touring with The Larry Parnes Tour and The Crystals next year and doing some Granada dates with The Ronettes."

13. RIGHT STRING BUT THE WRONG YO YO

Johnny Kidd
"Before I join Larry Parnes' Spring tour, I am looking forward to spending a couple of weeks in Sweden. I've never been there but I've heard a lot about the place - especially from Emile Ford when I met him at the Star Club. He raved about Sweden and everyone seems to be going there these days."
Hans Siden (Swedish Journalist)
"I was surprised that Johnny played in Boras which is a very small town and not like Gothenburg where all the big stars played."

below: Press advertisement (© Always N' Ever Archive)

bottom: Handbill - Granada Mansfield (© Always N' Ever Archive)

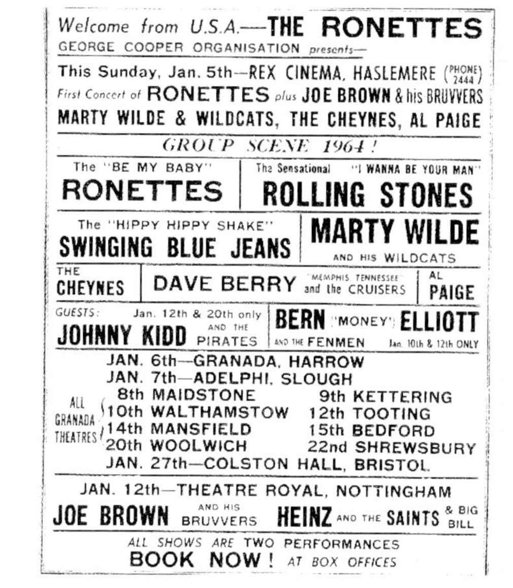

Johnny became very popular in Scandinavia. The following singles were released in Norway. 'If You Were The Only Girl In The World'/'Feelin' HMV POP674, Red Wax Company Sleeve, 'Shakin All Over'/'Yes Sir That's My Baby' HMV POP753, Red Wax Company Sleeve, 'I'll Never Get Over You'/'Then I Got Everything' Black Wax Picture Sleeve HMV POP1173.

The British group The Zephyrs recorded a fine version of 'I Can Tell'/'Sweet Little Baby' with Jimmy Page as session guitarist. They cited Kidd as the influence for recording the song.

During January The Searchers EP entitled 'Hungry For Love' Pye NEP2414 entered the top 5.

John NcNally (Searchers, Lead Guitarist)
"Although I enjoyed seeing Johnny and The Pirates at the Cavern they were very respected. We, in fact, got 'Hungry For Love' from its composer Gordon Mills before we heard the Kidds version.

The beat group era, especially Merseybeat had made it very hard for American artists to get a hit in Britain. The Ronettes arrived in early January '64 for a month long British tour which included top billing on ITV's variety show Sunday Night at the Palladium. Johnny and The Pirates and a host of top groups joined the tour, Joe Brown and his Bruvvers, Heinz, Swinging Blue Jeans, Cheynes and the Rolling Stones. The shows were promoted by George Cooper. Johnny broke from the tour on the 13th January to record 'Dr Feelgood' the ultimate British beat single.

Throughout February and March the Larry Parnes' Your Lucky Stars Show was bringing stars to every town, Finsbury Park, Worcester, Taunton, Mansfield. It starred Joe Brown, The Crystals (another Spector girl group), Johnny and The Pirates, Sundowners, Kevin Kirk, Mike Preston, Daryl Quist, Heinz and The Saints. Manfred Mann with compere Al Paige. Manfred Mann were having great chart success with 5,4,3,2,1. They went on to score countless hits. Their drummer Mike Hugg was really keen on the Pirates especially Frank Farley's simple technique and use of bass drums, more suited to a Bo Diddley beat than the Elvin Jones style that Hugg had tried to employ up to that point in his career.
The Larry Parnes' package shows were tremendous. There would be seven or more

Programme 'Your Lucky Stars' (© Always N' Ever Archive)

different acts all of whom were recording artists and they'd put on a two hour show with two performances every night of the tour. The star would do twenty five minutes, the second top about twenty minutes, third spot would have fifteen and all the others would have ten minutes each. Many of the tours ran for six weeks, a different town every night playing either a local theatre or cinema. Ticket prices on average were fifteen bob (75p) and 5/- (25p) for the back stalls. It was great fun for the fans but very hard work for the acts, and of course, the poor roadies.

The following review of one show proves once again that Johnny and the boys could outshine the best.

POLISHED TURN BY JOHNNY KIDD

"Leather clad Johnny Kidd proved a really polished performance in the package show at the Granada Theatre last night Friday although he only got third billing. His act outclassed that of Heinz and Joe Brown the stars of the show. The audiences of both full houses were comparatively quiet until those top Rhythm and Blues artists Manfred Mann entered the scene. America's foursome The Crystals brought many whistles of delight from male fans present. Their act however, was a replica of that given by The Ronettes at the last beat show in January. Johnny Kidd followed giving out with his oldies. This stylish singer, with the thigh length boots and lace shirt introduced his latest number 'Always 'n' Ever' and proved his versatility by breaking away from the 'Shakin All Over' type beat of previous records. Good backing from the Pirates provided a clever act.

Heinz came on amidst frantic screams and handkerchief waving. He sang, he played, he leapt, jumped and kneeled on the floor. His exit was echoed in mass screaming and chanting for more. Joe Brown with his mixture of music and humour will always he a hit and this was no exception. This six foot cockney is rapidly becoming an all round entertainer as did Tommy Steele a few years back. Supporting singers including Mike Preston and Daryl Quist all gave good performances. Altogether the show was good."

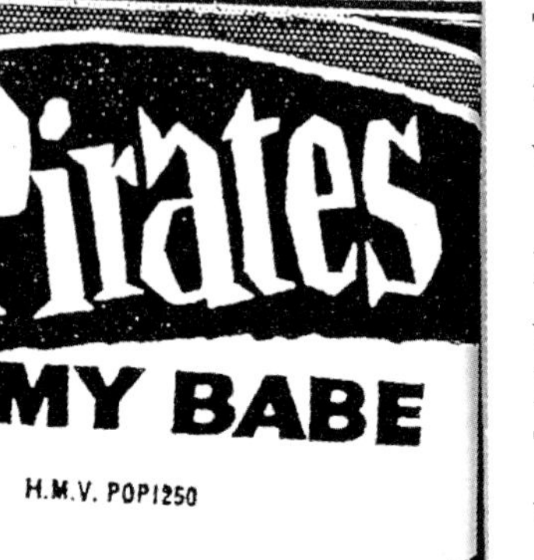

'My Babe' Press advertisement

Mick, John Spence and Frank were merry marauders on the 3rd January when they had a single released without their captain - 'My Babe'/'Castin My Spell'.
The young Jimmy Page with his group The Talismen recorded a fine version of 'Castin My Spell' for American release on ACTS22.

Feb 1st Roxy Cinema Ulverston along with Heinz and The Saints, Ricky Valance, Danny Rivers, Vince Eager, Nelson Keene and The Fabulous Flee-Rekkers.

Peter Flee-Reckers (Sax, Flee-Rekkers)
"We did this tour of the North for promoter Denny Boyce the former band leader. Agent Bob Alexander had recently joined up with The Boyce Organisation and helped us get this tour. Johnny played most of these gigs as well. I used to drive an Austin, Johnny had exactly the same van. I wouldn't let any of my group drive, there would be eight of us crammed in. We'd often pass The Pirates on the motorway. I will always remember Johnny saying "I must give up this travel-

ling it's going to kill me". Johnny was a nice bloke, happy go lucky, a big loss."

Ricky Valance
"All the members of the cast were looking for a way out of the theatre to get around the fans. Someone found a side window and a chance to get out and away unnoticed and would have done so to had it not been for Johnny! With one leg half way through the window Johnny started shouting loudly "look we can get out through here" which resulted in a large crowd running up and blocking the way. Great publicity man was Johnny!"

Johnny and the crew had recorded a wild version of Piano Red's 'Dr Feelgood' on Jan 13th. The studio was re-booked for the 4th Feb for a fun session, the recording of the colourful neapolitan song 'Santa Lucia'. This was given an English lyric, re-titled 'Always 'n' Ever', and featured a very catchy chorus line.

Alan Wheeler
"'Always 'n' Ever' had all sorts of people singing on the over-dubs Frank Farley, Mick Green, Johnny Spence, roadie Johnny Irving, myself and even George Cooper who was Johnnys' agent at the time."

'Always 'n' Ever'/'Dr Feelgood' was released on the 6th March. They starred on ITV's Ready Steady Go the very same day along with Adam Faith, Mike Hurst, Louise Cordet and The Marauders. Every TV company had a pop show - (Scottish - Dig This), (ATV Midlands - For Teenagers Only), (Ulster -Now Hear This), (Southern TV - Dad You're A Square), (Channel TV - New Look Here), (Television West and Wales - Discs A Go Go), (Border TV - Beat The Border), (Tyne Tees - Songs For The Swinging 60's), (BBC2 - Beat Room) which only lasted 6 months. Johnny and The Pirates co-shared an edition with skiffle King Lonnie Donegan and his group.

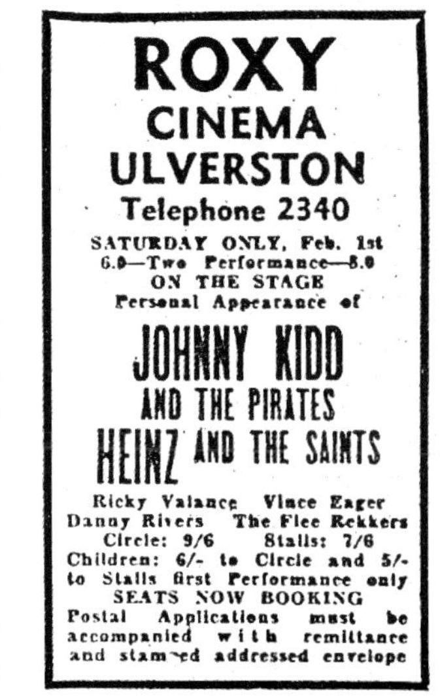

above top:
Advertisement - Roxy Ulverston

above bottom:
Advertisement 'Always N' Ever'

During April the A side was given another good plug on Ready Steady Go. The Pirates also proved that they were the best powerhouse trio in the land with their solo performance of 'My Babe'. Johnny and the boys also tele-recorded a spot for BBC1 Top Of The Pops but it was never shown. T.O.T.P. had started on New Years Day of 1964. It was televised from a converted church in Manchester.

Alan Wheeler
"I recall John taking the demo disc of 'Always 'n' Ever' that they had cut in Berwick Street Soho along to a gig that very evening at Leyton Baths for a try out over the PA system."

Ex-Freddie Heath Band member Pete Newman (sax) cut a demo of a song he had written called 'You Gotta Be Around' at the Regent Sound Studio. Johnny was pleased to hear that his ole sax man was recording a vocal and turned up to do some vocal backing.

Pete Newman
"Sadly the demo was lost but its just possible that Vic Clarke who played rhythm on the session had a copy but he went to Australia. I often wonder if he still has a copy."

Birmingham group Gerry Levene and The Avengers, recorded a Brumbeat version of 'Dr Feelgood'/'Driving Me Wild' on Decca F11815. This marked the recording debut of Roy Wood.

Roy later became a member of The Move and Wizzard. A tremendous songwriter, producer and multi-instrumentalist.
The earliest known version of 'Doctor Feelgood' was recorded by Willie Perryman under the pseudonym of Dr Feelgood. He was an Atlanta blues man who had recorded prolifically as Piano Red for RCA/Groove between 1950 and 1958. Although he is often credited for recording the original of 'Right String But The Wrong Yo Yo, it was in fact his brother Rufus Perryman alias Speckled Red who cut the original in 1930.
The long awaited album looked on the cards as they returned to Abbey Road to record eleven masters between the 6th and 7th April. Johnny said at the time "The songs will be in the R&B vein." They even added an organist to get a much fuller sound. 'Whole Lotta Woman', 'Your Cheatin Heart', 'Let's Talk About Us' (2) (released 1990), 'A Little Bit Of Soap' (released 1983), 'The Fool' (2) (1990), 'Oh Boy' (released 1983), 'Send Me Some Lovin' (released 1990), 'Big Blon' Baby' (2) (1990), 'Please Don't Touch' (2) (released 1990), 'Right String But The Wrong Yo Yo' (1983).

Shop Around.
Sadly due to the decline in Johnnys single sales the LP was shelved. Many of these superb recordings were to remain in the vaults for over 20 years. During his life time he never had an album released.

Peter Wilson (The Hustlers)
"I remember the period when Johnny and The Pirates were recording an album. I used to go to a record shop at the bottom of South Hill Avenue, South Harrow near Johnnys home. Big Jim Sullivan used to go and play there along with many others such as Ritchie Blackmore. There was much discussion about what was on it but only two tracks turned out to be right I found out later from Kidd. It was a great disappointment when it was put on hold and finally cancelled. The record shop was the only shop to have all those R&B records that later became staple parts of so many acts. Sullivan used to take his guitar in there and give impromtu performances. The other guys used it for obtaining and hearing all the great R&B stuff. Sullivan was then in a band with Jimmy Page, Bobby Graham (drums) and another ex Bruvver on bass. They played on countless hits in 1963/64. I clearly remember talking about the Kidd album that never happened. We heard stories of difficulty in the studio, that Green didn't like to play second fiddle to an organ which changed the sound (and the numbers). This may be completely untrue."

Friday April 10th once again at the very popular Central Pier, Morcombe 8pm - 2am. 5/- in advance, 6/- on the door.

More sessions were booked for May, 13th 'I Know' (rel 1983), 14th 'Jealous Girl' and on the 20th 'Where Are You' (rel. 1983).

Organist Vic Cooper, another ex Red Cap and good mate of Frank Farley and Johnny Spence had settled in well. He had been involved on the April/May recording sessions and now was a full time shipmate. Poor roadie Johnny Irving soon found that an organ is bloody heavy. It often proved a difficult item to move about to gigs it was extremely and cumbersome and took up valuable room in a cramped bandwagon. In fact they had to go in for a bigger van to accommodate it more easily.
Earlier in the year on March 29th the UK's first pirate radio station, Radio Caroline had started

broadcasting in the North Sea twelve hours a day 6am - 6pm. Johnny and his sea-rovers were invited on board and were proud to hoist the Jolly Roger whilst listening to the sounds of the sixties.

Johnny always laughed at the antics of Lord Sutch but he smiled from ear to ear when he learned that Sutch and his Savages had set sail from Leigh-On-Sea, Essex with a whole load of radio equipment aboard a 25 ton fishing trawler 'Cornucopia' on the 25th May '64.

The insurers of the 25 ton trawler ruled that the skippers insurance would be withdrawn if the vessel was used as a radio station. So they sailed to Shivering Sands a fort eight miles out at sea one of five built as anti-aircraft platforms during World War II off the coast of Herne Bay, Kent. Sutch grabbed a rusty iron ladder and climbed 20ft over the seaweed and barnacle - encrusted girders on to the first platform of the fort. The ironwork, corroded by sea and weather for twenty five years, broke under his weight and huge chunks crashed into the sea. Sutch was left screaming and clinging to a railing but he scaled a second ladder and minutes later the Jolly Roger fluttered from an old gun emplacement 100ft above the sea.

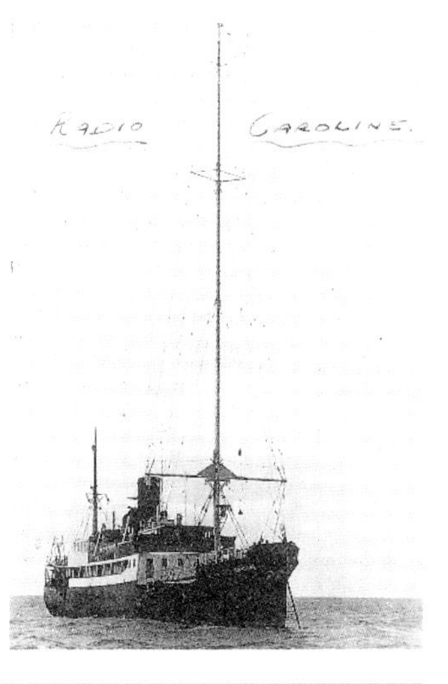

Another British pirate radio station was born. Sutch was planning to lure away listeners from Radio Caroline and Radio Atlanta by broadcasting rude bedtime stories such as Lady Chatterley Lover' and 'Fanny Hill'. Radio Sutch hit the airwaves through the sea waves on the 27th May. The first sound was the screams of 'Jack The Ripper' followed by various banned records and Joe Meek productions. Sutch was now a radio pirate. The transmission wasn't very strong 0.5 KW but he soon had a cult following. The rusty towers had advantages over other pirates, they couldn't sink, they had tremendous height which enhanced aerial performance and you never felt sea sick.

It was Reg Calvert (promoter) who had discovered the fort during April '64 while cruising off the Kent Coast. His wife Dorothy told the press "I think Reg and Dave are absolutely mad."

'Jealous Girl' and the final track recorded on their mammoth April sessions Smokey Robinson's 'Shop Around' were released on June 12th. Most of Johnny's singles were released on sheet music usually featuring a photo of Johnny without The Pirates. One of the most interesting was a booklet called 'The Johnny Kidd Album of Songs and Guitar Solos' released by Danver Music Ltd of Soho Square, London, who were linked and housed within the George Cooper Organisation. Six tunes were featured, 'I'll Never Get Over You', 'Then I Got Everything', 'What Shall We Do With the Drunken Sailor', arranged by Johnny plus three instrumentals written by Mick Green 'String Picnic', 'Spanish Armada' and 'Popeye'. These instrumentals were occasionally played at dance hall gigs not normally in the set with Johnny but on the sound run through. As time went on they were forgotten. The booklet also included nine photos featuring both Johnny and The Pirates. The following introduction was written by Johnny. "Hello. There are mainly two reasons why I am pleased to see this album go onto the market. Firstly, it is always pleasing to think that maybe you're good enough to warrant it.. maybe? Secondly, because I hope it is falling into the hands of some of my fellow musicians up and down the country. I have been fortunate in keeping a steady form of popularity over the past three years. I have always insisted that one of the greatest helps in maintaining this keeping the name alive was

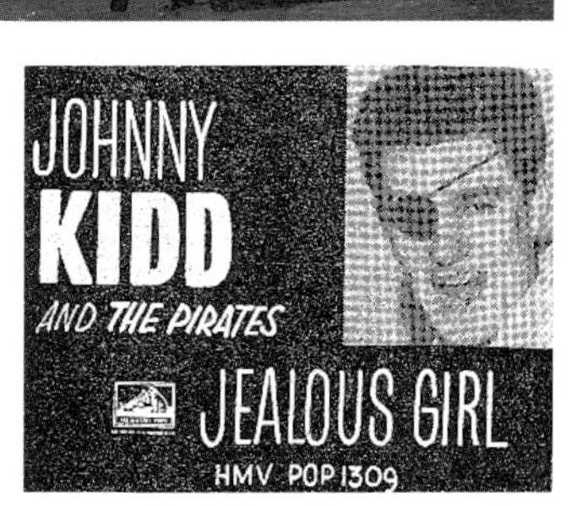

illustrations (in order)
Johnny & Pirates on the Bandwagon
Radio Caroline
Radio Sutch (Shivering Sands)
Press advertisement

because so many musicians in so many various groups all over the British Isles were kind enough to play my records at gigs. I have always favoured R&B music and hoped that one day it would reach the popularity that would enable us all to play it on our gigs without it falling on deaf ears. I think you'll find most of the numbers in this album are basically either R&B or, at least, very beaty. Whatever you find them to be, enjoy playing them."

Album of songs (© Always N' Ever Archive)

Johnnys producer Peter Sullivan was now becoming very much in demand with other stars. He formed Associated Independent Recordings (A.I.R.) along with George Martin, Ron Richards and John Burgess. Hiring themselves out as freelance producers they commanded a far better salary for themselves. A.I.R. went on to have tremendous chart success with The Beatles, Tom Jones, Shirley Bassey, Lulu, Manfred Mann etc.

Blackpool was full of the beat during the summer of '64. Promoter Larry Parnes presented a host of stars on his Summer Season shows.

The Royal Aquarium Theatre commenced on the 11th June with Billy Fury, Rolf Harris, Karl Denver Trio plus various other star names on The Big Beat Show. The Sunday Big Beat Show featured many stars, The Searchers, followed by Brian Poole and The Tremoloes etc. The Britannia Theatre commenced 21st June with The Sunday Special with Big Dee Irwin and Blues By Five. The Rainbow Theatre, South Pier commenced 26th June for the season with The Big Star Show starring Joe Brown and his Bruvvers, Johnny Kidd and The Pirates, The Tornados, Mike Preston, Lynne Perrie and compere Al Paige. The show was devised and produced by Ross Taylor in association with The George Cooper Organisation Ltd. They arrived at the Rainbow Theatre to find workmen and painters still in action. Reason was the theatre was burned down back in February but, in just twelve weeks, they had re-built the place. Tornado, Clem Cattini, and compere, Al Paige, used to pass the time between acts on the end of the pier fishing.

Blackpool star line up, August 1964

Clem Cattini
"I left my line dangling, nipped inside to do the act and when I returned I reeled in and found a dirty great fish on the end. Only it was a frozen fish - someone had bought it from the nearby fishmongers!"
Pirate Frank Farley recalls another fishy tale.
"This was a family show, singing and dancing etc. The opening began with Kidd, Joe Brown and Mike Preston doing a dance routine out front whilst we the musicians were barely visible behind a thin gauze type curtain. However when the curtain was raised at the end of the routine my drums disappeared up in the air as my bass drum spears were caught firmly in the curtains. I've always thought it was ex Pirate Clem Cattini then leader of The Tornados who did it."

Dave Lilley (Fan)
"I saw the show in early July. I missed Lynne Perrie but Al Paige was the MC telling the usual corny jokes. Followed by The Tornados, Clem Cattini. They played Telstar, Globetrotter, Exo-

dus and Robot and then there was an intermission.

Johnny and The Pirates opened the second half. They had a galleon at the back of the stage with nets all around. I seem to recall the numbers were 'I'll Never Get Over You', 'Shot of Rhythm And Blues', 'Hungry For Love', 'Always 'n' Ever' and concluding with 'Shakin All Over'. All sang impeccably with Johnny in his buccaneer stance and The Pirates playing note for note perfectly. They were followed by Joe Brown who did a good spot."

top: Al Paige, Johnny, Joe and Mike Preston
(© Jean Heath Collection)
centre: 'A Picture of You' - Joe and Johnny
(© Jean Heath Collection)
bottom: Mick, the Dakota (second left)
(© Always N' Ever Archive)

Bobby Elliott (Hollies Drummer)
"We actually went to Blackpool to see Johnny and The Pirates. Joe Brown was also on. I've still got the programme."

Blackpool was the place to be that summer. The Beatles recorded a TV Special at the ABC Theatre. The following week they starred at the Opera House. Stacks of stars called in for the special Sunday concerts. Dusty Springfield, Big Dee Irwin, Frank Ifield, Kathy Kirby, Jimmy Nicol and The Shub-Dubs, Blues By Five, Cilla Black, Applejacks, Danny Williams, Sound Incorporated etc. Even Brian Epstein who was proud to have Cilla Black topping a bill for the very first time. The same couldn't be said for Johnny and the lads. Johnny hated his spot which was sandwiched between jugglers etc. Guitarist Mick Green was even more fed up.

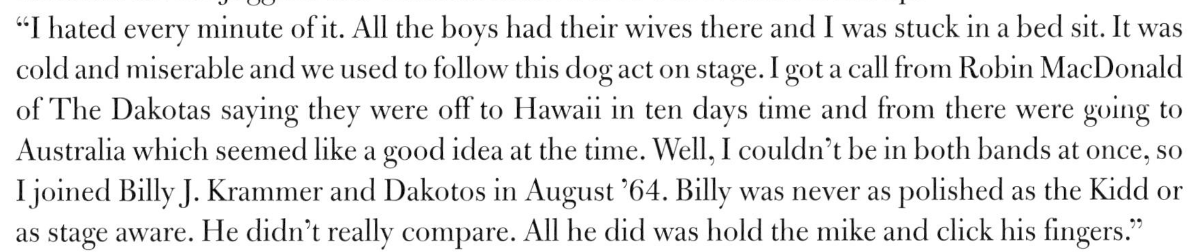

"I hated every minute of it. All the boys had their wives there and I was stuck in a bed sit. It was cold and miserable and we used to follow this dog act on stage. I got a call from Robin MacDonald of The Dakotas saying they were off to Hawaii in ten days time and from there were going to Australia which seemed like a good idea at the time. Well, I couldn't be in both bands at once, so I joined Billy J. Krammer and Dakotos in August '64. Billy was never as polished as the Kidd or as stage aware. He didn't really compare. All he did was hold the mike and click his fingers."

It was agreed that Tornado Stuart Taylor would help out until a replacement could be found. Johnny was soon smiling as his girlfriend Jean gave birth to a lovely little girl - Cilla, born 27/6/64. A kid for the Kidd the papers reported. Although he was over the moon having a little girl he was still unhappy with the show and it came to a head when Larry Parnes dismissed Johnny and The Lads for being late. They were sacked and told to walk the plank.

But it hadn't all been bad as roadie Johnny Irving recalls.
"After the shows all the cast would go to the local Top Rank Savoy bowling alley which they very kindly kept open especially for us until the early hours."

During July Johnny bought an interest in a Blackpool Club and named it The Picador. He had a great laugh playing football for the Blackpool Entertainers v The Northern TV All Stars. Dave King, Mike Preston, The Square Pegs were among the players. He also enjoyed dancing during the afternoons in the 'Twist 'n' Shake' contests on the central pier.

Johnny Kidd
"I flew to London for a replacement for Mick Green. I looked around and finally hired young Johnny Weider. We came back by car but we were held up in traffic in Preston. When I arrived back late at the theatre just before the show started I was

told the production manager had cut me out of the openin. I admit I was a few minutes late once before this session. Although I was changed and ready to go on when the curtain went up the stage manager had cut me out. Then he said impresario Larry Parnes had given me four weeks notice. I felt like walking out but I've got the rest of The Pirates to think about. I don't intend to stay in Blackpool I'll be returning to London when the four weeks are up."

Parnes wrote the following to Johnny dated 29th July '64
I'm going to be fair with you and give you four weeks notice to arrange alternative bookings for yourself and The Pirates.
They were sacked just three weeks before the season ended. Another promoter Bob Potter started putting a lot of work Johnnys' way and even gave the galleon backdrop' a home.

Bob Potter (Promoter)
"Johnny left the backcloth with me as he was joining my entertainment agency where I had around 15 other bands playing this country and Europe. The back-cloth hung in the Agincourt Ballroom, Camberley for many years and during this time Johnny played there many times. He also played my other venues the Atlanta Ballroom in Woking and the Palais De Dance in Aldershot. The main venue of mine he played was the Agincourt. As did many other acts of the time he also worked for me on a lot of one nighters up and down the country."

Johnny Irving (Roadie)
"The tours in those days were so different to the way they are planned now. We'd be in Cornwall and the next day we'd have to be up North. This would be like a 12 days tour and I'd be driving up ad down the country like a yo yo. I was driving a 20 hour day. Sometimes, they'd do two shows a night, jump in the motor, all the lads would sleep in the back, while I drove to the next gig. We'd often play a gig and not get paid on the night. With no money and not enough petrol in our bandwagon (a BMC 15 CWT mini bus) I'd go off on foot with my petrol can and plastic pipe to syphon some juice. One night we were stranded. I found this house with a posh car in the drive way. Just as I took off the petrol cap to insert my thirsty plastic tube. I noticed a sticker on the windscreen 'DOCTOR'. No way. I thought this is out of order. Just down the road I found a lorry parked up for the night. The driver was having a good sleep so the louder he snored the harder I sucked on the pipe and my can was soon full of petrol."

Bob Potter Entertainments
(Agency Licensed by Surrey County Council)
GT. BRITAIN AND THE CONTINENT
FOR FIRST - CLASS ENTERTAINMENT
Rock Groups, Dance Bands and Cabaret
(White and Coloured Artistes)
AMPLIFICATION SPECIALISTS
104 - 106 Mytchett Road, Nr. Aldershot, Hants.
Phone: Farnborough 2125

As a last resort Johnny's girlfriend Jean would be woken from a deep sleep with a frantic phone call from Johnny Kidd. "I'm sorry but could you bring me some money so we can buy some petrol and grub." Off Jean would drive in her Triumph to find five sorry looking rockers. Alan Wheeler sometimes travelled with the band. He saw the less spectacular side, travelling for hours on end in a BMC van.

top: 'Twist N' Shake' - Blackpool (© Jean Heath Collection)

centre: Johnny Weider joins the Crew (© Jean Heath Collection)

bottom: Bob Potter card

Alan Wheeler
"Travelling around with John and The Pirates one often bumped into other groups, musicians and singers especially in the transport cafes often the only means of eating in the twilight hours. Sometimes you would see other famous folk like TV wrestlers. It was not uncommon to bump into people like Jackie Pallo or Mick MacManus - big names in their day and sometimes wrestling in the same venue as John had just played or was about to play (you would see their names

on posters) like rock 'n' rollers. Such wrestling stars faced the same hard travelling, probably more so, as they drove themselves.

To give you an idea of the range of venues John and the boys played in those days one night it would be the plush Room At The Top in Ilford' (a private function) where they had to change in a kitchen. Then a cinema or ballroom (as opposed to a dancehall, there was a difference). Then a real grotty place like the Boathouse, Kew or a slightly larger venue like Leyton Baths where the acoustics were so bad the sound just bounced back off the walls and made things inaudible if the PA system was turned up loud. To say things were often a challenge would be an understatement.

The cinema package tours never paid much money but they afforded artists semi-luxury in allowing their sets to be seen in a good setting. Stage lighting and follow spots, 'tabs' (curtains to the layman) and stand mikes! Of course the in-house PA system was often of ancient origins and sometimes lacking but a million times better than what could be heard in most dancehalls at the time."

Bobby Graham (Drummer Joe Brown and His Bruvvers)
"With some of the poor equipment that was available in some of the dancehalls it became more important for a guitarist to have a better understanding of AC-DC than of A flat D flat."

Alan Wheeler
"Like them or loath them dance halls were the bread and butter work, the only means of earning good money outside of hit records. Most of them may have been on the lower run compared to a Granada, Odeon, Gaumont, Essoldo or ABC cinema, but they brought in the dosh!

They didn't suit everybody of course, Cliff Richard, Marty Wilde, Adam Faith, Lonnie Donegan were able to move in other realms of show business. Films, variety, pantomime, West End theatre etc. Some were protective of their image and wouldn't do them for love or money but years later could be found playing them! But for the less glamorous of performers, if I can put it in those terms like Johnny, Gene Vincent, Vince Taylor, Screaming Lord Sutch, with a more hardened image, were able to pull in the crowds and pack out the smaller venues, it was a good scene. It was worth putting up with changing in a corridor or a store room with a blanket hanging over a doorless entrance for the pay cheque or cash at the end of the evening."

No matter how bad the roads, time, distance, weather the show went on.

Roadie Johnny Irving has never forgotten trying to drive after a gig through a snow storm.
"The roads were so deep with snow we just couldn't move. We were stuck in this tiny place called Diggle not far from Huddersfield. It only had about eight houses and here we were desperate for sleep, hot food and a warm roof over our heads. Thankfully this kind lady let us stay at her home. We passed the time playing cards and eating her home made cooking. She loved to serve us raw onions in vinegar, a type of pickled onion. Pass the Diggle onions we'd cry. We left two days later full of good grub. Johnny and I would often laugh as we recalled the Diggle onions'.

Johnny Irving wasn't just an excellent driver/roadie he was a very close pal of Johnny. In fact he was the First Mate. They affectionately called him rag arse. Every line-up of Pirates thought he was just superb.

Mike West (original Pirate)
"Johnny Irving was an incredible roadie. We'd get gigs not knowing where they were. He always got us there on time, set up, everything under control.

Nick Simper (last Pirate line-up '66)
"I've seen Johnny Irving drive thousands of miles with no sleep Irvo was great."

Mick Green (Pirates 62-64)
"We were constantly gigging in ballrooms and theatres, lots of one nighters on the trot. There were hardly any motorways and the roads were rotten. To play in Liverpool you had to leave London at 4am in the morning to get set up for 6pm. It was 200 miles of bad road."

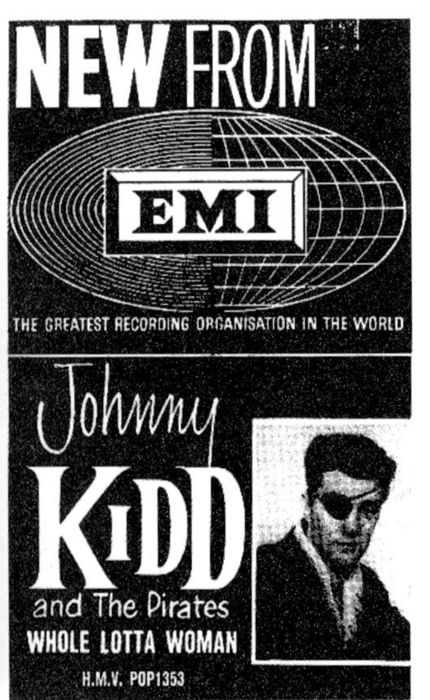

top: Roadie Irvo lets Johnny take the wheel (Spence, Kidd, Irvo) (© Sandy Regan)

bottom: Press advertisement

Johnny Irving (Roadie)
"I did some work for other stars Brenda Lee, The Ronettes (they were very nice they gave me a present as I left them at the airport), Little Eva, Big Dee Irvin, Dixie Cups, Billy J. Kramer."

Alan Wheeler
There was a cinema somewhere where everything and everyone had to go via the front entrance and through the auditorium so the artists had to arrive early so as not to upset or interfere with an act that may have begun their set. Another venue in Maidstone or thereabouts, was quite impressive looking from the outside. It was a dance hall run by the local council within a complex. Johnny had to change in a room designed for the purpose, then walk down a long corridor, down an even longer side road, round the back of the building, up a flight of iron stairs, and wait outside a door until he was announced over the PA by the MC, Phil Jay. The door was then opened and John rushed in and leapt onto stage (The Pirates had played 'My Babe' and 'Castin My Spell' prior to John's entrance)."

Lead guitarist Johnny Weider formerly of the Tony Meehan Combo was pleased to make his Pirate recording debut on the session of 'Don't Make The Same Mistake As I Did' on October 1st. He had replaced Mick Green back in July and soon proved he was a fine musician.

EMI culled 'Whole Lotta Woman' and 'Your Cheatin Heart' from the doomed album sessions and issued them as a stop-gap 45 on 30th October.

Once again Johnny wasn't given any credit. He was amongst a few British musicians performing country music. His rendition of Hank Williams 'Your Cheatin Heart' captures the emotional side of his lustrous vocals. His diamond voice of the finest cut combined with Vic Cooper's organ solo is just perfection. 'Whole Lotta Woman' was originally recorded by American Indian Marvin Rainwater who was the complete opposite of Johnny. He had crossed over from country to rockabilly.

Johnny loved American musicians. On guitar he admired James Burton (Rick Nelson band), Sonny Curtis (Crickets) and Cliff Gallup (Blue Caps). On keyboards Booker T, Ray Charles and Jerry Lee Lewis. Lewis had been amazed by the high standard of British rockers Cliff Bennett and The Kidd because back in the States Lewis was almost unchallenged.

Jerry Lee Lewis
"We kept on cutting the R 'n' R records, but nobody would play them. Boy, did they let R 'n' R down in those times. Elvis started singing like Bing Crosby. Don't get me wrong, I love Elvis, he was a great talent, but he let us down. All you could hear in the States was the name Bobby Vinton, Bobby Rydell, Bobby Darin, Bobby Vee."

Johnny's favourite vocalists were Elvis, Bo Diddley and Brenda Lee. His favourite group were The Beatles. He had a new hobby in boating. He was so keen he bought a boat and named it 'Kidnap 1' but his interest was short lived. After it sank he lost interest completely. He may have been the Admiral of British Beat but he just wasn't seaworthy.

JOHNNY ROCKS COUNTRY HIT

WHEN Marvin Rainwater scored a No. 1 hit with his self-penned "A Whole Lotta Woman," it was essentially a c-and-w number. Now HMV's Johnny Kidd and the Pirate transform it to the r-and-b idiom. A bouncy medium-fast shaker, with the boy maintaining a driving beat and organ prominent in the backing, it's totally different fron the original. But stands up to the adaptation admirably. And Johnny's in sparkling form

Another country speciality, Hank Williams' "Your Cheatin' Heart" is here handled as a big-bea ballad, with a thudding rhythm and organ again supplying an r-and-b quality.

SINGLES by DEREK JOHNSON

JOHNNY KIDD—new !

MARVIN RAINWATER—old !

above:
Press cutting

On October 31st Heinz broke from the Dixie Cups/Hollies tour to fly out to Brussels with Johnny for a special appearance on Belgian Television. Johnny now had many overseas engagements under his belt i.e. Germany, Holland, Sweden.

The crew played the Regal, Ammanford on November 6th and were supported by The Primitives. Their lead guitarist, Barry Hammett was surprised to be asked to join The Pirates for a month tour of German nightclubs starting January '65. Barry couldn't wait for the new year.

Friday November 13th, Johnny and the boys played the popular Floral Hall Morecambe and were supported by local group The Milestones, 5/6 (27 1/2p) on the door 8pm to 2am.

above: 'Kidnap 1'
(© Jean Heath Collection)

Barry Hammett (The Saints/The Primitives)
"I'll never forget November 6th 1964. We had previously played the Regal, Ammanford. The owner Denzil Price told us that Kidd was coming on the 6th. We begged him to let us play on the same bill but he made out he couldn't afford a support act with a major group. In the end we did play for just £5. I noticed their roadie Johnny Irving moving equipment about. I said to him, "We play a lot of Johnnys material. Can we perform some tonight or is it bad form?" Irving replied, "No mate, that's OK." I'd been a Johnny Kidd and Pirates fan since 1962 when our vocalist Billy Griffith first introduced me to Kidds singles. I would play their records especially with the Green, Spence, Farley crew. I'd study Mick Greens solos, I'd slow the speed from normal 45 down to 33 and 16 to get every last semi quaver. I copied this style until I sounded pretty close to him, I got pretty close as far as our band and public were concerned. There was nobody playing like that in those days. I don't think many can even now. The Pirates were a driving force, it was simplicity. There was some original element although it was simple three chord stuff. The bass lines were always very simple, always meaningful driving sparse but powerful. Same with the drums - wonderful! On guitar Mick is a legend and rightly so. Our group copied them, we changed our Shadows/Buddy Holly material for Johnny Kidds/Beatles. I used to put a banjo string for 1st, 1st on the 2nd string, 2nd on 3rd etc to get that thin clanging sound and to bend them of course. Kidd was our vocalists idol and Green was mine. They were gods to all us lads. I was just 20. So we went on as support feeling a bit nervous and it must have showed in my playing. Irving came up to me at the end and said "Ha! Mate I want a word with you, " I thought there was going to be a row, a telling off for playing so much of their material." I started to apologise, "Na, na mate come and

below: 'The Primitives'
- Barry (front left)
(courtesy of Billy Griffith)

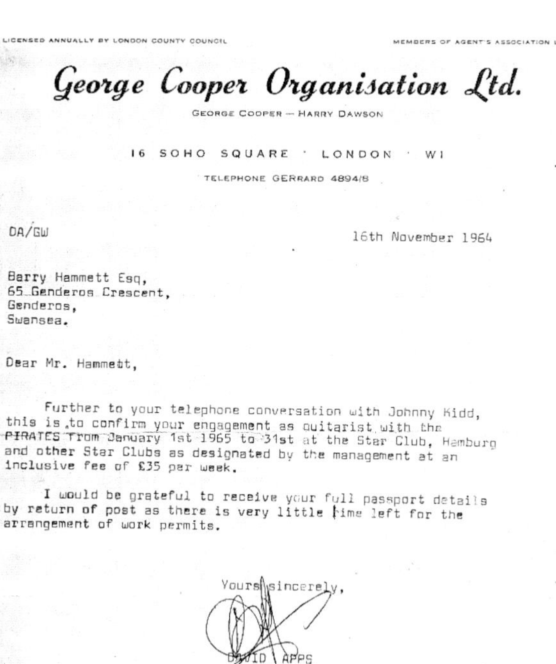

LICENSED ANNUALLY BY LONDON COUNTY COUNCIL — MEMBERS OF AGENT'S ASSOCIATION LTD

George Cooper Organisation Ltd.

GEORGE COOPER — HARRY DAWSON

16 SOHO SQUARE · LONDON · W1

TELEPHONE GERRARD 4894/8

DA/GW

16th November 1964

Barry Hammett Esq,
65 Genderos Crescent,
Genderos,
Swansea.

Dear Mr. Hammett,

Further to your telephone conversation with Johnny Kidd, this is to confirm your engagement as guitarist with the PIRATES from January 1st 1965 to 31st at the Star Club, Hamburg and other Star Clubs as designated by the management at an inclusive fee of £35 per week.

I would be grateful to receive your full passport details by return of post as there is very little time left for the arrangement of work permits.

Yours sincerely,

DAVID APPS

Barry's Old Address

ANY OFFER CONTAINED HEREIN DOES NOT CONSTITUTE A CONTRACT

ANIMALS ★ KINKS ★ BERRIES ★ TEENS ★ SHADS

Plus top pop news scoops

Sensational New Disc!
SHE UNDERSTANDS ME
JOHNNY TILLOTSON
On MGM 1252
WORLD WIDE MUSIC, 21 DENMARK ST. W.C.2
(SOLE SELLING AGENTS: GALLICO MUSIC LTD.)

new MUSICAL EXPRESS
WORLD'S LARGEST CIRCULATION OF ANY MUSIC PAPER —WEEKLY SALES EXCEED 275,000 (MEMBERS OF ABC)

NOW IN THE CHARTS!
WALK TALL
VAL DOONICAN
DECCA

WELCOME TO BRITAIN
★ BRENDA LEE ★

APPEARED ON THE ROYAL COMMAND PERFORMANCE LONDON PALLADIUM, NOV. 2nd

Recording Exclusively for BRUNSWICK

New Release November 13th
"CHRISTMAS WILL BE JUST ANOTHER LONELY DAY"
on BRUNSWICK 05921

Broadcasts:
SATURDAY CLUB NOV. 28th & DEC. 26th
EASY BEAT DEC. 6th
TOP GEAR Recording on NOV. 20th

Television:
ROYAL COMMAND PERFORMANCE NOV. 8th
BBC OPEN HOUSE NOV. 14th
THANK YOUR LUCKY STARS NOV. 28th
TOP BEAT, BBC 2 DEC. 7th

Also Recording:
THE JIMMY TARBUCK SHOW for A.T.V., NOV. 27th
READY, STEADY, GO! DEC. 11th

GEORGE COOPER ORGANISATION LTD.
★ ★ ★ ★ PROUDLY PRESENT ★ ★ ★ ★

(See local Press for times and supporting bills)

FINSBURY PARK, Astoria	—	Saturday,	November 14th
CHELMSFORD, Odeon	—	Monday,	November 16th
GUILDFORD, Odeon	—	Tuesday,	November 17th
TOOTING, Granada	—	Sunday,	November 22nd
MAIDSTONE, Granada	—	Monday,	November 23rd
BELFAST, A.B.C.	—	Wednesday,	November 25th
DUBLIN, Adelphi	—	Thursday,	November 26th
BIRMINGHAM, Town Hall	—	Monday,	November 30th
SHEFFIELD, City Hall	—	Tuesday,	December 1st
BRISTOL, Colston Hall	—	Friday,	December 4th
NORWICH, Essoldo	—	Saturday,	December 5th
WAKEFIELD, A.B.C.	—	Sunday,	December 6th
BEDFORD, Granada	—	Tuesday,	December 8th
KETTERING, Granada	—	Wednesday,	December 9th
WALTHAMSTOW, Granada	—	Thursday,	December 10th
SLOUGH, Adelphi	—	Friday,	December 11th
BLACKPOOL, Opera House	—	Saturday,	December 12th

ARTISTS SUPPORTING BRENDA LEE on dates include:
MANFRED MANN ★ BERN ELLIOTT
HEINZ ★ MARTY WILDE ★ BOB BAIN
JOHNNY KIDD ★ JOHN BARRY SEVEN
WAYNE FONTANA, Etc.

Publicity for BRENDA LEE · KEITH GOODWIN ★ British Representatives · GEORGE COOPER ORGN LTD 16 SOHO SQUARE LONDON W1 GER 4894/8

top: Barry Hammett contract (courtesy B. Hammett)

bottom: Brenda Lee tour announcement

meet the boss I think he wants to offer you a job." I started to feel faint, I was on cloud nine. I floated to the band room. There was the man himself, God, discussing with my parents and my young manager about me going to Germany as a Pirate in January '65. Here we are in rural Wales out in the sticks and there's Kidd offering me a job.l I can see him now sat dressed in white shirt, eye patch, durley curly hair, black leather trousers talking to my parents. Sadly Mick Green had already left. It would be wonderful to say I replaced Mick, but they had a very competent player in Johnny Weider, he was only seventeen, a loveable guy, tall, slim, always giggling, a heart of gold. A good player. All my boys were patting me on the back. I remember saying to the lads, 'I can't leave you. We were like a big family, but they insisted."

During November and December '64 George Cooper promoted a swinging tour starring Little Miss Dynamite Brenda Lee, supporting artists varied Johnny and The Pirates, Marty Wilde, Manfred Mann, Bern Elliot, John Barry Seven, Wayne Fontana, Heinz and The Wildboys with compere Bob Bain.

Tour Dates - November

Finsbury Park Astoria	Sat 14th
Chelmsford Odeon	Mon 16th
Guildford Odeon	Tues 17th
Tooting Granada	Sun 22nd
Maidstone Granada	Mon 23rd
Belfast A.B.C.	Wed 25th
Dublin Adelphi	Thurs 26th
Birmingham Town Hall	Mon 30th

December

Sheffield City Hall	Tues 1st
Bristol Colston Hall	Fri 4th
Norwich Essoldo	Sat 5th
Wakefield ABC	Sun 6th
Bedford Granada	Tues 8th
Kettering Granada	Wed 9th
Walthamstow Granada	Thurs 10th
Slough Adelphi	Fri 11th
Blackpool Opera House	Sat 12th

At the Chelmsford Odeon Alan Wheeler spoke briefly to Brenda Lee in the wings.

"Brenda was greatly impressed by John and The Pirates (which now included John Weider) (lead) and Vic Cooper (organist) and reckoned that they would do well in America. She also had a high regard for Marty Wilde who had the Johnny Barry Seven backing him on that tour and the guitar wizardry of Ritchie Blackmore (Wildboys) working with Heinz. Brenda had a good group backing her The Bobby Patrick Big Six as I recall."

Tour poster - Odeon Chelmsford (courtesy Brian Woods)

Brenda Lee
"My fondest memory of my British Tour was watching Johnny Kidd from the side of the stage. He was great."

The Wildboys were Heinz's' backing group, they featured a fine band of musicians Ritchie Blackmore (lead), Dave Adams (organ), Ian Broad (drums) and Brian Woods (bass).

Brian Woods (Wildboys)
"Johnny didn't play the whole tour, they only played odd dates. I never spoke much to him. Heinz being a fellow front line man spent more time with him. I and the other lads would mostly be talking to The Pirates about our musical instruments, swapping ideas etc. Brenda Lee was fab. I can see whey they named her Little Miss Dynamite. As small as she is she uses the stage to full. Her voice is very powerful for a wee one mind you they say there are good things in small parcels. She was only about 5' 2". Her husband was 6' 4" plus so we did not approach her too often.
One evening in the digs, for no reason at all, our guitarist Ritchie went almost made. He picked up an axe and was going to chop our heads off. Ritchie has got a very quick temper so you had to be careful what you said to him. As a guitarist he is one of the all times greats. I enjoyed every minute of those days because of the excitement of it all, and, of course, Johnny made it that way for us. They had a very tight fitting sound and were very respected on the rock scene. We toured with Johnny on quite a few occasions.
Brenda Lee was only 19 years old, a little, brown haired, freckled faced girl, yet she was so confident. Apart from her love of singing, her major interest in life was history.
Brenda Lee
"I tried to see as many old castles as I possibly could. Although I didn't actually attend school. I had a tutor on most of my tours. I was then still a high school junior. History, I was just crazy about that."

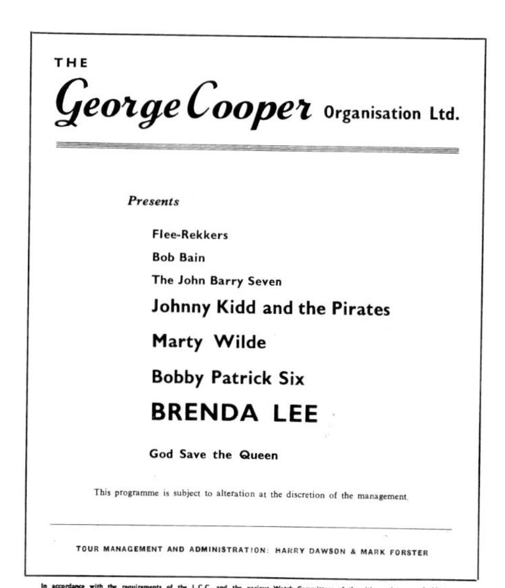
THE
George Cooper Organisation Ltd.

Presents

Flee-Rekkers
Bob Bain
The John Barry Seven
Johnny Kidd and the Pirates
Marty Wilde
Bobby Patrick Six
BRENDA LEE

God Save the Queen

This programme is subject to alteration at the discretion of the management.

TOUR MANAGEMENT AND ADMINISTRATION: HARRY DAWSON & MARK FORSTER

In accordance with the requirements of the L.C.C. and the various Watch Committees of the cities and towns of this tour:
1 The public may leave at the end of the performance by all exit doors and such doors must at that time be open. 2 All gangways, passages and staircases must be kept entirely free from chairs or any other obstructions. 3 Persons shall not in any circumstances be permitted to stand or sit in any of the gangways intersecting the seating or to sit in any of the other gangways. If standing be permitted in the gangways at the sides and rear of the seating, it shall be strictly limited to the number indicated in the notices exhibited in those positions. 4 The safety curtain (where applicable) must be lowered and raised in the presence of each audience. 5 No smoking shall be allowed to take place on the stage except as part of a performance or entertainment.

★ *Get your favourites to autograph their pictures* ★

Programme Line-Up (Always N' Ever Archive)

Another hardworking year, sadly no LP release, but Johnny was thrilled to have an EP released in France featuring 'Shakin', 'Whole Lotta Woman', 'Shop Around', 'Restless' on EP EGF813.

The following extract from the Reading Standard (18th Dec '64) give an excellent insight into the effect Johnny had on his many female fans. She rushed into our Wokingham Office. Her face was flushed, she screamed, "You will never guess who I met on Sunday, Johnny Kidd!" "Yes, really, he's lovely." The typical fan. She had met a favourite pop star. She would be living on the experience for weeks. "He gave me a lock of his hair, " she displayed a little tuft of black hair. She showed her other prizes, a butt of the cigarette Johnny Kidd had put out before her very eyes, an eye patch he had worn on stage during his performance, an autograph which filled a whole page of her book. The fan, Carol Collins (16) of 66 Greenwood Road, Crowthorne described how she had met the star during performances at Camberley on Sunday night.

"We were just writing our names on the groups van by the stage door. I had written, Carol loves John' in large letters on the side of it when this flashy white sports car drove into the courtyard. Then this chap got out. It was Johnny. The fabulous Johnny talked to Carol and her friend. After the performance he invited us back stage. Then he talked to us again. I thought he was a rocker with black greasy hair before I met him, but he is not, he's lovely."

Hundreds of screaming stomping teenagers danced the night away on Dec 19th at the first phase of Bolton's Press Ball at the Palais de Danse. The crew were proud to be guest artists for this special event to raise money for the Widow and Orphan fund of the National Union of Journalists. Also on the bill were The Peddlers, The Invictors, Les Moss Orchestra and Carl Ward Group. A last minute disappointment came in the shape of a news flash that pretty Sandra Gough, who played Irma Ogden in ITV's Coronation Street could not appear because of illness. But this was offset by the arrival of Bolton's Mike Haslam making his first home town appearance since signing a contract with Beatles manager Brian Epstein.
December saw the release of 'Ecstasy'/'A Shot Of Rhythm And Blues', Philips BF 1385 by Lee Curtis and the All Stars. 'Ecstasy' was originally recorded for the German market and was record of the week on Radio Caroline. A year earlier in December '63 two other great Mersey groups Rory Storm and The Hurricanes released 'Dr Feelgood'/'I Can Tell', Oriole 45 CB1858, and Kingsize Taylor and The Dominoes released 'Whole Lotta Lovin'/'I Can Tell' (as the Shakers), Polydor NH 52-272. In March '64 Taylor released 'Hippy Hippy Shake'/'Dr Feelgood', Polydor NH66-991.

Barry Hammett (Pirates Lead Jan-Feb '65)
"During December I was summoned to London to get a visa. I went up three times, the first two times Johnny never turned up. The third time he turned up drunk. I was told to change my guitar. I was pleased to get a Telecaster. Kidd took me back to his South Harrow home. I met his future wife Jean. They had a really nice, posh home. I stayed for a couple of days. The lads took me to Carnaby Street to get my stage gear, all on Johnny's account. I got two pairs of trousers, waistcoats, shirts, boots. On December 24th I got a telegram from Heinz' lead guitarist a guy called Richard. His

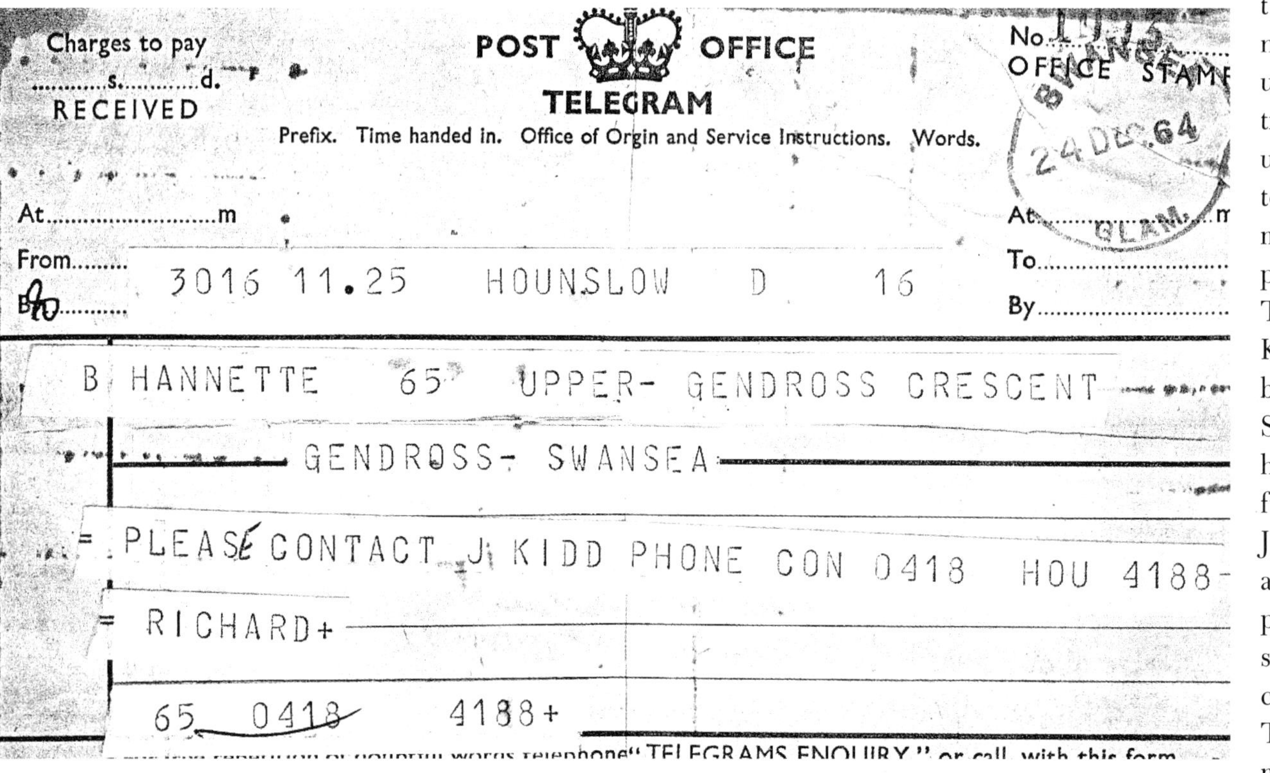
Charges to pay
..........s...........d.
RECEIVED

POST OFFICE
TELEGRAM

Prefix. Time handed in. Office of Orgin and Service Instructions. Words.

No.
OFFICE STAMP
24 DEC 64

At..........m

At..........m

From.........

3016 11.25 HOUNSLOW D 16

To.........
By.........

B HANNETTE 65 UPPER- GENDROSS CRESCENT
GENDROSS- SWANSEA
= PLEASE CONTACT J KIDD PHONE CON 0418 HOU 4188-
= RICHARD+
65 0418 4188+

telephone "TELEGRAMS ENQUIRY" or call with this form

Telegram for Barry
(courtesy B. Hammett)

wife was living in Germany and he wanted me to swap and back Heinz. I wouldn't swap for anything. This was a dream come true. We flew out on a Comet on December 30th. I'd never flown before let alone playing with a top band. Organist Vic Cooper was terrified of flying. I ate his breakfast because he couldn't face it. As we landed we could see snow on the ground. As we jumped in a taxi the boys were boasting about their previous visits. I was shocked to find that my Telecaster had got broken on the flight. I had no insurance. What a bad start to my Pirate debut!"

Charges to pay
s. d.
RECEIVED

POST OFFICE
TELEGRAM

No.
OFFICE STAMP

Prefix. Time handed in. Office of Origin and Service Instructions. Words.

At m
From
By 144 11.36 CONCORD HA 12 =

At m
To
By

BARRY HAMMET 65 UPPER-GENDROS CRESCENT
SWANSEA =

TELEPHONE EARLIEST CON= JOHNNY KIDD +

HAMMET 65 CON REPT CON+ TS 701

For free repetition of doubtful words telephone "TELEGRAMS ENQUIRY" or call, with this form, at office of delivery. Other enquiries should be accompanied by this form and, if possible, the envelope B or C

Telegram to Barry from Johnny
(courtesy B. Hammett)

14. GOTTA TRAVEL ON

This shipmates New Year Voyage harboured in Germany from January 1st - 31st. Guitarist Barry Hammett was enlisted for this short tour.

Barry Hammett (Pirates, Lead)
"We got to the Hotel Pacific in Hamburg. It was full of bands. Frank Farley and Vic Cooper took me under their wing, they were kind. I will never forget that. I've got a lot to thank them for. I didn't see a lot of Kidd until the gig and then after we all went partying together.

Barry with the Kidd (Bielefeld Star Club) (courtesy of B. Hammett)

Germany was a weird place. After our shows I'd have a couple of beers, see a strip show, nothing much else. All this talk of drugs, I've never taken drugs in my life and I don't recall the boys either. We played all the Star Clubs in Germany i.e. Hamburg (mostly), Bielefeld, Keil, about seven cities. We travelled in two cars, a Mercedes 190 and Citroen DS19. Kidd travelled in a separate car. We'd start about 10pm after the gig we'd travel through the night and sleep all day. We missed a few gigs - Kidd had to fly home to England due to family problems. Of the 4 1/2 weeks, I spent two weeks feeling very ill, I got bronchitis. I was so upset about my broken guitar. I had to borrow various guitars i.e. Fat Gibson Jazz, Hofner etc. They were all wrong for the job. Vic didn't take his organ, he relied on a piano being in the clubs.

The promoters complained about the act not using an organ, Kidd not bringing his cutless etc. I never rehearsed a single note with them. I knew all the records but, of course, they performed them differently on stage. The Pirates liked to do some instrumentals but I didn't know them. I was so upset about my broken guitar and Johnny Weider (Nutty) being flown over but being only 17 years old he could only stay for two days. The Pirates were not happy about the material. I was amazed when Kidd told me his favourite singer was Dean Martin and that he had turned down some songs written by the early Beatles. There were starting to be cracks in the band. The writing seemed to be on the wall. There was talk about leaving the Kidd. I just couldn't understand it, they were working for God. Kidd loved to have a giant 3ft Teddy Bear on stage. It had been given to him by a mentally retarded fan. One roughneck tried to jump on the stage and swipe the bear. Johnny caught him with the toe of his boot under the chin and knocked the swine senseless. I recall after a session ringing out my soaked shirt. Wherever we went restaurants, bars, bistros there was always a Jimmy Smith record playing. I bought a Jimmy Smith record so it would always remind me of the days in Hamburg with Johnny and The Pirates. I suppose Kidd was my mates' hero, mine was Mick Green, but of course it was great to work for his boss. I will never forget it. Some of the glamour rubbed off. Its something I'll always be grateful for." Being only seventeen years old Johnny Weider couldn't play the whole tour because no one under eighteen was allowed into the St Pauli area after 10 o'clock at night. The St Pauli area was the main place for clubs in Hamburg just off the notorious Reeperbahn. As soon as ten o'clock struck police patrols would raid all the clubs looking for young musicians and patrons. They would demand to see passports and identity papers. Every German carried an identity card which included birth date and photos. The patrols were called the Ausweis. This is why Barry Hammett was booked for the tour.

As one of the veterans of the British Beat scene Johnny spoke out about the lack of characters in the business at the beginning of '65.

Johnny Kidd
"When beat was first introduced to TV the producers really pulled out all the stops. All the acts were live and the business was better because of this. I owe everything to those early days. Up and coming stars were drilled and nine times out of ten the coaching served them well in later years. Cliff Richard, Adam Faith and others have all felt the benefit. Today... well make a disc, mime it and you're a STAR."

The BBC started broadcasting a unique TV series, a collection of documentary type plays under the slot of The Wednesday Play. Two of the best and most controversial were 'Cathy Come Home' and 'Up The Junction'. Both starred the young Carol White under the direction of the illustrious Ken Loach. Leading groups of the day were featured on the soundtrack of 'Up The Junction' e.g. The Searchers version of 'Hungry For Love' and 'Ecstasy' by Johnny Kidd and Pirates. A tale of three girls out for a good time in Clapham Junction South London. Its bad language and realism caused uproar.

During the first week of Feb, Johnny was not surprised to hear news of his ole drummer Clem Cattini walking out of The Tornados. Clem had been a founder member since 1961 and had got fed up with good musicians leaving the fold i.e. Brian Gregg (1963), Alan Caddy (1964) etc. Caddy, in fact, joined up with fellow Tornado, George Bellamy and vocalist Don Charles and ran the Sound Venture Studios in Highbury, North London. Alan cut a single called 'Work Out'/'Tornado' HMV POP1286. Come April Clem was back on the road with 'Division Two' backing The Ivy League.

HOTEL PACIFIC
30-31 NEUER PFERDEMARKT
HAMBURG 6
GERMANY
Jan 13th

Dear Bill
How is the group making out without the fabulous me. Hows the bookings hope you've got plenty, we are playing every night of the week. Tonight we are not playing, this is our own choice because J. Kidd has gone back to London to sort out some family trouble. He was crying his eyes out on stage when we (the pirates only) were playing last night. I sorry to tell you, I cannot bring back any pirate gear because I'm using Mick Green's stuff and so was Nutty, his other lead guitarist. I suppose you'd like to know something about J. Kidd & the pirates well first of all the boots they wear are specially made and cost more than £20 per pair and everything else is specially made. Johnny (Ollyburn/ Spencer has his Pirate clothes made for him by his wife. Frank is married also, to a German girl he met in Hamburg 3 years ago and has an 8 month old daughter. Frank speaks very slowly, is rather shy and self concious

Barry wrote to Bill Griffith, 13/1/65 (courtesy B. Griffith)

The original members of The Tornados tried to release a single 'Gemini'/'Pandora's Box' written by Alan Caddy but producer Joe Meek had the name Tornados under copyright and threatened to sue so the single stayed in the can. American group The Ventures released their version in 1968 'Flights of Fantasy'/'Pandoras Box', LBF 15075.

The sea-rovers were trying to find a new sound. More soulful material was being tried out. 'The World Is Round', 'Shotgun', 'The Whole World is Shakin', 'Out of Sight', 'Can't Turn You Loose'.

Raye Du-Val (Drummer Checkmates)
"Johnny was always experimenting with new tunes and lyrics and even thought of adding sax and piano to the '65 line-up."

If sax had been used Johnnys first choice would probably have been Pete Newman his old mate from The Freddie Heath Band. But during this period Pete was busy with Felders Orioles a sextet playing a blend of Jazz, R&B and soul. Originally called the Beat Society members included Peter (tenor sax), Barry Heiband (vocals), Paul Hodson (guitar), Rod Mealston (baritone sax), Mike O'Brien (bass) and John Halsey (drums). They recorded four singles for Piccadilly but never had a hit. By early '67 they had broken up. Drummer John Halsey later kept time for Timebox.

On February the 5th/11th/15th Johnny Weider made his second Pirate recording on the sessions of Jewel Akins 'The Birds and The Bees'. The 16th was Johnny's debut as a soul singer on Otis Reddings 'I Can't Turn You Loose'. Sadly this brave change of direction was to remain unreleased until 1983. 'The Birds and The Bees'/'Don't Make The Same Mistake As I Did', were released Feb 19th. Such haste did not result in a hit.

During February/March Johnny and the crew played a few gigs in South Wales. The popular Welsh group The Eyes of Blue supported them at Morriston on February 28th.

JOHNNY KIDD

JOHNNY KIDD

The Birds And The Bees; Don't Make The Same Mistake As I Did (HMV Pop 1397).

WE TACKLED the Jewel Akens' American hit last week and thought it was good enough for the charts. Now comes Johnny Kidd—and his chances on this catchy, blues-orientated number must be at least as strong. We hope so. Good group sound going, with plenty of fire in the lyrics. A foot-tapper, with more than average appeal. Flip is a fair-enough beat-ballad, sung well, but if it'd been the top side it probably would have got lost.

TOP FIFTY TIP

Record review

Barry Hammett (Ex-Pirate)
"I saw them working in Merthyr Tydfil. It was magic. Kidd and the boys often stayed at my mums home in Swansea. They'd often play cards all night and drink tea. Frank Farley stayed good friends with the family."

They played at the grand opening of Swansea's newest club The Rhythm 'n' Blues. About 300 people turned up. Promoter Martin Life was a very happy man.

On the 11th March the crew along with Heinz, Dilys Watling, The Hifis and Dodie West appeared on a special BBC Off The Record Show at the Daily Mail Ideal Home Exhibition. The previous Saturday they had played Morley Town Hall.

Thanks to Teen Entertainment local fans had the chance of seeing Johnny and his Pirates at Morley Town Hall. As usual they were all dressed in their appropriate attire. Johnny in his black leather skin tight jeans, above knee-length boots and frilly shirt and, of course, eye patch. The Pirates wore ordinary jeans with various styles of shirts, general loose fitting with hoops. Johnny was interviewed backstage for the Batley News and asked why unlike other groups they didn't just wear conventional clothes.
"I have gone through all kinds of changes but I'm still getting bookings. If the group and I dropped our outfits, it would be like starting over again. We once thought of changing to suits but it was not practicable. It just did not go with our names. At least now we are something different. We are original. We still have plenty of life left. I'm a little older than Cliff Richard and a bit younger than Gene Vincent."

On March 28th they played Bob Potters popular Agincourt Ballroom, Camberley followed by the Spa Ballroom (Yorkshire) with The Tennesseeans.

(© Jean Heath Collection)

Disc Weekly reported that the Pirates were due to record a number written by The Zombies entitled 'Somebody Help Me' but nothing was ever released.

A quick trip was arranged for Germany during April.

Ernst August Cordes (Fan)
"I saw Johnny and The Pirates at the Schuetzenhof dance hall in Wilhelmshaven during a Sunday afternoon. They were top of the bill. I first heard Johnny on Radio Luxemburg and the British Forces Network especially live on Brian Matthews' Saturday Club."

April '65 was an upsetting period in his life, Johnny divorced his wife Ada after nine years of marriage. They had two sons Tony and Russell. Johnny was ordered to pay costs.

On April 10th they were back at sea on The Central Pier Morecambe from 8pm - 2am 6/- (30p) on the door.

left: Vic Cooper organist (far right) (© Ernst August Cordes)

right: Johnny Weider and Kidd (Schetzenhof Hall) (© Ernst August Cordes)

Johnny's Blackpool club The Picador was becoming a popular place with musicians. Photos of Johnny and The Pirates were displayed down the stairway.

Mike Rudzinski (The Avengers)
"I went to the club a few times. There was a huge coloured cardboard cut out of Johnny in full pirate gear with raised cutless."

Sandy Hill (Friend)
"The Picador was near Blackpool Railway Station and a rather a sleazy sort of place but as these places go was full of character and intrigue (just like Johnny). The place was dark, disco, strippers, the usual thing."

Johnny bowed out of the club scene after only 18 months. The 24th April saw organist Vic Cooper make his TV debut on the popular children's Rediffusion show Five O'clock Club. The kids were soon boppin along with compere Stubby Kaye to Johnny and The Pirates latest single 'The Birds And The Bees'. Little Frankie was the other guest star. The girl with laughter in her voice the late Alma Cogan recorded a fine cover of 'The Birds And The Bees' with the exact same arrangement as Johnny's version. This was hardly surprising because her producer was Walter Ridley.

On the very rare occasion of having a day off Johnny loved to have a chat at Jim Marshalls shop at 76 Uxbridge Road, Hanwell W7. This was a very popular shop selling all the groups needs, guitars, strings, mikes, echo boxes, drums and amplifiers. On a Saturday morning the place was jam packed with the likes of The Who, Flee-Rekkers, Screaming Lord Sutch and The Savages, Buddy Britten and The Regents, Mike Dee and The Jaywalkers, The Eyes etc.

Johnny and The Pirates would meet up and chat over coffee with all the local bands. Jim Marshall was the man behind the legendary Marshall amplifier. He actually started out as a drummer during the forties. He went on to teach many great drummers in the 50's and 60's, including Micky Waller, Mitch Mitchell and even Brian Saunders of the Freddie Heath Group.

Marshall first opened a music shop in 1958 specialising in drums. Many of his former students brought in their groups and were soon asking Marshall to stock guitars and amplifiers. He started to sell and repair many American and British gear and amps. Many bassists were unhappy with the sound they were getting so he designed a compact 18" bass speaker cabinet. In 1962 he teamed up with Ken Bran and started designing a prototype 50 watt lead amplifier in consultation with guitarists like Big

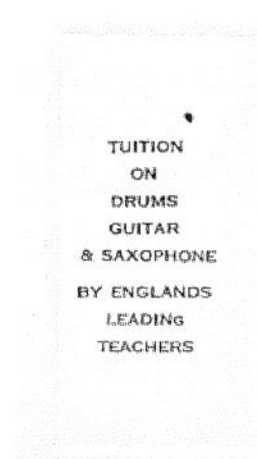
TUITION
ON
DRUMS
GUITAR
& SAXOPHONE
BY ENGLANDS
LEADING
TEACHERS

JMS
Jim Marshall & Son
MUSICAL INSTRUMENTS
EAL 1325
76 UXBRIDGE ROAD
HANWELL W.7

Business card - Jim Marshall & Son

Jim Sullivan and Pete Townsend. The very first Marshall amplifier, the MK1, was issued in the Autumn of 1962 and met with instant acceptance from young British musicians looking for a big rich tonality sound with smooth distortion. The 50 watt lead amps 4 x 12 Celestion equipped speaker cabinets became the dominant power behind most of the leading sixties groups. The forerunner of the pioneering Marshall stack concept. Marshall became distributed worldwide and was soon being used by famous musicians all over the globe. Ritchie Blackmore whose desire to be LOUD played a part in the addition of the 200 watt amp. The Who, Cream and Jimi Hendrix all helped Marshall get worldwide acceptance. Jimi Hendrix was introduced to Marshall by Mitch Mitchell who also worked in Marshalls shop. Hendrix was surprised to learn that they shared the same name (Jimi was born James Marshall Hendrix).

Unknown to Johnny his material was being recorded all over the world during 1965. Australian Normie Rowe and The Playboys cut a version of Shakin All Over on Sunshine 45 QK1103 it made No 1 in the OZ hit parade. Normie also issued a longer version on his album 'It Ain't Necessarily So' Sunshine QL31, 734. Another Aussie group Billy Thorpe and The Aztecs recorded 'I'll Never Get Over You' on their first LP on Parlophone PMCO 7525.

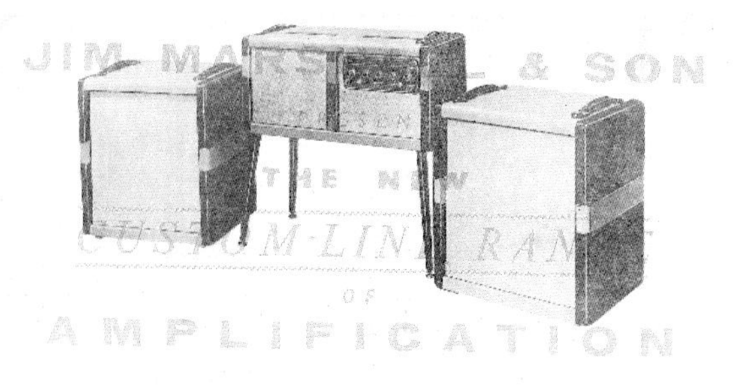

Leaflet - Jim Marshall & Son

American surfin group The Surfaris cut 'Shakin' for their vocal album 'It Ain't Me Babe' (MCA CORAL). Cambridge group The Phantoms released 'Shakin'/'Twilight Time' on Nashville N5803. Another British group The Eyes also recorded 'Shakin'.

Barry Allchin (Bass, The Eyes)
"I first saw Johnny Kidd at the Greenford Granada in Oct 1963. I was a great fan. I still am. George Cooper and his organisation were The Eyes' agents. It was my idea to record 'Shakin' All Over' as it was always a good dance number. We descended upon Rayrik Sound Studios in Central London to record a demo disc. Four tracks were recorded 'When the Night Falls', 'The Immediate Pleasure', I'm Rowed Out', and 'Shakin'. (Released in 1985 by Bam Caruso 'Scene But Not Heard' MARI 038). It is crap!! These were very early demos from '65 and should never have been released. Try to obtain our 'Blink' LP - 100% better!"

Johnny did hear news that Canadian group 'The Guess Who' were going to release 'Shakin All Over' Scepter 1295/'Till We Kissed' so he quickly decided to re-record his classic on the 20th April. 'Shakin All Over' (65) coupled with the traditional 'Gotta Travel On' was rushed released on May 7th. Two other tracks were tried out on May 25th 'Bad Case Of Love' and 'You Can Have Her' but never really completed. They were released in Sept '92.

Australian band 'The Missing Links' recorded a one sided demo on Alberts of 'Shakin'. It was released years later in 1980 on the compilation album Alberts Archives EMI APLP037.

Also released was a fine version by Ray Columbus and The Invaders on Zodiac EP in New Zealand.

Johnny Weider had now settled down on lead guitar. He was a very talented musician who had mastered guitar, violin, organ and piano. Born April 21st 1947 in Shepherds Bush, London he loved music from a young age. He made his first public appearance at the Festival Hall, London playing violin at the tender age of 9.

John Weider (Lead Guitarist, Pirates)
"One of the first bands I played in was The Moments with Steve Marriott, Jimmy Winston and Kenny Rowe. (Jimmy Winston and Steve Marriott later formed the Small Faces. Kenny Rowe joined the underrated Capability Brown). Before that I was doing a lot of session work with various people like Brenda Lee and all the people of that time plus I did a thing for The Stones once on 'Not Fade Away' playing one of the two rhythm guitars. Also a lot of the time I was doing residences in night-clubs. I did a thing at the Tottenham Royal for about six months, then I did a years residency at the Van Gogh Bar in Piccadilly with a trio, playing old standards and sort of schmaltzy jazz. I did a couple of stints like that which at the time were paying really good money. I was playing guitar then and a little bit of bass. It was called the Eddie Richardo Trio and he was the accordion player, I was the guitarist and there was a drummer. We actually made a couple of records under that name for Parlophone or something.

I played with Johnny's Pirates, but I can't really remember which year it was. We did record 'Birds And The Bees', 'Gotta Travel On' and the revised version of 'Shakin All Over '65.'"

'Gotta Travel On' had previously been a huge hit for American C&W guitarist turned vocalist Billy Grammer in 1958 on Monument 400. It sold a million. It was released in Britain on the London American Series 45HLU8752. This is how the song came to Johnny's attention. Sadly the Kidd's version didn't sell very well.

Weider had taught himself the guitar at 13 and left the Christopher Wren School, Shepherds Bush to go straight into the world of pop. He started learning the violin at the Royal College of Music at the tender age of seven. He passed all his exams and left the college by the time he was 12. At 14 he played with a group called The Canons, at 15 he played with the Laurie Jay Combo and at 16 he was playing the lead guitar with Jet Harris and Tony Meehan.

Johnny Weider
"I chose the pop world because there was more money in it and a bigger future. I played on Jet and Tony's hit Diamonds."

For his 16th birthday his father gave him a £500 guitar. He only used it to practise on. He wouldn't dare use it on stage because it was gold plated. He later joined The Wild Ones and at 17 signed up to be a Pirate. While with The Moments, they released a version of the Kinks 'You Really Got Me' on World Artists 1032 for the American market only. This very rare single only sold a few, it features the unique vocals of a young Steve Marriott.

(© Jean Heath Collection)

Former Pirate Johnny Patto was now playing lead for The Frays. During May '65 they released a bluesy medium paced number entitled 'Walk On' Decca F12153. Another ex Pirate, Ken McKay, (drums) was now playing bass for The Muldons with Chris Brough (piano) son of ventriloquist Peter Brough, Jim Cregan (guitar vocals), Andy Steele (drums). They released a debut single on the 21st May 'I'm Lost Without You'.

Their managers were John and Malcolm Jackson sons of show business personality Jack Jackson. Cregan later played for Julian Coway and The Machine, Blossom Toes, Stud and Family. Andy Steele had recently left the brilliant, but underrated, Gary Farr and The T-Bones.

Alan Wheeler

(© Jean Heath Collection)

"It was not usual for John to go to parties in his Pirate garb but I can remember two instances. He went for a promotion spot on the EMI SPECTACULAR and having donned the gear to appear before a tiny audience at E.M.I. House, Manchester Square, W1, where the Radio Luxemburg show was either broadcasting 'live' or bring recorded. John went straight off to some party afterwards without changing back into civvies. Another time was, after guesting on the BBC radio show Easy Beat he went off in his Pirate outfit with his agent George Cooper and his wife to a party somewhere."

The 27th May saw Johnny on E.M.I.'s spectacular Friday night Radio Show, Luxemburg Show promoting 'Shakin All Over 65' along with The Tornados ('Early Bird') Faye Fisher ('Our Love'), Little Frankie ('Make Love'), Harbour Lites ('Come Back Silly Girl'), Hollies ('I'm Alive'), Four Tops ('I Can't Help Myself'). The following night the crew had Torquay's teenagers shakin' and boppin' at The 400 Ballroom.

Early in July they were supported by The Cygnets at the Coronation Ballroom, Ramsgate. On the 31st they played on the Isle of Wight supported by the young David Bowie.

WINTER GARDENS
VENTNOR
Saturday, July 31st
JOHNNY KIDD
and the PIRATES
plus DAVY JONES and the LOWER THIRD
and NEIL ANDERSEN
Late Coaches to and from Cowes, Ryde, Newport
8 - 11-30 Fully Licensed Admission 7/6
Next Saturday: THE PRETTY THINGS!!

WALDBÜHNE
Sonnabend, den 14. August, 16 und 20 Uhr
Dieter Behlinda presents:
DIE SHOW DES JAHRES!
THE KINKS
mit ihrem Hit „You really got me"
PRETTY THINGS
JOHNNY KIDD
and the Pirates
mit „Birds and the Bees"
SCREAMING LORD SUTCH
and his Seven Savages
(Der wildeste Mann der Welt)
THE FORTUNES
mit ihrem Hit „You've got your troubles"
CHERRY ROLAND
DICK SCOTT
THE BOOTS
Vorverkauf an allen Theaterkassen und Liverpool-Hoop am Nollendorfplatz täglich von 17–24 Uhr. Einheitspreis 5,- DM, an der Abendkasse der Waldbühne 6,– DM
Gastspieldirektion Behlinda

above and right: Press advertisements

They met up with their pal Screaming Lord Sutch on Saturday August 14th at the Waldbuke Club in Germany along with The Kinks, Pretty Things, The Fortunes, Cherry Roland, Dick Scott, The Boots.

On returning to England. Johnny was handed two cathy outright pop numbers, one composed by Mr 'How Do You Do It' Mitch Murray, entitled 'I Hate Getting Up In The Morning' and a superb Greenaway/Cook classic 'This Golden Ring'. Both were recorded on Friday September 10th but withheld. The lads were very disappointed (the two tracks weren't released until 1983).

Morale in the crew was at an all time low.

Johnny Weider (Lead Guitarist)

"We did some shows at Blackpool and I left after that because it sort of did me in On the bill with us were Heinz, Tornados and Lord Sutch. I joined Eric Burdon and The Animals in 1966, in '69 I replaced Ric Grech in Family when he left to form Blind Faith."

During June '71 Weider joined Stud and in '74 was working with Nicky James. The Pirates new lead guitarist was Jon Morshead.

The Palace Ballroom Douglas, Isle of Man lined up a star line-up of groups every Thursday throughout the summer of '65. The Tornados, Hermans Hermits, Cliff Bennett, Dave Berry, Wayne Fontana, Animals, Ivy League, etc etc. Johnny and The Pirates raided the Palace on June 25th. A capacity crowd danced at the Winter Gardens Pavilion, Weston-Super-Mare on Saturday July 3rd to the pop pirates along with The Krestas and house band led by Ken Birch.

For a short period John Weider replaced Eric Clapton in John Mayall's Bluesbreakers. Eric played his last date for Mayall on August 30th '65 at the Black Prince, Bexley.

While appearing at the Civic Hall, Barnsley Alan Collins the guitarist with local group Little Midge and The Kritios presented an oil painting of Johnny and The Pirates to a surprised Johnny. (Jean Heath still has this proudly on display in her home).

At the Star Ballroom, Maidstone the crew backed an unknown local singer, 19 year old Diane Hannan. "My friends used to dare me to get up and sing - and so I did with The Pirates, Bruvvers, Outlaws." The experience must have helped because Diane won the Search For A Singer competition in July '65.

The Hollies had always been keen fans of Johnny and during September '65 they told the New Musical Express that they had written a song for Kidd.

Tony Hicks (Lead Guitarist)
"We have this song which we are sure would be right for Johnny. It could bring him back to the charts. I wonder if he would contact us."

Their drummer Bobby Elliot told the paper that his rave singers were Dakota Staton and Johnny Kidd.

The crew in Mid September was now Frank Farley (drums), Johnny Spence (bass), Vic Cooper (organ) and new boy Jon Morshed (lead).

Jim Evans of Lord Sutchs' Savages sat in for Big Frank Farley for a couple of gigs. Jim was a very competent drummer he was one of a rare breed (he could read music). He had played with Harry Gold and his Pieces of Eight, an old dance band prior to his Savages days. He, in fact, gave lessons to various young percussionists including Peter Jay, leader of the Jaywalkers.

Thursday October 14th back on the Isle of Wight at the Ryde Castle Hotel.

Keith Roberts
"I played in the support band, we spent the whole day with Johnny, Spence, Farley, Morshed and Vic Cooper and struck up quite a friendship with them."
Having such a first-class roadie in Johnny Irving they nearly always made their gigs on time but one very rare non appearance nearly got them sued. Between 350 and 400 fans at the Market Hall, Abertillery demanded part of their money back when the band failed to appear.
William Williams (Manager)
"I had no idea where they were. Johnny Kidd rang an agent at five o'clock and said he was having trouble with his van but would definitely arrive. He didn't I just didn't believe any yarn about

breaking down. I was so mad I went to my solicitor about suing him."

Johnny Kidd
"We had a breakdown on Thursday night. We toured London looking for new parts and spent the night in a Camberley garage while the van was being repaired. The work was unsuccessful and we tried to cancel the show but were told we must appear. After great difficulty I borrowed a van on Friday evening and we got as far as Slough but turned back because we had no chance of reaching Abertillery until the early hours of Saturday morning. I feel really bad about this but I really did my best. I have a record for getting to places early. I might now give a free show."

The group would have been paid £90 for two thirty minute spots. Extra stewards had been engaged, an extra bus laid on and extensive publicity arranged throughout the valley. Although the fans were disappointed they enjoyed The Sultans from Brynmawr and The Hitchhikers of Ebbw Vale.

Throughout December Johnny was pleased to help his mate Joe Brown. Joe had secretly bought his mother a house in Woodbury Close, Wanstead. So with the help of Johnny, The Bruvvers, Vince Eager, Marty Wilde, Tornados and Manager George Cooper they secretly furnished the place.

French magazine advertisement (courtesy Phil Guidal)

The lateMrs Norah Brown (Joe's Mother)
"I was invited to the home of George Cooper while all the moving was going on. I was entertained by Johnny and Vince Eager. I remember Johnny lifting his patch from his eye to wink at Vince. I didn't know what was happening. When I was taken to my new home. I was presented with house-warming gifts from all the pop star friends. For the rest of my life I will never forget the kindness of all the boys I have met in show business. They were wonderful."

15. THE DAY THE WORLD TURNED BLUE

1966 kicked off with a short tour of Germany, back home on Wednesday 19th. The J Club Leominster was soon shakin.

Johnny Kidd
"I flew back to England for two reasons, one to get married and two to make a new record. 'It's Got To Be You' which is written by a girl group from Liverpool called The Liverbirds."

Johnny gave notice at Caxton Hall on the 11th February that he was going to marry Jean Yvonne (Complin) Heath of Rampayne Street, Westminister.

above: Johnny was admired by many German musicians (© Jean Heath Collection)

Johnny Kidd
"I met Jean on a blind date in 1961. I'm usually suspicious about blind dates but I'm glad I turned up for that one. It was when I was playing a one night stand in Aylesbury."

WEDDING DAY Friday February 18th (Mid-day)
The service was at Caxton Hall in London, with the reception at the Constellation public house at the corner of South Hill Avenue and Northolt Road, South Harrow and finishing up at Johnny's

above (top left): The Hollies 'stay' for the party
above (top right): The head table
above (left) Viv Prince (Pretty Things), Tito Burns, Tom Jones and Johnny
above (centre): 'Treasure Chest' Wedding Cake
right: Baby Cilla with Mummy and Daddy
margin (top): Only girl in the world
margin (centre): The Constellation
margin (bottom): Johnny and Jean
(all © Jean Heath Collection ex 'The Constellation' Always N' Ever Archive)

home at 74 South Hill Avenue. Jean told the press - "There's nothing wrong with his eye but the eye patch will stop him from winking at other girls. His pals Lord Sutch, Tom Jones, Georgie Fame, Eric Delaney, The Caravelles, Big Jim Sullivan and members of the Hollies were among the guests.

Wedding Day press report

EBRUARY 1[illegible] 1966

Shiver me guitar! Pirate Johnny gets himself spliced to Jean

By PHILIP FINN

THERE were no peg-legs, cutlasses or rum-swigging buccaneers about yesterday when Pirate Johnny Kidd got married.

But, then, things have changed a lot since the fearsome days of Blackbeard and the infamous Captain Henry Morgan.

Yesterday the names that brought forth many a startled gasp were those of a new brand of romantic swashbuckler—Screaming Lord Sutch *(imagine him on a pirate ship)*, Tom Jones, Georgie Fame, The Hollies, and Eric Delaney. Heroes of the world of pop.

They went to Johnny's £12,000 home in Harrow, Middlesex, last night to help him celebrate his marriage earlier in the day.

Delayed honeymoon

Only a handful of relatives and close friends were at London's Caxton Hall to see Johnny—real name Frederick Albert Heath—26-year-old leader of the Pirates pop group, and his bride, Jean, a 23-year-old blonde hairdresser from Harrow, sign the marriage register.

Johnny, whose first marriage ended in divorce last year, and Jean will wait for their Spanish honeymoon until May.

Tonight the former painter, plumber's mate, fairground attendant

PICTURE BY EXPRESS CAMERAMAN MICHAEL MCKEOWN

Bobby Elliot (Drums, The Hollies)
"That particular day we were doing Ready, Steady, Go in Wembley. We got a phone call inviting us all to the do at John's house after R.S.G. We didn't go to the wedding. I remember playing drums with Georgie Fame on organ. Johnny was singing 'I'll Never Get Over You' with his two sons singing back up vocals. Tom Jones also did some singing, a good do!

The day after his wedding Johnny was back on the road performing in Wrexham.

Don Craine (Downliners Sect)
"I got married on the same day as Johnny. Our pictures were side by side in that weeks NME Like the Kidd we worked for George Cooper, Bob Alexander and Bob Potter. In fact most of the 'Sect' work at this time was through them and I'm pleased to say we usually got our money."

JOHN STOKES, of the Bachelors, looks proudly at his 9 lb. son, held by his wife CELINE, as fellow-Bachelors CON and DEC CLUSKY look on. Stokes junior will be the only youngster who can proudly say: "My father is a Bachelor"!

BIRTHS AND MARRIAGES

Left: Downliner Sect's leader DON CRAINE married group's fan club secretary, JACQUELINE STARR, at Twickenham. And JOHNNY KIDD, of Pirate fame, married JEAN HEATH at Caxton Hall.

Press report

Ex Pirate Johnny Weider was now playing lead for Jimmy Winston's Reflections. During Feb '66 they released their debut single 'You Ought To be Ashamed'.

Johnny Weider (Lead Ex Pirate)
"I felt I wanted to start afresh with a new, young, mod group. We had quite an original sound, we called it pop jazz. The other members were Terry Slade (drums), Alex Paris (bass), Tony Kay (organist) and Jimmy Winston (vocals)."
Weiders main hobby was clothes. He spent most of his spare time in Carnaby Street trying out all the latest mod gear. He was a good mate of John Stevens who more or less owned the famous fashion street.

Band leader Eric Delaney who was a guest at Johnny and Jeans wedding had some very inventive ideas. Apart from carrying around his own backdrop and lighting (which influenced Johnny) he was the first drummer in Europe to play with two bass-drums after an original idea by American drummer Louie Bellson. He was at the birth of British Beat. As early as July '56. Delaney was announcing that he was soon to form Britain's first rock n' roll band.

Another version of 'I Hate Getting Up In The Morning' with the accompaniment directed by Johnny Harris was recorded on Tuesday 22nd February. The A side, 'It's Got To Be You', was also directed by Harris and released on April 7th.

Johnny Kidd
"This record is a real sink or swim disc for me. It's going to mean everything or nothing to my future. If it isn't a hit of some sort I shall consider giving up the pop business as an artist and go into the club business on the promotional side."

The Marionettes who supplied vocal backing for the single were very much in demand supplying backing to no less than 10 singles released during the months of April/May '66. Johnny had been very impressed by their vocals when he first met them on the Rising Stars spot at the Ideal Home Exhibition in March '65.

Michael Cox also recorded the flip side with 'Love 'Em And Leave 'Em' (Parlophone R5436). Crispian St. Peters' wrote in the Blind Date spot of the Melody Maker week ending April 16th. "Chris Andrews? No Johnny Kidd. Its about time he came out with a new one. One of my favourite artists. He and The Pirates have got one of the best stage acts in the country. I like the backing - that double rhythm guitar is great. The backings better than the song, I think it'll be a hit. He needs a hit."

The single made no commercial impression. Sadly there had been a huge drop in Johnny's popularity and work load since the end of '65. After an April gig at Bletchleys Wilton Hall Johnny and his Pirates broke up. Johnny felt it was time to try a new career in cabaret and decided to kill off the Pirate image. He gave up his trademark eye patch but his loyal fans and friends objected so strongly that he turned back and proud to his original gear.

Raye Du-Val (Checkmates)
"Johnny told me that he was going to the cabaret circuit and night clubs and getting rid of the pirate image but the fans 'no like' so he reverted back. I went with Johnny to the Rush Studios in Soho and played drums for him. Johnny wanted to see if it was worth updating his hits."

Johnny Kidd
"I'm getting rid of the Pirate kit, we want to make a fresh start, the fancy dress days are over. I am old for a pop singer and I know it. So now we are discarding the pirate gear and from now on we will be wearing suits on stage. I won't even wear an eye patch. When we started I thought the dressing up idea was a bit false. I just wanted to be myself but in those days groups had to have an image and a gimmick. It is not so important now. Kids were always coming up to us and asking where we bought it all. I would like to give it all to a deserving charitable organisation so I know they will serve a useful purpose. I've got eye patches by the dozen, leather waistcoats, coloured shirts and very costly leather thigh boots."

Johnny Spence (Bass)
"We decided to walk the plank, and sink or swim by our own efforts as The 'Pirates to try and get into the big time."

Seeing The Fortunes version of 'This Golden Ring'/'Someone' entering the top twenty in March didn't do Johnny's ego any good. His own version recorded in September '65 should have been released, but E.M.I. decided that 'It's Got To Be You'/'I Hate Getting Up In The Morning' would make a better single.

The Fortunes sound was far removed from the raw driving R&B style of Johnny and his crew. The song was perfect for their vocal harmonies, as they specialised in dramatic ballads in the pop mainstream tradition with large orchestral arrangements. Their greatest hit 'You've Got Your Troubles'/'I've Got To Go' like 'Golden Ring' was a Greenaway/Cook composition. Since leaving The Pirates drummer Clem Cattini had kept very busy.

photo by Philip Gotlop
(© Jean Heath Collection)

Clem Cattini
"I started doing sessions in '66 I couldn't read a note so I bluffed my way through it. It was a case in those days of playing better than they had written. It was the early days in pop and nobody knew what to write and most writers didn't know what to write and most writers didn't know about pop anyway. So I managed to get away with it. About 66/67 I was working with Jimmy Page, Jim Sullivan and John McLaughlin. They'd never tell you what session it was in case you turned round and said that you didn't want it."

As a studio musician he drummed on no less than 42 No 1 hits. Clem is on discs by The Kinks, Ivy League, Edison Lighthouse, Bay City Rollers, Love Affair etc.

Clem Cattini
"I played on LP's by Paul Jones, John Kongos, Lou Reed, P.J. Proby, Nirvana, Bee Gees, Jimmy Witherspoon, Clodagh Rogers, Kinks, etc. At one time I was playing on 8 of the top 20 singles. I've backed Roy Orbison at the Talk Of The Town, Englebert, Dixie Cups, Gilbert O'Sullivan, Stevie Wonder on Top Of The Pops, (I did that show for years), Gladys Night who is one of the best singers in the world, you don't have to play, she just pulls you along. I recall backing the young Lu Lu. The rhythm section was John Paul Jones (bass), Nicky Hopkins (piano), Jimmy Page, Alan Parker (guitars) and myself. Of all the singles I played on 'Shakin All Over' and obviously 'Telstar' are my favourites."

"Andy White was tremendous to me when I first started to do sessions. It was down to Andy that I learned to read. He was teaching me to do things and I was taking his work from him."
Andy White was a very respected drummer he worked on sessions for The Beatles, Tommy Steele, Lord Rockinghams X1 etc.

During April Johnny arrived at a venue and found the hall in darkness. He found a poster on a wall which pointed out that he was a week late. Johnny dropped a note to a local paper to apologise. Later he found that the week before the man running the event had run off with the takings and no-one had been paid.

It wasn't long before the news spread that Johnny was once again without a crew of Pirates. Mike Rudzinski of the Merseyside group The Avengers was ready to enlist as a Pirate.

Mike Rudzinski (Bass, The Avengers)
"We played all the dance halls and cellar clubs on Merseyside and in the North West area. I idolised Johnny Kidd and The Pirates in particular the Mick Green, Johnny Spence, Frank Farley line up. We would play all their numbers and rush out and buy their latest records.

One day I was reading through the Melody Maker and I spotted an advert from Johnny Spence saying that he had recently left Johnny Kidd and wanted to form his own band. He was advertising for musicians, so I rang him up. My knees were knocking while speaking to one of my idols but cheekily I asked him if Johnny Kidd wanted a new bass player. Johnny Spence was great he understood how nervous I was. He gave me Johnny Kidd's phone number and wished me the best of luck. So with great apprehension I phoned Johnny Kidd. After a long conversation he made arrangements with me to come to Wallasey to listen and rehearse with my band. This was beyond my wildest dreams and as an 18 year old at the time I could not take all this in. A few days after our telephone conversation Johnny arrived with his road manager Johnny Irving. We spent most of the day rehearsing and at the end of rehearsal Johnny decided that we were to be his new Pirates. He phoned Wally Ridley to book some studio time at the Abbey Road studios. This was unbelievable, first meeting my idol, then rehearsing with him in my dads garage and being accepted as a Pirate with the chance of a recording contract. The following day we left for a short tour of Devon and Cornwall and it was just great for me to sit and talk to Johnny on our journey to Devon. I remember one of the places we played was a town called Seaton and Beer. We were told that the whole of our spot was filmed. I don't know for sure if that was true but I do remember the film cameras set up in the balcony of the dance hall. I was told about the film by the management of the hall but I was too excited at the time to take it all in. I remember starting our set with 'Hello Josephine' into 'My Babe' then we would go into the intro of 'Shakin All Over'. The roar from the fans was fantastic then Johnny would stride out on stage and stand there with hands on hips and looking very menacing in his pirate gear and again the roar from the crowd as Johnny would throw his cutless into the floor boards of the stage where it would sway from side to side. Then he would grab the microphone and go into 'Shakin All Over' or 'I'll Never Get Over You'. What a great great vocalist and the way he worked an audience, played with them and in the end he would have them eating out of the palm of his hands.

The Avengers (Pirates)
Les Hall (Drums)
Mike Rudzinski (Bass)
Bill Knaggs (Lead)
(courtesy M. Rudzinski)

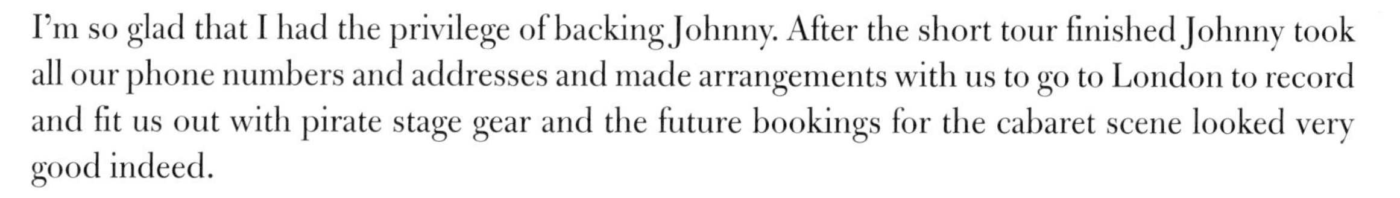

I'm so glad that I had the privilege of backing Johnny. After the short tour finished Johnny took all our phone numbers and addresses and made arrangements with us to go to London to record and fit us out with pirate stage gear and the future bookings for the cabaret scene looked very good indeed.

Sadly none of this was to be. The main reasons was because our lead guitarist, Billy Knaggs, was married with two very young children and he had a steady job and was very unsure of the future if he gave up his job and went full time professional. Les our drummer was on the point of getting married he also had a steady job at Cammil-Laird the ship builders so he also wasn't too sure. In looking back I don't blame them for turning down this opportunity. I think I would have done the same if I was in their situation but as an 18 year old working in my father's garage business I had nothing to lose because if things had not worked out with Johnny I would have returned to the garage. Johnny did contact me a few times saying that he wanted us to back him and that how much he loved the Liverpool group scene. Then Micky Stewart, Roger Truth, Ray Soaper and Nick Simper came along to be the very last Pirates line-up."

Nick Simper (Bass, The Pirates)
"The first band I joined was The Renegades, while still at school. They were started by a pal, Neil Nelhams, who used to live around the corner from me. Neil, in fact, was Adam Faith's cousin. It was the usual thing when news got out I'd got a guitar. I was 14. "Wanna join a group?". They asked me to join 'cos they wanted to use my guitar. I was told I could be the bass player on this home made bass. We did a couple of basement jobs, youth club hops, got the taste for being on stage, a fiver between four of us. I originally played lead, wanted to be Hank Marvin and I was learning that kind of stuff but it was a case of if you want to join play this. The Renegades didn't last very long, had a few line-ups and then I was asked to join The Delta Five, who's big claim to fame was having supported Jerry Lee Lewis at Southall Community Centre!"

They played all pop stuff. The lead guitarist opted to play rhythm 'cos I said I wasn't going to. I was a lead player and I was sold on Johnny Kidd, trying to play like Mick Green and Micky King (Rebel Rousers) but there was no way I was going to be good enough. During this period Ritchie Blackmore used to play at Southall Community Centre with Micky Dee and The Jay Walkers. Everybody noticed Ritchie because he was so fast.
Around this time I was knocking about with a guy called Cliff Barton a legendary bass player. Cyril Davies who died in around '68/'69, lived in Ealing not far from me He said forget about this two guitars business. I'll show you a real band and this was Buddy Britten and The Regents. There was just guitar, bass and drums behind him and I couldn't believe the noise they were making, doing tracks like 'Money', 'Tricky Dicky', American R&B stuff the Beatles latched on to later on. The following week he took me to see Johnny Kidd and The Pirates and I was blown away. Like I'd seen them on telly but live that was it. That was the direction I wanted to go in and what I wanted The Delta Five to do but they didn't want to know. So I formed a splinter group called Some Other Guys. They were a bloody marvellous little band although there was no-one really famous in it.

We used to rehearse in Hayes Church Hall right next door to this place called Whistow House where Jess Gillian and The Javelins used to play. This school mate of mine Tony Tacon (rhythm) formed The Javelins and sort of discovered Gillian. When Some Other Guys got together I was still playing lead. Trouble was we couldn't find a bass player and everyone who came along was playing lead better than me. So in the end I went up to Jim Marshalls shop and he'd just brought out that big 4 by 12 which was the most amazing thing I'd ever seen. So I traded my Fender amp and Gibson Melody Maker and I turned to bass full time and loved it as you know."

WITH THE COMPLIMENTS
of
" The Delta Five "
Weddings, Parties, Socials, Dances.
WEMbley 8523. PERivale 8343.

(courtesy Nick Simper)

It was Tony Ross (Rupert) The Flintstones superb bass player who taught Nick how to handle the bass. Tony lived in the next street to Nick and from time to time gave Nick lessons. Sadly in 1964 Tony died of cancer. His mother gave Nick his old bass guitar as a momento. Nicky has treasured that Fender bass ever since. It still has Rupert painted on the body.

Nick Simper (Bass, the Pirates)
"The Some Other Guys added sax players. Our cards read Some other Guys American Beat. We

did about half a dozen gigs and everyone went potty. Then someone phoned up out of the blue and said would you like to go pro with Buddy Britten, and that was it, good-bye boys. They carried on for a few months and I went on the road with Buddy and The Regents. In fact it was Jim Marshalls son Terry who told me about the job with Buddy. Terry rang up and said Buddy's drummer has been in and they're looking for a bass player, are you interested? I asked who the drummer was and he said Roger Pinner (Roger Truth) the same guy who became a Pirate. He gave me his address, I went round and banged on his door as we knew one another 'cos he'd sat in with The Delta Five sometimes and that was it. I was in with Buddy. That was fabulous, tearing up and down the M1 for five quid a night, two or three gigs a week. I was earning more than my dad after twenty years a the top of his trade. We went off to Jersey for a summer season which was fun 'cos he was a big star there. He'd been over in '63 causing riots. He'd been banned for a time but we went back and it was amazing. Huge crowds, my first taste of stardom. He made good records, his producer and bass player before me Tony Clarke went on to produce some brilliant LPs especially with the Moody Blues. When we came back from Jersey Buddy was getting into sort of pop art. In fact Keith Moon was going to join Buddy but went with The Who instead. Great for him or maybe not as it turned out. So Buddy said, 'right', get your hair cut and wear these jumpers with circles on. He decided to change his name to the Simon Raven Cult 'cos he'd read books by the author Simon Raven and thought it was a good name. I thought it was a good idea actually 'cos we had a pretty wild act. When we came back though rather than go back on the road which I always wanted to do. He got a residency in the Latin quarter of Soho which destroyed me being in the same place six nights a week.

We'd had an organist Richard Honour and so I packed it in and with Richard and drummer, Roger Truth, we formed a group called Cyrano and The Bergeracs, Cyrano was Dave Langston who went on to be The Who's engineer. I went back to playing lead and it was a good exciting act. Then we went back to Buddy for a while. Cy became The Who's roadie. We got rid of the organist Ray Soaper because it was a lot cheaper and easier to take a trio on the road."

Tony 'Rupert' Ross
- The Great Bass Man
(courtesy N. Simper)

Buddy Britten and The Regents (64-'65)
Roger Truth (drums), Nick Simper (bass), Buddy Britten (vocals/gtr), Tony Lost (piano)

Simon Raven Cult (65-'66)
Roger Truth (drums), Nick Simper/Kid Freedom (bass), Richard Honour (keyboards), Simon Raven (Buddy) (vocals).

Cyrano and The Bergeracs ('66)
Dave Langston (Cyrano, vocals), Nick Simper (lead), Roger Truth (drums), Richard Honour (keyboards).

Buddy Britten was one of the few British rockers to actually meet Buddy Holly and The Crickets on their British tour in '58.

Buddy Holly
"I've never seen anyone who resembles me like Buddy Britten."

They had photos taken together. Britten with his black curly hair, glasses and 6ft 2ins frame tried to carry on the Holly sound after Buddy was killed in Feb '59.

Nick Simper (Bass, the Pirates)
"Organist Ray Soaper rang me up and said "I'm doing some gigs with Johnny Kidd."
I said, "Your joking!" Because he knew I idolised Kidd. I asked him "Who else was with him?" and he said he'd got a little group working with him on odd dates. So I got our drummer Roger Truth and we went round and knocked on Johnny's door 'cos we all knew him, seen him at gigs and so on, and said "were The Pirates, " and he said, "You've saved my life" and we went on the road as Johnny Kidd and his New Pirates."

During this period Johnny was managed by Kennedy Street Artistes in Manchester. Two girls took over the running of the fan club. They hailed from the Manchester area. Alan Wheeler (fan club secretary) just couldn't get any co-operation from the new agency so he ended his association as far as the fan club went. Freddie and The Dreamers were also handled by Kennedy Street and for a couple of gigs Johnny and The New Pirates supported the frantic Freddy. Johnny got a tremendous reaction much to the annoyance of Freddie and Co!

The new Pirates were Nick Simper (bass), Micky Stewart (lead), Roger Truth (drums) and Ray Soaper (organist).

Nick Simper (Bass)
"After our first rehearsal Johnny said to us, "Your the best band I've ever had." I was very, very proud but I said, "We haven't got a Mick Green, " he replied "You don't have to worry about my ex-musicians, you are the business." I don't know if he just said that to be nice but he was always telling promoters "That these were the best Pirates I've ever had." Even Irvo our roadie said Johnny was well please. I recall this dance hall up North when this excited fan came into the dressing room and said "they are the greatest Pirates I've ever seen." Johnny told us a bit later on that the bloke was a loyal fan who had been following his career for years. I felt really pleased and proud. Here I was working with my idol, a dream come true. I think us being a little younger we had much more enthusiasm than the last line-up. I had seen Green/Spence/Farley many times. I was always excited by the atmosphere but they never moved. Our drummer Roger Truth was wild like Keith Moon, spinning his sticks. I used to leap about all over the place. Kidd and I would have crazy times trying to see who could leap about the most. When we first joined he said, "Lets forget about the pirates gear, I'm never going to wear the eye patch again, " but on the way to the gig he yells "Irvo drive us to a Boots chemist quick." He comes out of the shop with a handful of patches. He gave me a pair of Mick Green's old boots. Here I was working with my idol and wearing the boots of a great guitarist. I felt great!"
On Saturday May 7th Johnny attended the annual Festival Gardens Star Gala which was organised by the Variety Club of Great Britain. New Musical Express readers had the chance to meet various stars host Roger Moore, Trini Lopez, David Frost, Ivy League, Jonathon King, Tony Jackson, Roy Castle etc. Johnny was pleased to mix with other stars and chat to his fans. One of the highlights was a draw for an autographed album signed by every star who attended this Battersea Pleasure Gardens Gala.

Ex Pirate Johnny Weiders new group Jimmy Winstons Reflections released their second disc on June 3rd 'Sorry She's Mine'/'It's Not What You Do, Its The Way That You Do It' (Decca). To coincide with its release they appeared on ITV's Ready Steady Go. They were managed by Don Arden.

below: Press announcement

bottom:
Micky, Kidd, Nick, Ray and Roger
(courtesy Nick Simper)

KENNEDY ST. ARTISTES LTD.
have pleasure in announcing that they now solely represent
JOHNNY KIDD & THE PIRATES
Enquiries invited to:-
KENNEDY STREET ENTERPRISES LTD., KENNEDY HOUSE, 14 PICCADILLY, MANCHESTER, 1 Tel: MANCHESTER CENTRAL 5423

The crew were pleased to make a surprise performance for the Saturday Morning Children's Club at the Odeon Cinema Kingsbury in Middx on May 21st. The event was a publicity booster for the film Stagecoach which was shown at the Cinema. They met all the children after the film show and were pleased to meet Radio Luxembourg disc jockey PeteR Aldersley.

The Pirates had returned colours aloft and sailing close to the wind.

Nick Simper (Bass)
"We used to go down a storm. Kidd was really rejuvenated. He'd been going through some pretty thin times but now he was back to his old cheerful self. We started trying out different numbers, we even tried our various Beatles numbers but we weren't really happy with them.

I remember the occasion when we got a late call to dep for Georgie Fame at Weston -Super-Mare. On the way we got lost and ended up at Cheddar Gorge. We went in this cafe and who should come walking in but Eden Kane and his group. He says, "Johnny Kidd, " Johnny replied "Where are you going?" Eden says, "I'm going to Weston- Super-Mare to dep for Georgie Fame, " "So are we " came our loud reply so we all ran to our motors and raced to see who could get their first. On arrival we could see a big banner starring Johnny Kidd and The Pirates, Eden Kane was the support band. Peter Sarstedt, Eden's brother was on bass, I remember him coming in our dressing room and saying "nobody in the land could follow your show." We used to have a joke on Johnny he never used to pull on his boots until the very last second. I used to sing a couple of numbers, then the compere would announce, here he is star of stage, screen etc. a really great build up and Johnny would wait until the last second before he pulled on his wailers,. We used to stuff them up with beer bottles, coke bottles, anything. He'd come hopPing on stage "you bastards."
Since April the mutineer Pirates - Farley, Spence and Morshead had stayed afloat and even recorded a single on Polydor 'Shades of Blue'/'Can't Understand' M56712 but in July they cast anchor. They were no longer seaworthy without their Admiral of the Beat, Captain Kidd. They all abandoned ship, their voyage left like a drift net. The commander less crew were nearly lost at sea. They landed in the harbour as land-lubbers. One of their last gigs was Morecambe Pier on Sunday July 10th (Tip Top Club). Frank Farley (drums) soon joined up with ole pal Mick Green (gtr), plus Mike Maxfield (gtr), Robin MacDonald (bass) in the Dakotas backing Billy J. Kramer.

Everything was now in good ship shape. With his new crew it looked like the start of a revitalised career and an exciting new voyage. E.M.I. studios were booked for August 18th and 23rd for the recordings of 'Send For That Girl' with orchestra and accompaniment by Harry Robinson plus Johnny's favourite 'The Fool.'

Nick Simper (Bass)
"Our producer Norman Smith asked us "What are you going to record for a new single?" Johnny had been sent an advance copy of The Beatles 'Revolver' LP during July. He was very impressed with the psychedelic sound on 'I'm Only Sleeping'. So we had a go at it plus others but we didn't really like the result so Johnny suggested 'Please Don't Touch' in an Indian style with sitars but it didn't work. It was bloody awful.

We kept rehearsing different material at Manchester Square until we were given a demo of 'Send For That Girl' and we all liked it. Johnny wanted 'The Fool' for the B side. We used to do it on stage because Johnny had taught it to us. I'd never heard the original by Sanford Clark so I never really knew how the song went. I don't play it right and, of course, it's nothing like the original. I got £9 for the session. We really enjoyed the recording session but we were a little on edge because we were leaving for Scotland for a tour with David and Jonathon right after the session."

Press advertisement

David and Jonathon's bassist, Rowland Barter, (The Issue) wrote 'Send For That Girl'.

The singing duo topped the bill at the Caird Hall, Dundee the following night. The supporting groups included Johnny and the Pirates, The Red Hawks, Dunfermline Boys, Jay-Birds, St Louis Union and the Ivy League.

The St Louis Union along with Johnny and his crew were reported to have been signed for a French film 'La Musique Est Mort'. Shooting was due to start on September 10th. During the shooting The Union' were to play the Paris Olympia while Johnny and the lads were to play a week at the Locomotive Club followed by three days at the Olympia. The French thriller roughly translated 'The Music Is Dead' was to be the story of a group playing in a Paris club until a compere gets murdered. Sadly the film didn't see the light of day but The Union did make their movie debut in '66 along with Spencer Davis Group, Acker Bilk, Lorne Gibson Trio, The M6, Dave Berry, The Three Bells in the British Pathe production 'The Ghost Goes Gear' which was filmed on location at Cookham on the Thames.

The boys at E.M.I. Manchester Square
(© N. Simper)

Nick Simper (Pirate)
"Unfortunately the French film saga was just a publicity stunt made up by Keith Goodwin and Kaygee Publicity. They often invented headlines just to keep us in the leading pop papers. Sadly Johnny's amazing act never made it to the big screen."

So it was back on the rocky road with the amazing Johnny Irving at he helm. He'd bring the van to leeward and off they would sail on yet another voyage. Irving was an amazing helmsman. He'd weigh anchor, set sail, before Johnny could say 'rag arse'.

Nick Simper (Bass)
"Our roadie Johnny Irving was like Iron Man. Straight after 'The 'Fool' session, he drove us all to Kidd's home. After a quick cup of tea and sandwich we left for Dundee in Scotland. Irvo drove all the way, he wouldn't let anyone take over. He drove all through the night, all the band went to sleep. He was as safe as houses. Irvo is only a little bloke but he is one of the toughest guys I've ever met. I love him like my own brother. When we get together and talk about the ole Pirate days we start laughing. It's hard not to start crying we get so emotional.

The Pirates had their own language, our own cockney type rhyming slang. Kidd and Irvo were totally over the top. Kidd made up his own i.e. there's a Cheddar in here, meaning Cheddar Gorge = George = George Raft = Draft. Kidd and Irvo had their own words, nobody could work out what they were talking about. To pass time in the van Kidd used to keep a sketch block with poster paints. He would draw weird figures like men with pig heads, pure surrealism. He used to hang them in the van. Sadly they were all thrown away."

Johnny was keen on buying a new car so on September 25th he went to see his good mate the ole Five Nutter Frank Rouledge who now worked for Downes Car Sales in Malvern Road, Kilburn NW6.

Frank Rouledge (Five Nutters)
"I'd been working for the brother of ex-boxer Terry Downes in his car showroom ever since I left Fred's band. I spied this lovely blue Ford Sunliner. I knew Fred would fancy it. I arranged for him to do a part exchange plus cash for it. He loved it and said that he'd collect it when he came back from a trip up North but sadly he never came back."

(courtesy N. Simper)

Ex-Pirate lead guitarist Johnny Weider was now playing bass along with Danny McCulloch (gtr), Barry Jenkins (drums), Dave Rowberry (organ), in the New Animals behind the powerful vocals of Eric Burdon. Rowberry soon left and was replaced by guitarist Vic Briggs.

In '67 they would record classic singles full of peace, love, hippiedom. 'When I Was Young' MGM 13721, 'Good Times' MGM 13769 which featured the classic chorus 'When I think of all the good times that I wasted having good times....!', 'San Franciscan Nights' MGM 13769 and 'Monterey' MGM 13868.

Nick Simper (Bass)
"Johnny was surprised to hear from his ole manager Georgie Cooper. Johnny had fallen out with him but he always said that Cooper was like a father to him. Cooper phoned Johnny up and said they are all doing cabaret Tom Jones, Billy J. Kramer, Engelbert. I'd like to book you for a week in Darlington. You will enjoy being based in one place instead of racing from venue to venue. Johnny wasn't very keen but decided to give it a go.
Johnny said we had better play 'If You Were The Only Girl In the World' and 'Sunny Side of The Street' for the mums and dads. We weren't very keen but when we got there it was full of teddy boys so we just played our usual rock n' roll set. We went out every night for 45 minutes and played non stop rock 'n' roll. The place was packed every night. That was his future. We could have worked for 'Always n' Ever'. We probably could have taken the act to Las Vegas, who knows.

Our guitarist Micky Stewart would sing 'Something You've Got', 'Sticks and Stones', 'She's About A Mover', about six numbers before Kidd came on. Johnny really was a rock pioneer. He held his mike at arms length at a certain distance, a great technique. During 'Shakin All Over' he would shake from head to toe. I've never seen anyone else who can do this except the original Pirate, Mike West.

Irvo would flash the spot lights on and off as Johnny would pull on his belt and shake his hips at the girls in the front. Amazing. We used to turn

74, South Hill Ave,
Harrow,
Middx

Received from Downes Car Sale the sum of £10-0-0 being the agreed repayment in respect of intended agreement on Sunliner which is now cancelled

[signature]

'The car he never had'
(courtesy F. Rouledge)

DOWNES CAR SALES
117 MARVERN RD
25-9-66 NW6.

Received from Mr F. A. Heath 74, South Hill Ave Sth Harrow Middx the sum of £100-0-0 making a total value of £245-0-0 so far on Ford Sunliner sold at the agreed price of £495-0-0 a further balance of £250-0-0 to follow partly by cash & partly by hire purchase within seven days of the above date

F. Rouledge

up for gigs, set up our amps, mikes and drum kit. We never bothered with sound checks. As we came out of our dressing rooms in the Pirates gear, no matter who was there - toughs, teds, rockers, bikers they would just melt away as if we were real buccaneers. While on the road Johnny always brought his portable TV as he just loved horse racing. Near to his home in South Harrow Johnny was always betting in Patsy Rays, the bookie. If he had a winner he would treat us Pirates. He was kind to us all. Patsy Ray had a Jag MK2 which he kindly lent to Johnny for special posh events. I recall watching the '66 World Cup on Johnny's TV plus the Ready Steady Go special with Otis Redding. Johnny was really excited about the new soul sound. He loved Sam and Daves 'Hold On I'm Coming' and Gene Vincents' 'Bird Doggin'/'Ain't That Too Much', He nearly wore those records out. Brook Benton was another of his favourites, so was P.J. Proby. He had a Proby LP which his little girl Cilla would point at and yell "daddy, daddy."

Johnny and his new crew started in cabaret in September. Before their gigs at Darlington and Middlesborough he told the press.
"Hell I feel so nervous" but he soon got over his shaking with Nick, Ray, Roger and Mick in support they soon had the crowds 'Shakin All Over' with excitement."

Nick Simper (Bass)
"In September we made our cabaret debut (rather nervously) doing a week at both the Flamingo Darlington and a Middlesborough club the name of which I've forgotten. The scenes were so tremendous as to be unbelievable! We received tremendous applause and demands for encores throughout the week. Of course the show-stoppers were 'I'll Never Get Over You' and 'Shakin All Over'. After the last appearance the fans were so enthusiastic that Johnny had to leap from the rear entrance into the moving van to escape. So it seemed that Johnny had a future in cabaret."

Another interpretation of 'Send For That Girl' was recorded on September 6th but it was the first with Harry Robinsons' orchestration which was chosen for the A side. Version 2 remained unreleased until 1983.

(courtesy N. Simper)

They also put down a version of 'Send For That Girl' plus 'We Will Come Together', 'I Love You' and the Beatles 'I'm Only Sleeping' on Johnny's home tape recorder. He was always happy to get home to his wife Jean and family and always thrilled to see ole pals. He was over the moon when his ole mate Pete Newman (sax player with Freddie Heath band) came knocking at his door.

Pete Newman
"I was with Fred in the late '50's. He, in fact, gave me my first break in the business and I have been in the music game ever since. I last saw Fred at his home a week before he died and I remember we talked all night about the very early days and all that happened between 1959-66. He showed me loads of old press cuttings even of the Freddie Heath Band/original Pirates."

Nick Simper (Bass)
"I remember a gig at the Flower Show, Ainsworth at the time when some police had been shot in Shepherds Bush, London by Harry Roberts. As we drove in there was a copper at the gate. He

said "Who are you?" and we replied, "Johnny Kidd and The Pirates." You had to have a pass to get in and we couldn't find ours. So this copper starts to give us this big lecture. Next second our drummer Roger pokes his head out and yells, "Have you caught Harry Roberts yet?" The copper was suddenly lost for words. Supporting us on the show was Tony Jackson and The Vibrations. After the gig Tony's van broke down so we let him squeeze in with us. We all ended up at Johnny's South Harrow home. I'd never met Tony before, I was impressed, a nice bloke."

(courtesy N. Simper)

Johnny was well pleased with his new crew because they blew up a storm at every venue.

May 14th	Bromley
May 20th	Walton on Naze
May 21st	Odeon Kingsbury
May 26th	Folkeston, Leas Cliff Hall
May 27th	Abergavenny
June 2nd	Wantage
June 3rd	Newbury
June 25th	Folkeston, Leas Cliff Hall
July	Oxford
	Prestatyn, Clwd
	Seaton
August	Grimsby
	Western Super Mare
August 18th	Recording Session
August 23rd	Recording Session
	Dundee
	Ripley
August 26th	Clacton (Special Police Do)
	Nantwich
Sept 3rd	Orpington
Sept 6th	Recording Session
	Putney (Le Caer Club)
Sept 19th-25th	Darlington (Flamingo)
Oct 1st	R.A.F. Waddington (last ever gig)

Johnny tried hard to get a tour of Sweden for the week commencing 24th September.

Alan Wheeler
"During June '66 I had a three minute telephone call with Gene Vincent at his home in Albequerque, New Mexico. He said he was cutting a new record in a week or so and hoped his ole drummer Dickie 'Be-Bop' Harrell would be on the session. He said how anxious he was to come back to Britain and specially asked how Johnny Kidd and Marty Wilde were getting on."

Nick Simper (Bass)
"After a disappointing gig we stopped off at the Blue Boar for a nosh and natter. Johnny suddenly said he was thinking of retiring and becoming an agent. I was dumb struck but thank God he

soon snapped out of it and was back to his usual self looking forward to the next gig. We now started playing more gigs without our organist Ray Soaper. We all liked Ray, he was a smashing fella but we all had to admit, no matter how much we loved ole Ray, The Pirates sounded better as a trio. Micky Stewart (lead), Roger Truth (drums) and myself bass. Johnny, of course, based his sound on the superb Johnny Burnette Trio. My ole boss Buddy Britten also loved the same line-up but he did it because of his idol Buddy Holly and the Crickets. On one of my first gigs with Buddy Brittens Regents we were supported by The Who at Exeter University. Their bassist John Entwhistle said I see you've got the late great Rupert Ross's (Flintstones) bass and you play just like him. I felt very flattered but although I played in Ruperts' thumb style I, of course, couldn't play half as good as Rupert. He was a genius. Another member of the great Flintstones was Rod Freeman (guitarist). He was a smashing bloke I recall taking him round Johnny's home and later on he came to our gig at the ex-boxers Terry Downes club in Harlesden. A great day in the life."

Johnny had always admired Johnny Burnette, even his ballads 'Dreamin' London HLG9172, 'You're Sixteen' London HLG 9254, 'Little Boy Sad' London HLG315 but it was his early frantic rockabilly with The Rock n' Roll Trio that Johnny loved most. Johnny Burnette (vocals, acoustic guitar) his brother Dorsey (string bass) and the torrid chunky guitar of Paul Burlisson were the first real creators of the powerhouse heavyweight trio sound. Their material 'Tear It Up' Vogue Coral Q71177, 'Lonesome Train'/'Honey Hush' Vogue Coral Q72227 and 'Sweet Love On My Mind' from the LP Rock 'n' Roll Trio (10" Coral LVC 10041) played a big part in the Pirates rebirth. Paul Burlison, along with Scotty Moore and Cliff Gallup was one of rocks first guitar heroes. Burlison's distinctive, over amplified, Fender Telecaster sound had first been achieved by accident when he dropped his amp and knocked a valve loose and created a fuzz tone sound. Burlison's first claim to fame was backing blues legend Howlin' Wolf on Radio KWEM between 1949-1951. The Kidd had been very upset when he learned on August 14th 1964 that Johnny Burnette had been killed in a boating accident. He really was a rock pioneer, Johnny used to over-dub the drums on the Trio's sessions before most others had ever heard of dubbing.

(courtesy N. Simper)

Nick Simper (Bass)
"When we played The Lido Ballroom, Prestatyn our support were Amen Corner. We would see these new bands coming up. One thing Johnny couldn't grasp was how the business was changing. I remember driving down Carnaby Street and seeing posters of The Move, The Who, The Action. I said to Johnny there's a lot of new faces coming up. He replied "They are not doing anything, don't worry about it." But they were, they were kind of taking over from us and The Gladiators, Lord Sutch, Joe Brown etc. All of a sudden these younger groups were making a name."

Cromer Norfolk was one of Johnny's last ever appearances. The press said -
"Always a very visual performer his voice sounded more powerful today then when he was in the charts! A really tight backing was provided by The Pirates for this legend of British rock 'n' roll."

Nick Simper (Bass)
"Johnny's last ever performance was at R.A.F. Waddington on October 1st 1966. It was a tremendous gig. Johnny was in top form."

Johnny was keen and excited looking forward to the next gig at Bolton.

Nick Simper (Pirates Bass)
"We were booked for Bolton on Friday 7th October. We had another gig on the Sunday night but we didn't have a gig for the Saturday. We were just about to set off for Bolton but at the last minute Johnny's wife, Jean, decided to come because we were staying with the two girls who now ran the fan club. We were well late getting away. When we got there our guitarist Micky Stewart said he'd been there since about 4 o'clock. We didn't arrive until about 7.30pm, we were due to be on at 7.00pm. The Manager had put up a cancelled sticker and moaned "You're too late, its a breach of contract." Johnny quickly said "sorry but the punters ain't about yet - take the sticker down and forget about my fee, I'll do the gig for nothing. Just give my boys a fiver each, I don't want anything, I just want to perform." The Manager still didn't want to know. He was being bloody funny, a real little Hitler. The show was off. Kidd was upset but suggested while we were up there "Why don't we go up to the Nelson Imperial. We're due to play up there in a few weeks and the Manager, Bob Kane, is a good mate of mine. He books a lot of venues in the area so perhaps he can get us some future bookings. It will make up for tonight's let down." We all agreed and travelled up to the Nelson. We had a beer with Bob and he said he would phone up a few people to help us get gigs. He promised to let us know the next day. Our drummer, Roger Truth, didn't come with us he went to see an old flame in Manchester who was a secretary for Kennedy Street Artistes. Micky Stewart and I were to stay together while Johnny and Jean were going to stay with Wilf our driver and his wife Chris in Atherton. Our usual driver Johnny Irving was very busy running a breakers yard. As we came out of the Nelson Imperial this guy came running up to the car and asked Johnny for his autograph. He was really excited. He said "you're coming here in a couple of weeks, I'll bring all my mates." Johnny said "I'll look forward to seeing you, come back stage and say hello." That was the very last autograph Johnny ever gave. I've often thought that perhaps if we hadn't stopped for that guy we wouldn't have hit that Mini or perhaps if we hadn't stopped for a leak behind a tree, its all IF... but I think Johnny's number had come up, who knows why these terrible things happen, we never really knew what caused that crash. Our driver Wilf had only had the G.T. Cortina a couple of days. In those days no one wore seat belts, no speed limits, no M.O.T.'s.

Johnny Burnette's 'Rock 'n' Roll Trio' 10" L.P.

Probably the final photo (courtesy N. Simper)

We were on a big main road about, 12.30am - 1.00am. We hardly saw a car, we were going along a steady 70mph, there was nothing dangerous about it. All of a sudden the car started to veer across the road, the steering just wouldn't respond. The Kidd was in the front turning round talking to me about going back to Hamburg in Germany. I was leaning forward talking to him, all of a sudden Wilf cried out. It was only a split second but it seemed like it was an hour. Wilf was trying to handle the steering but the car just swerved across the road. There was a chain link fence coming towards us. I remember thinking he's got a brand new car and he's going to hit the fence and carve it all up. All of a sudden out of no where there was a Mini coming towards us. He had turned out of a road and was accelerating up the road. By the time he saw us we were on the wrong side of the road, he kept coming and flashing his lights. We just couldn't avoid him and BANG! There were two people dead. I just couldn't take it in. As I was being wheeled into hospital I thought fractured skull I'm dying, I was really calm, I thought I'm not going to live very long, it doesn't seem so bad if this is dying, it doesn't seem too bad. The next thing they've stitched me up and said you can go home now. I said "Johnny's dead, he's gone isn't he?" she replied, "I'm afraid so." The next second I'm saying we've got all these gigs next week, Johnny can't be dead he's playing all these shows. Shock took me over, I just couldn't except that the Kidd was gone. I knew the second I saw him that he was dead. I took a long, long time to get over losing him." Johnny died in the early hours of Saturday 8th October.

Johnny, Nick and Wilf were travelling on the A58 to Wilf's (driver) house in Atherton. They hit a Mini driven southwards by a Chris Metcalf. It was a quiet area, a green belt area between two pubs The Bull and Three Arrows, a half mile from the Bury boundary. Johnny was dead on arrival at Bolton Royal Infirmary. Bassist Nick Simper received head, back and arm injuries, driver Wilf Isherwood was badly cut. A passenger in the other car, Helen Read, was also killed. She was only seventeen. Helen had lived at Sunny Bowers, Tottington, Bury. Firemen, police and ambulances sped to the scene. Traffic was diverted while firemen released the injured from the wreckage. Weeping teenagers gathered the next day near the home of Wilf Isherwood in Marlborough Road, Heaton Mount, Atherton, Lancashire. Johnny's funeral took place the following Wednesday at Golders Green Crematorium.

Press report

POP STAR JOHNNY KIDD KILLED IN CRASH

Singer who wore a pirate patch

Johnny Kidd and his bride Jean on their wedding-day at Caxton Hall in February.

"Evening News" Reporter

Johnny Kidd, the 29-year-old pop singer who wore a pirate-style eye-patch, was killed today when two cars crashed head-on near Bury, Lancs.

A woman passenger in the other car was killed and three people seriously hurt.

The singer, former leader of "The Pirates" group until he went solo seven months ago, was a passenger in a car driven by Mr. Wilfred Isherwood, of Marlborough Road, Atherton, Lancs.

Johnny Kidd's real name was Frederick Heath. He lived in South Hill Road, Harrow.

The dead woman was named as Helen Read, of Sunny Bowers, Tottington, Bury.

She was a passenger in a car driven southwards by Peter Metcalfe, of Quarlton Drive, Bury.

Mr. Isherwood and a rear seat passenger, Mr. Nicholas Simper, of Brookside Road, Hayes, were taken to Bolton Royal Infirmary.

The crash happened on the A.58 Bolton-Bury road, about three miles south of Bury.

Firemen, police and ambulances sped to the scene after the smash. Traffic was diverted while firemen released the injured from the wreckage.

Mr. Simper was lead guitarist with the singer's group, The New Pirates.

BEGAN IN CHOIR

Twice-married Johnny Kidd started his singing career as a choirboy with the Band of Hope when he was evacuated to North Wales during the war.

When he returned to London he turned to pop and cut his first disc in 1959 with the songs "Please Don't Touch," and "Growl."

He came into fame in the first few years of the sixties. His greatest hit with the Pirates was perhaps "Shaking All Over."

He followed up this early success with "Hungry For Love" and "I'll Never Get Over You."

In April this year Johnny, who projected the Pirates image by wearing his black patch, decided to go solo.

FIRST SOLO DISC

It would appear to have been a mistake. His first solo disc "It's Got To Be You," currently on release, has failed so far to make the charts.

In April last year Johnny was divorced by his wife Ada for adultery. Less than a year later—in February this year—he married again.

His new wife, the co-respondent in his divorce, was blonde hairdresser Jean Heath. He had three children by his first marriage.

For the wedding reception, Johnny threw open his £12,000 house at Harrow and many leading pop singers attended. Among them were Tom Jones, Georgie Fame, the Hollies and band leader Eric Delaney.

Zu schnell

Johnny Kidd kam bei einem Autounfall ums Leben. Er war 30 Jahre alt. Mit seiner Beatgruppe The Pirates hatte er mehrere Bestseller, seine letzten Hits liegen jedoch schon einige Zeit zurück. Das Unglück geschah in der Nähe von Ratcliffe, Lancashire. Es war ein Frontalzusammenstoß mit einem anderen Personenwagen. Dabei wurde auch ein junges Mädchen getötet, drei andere Insassen erlitten schwere Verletzungen. Die Ursache: Stark überhöhte Geschwindigkeit!

Nick Simper (Pirate)

"It took ages and ages for me to get over losing Johnny. I used to dream about him every night as soon as I went to sleep he was there. I had to go to the doctors to get special pills. It was as if he was still alive and we were travelling the astral plane together. I remember one night I always had this dream of us walking into a pub and there's my girlfriend who later became my wife and her mate. When we walked in they couldn't see us. I said "tell me something John, how come we can see these girls but they can't see us?" He turned around and looked at me and said, "I wish you hadn't asked me that, you shouldn't have asked me that." Then he vanished, I never dreamt about him again. I'm convinced somehow I was out of my body and actually with him. It was real. I went to my doctor and spoke to a spiritualist about it. I even woke up one night and felt my hand being held. I knew it was Johnny. It made me really ill for two or three weeks. They say when someone dies suddenly they don't know that they are dead, they just can't accept they are dead. I just know he was around and hadn't gone. I'm sure I wasn't dreaming. I don't know where we were or what plane we were on. I'll never forget it."

Without a doubt Johnny and The Pirates would have had a good future on the cabaret scene and may even have followed Engelbert Humperdinck (with Mick Green) and Tom Jones to deserved mega status in Las Vegas, USA. During my research many of Johnny's musicians have mentioned what a tremendous influence the Kidd's stage act had on a young unknown called Tom Scott. Tom later found fame and fortune as Tom Jones.

Nick Simper (Bass)
"I recall the night before I left for Jersey with Buddy Britten as a member of the Regents we were all watching the young Tom Jones and The Squires on TV. Roger Truth and I looked at each other and said who is that on there? Johnny Kidd!! The way Tom held his mike, the movement of his hips, every pose was copied from the Kidd. Tom Jones idolised Johnny Kidd and so did I."
Keyboard player Vic Cooper joined The Squires after leaving The Pirates. A few years later Big Jim Sullivan became lead guitarist in Jones' touring band. He stayed for five years (he'd already played on Jones' records). In 1974 Jim formed his own record label Pacific Eardrum.
Peter Wilson (Hustlers)
"The final time I met Kidd was in Marshalls shop in Hanwell. We chatted away and he said he was rehearsing in a pub just down the road. I drove him to The Viaduct pub near Wharncliff Viaduct in the Uxbridge Road. I met the band, and listened until lunch time. Then went off with Kidd plus three of the band to an Indian restaurant in West Ealing. I remember the Kidd talking not only about his ole Pirate Mick Green's driving lead and rhythm work but also about the way he really used the A and E bass strings. A very hot lunch and a few pints later we returned for a couple more hours of rehearsals. He gave me his telephone number of his home at South Harrow. We said we would be in touch soon and three days later he was dead!"

Roy Carr (Contributor and writer for Music Press)
"I'd just come off stage at the Imperial Ballroom, Nelson where my band was supporting the Alan Price Set. The time was about 9pm when the hall manager informed me of the tragedy and asked me if we'd be prepared to rush straight to the Bolton Nevada to dep for Johnny and the Pirates. We did, but it was a sad occasion - filling for a man who helped change the face of British rock. This man Johnny Kidd changed the face of British rock when Cliff Richard and Co. cleaned up their sexy ways.

Tony Jackson (Vibrations and Ex Searcher)
"Our van had broken down. Johnny very kindly gave us a lift and put us up for the night at his house. Sadly that was the last time I saw him. About a week later we went to Hamburg and that's when I read in this German paper about his death."

Tony Dangerfield (Savages)
"We were on tour in Germany. Dave (Lord Sutch) popped out to get the previous days Evening Standard. He returned deeply shocked, his mate the Kidd was dead. He showed us the write up, we just couldn't take it in. I've never seen Dave so sad, he had lost a very good mate."

Nick Simper (Bass)
"We really thought 'Send For That Girl'/'The Fool' was going to be a hit. We thought the public

would make it a memorial hit for the Kidd. Alas no money was given for publicity so sadly it didn't get much air play. Not long after we lost Johnny we had a tribute show in Putney with Robert Stigwood, Lord Sutch and Savages, (Carlo Little, Tony Dangerfield, Ritchie Blackmore, Matthew Fisher) etc. and, of course, various crews of Pirates. It was a real sad time."

Gene Vincent was terribly upset about Johnny. Only a week before the crash he spoke to Johnny and Johnny said he was thinking of going to the States to live. He also asked Gene if he would do a tour with him.

Nick Simper (Bass)
"Just before Johnny's death E.M.I. had agreed to record an L.P. and believe it or not it was to be titled 'Johnny Kidd Sings Gene Vincent'. What a gas it would have been! The Kidd was a great friend and admirer of Gene and we spent many enjoyable hours on the way to gigs discussing him and playing his records on our record player. In fact hardly a day passed without Johnny saying "Wait until you meet Gene." Shortly before the accident we were in cabaret at Darlington when we first heard his 'Bird Doggin' on the radio which knocked us both out."

16. I'LL NEVER GET OVER YOU (THE LEGEND LIVES ON)

Nick Simper
"After the Kidd died I couldn't work for a while 'cos my arm was smashed up. Micky Stewart went off to back Jerry Lee Lewis."

Between October to November '66 Jerry Lee came to Europe for a quick tour. Various ex Pirates made up the band - Johnny Spence (bass), Vic Cooper (organ), Roger Truth (drums) and Micky Stewart (lead). They went on the tour unseen and uncredited. This was because there had to be at that time an agreement with the musicians union over Jerry Lee Lewis's backing group. He wanted to use the Memphis Beats (his own American band) and the only way this was allowed was for British musicians to be paid to stand in if need be. So ex Pirates were signed for the tour but never appeared. Once again Lewis never mixed with the rest of the bill except for fellow American, Lee Dorsey."

Nick Simper
"Morris King brought over Bobbie Hebb and they got a special backing band together - Kenny Slade, Johnny B Great and me. When Hebb went back to America I said lets get The Pirates going again. I phoned Tony Jackson up and asked him if he would like to be a Pirate. He said Yeah! We kept trying to arrange a meeting to have a blow to see how we would get on musically to see if it would work. The trouble was we were working and he was busy and we just couldn't get it together. It just fizzled out. I thought it would have been a good combination The Pirates with Tony Jackson the ex Searcher.

During December Nick (bass), Mick Stewart (lead), Johnny Carrol (organ) and Johnny Kerrison (drums) toured all over Scotland. At the very last moment drummer Roger Truth decided to leave and join the Freddie Mac Band. The Pirates were upset but they soon found an excellent replacement in John Kerrison.

The Final Voyage - Nick, Mick, Roger and Johnny Carrol (courtesy N. Simper)

Nick Simper
"We got to the theatre and were pleased to see our mates Lord Sutch and the Savages on the bill plus, of all groups, The Freddie Mac Band including Roger Truth. Dave Sutch (Lord) said "Your ole drummer Truth is hiding from you all, he won't show his face." I said "If I get my hands on him I'll kill him for letting us down." Anyway we went on stage, I sang some vocals, we played a lot of Kidds material. We went down well, some girls started screaming this gave us more confidence. It was a very hard decision to carry on The Pirates without the Kidd but we felt he would have wanted us to keep flying the jolly roger.

Roadie Johnny Irving was offered the tour but he decided that when his buddy Johnny Kidd died that he would never be involved in music ever again. He was offered jobs with many leading groups including The Shadows and The Who but he declined.

Johnny Spence (bass) messed around with a couple of groups one of which featured the multi-talented pre-traffic David Mason. Johnny then joined Jon Morshead, Pete Stolley, Keith Webb and Julian Covey (Phil Kinorra) in Julian Covey and The Machine. They cut a single 'A Little Bit

Hurts'/'Sweet Bacon' WIP6009 and were offered a five year deal with Island but they split up in '67. Spence left the music world and slowly built up a lucrative used car business.

Nick Simper (Bass)
"Sadly The Pirates folded in May '67. I went on the road with Billie Davis and then the Flowerpot Men, Deep Purple, Warhorse, Survivors, Rocket, Dynamite, Fandango, Flying Fox and most recently The Good Old Boys who feature Alan Barratt (vocal), Peter Parks (gtr), Simon Bishop (gtr), Terry Sullivan (drums) and, on some gigs, ex-Pirate Johnny Kerrison (drums)."

May 25, 1967

Dear Nicky,

I was so pleased to hear from you. The pictures and the news articles are just great. Thank you very much.

"Love Me" was a king size drag to me also. If you recall our discussion,on "copyism", you'll see that there is no substitute for truth and love.

I'm sorry things are at rock bottom for you at the moment. I wish I knew something I could do to help. At any rate, please don't hesitate to call on me if there is anything I can do.

Yes! I remember the guy in the shades at Blaise's (he was the guy with the censored looking girl!) I hope things will be better now that you have your original drummer again.

I suppose Ken Slade went with a big band --He had such a big band sound.

Since Johnny B. was married, I suppose his responsibilities would not allow him to gamble. Since you and Mick are the backbone of the group, I'm sure you'll eventually find everything "Sunny."

Enclosed please find a picture of myself and one of the "former" Pirates when we played at all those groovy (?) places.

Please keep in touch, it's so nice to hear from old friends.

Sincerely,
Bobby Hebb

S. Penny sends her regards. And listen for a March!

Letter to Nick from Bobby Hebb (courtesy N. Simper)

John Kerrison (Drummer)
"I joined Episode Six for about a year then I backed The Flirtations with John Savage and Mad Bill." After leaving Julian Covey and The Machine Jon Morshead (lead) joined Shotgun Express then the Aynsley Dunbar Retaliation.

During February '67 Jean Heath moved out of South Hill Avenue. Jean lived for a time in a flat in Sudbury Hill before finding a house in Kenton, Middlesex.

Frank Farley and Mick Green stayed in the Dakotas until March '68. 'Sneaking Around' and 'I'll Be Doggone', feature Mick Green's best work behind Billy J Kramer. Without vocalist Billy J. they cut some excellent singles 'Oyeh'/'My Girl Josephine' Parlophone R5203. 'I'm 'An Ard Working Barrow Boy'/'7lbs Of Potatoes', 'Page One! I Can't Break The News To Myself'/'The Spider And The Fly' Philips BF1645.

Both B sides of the last two singles were experimental psychedelic. Mick Green recalls an amazing backstage incident during his Dakotas days.
"Jimi Hendrix was desperately trying to sell Billy J. on the idea of recording 'Purple Haze.'"
Perhaps Jimi wanted to cover 'Little Children'?!?!

On leaving Billy J. they backed Billy Fury for three months.

Mick Green
"Billy was great, a one off, a hell of a guy. He was a real animal lover. When I worked with Billy we worked a club and one of the acts was a magician who used lots of pigeons in his act, maybe 50 or 60, he used to leave his trained pigeons overnight. One morning Billy arrived early to rehearse and decided he didn't like to see them cooped up in cages so he let them out inside the club. They were flying about for half an hour until they all managed to fly out of a window. When the magician came back to find his pigeons gone he was shocked and very annoyed, raving about how he couldn't carry on his act without his birds. All Billy said was that he had let them go and

it was cruel to keep them locked up in a cage all night. Billy knew that he didn't have long to live. He never planned too far ahead but when he did 'Deborah' in 1982 for his last album which I produced his voice was terrific. I for one miss him, he was a great talent and a great pal."

In June '68 Mick and Frank both joined the Cliff Bennett band. They both played on Cliff's wild version of The Beatles 'Back In The USSR'/'This Man' Parlophone R5749. Mick left with Robin MacDonald (bass) for Las Vegas USA to back Engelbert Humperdink. Mick stayed in the States for the next four and a half years. Frank kept the beat for Bennett until June '69 but left the crazy world of rock 'n' roll for the next few years. He did various jobs and occasional drumming stints with different rock 'n' roll bands i.e. Houseshakers and Fifth Avenue. Johnny Spence played the occasional gig for Avenue. During this period a band called Johnny C and The New Pirates was based in the Portsmouth area. After a few gigs they dropped the 'New' and became The Pirates but quickly disappeared. Who were they? Was it Johnny Carrol?

Mick Green
"I left Engelbert because I was losing touch with reality. When you spend half of every year in Las Vegas - with just about everything you want laid on you feel you are in Disneyland. Life becomes too easy for your own good. I returned home in '74 and formed Fresh Meat who later became Hard Meat before evolving into Shanghai. I learnt to read music while I was with Engelbert."

During April '69 ex-Pirate Johnny Weider replaced Ric Grech (who had quit to join the ill fated super group Blind Faith) in Leicester band Family. Weider doubled up on bass and violin as Grech had done before. He soon became one of the family playing alongside some of the most creative musicians on the underground circuit' Jim King (flute, sax), Rob Townsend (drums), Charlie (John) Whitney (guitar) and the unique haunting quivering vocals of Roger Chapman.

Keith Hunt"I saw their historic performance on July 5th ' 69 at the Rolling Stones Hyde Park concert. I can still hear Chapman's super weird vocals. They, along with the thousands of butterflies released in memory of the late Brian Jones, will haunt me forever. So will the 250,000 music loving fans. I'm proud I was there 'along with' The Weavers Answer."

Clem Cattini (Ex Pirate Drummer)
"I worked with Jimmy Page and John Paul Jones on quite a lot of sessions. One day in 1968 Peter Grant, their manager, called me and said there was something he wanted to talk to be about but I never had time to call him back. About a year later I bumped into him and said "Was It?" He said, "Yes." I'd missed out on the chance to join Led Zeppelin."

In September 1971 Johnny's idol and mate Gene Vincent arrived in England to undertake a few dates. His former English wife Margie took him to the law courts over money on October 4th. Ill health cut short his stay and the cancellation of the remaining shows. He flew home to California to his parents and was taken very ill. He died in hospital on Tuesday October 12th 1971 of internal bleeding from a burst ulcer. Gene like Johnny had tremendous talent, both had the making of real superstars, both were great showmen. Why they never got the success that many people thought they deserved will now remain one of those unanswered questions of show business. Both could performed ballads and rockers superbly. Both were due to die very young, Gene was 36, Johnny only 30. Many people have said Gene drank himself to death. He was once asked how long he would go on singing "For as long as the fans want me to. Perhaps I'll go on until I die, in a car crash or a plane crash." Gene is now somewhere over the rainbow, but he left us some classic music and memories. He was an original, just like the 'Kidd'.

Nick Simper had a few approaches to reform the very last crew during 1975 but as some of the lads weren't available he refused the offers. A short while later in '76, Nick and Roger Truth (drummer) decided to record aS The Pirates but news reached them that Mick Green, Johnny Spence and Frank Farley were all in it together to re-hoist the jolly roger but that's a different voyage and another ole Pirates Tale.

Nick Simper (Bass)
"Johnny and Gene Vincent they were good pals. When they were together they were like brothers and they really admired one another. Both lived by the same motto, if someone wanted to see them they would be there. More or less when the rocky road runs out they die and that's the true spirit of rock 'n' roll. Chuck Berry, Bo Diddley they still roll, great! I often wish that I was involved a few years earlier during the Two I's and Six Five Special era. I watched it all on TV but that's not the same. Johnny loved rock 'n' roll, he always used to say "If I dropped dead or something there's only three people I would wish to front the Pirates, Gene Vincent, Little Richard, Jerry Lee Lewis. Anybody else forget it!"

While a member of the Outlaws Chas Hodges backed his idol Gene Vincent.
..."I soon found out that Gene would put on a show if he knew an old mate had come to see him. One of his best shows was when Johnny Kidd turned up one night. Gene had that way about him. He decided when to put on a good show."

Mick Green worked for a while backing the zany Freddie Starr.

Pepe Rush (Recording Engineer)
"The last time I had any contact with Mick Green was in about 1975 when we went to the Circus Tavern in Grays, Essex with Chris Hutchins the publicist who was Mick's partner in a record company. I was going to arrange to do a location recording for an album of Freddie Starr's live show. This did not unfortunately materialise. I remember Joe Brown was there and they all went back to Joe's home studio to do some recording. I, unfortunately, had other commitments and could not go with them."

Led Zeppelin recorded 'Shakin' All Over', 'Hungry For Love', 'I'll Never Get Over You' at the Metropolitan Sports Centre, Minneapolis in January '75 during rehearsals for a tour. Released on Brigard Records Brig 012 on a bootleg album entitled 'A Tribute To Johnny Kidd And The Pirates'.

'Shakin' All Over'/'A Shot of Rhythm And Blues' was released in France in '73 on Columbia 2C 006-05 255 by Johnny and the Pirates in a picture sleeve depicting Hells Angels.

Vince Eager released the Album 'Twenty Years On' on Nevis NEVLP 143 featuring a fine version of 'Please Don't Touch' which was dedicated "J.K. my good friend this is for you" and also 'Days Of Rock 'N' Roll' which Vince wrote and dedicated to Johnny and the Pirates, Gene Vincent, Elvis, Tommy Steele, Guy Mitchell, Buddy Holly, Eddie Cochran. The album featured superb musicians Eric Ford (guitar), Alan Weighall (bass), Rex Morrix (sax), Bobby Orr (drums) and Kenny Brown (piano).

The Memory Lives On.

(© Always N' Ever Archive)

In 1976 ten years after we lost Freddie Heath (Johnny Kidd) The Edwardian Club at The Loughborough Hotel, Loughborough Road, Brixton, London SW9 put on a tremendous tribute show to the memory of The Kidd. The club was run by Len Jinks who well remembers that fantastic evening.
"The time is 7.15pm. I'm standing in the Edwardian Club Room on Oct 9th 1976. I have seen this weekly rock 'n' roll venue slowly growing in status. For the last two months arrangements have been made by the hundreds for this Johnny Kidd tribute. At last the night has arrived. In the club room are members of 'Flashback' who are arranging their equipment on stage alongside Geoff and Stu of Timespan disco. At around 8 o'clock I called all the stewards round a table. We quickly ran through the arrangements. That done a final check with the bar staff, they are ready. At 8.45 the word comes through that there is a queue of over 200 yards long formed at the door and the public bars are packed. Timespan spin the first record of the night with shaky knees and nerves on edge in a shaky voice I whisper OK open the doors THE JOHNNY KIDD MEMORIAL SHOW has started. After half an hour all dancing has stopped with the club room packed solid and people still rolling up, not just from London but from all over the country. In the saloon bar are Wee Willie Harris, Screaming Lord Sutch. During Flashback's second act Stu (Coleman) remarks that if he's ever seen a band with a big future in front of them, this is it. Heads nod in agreement all around the dressing room. They go off stage to a deafening roar of approval. On the disco Geoff (Barker) and Stu are intensifying the atmosphere to breaking point with just about every record available by Johnny Kidd being blasted out and now its time. The room is silent as four people walk on stage. All ears are listening to Stu. Here tonight in tribute and to the memory of Johnny Kidd are.... and then a fifth person climbs on stage he proceeds to introduce each one to deafening cheers. Big Al on sax, on keyboards Neil McArthur, on drums Carlo Little, lead guitar Mick Nash, on bass guitar the man who was present when we lost the Kidd, Nicky Simper. Stu then introduced Wee Willie Harris. He and the band went on to bring the crowd to fever pitch with non stop rock 'n' roll. As the crowd were going frantic the figure of a man, tall and dark, stripped to the waist and climbed on to the stage. It was Roger Truth who took over his rightful place on drums alongside his old buddy on bass. He set about the drums with such venon he had the crowd roaring their approval. He also had Mick Nash taking evasive action from flying drum sticks. The crowd were wild with excitement not seen in London since the fifties. I thought this is truly a worthy tribute to THE KIDD...."

After 40 minutes an exhausted Wee Willie Harris left the stage with these words: LONG LIVE THE MEMORY OF JOHNNY KIDD... Later Bass man Nick Simper took vocals and went into the bass part of 'Shakin All Over'....When the applause died away Sutch introduced Johnny Kidds life long friend and roadie, Johnny Irving who gave his tribute to Johnny in an emotion choked voice. Another five or six songs and the stage was left empty for Geoff and Stu to bring the show to a close. The club room was slowly emptying, the thoroughly shattered but contented crowd were on their way home. I was standing near the exit getting my breath back. My mind went back to the earlier comment made by someone: "If only Johnny was here" Somehow I felt

he was." Although a sad occasion Johnny Irving, Nick Simper and Roger Truth all enjoyed meeting up.
To mark the 20th anniversary of Johnnys death - '86 The London Rock 'n' Roll Club paid a smashing tribute to The Kidd. The Shakin' Pirates of Clem (drums), Alan (guitar) and Brian (bass) played together for the first time in over 24 years as The Pirates. The show got rave reviews in the rock 'n' roll magazines.

The greatest honour of the evening went to rocker Dave Sampson who sang vocals. This led to Dave appearing at the '87 Weymouth Rock Festival alongside Gene Vincents fabulous Blue Caps.

Nick Simper
"Roger and I were talking about getting The Pirates back on the road. I used to sing a few numbers so I was quite confident about reforming but Dave Sutch (Lord) informed us that Mick Green, Spence and Farley were about to re-hoist the jolly roger. So Roger and I weren't so jolly. Although they returned a super heavier trio they always missed having the Kidd on vocals. He really was a super front man, no one else could compare.

below left: Brian Gregg at Tribute Show (© P.Smith)

below right: Clem Cattini (© P. Smith)

bottom: Alan Caddy (© P.Smith)

During my 1966 tour with Bobby Hebb it was really weird when we played the Nelson Imperial. It was only a matter of months since we left there and Johnny died. I had a real bad feeling especially because we were travelling in a Cortina. I kept thinking cars were going to come across and hit us. On one gig we met Billy J. Kramer and The Dakotas. I will never forget what Mick Green said to me that night. "I can't ever think of Johnny being dead, to me he's just on the road somewhere doing another gig." We will never except he is gone, its a nice way to think that Johnny Kidd is still singing somewhere."

In April 1978 Alan Wheeler formed the excellent Johnny Kidd Appreciation Society. Johnnys widow Jean Heath gave Alan permission to run this official society. Alan ran it superbly until February 1980. During the same year The Revillos released a good version of 'Hungry For Love' Din Disc DINZ 20 SP703.

Over the years Alan and myself have written to the BBC and ITV for footage of the Kidds TV performances. Sadly nothing has ever been found. In recent years the thumping leader of the Dave Clark 5 has bought the copyrights to many leading 1960's musical TV shows including Ready Steady Go.

Dave Clark Productions
"Unfortunately so far, not a single performance has been found. Should such a performance be found we will contact you."

Cyriel van den Hemel (Producer CCTV)
"We are not aware of having any footage but we will let you know if we do ever come across any."

JOHNNY KIDD
APPRECIATION SOCIETY
SAE for full details to:
ALAN WHEELER (Sec)
6 PEDLARS END
MORETON
ONGAR, ESSEX, CM5 OLR
(courtesy A. Wheeler)

Hemel was the Producer of the rock 'n' roll videos released in 1988 'The Greatest Years' and, surprise, surprise, Suzanne Heath the niece of The Kidd worked on the series.

Suzanne Heath
"This connection with the music industry led me into music management. I set up a company called Melody Music at the age of 21. The real star of the Heath family is my sister Juliette (23). At the age of fourteen she received the gold medal for achieving the highest mark for grade 8 on any instrument in the country. This gave her an automatic place into the Royal Academy. At the age of 18 she went to Middlesex Polytechnic to study electronic music and Stephane Grappelli Style jazz (violin). In the meantime she also discovered the art of song-writing and that she could play practically any instrument. Juliette is currently a professional musician with Divided Opinions. She also teaches the violin and the piano and, of course, what everyone wants to know - yes she does have plans to record 'Shakin' All Over'."

Along with Juliette and Suzanne Heath, the two sons of Clive Lazell (drummer with Five Nutters) are also involved in music. Peter like his father plays drums with Oxford band Workhouse while brother Jason plays bass for Leyton group Hunky Dory. Now in the nineties these are the Kidds of the future.

The superb rhythm section from the 'Shakin' Pirates Brian Gregg (bass) and Clem Cattini (drums) rejoined the Dene Aces in March '85 along with Mitch Keynes (guitar) to back Terry Dene for a North East mini-tour. The highlight of the shows was a pounding version of 'Peter Gunn' during which Terry introduced the band members. As soon as Brian Gregg's name was mentioned the riff switched to the haunting opening bars of 'Shakin All Over'. Terry would then rush off stage to return dressed in a white sports coat complete with a pink carnation. The band really rolled through 'Pretty Little Pearly', 'Start Moving', 'Baby She's Gone' and a medley of rock 'n' roll standards. Brian Gregg apart form playing a mean bass was also Terry's manager - until John Aldridge (Swindon businessman) took over in 1986. The Dene had a new line up Steve Smith (bass), Richard Leech (drums) and Mitch Keynes (guitar) but still featured 'Shakin All Over'.

On the 7th June '91 Joe Meek fanatic, John Repsch, created musical history by bringing Screaming Lord Sutch and The Savages, Cliff Bennett and The Rebel Rousers, Honeycombs, Mike Berry, Heinz, Moontrekkers, Clem's Tornados, Danny Rivers and the original Tornados together to celebrate the memory of Britain's greatest recording genius Joe Meek at the Lewisham Theatre. Repsch paid £2, 475 fees for the performers all except Alan Caddy, who insisted on nothing more and nothing less than the payment he had received for his very first gig with Johnny Kidd : 3 half crowns and 2 bottles of Coca-Cola. The Tornados - Alan Caddy (lead), George Bellamy (rhythm), Heinz Burt (bass), Roger Lavern (keyboards) and Clem Cattini (drums) were full of animosities and long held resentments but they did perform 'Telstar' for the first and last time since 1963 thanks to John Repsch.

During the nineties sessions have been harder to come by for Clem Cattini. He's kept busy touring with his Tornados (a new line-up) and playing drums in the West End production of The Rocky Horror Show. He also works as a limousine driver.

Clem Cattini
"I've played on one of the biggest records ever but I'm out driving because that's the only way I can pay the rent. If I'd known how important the business was going to be 30 years later I'd have played a little better in the first place. At the end of the day you are a musical navvy."

Clems' love of music and football will never die. He is an Arsenal season ticket holder and shareholder. For the 94-95 season he enrolled his grandson for the Junior Gunners. On Friday 5th August 94 Clem was looking forward to meeting up with Alan Caddy plus other original Tornados, Screaming Lord Sutch, Mike Berry and The Honeycombs to sign copies of the album 'The Adventures of Joe Meek' but sadly Alan Caddy had recently been mugged and suffered a broken jaw so of course he couldn't meet up with a fellow ex-Pirate. Most others showed up to celebrate the works of the legendary Joe Meek, the Telstar Man at HMV 150 Oxford Street, London.
In 'Shakin All Over' Johnny wrote a classic rock 'n' roll song. The number of artists who have featured it in their act is countless. Many famous musicians have recorded their own versions of the classic - The Pirates (without Johnny), Shanghai, the Swinging Blue Jeans, The Who, Wild Angels, The Pretty Things, Vince Taylor, Surfaris, Tommy Bruce, The Guess Who, CC Riders, Chris Spedding, Van Morrison, Little Tony, Generation X, The Searchers, Alex Harvey, British Invasion All Stars, Steve Marriott, Manyana (disco version), Led Zeppelin, Flaming Groovies, Wild Bob Burgos, Stray Cats even Mae West, etc, etc, .

Les Richards (La-De-Das)
"I saw the Flaming Groovies in Australia in around 1991 they played 'A Shot of Rhythm And Blues' plus 'I Can Tell' and dedicated it to Johnny Kidd, then started playing 'Shakin All Over' but turned it into a medly which ended up as 19th Nervous Breakdown the Stones song."

Wild Bob Burgos the tattooed sledgehammer of rock 'n' roll has recorded some tremendous versions of 'Shakin'/'Talking Bout You' J B 45 061.75. 'Please Don't Touch'/'All The Boys Love My Baby' Charly 45 CYS 1674. Even Cliff Richard 'Daddy's Home'/'Shakin'' EMI 5251. Due to the folding of Mills Music and Film Gems the rights of all Johnny's (Heath) compositions are now with E.M.I. In recent years Rowntrees Jelly used 'Shakin All Over' for the sound track for an advertising jingle.

Rock writer Spencer Leigh presented a superb radio series entitled 'Shakin All Over' which traced British rock 'n' roll from '55 to '63. This series ran for 12 weeks and was broadcast on many local radio stations. During the 60's Leigh, a Liverpudlian, saw many great bands at the Cavern. He is now an expert on the history of Merseybeat. He interviewed over 300 musicians who played the Liverpool scene and Hamburg for his excellent book 'Lets Go Down The Cavern' (Vermilion) (1984).

Spencer Leigh
"When Johnny and The Pirates combined Arther Alexander's 'A Shot Of Rhythm and Blues' with Bo Diddleys 'I Can Tell' they made one of the best double sided singles of all time. That single, more than any other, marks the transition from British rock 'n' roll to Merseybeat."

17. ALWAYS AND EVER

Les Dawson (Comedian June '93)
"Nothing dies in this world. We create an aura around us and somewhere along the line it carries on."

Johnny had a gift, a unique talent, he was amongst a rare breed of young rockers in Britain during the late fifties writing his own material. He wrote classic numbers years before the Beatles proved that groups could write their own material. To this very day Johnny's material is still played by many musicians all over the world. The Rapiers are one of many groups still flying the jolly roger for Johnny Kidd, and in fact, are one if not the best at re-creating the magic sounds of Johnny and The Pirates.

The Rapiers
(© Rapiers)

Colin Pryce Jones (Lead Guitar The Rapiers)
"The atmosphere in England of the late 50's and early 60's was socially different in every aspect of life. In particular the emerging talent in the music scene was over shadowed by the American rock 'n' roll giants of the era. Nobody thought at that time that good rock 'n' roll numbers could be written outside America! I feel its fair to say that early efforts by British rock 'n' rollers proved this to be true. However all of that seemed to change around the time of '58 when a handful of people started writing really good British rock 'n' roll i.e. Ian Samwell, Billy Fury. In May 1959 Johnny Kidds' 'Please Don't Touch appeared. From the opening riff into the first vocal line there is a raw power and energy that came through. For a debut single at that time I would call it astounding! The lyrics in rock 'n' roll songs have always been about fun boys and girls, cars etc. These lyrics still have the magic of an era never to be repeated. Please don't touch, I shake so much, what a line!! 'Feelin' followed with the same power house vocal and musical arrangement. 'Shakin All Over' has gone down as one of the Best British rock 'n' roll 45's ever. Who could argue with that? To be able to write that number is more than just talent I would say a unique feeling for the musical genre of his chosen field. Ask who else was coming up with that much good stuff in 1959/60? 'Restless' was another lyrical plea to the ladies, showing Johnny Kidd's emotions toward the opposite sex. I can certainly identify with most of his songs in one way or another! Always remember that he was writing these songs whilst touring the A roads going from gig to gig in a Bedford van doing radio, TV etc. In those days work followed by more work was normal not like today when songwriters have studios packed with gadgets and modern technology to relax in. Johnny Kidd's songs came out of his head and were heard in the most convenient form available - one guitar. So there was little time to refine or change what he had first thought of. Judging on the wonderful output, he got it right first time. 'Growl' was a perfect example of hard hitting rock 'n' roll, his vocal treatment is superb and at the same time unusual. Johnny Kidd sang not only lead vocal on his records but also harmony lines and backing vocals on some sessions, again innovative at the time. From all of this I would say he had a good ear for music generally which must, of course, help in the writing and arranging of songs. I think that he had that a certain touch in his ability to keep a flow going through each of his songs, which made each Johnny Kidd track instantly recognisable. Listen to 'Please Don't Bring Me Down', 'Then I Got Everything' and hear the ideas in the songs reach out. The true test of a good song is can you remember the tune? I know most of you reading this will be able to do that for an awful lot of Johnny Kidd's songs."

above top: Brian Gregg and Colin Pryce Jones - Ace Café Re-union 4/9/94)
(© Always N' Ever Archive)

above centre: Frank Rouledge plays Johnny Gordon's original guitar
(© Reed Northern Newspapers)

above bottom: Keith Hunt, Mike West, Don Toy
(Always N' Ever Archive}

right:
Johnny's unfinished song
(© Jean Heath Collection)

Johnny Kidd
"Once I get an idea for a song, I work on it until its finished. Then I only have to play it over once on my guitar and it sticks in my head like glue."

Alan Carter (Teenage Pal)
1956 - "He was very keen and told me he was writing songs and he was going to make it big in show time."

Frank Rouledge (Guitarist, Five Nutters)
1957 - "Fred was always writing catchy little tunes, many a time I found him sitting beneath a tree in Roundwood Park with his banjo on his knees, working on a new song."

Mike West (Backing Vocalist Original Pirates)
1958-59 - "Fred sat down in the studio and between us all we quickly wrote 'Growl'."

Brian Gregg (Bass Pirates)
1960-61 - "After a night out going around the coffee bars we'd often end up at my place and we'd sit there half the night listening to music I'd get a guitar out and we'd write some songs."

Mick Green (Lead, Pirates)
1962-64 - "I used to really nag Johnny to write songs. I remember waiting for him at home one time so we would do some writing. I waited two hours for him to turn up and when I eventually rang him he said he'd decided not to come but go to bed instead! He had the talent to write songs but whether he had the talent to bring it out and do it, I don't know."

Frank Farley (Drums, Pirates)
1962-66 - "Johnny used to write a lot of material. He'd write it on the back of a bus ticket or something. We'd just go in the studio and play with it. In those days we were recorded direct, there were no over-dubs there was none of that 32 track rubbish."

Are you ~~just~~ having ~~your fun~~ me on.
Do you really want me
Am I the only one
Do you really need me
I hope and pray you do.
Cos I love you

Are you ~~just~~ playing around
Do you really want me
Am I ~~just~~ someone you've found
Do you really need me
I hope and pray you do
Cos I love you yes I do.

And if I promise I will leave you never
Will you give your heart to me forever and ever.

Nick Simper (Bass Pirates)
1966 - "He always came up with hook lines, just before he died he came up with a good idea, knocked about with it, it had the making of a good number. Sadly nothing came of it."

Clive Lazell (Drums, Five Nutters)
"Fred was a friendly down to earth man, he had a great voice and was a smashing fella. He wasn't big headed or anything we had some fun times."

Alan Carter (Teenage Pal)
"I always used to boast to everybody that Johnny Kidd was my mate. The day he was killed will live in my memory forever. I was driving along the Willesden High Road when over the car radio it was announced that he had been killed in a road accident. I pulled over in total shock and cried my eyes out. I still think of Fred, because every now and again I hear 'Shakin All Over' played on the Golden Oldies Show here in Dallas, Texas my new home."

Ron and Yvonne Everard (Friends)
"Freddie was a very warm and likeable friend. It was tragic that he lost his life so young and at the beginning of what we thought would be a very promising career."

Brian Saunders (Drummer Freddie Heath Band)
"I was living in Ealing at the time, standing on the kitchen table putting cladding up in the wall, when it came over the radio that Fred had been killed. I went all cold. He was a down to earth, nice chap, never miserable always keen and happy looking forward to the next gig. He worked very hard to get success."

Mike West (Backing Vocalist, Pirates)
"Although I had worked hand in glove with Johnny I always stood and watched him because there was just something magic about him. He was very exciting. It was because of Johnny's image that I became Robbie Hood. It was Reg Calvert's idea but at the same time it was a kind of tribute to the Kidd."

Nick Simper (Bass, Pirates)
"Johnny was such a nice guy that lots of doors would have opened for him. It was a great feeling playing along with Johnny ...., no matter who else was on the bill there was no way you'd be overshadowed."

Alan Wheeler
"John's end was tragic, being at what looked like the start of a revitalised career. (New Pirates, re-found enthusiasm, new 45). I shall always remember Johnny Kidd as a great character, good rocker, a warm human being I am sure others will too."

Clem Cattini (Drums, Pirates)
"Even to this day I think Johnny was one of the best rock singers to come out of England. He was great."

Brian Gregg (Bass, Pirates)
"Out of all the guys I worked with he was definitely the best singer in rock 'n' roll. Johnny Kidd was the nicest guy, the most down to earth, natural, friendly guy, out of the lot of 'em. We were very good friends."

Frank Farley (Drums, Pirate)
"I think he'd be pleased that we're still at it - and I think he'd still be at it himself. I think he'd still be having hit records as well. Sounds change but the feel stays the same and he had a very unusual feel. It's good that he's still remembered but not really surprising after all 'Shakin' All Over' is really the only British rock classic and Kidd wrote it as well."

Jimmy Saville O.B.E. (Leading Disc Jockey)
"I'm not really into writing articles and such like but Johnny was one of the most exciting people on the scene in those day, and his loss was a shock that a lot of us never got over."

Keith Goodwin (Publicist)
"Johnny was one of the nicest and most genuine people I have met in the business. Stories that he had had his day were a load of rubbish - he was doing really well in cabaret."

the late Kenneth Connor (Actor, Carry On film star)
"No I never met or even had sight of Johnny Kidd in spite of him only living a few doors away from me. Therefore my tribute is, He kept a fine lawn. I always admired it and still do."

No. 74 South Hill Avenue
(© Always N' Ever Archive)

Raye Du-Val (Drummer, Checkmates)
"Johnny Kidd was a king of rock 'n' roll in his own right and his band were the tops. A lovely guy, a true friend. He may not be with us on earth but his is that great rock 'n' roll arena in the sky."

Pete Searles (Mark Shelley and The Deans)
"We still drag out the old band twice a year for sixties charity gigs. They are sold out each year and the most requested song is still 'Shakin All Over'."

Bruce Welch (Guitar, The Shadows)
"Johnny Kidd and The Pirates without doubt were one of the finest British rock 'n' roll bands of all time. 'Shakin All Over' is a classic record which had weathered the test of time magnificently well."

Peter Wilson (The Hustlers)
"I still miss his music! He was certainly in very good humour the week he died saying he had sorted out his direction problem and was very positive of popularity with a new audience he was building."

Don Toy, Pete Newman &
Johnny Irving - 25/1/92
(© Always N' Ever Archive)

Sandy Regan (Friend)
"Johnny could be very quiet and withdrawn, he could be completely mad, a real laugh at times. He loved his time on my dad's farm driving around on the tractor. He never acted like a 'pop star'. I was proud to have been a friend, he really was a great guy."

Les Richards (New Zealand Group, The La De Das)
"Johnny and The Pirates had a great influence in NZ and OZ. I love Johnny and The Pirates as I feel it was his influence at an early age that go me involved in rock music. I wish he had been more widely released i.e. USA, OZ and NZ as I'm sure he would have been much more popular but that's life. Lets make the greatest rocker live musically forever, long live JK, and The Pirates of course."

Mick Rudzinski (Bass, The Avengers, The Dees, Mersey Cats)
"Since those far off days I have kept playing and trying like everybody else connected with Johnny Kidd to keep his name alive by playing most of his numbers, 'Shakin All Over', 'I Can Tell', 'Shot Of Rhythm And Blues', 'I'll Never Get Over You', 'Hungry For Love' and 'Ecstasy' and we get a

great reaction because of them. I also play for various children's rock 'n' roll charities i.e. New Brighton Rock/Mersey Cats which raises funds for very sick children in the Merseyside area. Within this charity Johnny Kidds name is very much respected and I think he would have been involved in it."

The Dees are well-known locally for their support of Local Charities. - They were in fact the founders of 'NEW BRIGHTON ROCK'.
Guitar / Vocalist DON WOODS has penned and recorded many songs of the locality. He was a member of a number of local bands in the early sixties.
Bass Player MIKE RUDZINSKI started playing in local bands including THE AVENGERS in the '60s, and in 1964 he joined JOHNNY KIDD'S PIRATES.
Drummer / Vocalist TOM BENNETT played with a number of well-known Merseybeat groups including The UNDERTAKERS & The PATHFINDERS, but is best known as the drummer with Wallasey band THE PRESSMEN.
All three have been friends since they were teenagers.

The Dees (Mike Rudzinski centre) proud to feature Kidd's material during their endless charity work throughout the 1990's

Colin Richards (Rhythm Guitar, Terry Franks and The Avalons)
"We played up and down the country sometimes lead billing but on many occasions we supported many of the big names of the ballroom circuit Joe Brown, Lord Sutch, Cliff Bennett, Nero and The Gladiators, Shane Fenton, Gene Vincent, Neil Christian, Jackie Lynton, Chris Farlowe and many others but my favourites were Johnny Kidd and The Pirates. We supported them, it was a great era, I'm glad I was there. I'm back now with Terry Franks as lead guitarist and we still reminiscence about the old days, especially the time we spent with Johnny Kidd."

Tony Jackson (Bass original Searchers and Vibrations)
"We still do a tribute to Johnny during our act i.e. 'Shakin All Over'. It really goes down well. I'd like to do 'I Can Tell' which I thought was one of his great songs."

Colin Pryce Jones (Lead Guitar, The Rapiers)
"I have the utmost respect for Johnny Kidd both as a songwriter and performer. In his song book Johnny wrote "I have always insisted that one of the greatest helps in keeping the name alive was because so many musicians in so many various groups all over the British Isles were kind enough to play my records on their gigs." I assure you all I shall carry on the tradition of playing his material at all the Rapiers gigs as well as recording them as we have done on our records. We lost a very talented man."

Screaming Lord Sutch
"Nobody could follow Johnny Kidd and his Pirates amazing act not even. The Beatles or Rolling Stones. He was an original performer, singer and a great man."

Heinz
"What a shame the way he went, he was one of the best and he would still be at the top now if he was still alive."

Marc Bolan and his percussionist Micky Finn both loved playing Johnny Kidd and early Johnny Burnette records.

Noel Redding of the Jimi Hendrix Experience was a keen fan of The Pirates.

The late, great Steve Marriott (Small Faces, Humble Pie, Packet of 3)
"I always thought that Johnny and The Pirates were incredible together for their day." Steve loved 'Shakin All Over' so much that on Humble Pie's first UK tour with David Bowie in 1970 they opened the 'Pie' set with a heavy version of the classic. On his final album '30 Seconds To Midnite' Trax Music MOD 1037 CD released in 1990 he couldn't resist recording a very original arrangement of 'Shakin'."

Bobby Elliott (Drums, Hollies)
"We've busked 'Shakin All Over' on a couple of tours. The rock 'n' roll spot at the end of our show is full of surprises, we never rehearse that stuff. Clarkey (Allan Clarke vocalist) starts up and tries to catch the band out - Great fun! That's what rock 'n' roll' should be - FUN!"

Mrs Jean Heath (Johnny's wife)
"I find it hard to play his records because his singing voice was too much like his speaking voice. If I'm in a shop and 'Shakin' comes on the radio it always gives me a twist in the stomach."

Mick Green (Lead guitar, Pirates)
"Johnny was one of the first British rock 'n' roll singers, he had it all going, the image, Pirate gear, patch, backdrop and he wrote songs like 'Shakin', 'Touch' etc. He really was a great live performer, it was a real blow to us when he got killed in that car crash."

Bert Weedon (Mr Guitar)
"I enjoyed Johnny's company, he was quite unique. He is sadly missed."

Malcolm McLaren (Manager, Sex Pistols, Adam and The Ants)
"Kidd had a greater sociological impact on British youth than Bob Dylan."
McLaren suggested a look based on Kidd with a dash of Red Indian to Adam Ant. Adam's finest videos were full of buccaneer dramatics.

Pete Rush (Recording Engineer)
"I was very upset at the time when I heard of his death and he has come into my thoughts very often over the years. From this you will realise that his manner must have made a very great impression on me. I must say in all honesty that Freddie Heath, he used his real name, was one of the most pleasant, friendly, polite and genuine people I ever met in the music business the whole time I was involved with it."

top: Jean and Johnny
(© Jean Heath Collection)

centre: Mick Green - 'Still Castin' A Spell'
(© Ray Johnson)

bottom: Frank Farley and Bob Burgos - 1991
(© R. Burgos)

Wild Bob Burgos (Drums)
"It was back in the 60's when I first heard that unforgettable sound of Johnny Kidd. At that time I was playing in the small clubs of South London where every juke box was rockin' with the music of 'Shakin All Over'. After many years of playing with several different bands this song had definitely registered in my mind as being an all time classic. The years went by and in July 1975, when, with a band called Kick-start, we cut our first ever record 'Shakin All Over' as a tribute to the great Johnny Kidd. We went on to record another record before splitting up to go our separate ways. It wasn't too long before I was recording again this time with the original Matchbox.... After many tours across Britain and Europe we released our debut album 'Riders In The Sky' in 1976 featuring Johnny Kidd's 'Please Don't Touch'. On turning gold, a single ('Please Don't Touch') was cut and released in three different countries. The rock 'n' roll revival boom of the 70's was here and so was Johnny Kidd's music...

A great talent, a great artist and a great British rocker whose name and songs will never be forgotten.
Long Live Rock n' Roll .... and long live Johnny Kidd's music."

Suzanne Heath (Johnny's niece)
"The family had spoken about Johnny Kidd on many occasions but the first acknowledgement of it for me was when I was at school and all the kids were discussing who we knew that were famous and who had famous family. I said that I was related to Johnny Kidd and no-one believed me! It didn't take me long to realise exactly how well known his music was and still is. I soon began to appreciate the music of the great man. I am a lover of music anyway and pleased to realise that it is actually in the blood."

top: Keith Hunt, Pete Newman, Nick Simper, Johnny Kerrison - Xmas '93
(© A. Jarrett)

Bottom:
(© Jean Heath Collection)

Wilko Johnson (Guitarist and Pirates Fan)
"Our old band's name Dr Feelgood came from Piano Red who was Dr. Feelgood and The Interns - but it was the song. I had a record of it by Johnny Kidd and The Pirates. Kidd and The Pirates were my people you know. So it was one of the numbers we learned and then Sparko thought of calling our group Dr. Feelgood which seemed good enough because it seemed to fit the music. We didn't worry particularly about it not being original because at the time we seriously didn't think of going any further than the Railway Hotel, Pitsea. Johnny Kidd and The Pirates were really good. There's no doubt about it Mick Green is the best rock guitarist this country has ever produced and if anyone ever mentioned any other name I just laugh at them because nobody can play like him. These people who are living in bloody mansions now - they can't hold a candle to him."

Pete Newman (Sax, The Savages, The Bizz)
"I have never forgotten Freddie Heath and will always be grateful to him for giving me my first real chance in the music business and of course introducing me later to musicians like Clem Cattini, Alan Caddy, Heinz etc. people who I still see today on gigs and other social events."

Joe Waite (The Dolly Blues)
"I became a guitar player in the early sixties after being knocked out by JK's guitarist Mick Green and bought a Fender Telecaster in 1963 which I still have. The first Kidd record I bought was 'Restless' (still got it plus a few scratches). My brother John and I played it on our Dansette a million times. Kidd was someone you never forget, the backdrop, the band, the act. He was just in the wrong place at the wrong time all the time. He was on par with Lord Sutch up against the wishy washy safe beat. He certainly beat the shit out of Wayne Fontana and the Mindbenders etc. - they all played safe!

We used to catch Johnny at the Floral Hall, Morecambe. I played there '64 and '65 I was always there, playing, sometimes standing in, swapping gigs due to double bookings or just watching but The Pirates were the greatest. An act only rivalled by Sutch. I also played the Imperial Ballroom, Nelson which I believe Johnny was travelling from. I gave up playing pro in 1971 leaving my brother's band. My brother John went on to be singer and bass player with The Babys in the 70's, then solo when he had a hit in the American charts with 'Missing You' EMI America 8212. In recent years he sang with with Bad English. He agrees with me it all came from Johnny Kidd. I've got the old stars dressing room mirror from the Floral Hall. They all combed their locks in it. Even the Stones, Beatles, Hollies not to mention Johnny Kidd. Kidd was a real character."

Keith Hunt (Fan)
"On Saturday 8th October '66 I was on the tube travelling to my beloved Queens Park Rangers F.C. My brother Dave was reading the sports page of his newspaper. On the back page stop press "Johnny Kidd killed in car crash, " I was so shocked. A few months earlier Mike Millward the giant guitarist with The Fourmost had died of leukaemia. This had upset me, but Johnny was my first pop idol to die. Years later in the 1970s I met Billy Hatton, Brian O'Hara, Dave Lovelady, Joey Bower of The Fourmost. Great guys with loads of talent. They told me that Mike Millwards father still feels the Mike is there with the lads on stage. I think that was a lovely way to look at things. Throughout my research for this book I have met hundreds of musicians who admired and worked on the same bill as Johnny Kidd and The Pirates. Many have admitted that Johnny and his various crews had the greatest stage act they'd ever seen.

The curtains would part, a twenty foot high and forty foot long galleon painted with ultra violet paint would hit you between the eyes. A crew of Pirates would set the swinging beat for the arrival of Capt. Kidd. On he would stroll the Buccaneer of British rock 'n' roll, clad in jet black leather, looking very sinister wearing an eye patch, and with chains hanging from the wrists of his jacket. Swinging a huge cutless he would chop props in half. He was wild, his vocals superb as he smashed his rapier to the beat. He was a unique performer and that's why I will remember him for Always n' Ever."

below top: Nick Simper, Keith Hunt, Pete Parks (© A Jarrett)

below bottom: 'The Good Old Boys' (Nick second left) (© A. Jarrett)

Mick Hill (Rock You Sinners magazine)
"Johnny Kidd - even the name sends a shiver down your spine. I can remember listening to him on the radio. I bought his 'Please Don't Touch' in June 1959. I was crazy about that record. Even today its still my favourite Kidd track. A few years ago I held a readers poll to find the Best of British' top 20 records from the 1950's and early 60's. Readers sent in their Top 20 lists. The response was tremendous and over 250 different records were listed! In the end I had to print the Best of British Top 50! - and what was the top voted British record? 'Shakin All Over' and not only that his 'Please Don't Touch' was number four! - Johnny Kidd was number one... and still is."

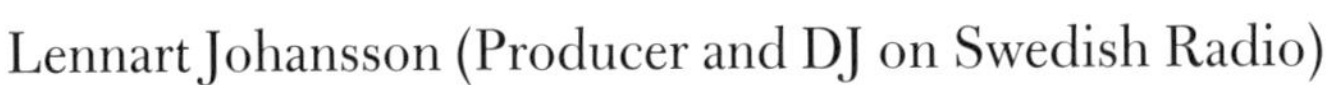

Lennart Johansson (Producer and DJ on Swedish Radio)
"I run a rock history show on Sunday mornings called Backtracks on Radio Skaraborg. I have played Kidd tracks from the start several years ago. A while back I got a phone call from a 15 year old who thought Johnny was the best thing he's ever heard. It feels that he finally got the acknowledgement he deserved. Johnnys' music surely lives on..."

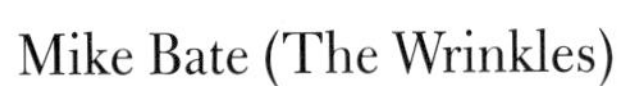

Mike Bate (The Wrinkles)
"It is very exciting a book dedicated to Johnny Kidd. He has been my idle for many years. Our 60's show band still feature at least three Kidd songs."

Wally Ridley (E.M.I. Record, A&R Manager)
"I always thought that Johnny was a good singer for his time. It was a tragedy to die so young and too have left so little behind him."

Nick Simper (Bass, Pirates)
"He never treated us as a backing band, that's why people were so loyal to him. He never pulled

rank. He was such a unique human being. So were Rod Freeman (Flintstones) and Tony Ross (Flintstones). If you lived to be 200 years old you'd never forget such special people. Every day they come into my mind. Other people get lost in time but these were special. Tony Ross was a legend on the bass, light years ahead of his time. The Beatles, Searchers everyone at the Star Club in Hamburg were just spellbound by Rupert Ross's thumb style technique - amazing talent. I didn't think Irvo (Johnny Irving, roadie) would survive after Johnny died. It was like having his twin cut away. They were so close. I remember his mum saying that he didn't cry when his dad died but he cried when we lost the Kidd. I'm quite proud of my work with Deep Purple but if I had to choose my time with Johnny and his Pirates or Purple there's no contest, Johnny Kidd was the Governor."

Arron Kane (Johnny Kidd 'Fan')
"Well let me tell you the sounds of Johnny Kidd live on for now we have the 1990's tribute version of the great Johnny Kidd and The Pirates with my band Kidd Kane and The Buccaneers. We are making a big name for ourselves in the West country. We feature over 20 Kidd classics including the rare version of The Fool."

Mike Bate (Wrinkles)
"An attempt to bring out a Johnny Kidd tribute band' is under way and we are in the middle of rehearsals. I hope it works because I'm very involved in this as drummer and lead vocalist. Our lead guitarist is none other than Barry Hammett (Pirate, Jan/Feb '65) plus a bass player. At the moment we are calling ourselves Only Kiddin but we may change it at a later date."

18. JOHNNY KIDD - RETROSPECT

Alan Wheeler

"Looking back, it would be hard for me to distinguish any difference between Johnny Kidd - The Star and Johnny Kidd - The Person. By that I mean that he did not adopt any of the superficial airs and graces that some of his contemporaries did back in those days. He was and always remained an ordinary guy. Someone with his feet firmly on the ground. There would be the likes of Billy J Kramer or Joe Brown fighting to leave a cinema or TV studio, and along would come Johnny and stroll right past! Not that he didn't have time for his fans, he most certainly did and often spent quite a while after a show signing autographs and pics but he liked to take advantage of the freedom other stars of similar standing never enjoyed.

He frequently went back to his roots in Willesden, North London where he liked nothing better than to chat to some of the locals that he knew. He would sometimes sit on a doorstep and pass the time of day with former neighbours and friends in the area happily signing autographs for their children. It wasn't Johnny Kidd - the star here but a local lad that had got on. During the time I knew him Johnny mostly lived in Perivale (later South Harrow) but there was no big star scene there either - he would go into the newsagent or cafe to buy some cigarettes himself - he didn't need someone to buy them for him. Of course he couldn't do that when dressed in the gear - at a venue for instance when his roadie Johnny Irving would take care of it. Soho was another of Johnny's haunts - he would often drop into the famous Two I's Coffee Bar in Old Compton Street or pop round to Leeds Music and other publishers. He and The Pirates would cut the odd demo disc in a tiny basement recording studio in Berwick Street - close to where skiffler Chas McDevitt had a coffee bar. When in Soho Johnny didn't just have time for a chat with other notables such as Adam Faith, Terry Dene, Wee Willie Harris, Vince Eager etc, who came along. Equally he would stop to speak to less recognisable singers and musicians whom he also knew from way back but then that was the kind of man he was - he liked to remember his mates. Quite a few Soho faces hit the big time but several remained in the second division. Johnny once commented on those on the lower rung by saying that they were just unlucky. He didn't regard it as a talent issue.

Johnny lived for music but not the road - travelling hundreds of miles each week for most of the time in a cramped Austin-Morris J2 van was hardly a luxurious way of getting around. There was only one motorway (the M1) back in those days so getting to and from the more far flung part of the British Isles was often an endurance test. Eating was often a problem, not so bad if the M1 was being used, but invariably it meant the transport or road side cafe. Coming back from a gig reduced the options still further most of the time. Johnny and company would be grateful to find a milk machine at a garage in the middle of nowhere! Such was life on the road!
The sparse conditions of some of the dancehalls and ballrooms, where Johnny and the boys sometimes had to change in a storeroom or kitchen, and the battle against terrible acoustics in a hall devoid of proper stage lighting or adequate sound system left a lot to be desired. The worse thing when playing such places was to arrive late after a long drive and go on cold. The sound would be bouncing all over the place. That Johnny and the group were always able to put on a great show despite such appalling odds was a tribute to their professionalism. But it was no easy task. Johnny played a higher percentage of dancehalls and ballrooms than other venues simply because they brought in the money. From a purely financial aspect it was worth putting up with the inconvenience and, in the itinerary somewhere, would be the more plusher ballroom which

would be a bonus. The right setting, of course, was in the cinema or theatre where the visual impact was helped with backdrops and follow-spots. There was usually a higher degree of comfort back stage with proper dressing rooms and toilets and the overall effect created a more sinister performance. A great pity that Johnny and The Pirates were never filmed in their environment. In real money terms the package show tours that Johnny went out on were not very lucrative but offered great promotional opportunities for a new 45 together with guaranteed press coverage. It usually meant playing to larger and often packed audiences - the early Gene Vincent and Jerry Lee Lewis tours and later The Ronettes, Billy J Kramer and Brenda Lee packages were no exception. To deal with the inadequacy found in some dancehalls Johnny took to rigging up his own galleon backdrop and using ultra-violet light strips as a substitute for non-existent foot lights. It proved an effective move.

Less so was Johnnys' experiment with an echo-box to put an edge to the sometimes distorted P.A. systems he had to contend with. This was abandoned after a brief encounter as was his use of a cutless thrown into the stage floor. Mixing the texture with rock 'n' roll was a good idea - way ahead of people like The Who and Adam Ant but unfortunately not shared by insurance companies - at least not at that particular time! A great shame as it proved a highlight of Johnny's stage act whilst it lasted. But the undoubted surprise, night after night was his rendition of the old music hall song 'If You Were The Only Girl In The World' which, recorded with an orchestra, was a rather insignificant follow-up to his first single 'Please Don't Touch'. However, on stage, Johnny would transform the number from lightweight to a pounding version, almost reminiscent to Gene Vincents' 'Baby Blue'. It would provoke a tremendous reaction whether in a working men's club, cinema, dance hall or plush night-spot. It never surprised me that something of Gene Vincent rubbed off on Johnny given that he was one of the American singers' greatest fans. When the subject came round to Gene, Johnny would defend him to the hilt - quickly dismissing any claims or suggestions made by promoters or anyone else that he and The Pirates had done better business/given a better show than the American. Johnny's view that 'Gene can always pull it out of the bag when he wants to' never diminished and was strengthened, in 1963 when Gene supported Johnny and The Pirates at Birmingham Town Hall. Backed by the Rockin Berries, as I recall, and appearing in the role of Guest Star. Gene did a marvellous act very much akin to his hey day. It was certainly watched and appreciated by Johnny and the trio. Later Johnny talked seriously of recording a tribute to Gene Vincent album and I believe it was discussed with Walter Ridley at Abbey Road Studios, where he and The Pirates laid down a cut of the Vincent song 'Baby Blue' - so far undiscovered in the E.M.I. archives. Johnny also slipped 'Be-Bop-A-Lula' into his act on one occasion, so yes, he was a great Gene Vincent admirer.

In the recording sessions held in St Johns Wood most would be light hearted affairs. All the same, professional that he was, Johnny would like to get the job done and in those days at E.M.I. time was precious. Both side of a 45 could be completed quickly by today's standards. Usually in a morning or an afternoon or sometimes in the early evening depending on how busy Abbey Road Studios were. As I recall, Studios 1 and 2 were used. Johnny and The Pirates would alternate between the two, cutting one 45 in 1, the next in Studio 2. Normally there would be a run through for a sound/balance check and then cut on the first or second take. Rarely did it go to three takes. There might be a little time spent on over-dubbing the lead vocals (to give a double vocal effect) and occasionally re-recording the ending of a particular number but it was all rather hurried back in those days. The Pirates were treated as session musicians and paid at the end of a session (as I remember it was £6 whilst Johnny being the contract artist received royalties in due course of a release. He never spoke of getting any advance payments. The man in overall control of HMV sessions was Walter J Ridley - a guy I always throught better suited to other signings such as Ronnie Hilton or the Joe Gordon Folk Four - not to rock 'n' roll or R & B. He didn't really understand it and I doubt if he could have recorded Johnny and The Pirates with the same punch were it not for his assistants such as Peter Sullivan (early on) and Norman 'Hurricane' Smith (later).

If anything BBC Radio recordings for the old Light Programme could be slightly more humorous and, in the case of Saturday Club, less hurried. Johnny and The Pirates would amble into the Old Playhouse in Charring Cross and usually have to wait around until it was time to record a five song set for the 'club'. Sometimes Johnny would be interviewed by Brian Matthew, or read out a request. This was no mean feat as it was often against a background of The Pirates pulling funny faces at him! Other radio sessions for the Beeb took place at The Paris Theatre in Piccadilly, and more often than not, like an actual stage show in front of an invited audience.

Everything about BBC radio in those days was fairly primitive, from ancient stand microphones and 'boom' mike (these were taken off the boom and suspended in mid air over the drums along with a mic on the bass drum and another picking up the cymbals) to the two-track tape recorders. Sometimes there would be a baffle board in front of the drums but only as high as the drum kit itself. Not like in commercial recording studios where the drummer could be skimmed as well (as Frank Farley sometimes was at Abbey Road). There was no chance of over-dubbing at the Beeb - sessions were recorded on the straight with Jimmy Spencer helping Johnny to capture the double vocal sound on numbers like 'I'll Never Get Over You', 'Hungry For Love', 'Always 'N' Ever'. The Beeb had their own way of doing things as well. Mick Green would turn up the volume on his amp (only 30 watts! later graduating to 70 watts!) only to have the Beeb engineers turn it down again! They would also come and adjust the stand mike on it. It would be usual for Mick to run through an intro or two to get the guitar being picked up right and the same for Johnny Spence's bass guitar. There would be a little burst of activity from Frank and they would be ready to go. Johnny had to adopt a slightly different technique in a studio setting than when on the road and using a hand mike. A static microphone obviously restricted movement and the greatest difficulty for Johnny was in keeping still! (Thank goodness for mimed TV appearances when he would freely move!) Whilst an unusual broadcast of 'Shakin All Over' played by the Northern Dance Orchestra springs to mind as a rare radio slot, I can also recall Johnny making a guest spot on Parade Of The Pops to perform 'I'll Never Get Over You' backed by the resident house band - Bob Miller and The Millermen and just Johnny Spence helping out on the double voiced chorus. Probably the only time Johnny Kidd has broadcast live without The Pirates playing behind him (excluding Radio Luxembourg's E.M.I. spectaculars which had a live interview). Radio was fine but at seven guineas a programme it was hardly a fortune! Not that BBC Television paid the earth either in those days. I believe things like Crackerjack and Juke Box Jury earned Johnny around £21 whereas ITV companies were more generous - A spot on Thank Your Lucky Stars or Ready Steady Go paid nearer the £50 mark but it was the exposure factor that mattered to Johnny not the monetary value of a booking. I think he would have gone on Gardening Club if it would have helped him up the charts! He certainly had some bad luck with Top Of The Pops. As far as I can remember the show hadn't started until 'I'll Never Get Over You' had reached its highest position in the hit parade. With the disc standing at No. 4 Johnny and The Pirates were hurriedly invited over the Television Centre where they telerecorded a performance of the song in front on a specially gathered teenage audience (and DJ Jimmy Savile) after having done the rounds of other and, at that time, more established programmes. Alas this particular contribution was never shown! Having banked on the disc remaining static or going up Top Of The Pops dropped Johnny from the show when chart placings were received from the Record Retailer' which showed that 'I'll Never Get Over You' had gone down! The format of the programme was different in those early days - it was centered purely around the top twenty - no bubbling under or even the best of the Record Retailers top 50. So although further interest was aroused when 'Hungry For Love' made it to No. 20 it quickly waned when the disc dropped below.

Johnnys last television appearance was during 1965 promoting 'The Birds And The Bees' on Granada TV's 'Five O'clock Club' with an outdoor location. Although these television bookings pleased Johnny he became increasingly despondent with the lack of chart success and as stage engagements decreased coming to a head when The Pirates decided to go their own way and cut a disc with Polydor and the ending of his management contract with Kennedy Street Artistes in Manchester in 1966. It proved a lean time for Johnny. A stab as a solo performer built around a 45 ('It's Got To Be You') did not revive his fortunes unfortunately. It seems dancehall crowds were not ready to accept Johnny with indifferent groups backing him. Despite, or maybe because of, as Johnny said, "Exaggerated reports in the music press that he was thinking of quitting the business, moving over to management or whatever." Johnny came back with The New Pirates including a keen Kidd follower, bass-guitarist Nick Simper regaining much of his enthusiasm if not the work. Although back with a regular trio again and able to stamp the Pirate images on P.A.'s, bookings were not plentiful. However Johnny was optimistic of turning things around with a new single he had cut at Abbey Road with the new three piece unit - 'Send For That Girl' and an old standby number - 'The Fool'.

Talking on the phone, Johnny seemed more perky than he had been for sometime although he was obviously troubled by the lack of work and a worsening financial situation. That aside, he said he was well pleased with The New Pirates which he described as a very tight group - he urged me to come and see them in action and that I would like them for sure. He said that he hoped the fans would go for the A side of the forthcoming 45 which had added accompaniment to broaden out the sound and make it more distinctive'. Johnny said that he enjoyed spending more time with his wife, Jean and their young daughter Cilla (then 2 1/2 years old), and going round to his old house (in Perivale) to see his folks and his two boys (from his first marriage). But he ought really to be bringing in the bread! For one thing his larger house in South Harrow was expensive to heat. In a bid to generate some engagements ahead of the new record release, Johnny said he was taking the group up to a Lancashire promoter/friend for what he said was a Surprise Guest Spot at one of his clubs. He was hopeful of obtaining some more gigs at his other clubs in the North. He said he still saw his old mate and former roadie, Johnny Irving, but he wasn't going with him on this trip. Tragically, it was to be the last time I spoke to Johnny.....

Most people, I'm sure, will remember Johnny Kidd as the hard-hitting original performer and recording artist that he was but we should also spare a thought for Johnny Kidd - songwriter. Few, if any, British singers emanating from 1959 can lay claim to having one of their songs recorded by a legendary American film star with Mae West putting 'Shakin All Over' on an LP in the States. Pure novelty, of course, but not for the first time since earlier in Britain Tommy Bruce had treated record buyers to a gravel-voiced version of the song on Columbia. Johnny was always knocked-out about other artists recording or performing his songs. He would sometimes reflect on the fact that an American singer called Chico Holiday had waxed 'Please Don't Touch' in the States and in particular that the version was released in the UK on the same label as Elvis Presley - RCA/ Victor! - Johnny was quite chuffed about that as he was that another Stateside act - The Surfaris (of 'Wipe Out' fame) had also done a cut of the song on an LP - coming out here on the famous London/American label. He also reminisced about Vince Eager performing 'Please Don't Touch' on the early Larry Parnes package tours when Marty Wilde headed one show and Vince the second (before the emergence of one Billy Fury). In '62 and '63 Johnny became aware of some of the Northern groups putting one or two of his self-written numbers into their sets - not only in this country but also in Hamburg - an early 'In' place for many British beat groups - playing and congregating at the Star Club or Top Ten Club, in pre-Merseybeat days and after. Amongst those putting a Kidd tune on disc whilst in Hamburg - The Searchers performing 'Shakin All Over' on a live LP recorded by Philips and issued in the UK. Johnny was flattered by the recognition (and, incidentally, by the reception he and The Pirates received when playing in Hamburg) but sadly and regrettably he was to miss out on much recognition that came in later years. I have no doubt that he would have been delighted with the Canadian group The Guess Who taking 'Shakin' into the American Billboard and Cashbox charts which was quite remarkable. Of The Who for including the song on a hit LP ('Live At Leeds') and to know the song transcended the underground and punk movement with cuts by the Sensational Alex Harvey Band and Generation X. Just what he would have made of a heavy metal version of 'Please Don't Touch' by Motorhead I don't know. Still it got into the charts so there's something in that! I am sure Johnny would have been touched by Cliff Richard having 'Shakin' on the flip of a No 2 in 1981 ('Daddys Home') as he would have been with ex-Small Faces star Steve Marriott, now no longer with us, finally putting the number on an album after first performing the song with Humble Pie back in 1969. Equally I feel sure Johnny would have smiled at a version of the song recorded by the 70's glam-rock band, Mud, but much later which featured Mick Green as guest guitarist. But even with the presence of a distinguished musician like Mick I don't think their version was meant to be taken too seriously! Much more akin to what he was doing at the beginning of 1960's was a little known 45 of 'Please Don't Touch' by the Wild Angels. This cut would have pleased him coming as it did from a band associated with Gene Vincent in the UK. But above all else, Johnny would have appreciated the efforts over the years by some of his old friends and contemporaries such as Bert Weedon, Little Tony, Cliff Bennett, Tommy Bruce, Ricky Valance, Vince Eager, Alvin Stardust, Danny Rivers, Graham Fenton, the Swinging Blue Jeans and Mick Green who deserves a credit for laying down the most recorded versions of 'Shakin All Over' with Shanghai, Pirates, Mud and his own solo album. Another ex-Pirate, Nick Simper and his band The Good Old Boys, and other vocalists and musicians who have kept his most famous songs and his name a part of the music and entertainment scene.

Some people in the music business and among the journalistic fraternity described Johnny Kidd as being a dated performer. Times were indeed changing but I am of the opinion that Johnny would have come back to his own via the cabaret circuit and the rock 'n' roll revival shows that materialised later.

In closing, may I say that my memories of Johnny are as vivid as ever. On stage there was something about him that made you sway and your feet tap. Off stage there was a genuineness about him that made you warm to him. There is little doubt that the reformed Pirates of Messrs Green, Spencer and Farley did a tremendous job in reviving something of the old days with Johnny, even getting into the album charts, but as great as they could be, to my mind, there was always one spark and ingredient missing...."

Nick Simper (Bass, Pirate)
"Rock historians of the future, so called rock 'n' roll writers and all those spotty arseholes who write for the papers, there's no way that they can say that his Pirate stage gear can distract from his talent. He wrote the best record that ever came out of Britain, 'Shakin All Over', its still the best and always will be I think. He had a superb voice, he was totally open to suggestion, if it was a good tune he would do it, no matter what style.

He phoned me up one day and said "I had a dream about you last night because you're like my thing", I shockly replied, "What do you mean?" He said, "All the big stars have a thing i.e. Dave Clark has got his sax player Dennis Peyton, a member of the band to latch on to. I feed off you when I'm on stage." I said, "That is a great compliment." There was always something special between us, he really was a nice bloke."

Clive Lazell (Drummer, Five Nutters)
"It's funny how Freddie finished up being Johnny Kidd as my mother bought us all Pirate stripped jumpers when we first got going in the skiffle era. My mum must have known something, eh!"

Keith Hunt
"In the late 1960's Alan Wheeler completed a draft manuscript of a book on Johnny and Gene Vincent which was submitted to a number of publishers. None of the publishers were interested due to a changing music scene!

Years earlier Alan also produced a six page biography booklet, complete with photographs and artwork. During the fan club era the excellent Johnny Kidd mag which often ran to 24-30 pages was a tremendous read. In fact it was Alan's first class inscriptions plus Screaming Lord Sutch giving me Johnnys ole Vortexion amplifier that encouraged me to put pen to paper in the first place. I must have asked Alan hundreds of questions during my research for this tribute. Amazingly he answered every question!

Johnny Kidd (Freddie Heath)
"With me ambition goes in stages. I start with a small ambition, gain it, then build up to a greater ambition. One should reach up all the time, and when disappointments come, as they do, forget about them, never dwell on them, just cherish one's hearts desire and struggle to make it come true. Tucked away I have a secret dream to star at the London Palladium and to meet Elvis Presley."

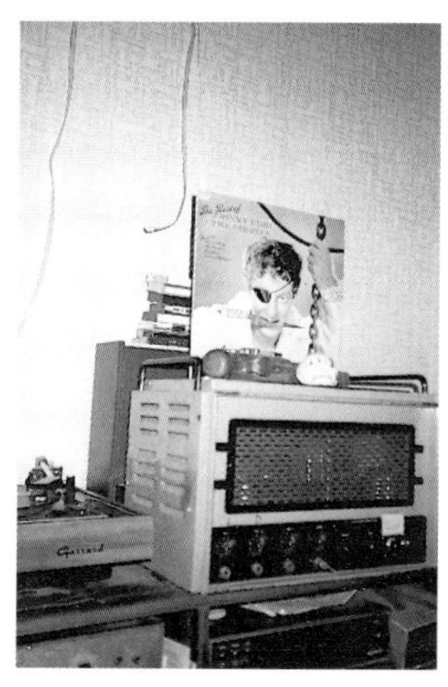

top left: Clive Lazell - Xmas '94
(© C. Lazell)

top right: Brian Gregg and Keith Hunt - Ace Café Re-union 4/9/94)
(© Always N' Ever Archive)

bottom left: Kidd's vortexion amp
(© Always N' Ever Archive)

bottom right: Lord Sutch and Brian Gregg - Ace Café Re-Union
(© Always N' Ever Archive)

JOHNNY KIDD AND THE PIRATES DISCOGRAPHY
SINGLES 1959-66
HMV LABEL

RELEASE DATE	TITLE	NUMBER
8/5/59	Please Don't Touch	POP615 (7XEA 19482)
8/5/59	Growl	POP615 (7XEA 19483)
4/12/59	If You Were The Only Girl In The World	POP674 (7XEA 19633)
4/12/59	Feelin'	POP674 (7XEA 19586)
22/1/60	You Got What It Takes	POP698 (7XEA 19662)
22/1/60	Longin' Lips	POP698 (7XEA 19664)
10/6/60	Shakin' All Over	POP753 (7XEA 19764)
10/6/60	Yes Sir, That's My Baby	POP753 (7XEA 19765)
30/9/60	Restless	POP790 (7XEA 19846)
30/9/60	Magic Of Love	POP790 (7XEA 19847)
24/3/61	Linda Lu	POP853 (7XEA 20012)
24/3/61	Let's Talk About Us	POP853 (7XEA 20013)
15/9/61	Please Don't Bring Me Down	POP919 (7XEA 20072)
15/9/61	So What	POP919 (7XEA 20110)
19/1/62	I Want That	POP978 (7XEA 20178)
19/1/62	Hurry On Back To Love	POP978 (7XEA 20177)
9/11/62	A Shot Of Rhythm and Blues	POP1088 (7XEA 20477)
9/11/62	I Can Tell	POP1088 (7XEA 20465)
14/6/63	I'll Never Get Over You	POP1173 (7XEA 20643)
14/6/63	Then I Got Everything	POP1173 (7XEA 20644)
8/11/63	Hungry For Love	POP1228 (7XEA 21108)
8/11/63	Esctasy	POP1228 (7XEA 21121)
6/3/64	Always and Ever	POP1269 (7XEA 20812)
6/3/64	Dr Feelgood	POP1269 (7XEA 20813)
12/6/64	Jealous Girl	POP1309 (7XEA 20847)
12/6/64	Shop Around	POP1309 (7XEA 20848)
30/10/64	Whole Lotta Woman	POP1353 (7XEA 20880)
30/10/64	Your Cheatin' Heart	POP1353 (7XEA 20881)
19/2/65	The Birds and The Bees	POP1397 (7XEA 21402)
19/2/65	Don't Make The Same Mistake As I Did	POP1397 (7XEA 21403)
7/5/65	Shakin' All Over '65	POP1424 (7XEA 21415)
7/5/65	Gotta Travel On	POP1424 (7XEA 21416)

RELEASE DATE	TITLE	NUMBER
7/4/66	It's Got To Be You	POP1520 (7XEA 22023)
7/4/66	I Hate Getting Up In The Morning	POP1520 (7XEA 22024)
11/11/66	Send For That Girl	POP1559 (7XEA 22277)
11/11/66	The Fool	POP1559 (7XEA 22278)

EXTENDED PLAY

1960	Shakin' All Over	7EG8628

	Please Don't Touch, Shakin' All Over Restless, You Got What It Takes	
1964	Johnny Kidd and The Pirates I'll Never Get Over You, Then I Got Everything, Hungry For Love, A Shot Of Rhythm and Blues.	7EG8834
2/12/60	LP Parlophone Saturday Club (two tracks only) Big Blon' Baby, Weep No More My Baby	PMC1130

PIRATES SINGLES

3/1/64	My Babe	POP1250 (7XEA 22155)
3/1/64	Castin' My Spell	POP1250 (7XEA 21156)
1/7/66	Shades of Blue	POLYDOR BM56712
1/7/66	Can't Understand	POLYDOR BM56712

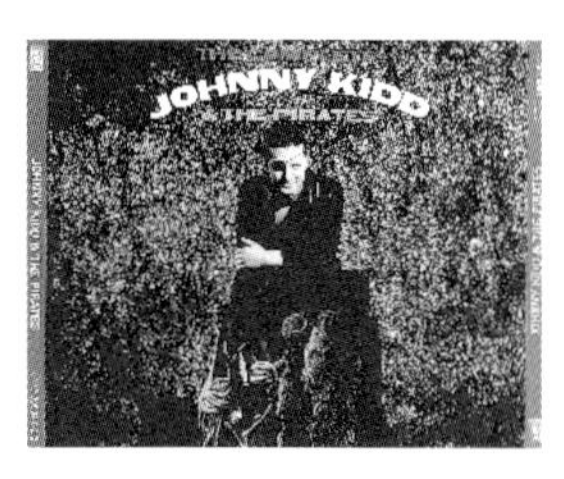

BRITISH RELEASES LP'S

Shakin All Over	Starline SRS 5100 Stereo Re Channeled	1971
Best Of	EMI NUTM 12 0C05406613M	April 1978
Rarities	See For Miles CM120	March 1983
Best Of	EMI EMS 1120	1986
Classic and Rare	See For Miles See 287 also on CD SEE CD287	1990
The Complete	EMI 79994 823 Double CD	Sept 1992

62 tracks containing most of his work for E.M.I. between 1959-66 featuring two previously unreleased tracks Bad Case of Love, You Can Have Her plus a Little Bit Of Soap first time edited and completed as per producers notes.

GOLD IN EMI VAULTS UNRELEASED TRACKS

Baby Blue, Tricky Dicky, Be Bop A Lula, Feel So Fine, Baby That's All You Gotta Do, Fortune Teller, If You Were The Only Girl In The World (original Pirates) Box 8849, Magic Of Love (original Pirates), Buddy Holly Style possibly E39683, Always and Ever (in Blue Beat Style) E57419Z, Spanish Armarda and Popeye (intrumentals written by Mick Green E48829), The Fool (very short demo) E48828/9.

BELIEVE TO HAVE BEEN SCRAPPED

Test 1959	If You Were The Only Girl In The World	E35975 BOX 8849
Test 1959	Yes Sir That's My Baby	E35975 BOX 8849
	Always and Ever (Bluebeat Style)	E57419Z

NOT RELEASED UNTIL 1983 (ALL MONO)	RECORDED
I Know	13/5/64 20/5/64
Oh Boy	6/4/64 13/4/64

Where Are You	6/4/64	20/5/64
A Little Bit Of Soap (Incomplete Session)		6/4/64
Steady Date		2/11/59
More Of The Same		31/1/61
I Just Want To Make Love To You		31/1/61
This Golden Ring		10/9/65
Right String But Wrong Yo Yo		7/4/64
Can't Turn You Loose (Reading) S. Bernstein Lt		16/2/65
I Hate Getting Up In The Morning (2)		10/9/65
Send For That Girl (2) Mills Music Ltd		6/9/66

NOT RELEASED UNTIL 1990

(M) Some Other Guy		31/1/63
(S) Let's Talk About Us (2)		6/4/64
(S) Send Me Some Lovin		6/4/64
(S) The Fool (Ford Hazlewood) (2)		6/4/64
(S) Please Don't Touch (2)		7/4/64
(S) Big Blon' Baby (2)	6/4/64	7/4/64

Over the years various compilations have featured Johnnys hits along with other Rockers i.e.
Rocking Again At The 2 I's ACE CHA77 1984
(So What)

Made In Britain DECCA 3093 1983
(A Shot Of R n' B)

Made In UK EMI VMP 1092/3 1980
(Shakin' All Over)

Testament Du Rock Vol 2 MFP 2M126 85573/4/5 1974
(I'll Never Get Over You/Shakin' All Over)

British Beat Before The Beatles EMI 07777
A set of seven CD's 1955-62
Total 140 Tracks by various British Rockers

Vol 4	Please Don't Touch
Vol 5	Shakin' All Over, Restless
Vol 6	Please Don't Bring Me Down
Vol 7	A Shot Of Rhythm & Blues

each CD contains 20 tracks.

RE-ACTIVATED RELEASES

Shakin' All Over/Yes Sir That's My Baby	EMI2414	Feb 1976
Please Don't Touch/I'll Never Get Over You	EMI2667	Aug 1977
Shakin' All Over/A Shot Of Rhythm & Blues	HMV POP2005	June 1980
Shakin' All Over/I'll Never Get Over You	OLD GOLD 9366 1983	

Yes Sir That's My Baby EMI 2414 recorded 9/7/59.
This is a different version of the song first released in 1960. A much faster and untidy cut. Johnny would not have been happy with this being issued. It is obviously a warm-up version and is not up to the standard of the 13/5/60 recording. Incorrectly placed as track 10 on 'Complete JK' CD - should be track 3.

OVERSEAS RELEASES (INCOMPLETE)

Shakin' All Over/Yes Sir That's My Baby	USA APT 25040	1960

Shakin' All Over/Yes Sir That's My Baby	Portugal A V0Z DO DONO EQ5030	1960
Shakin' All Over/A Shot Of R/B	French 2C00605255 Pathe Marconi	1973

I'll Never Get Over You/Then I Got Everything USA Capital 5065 1963

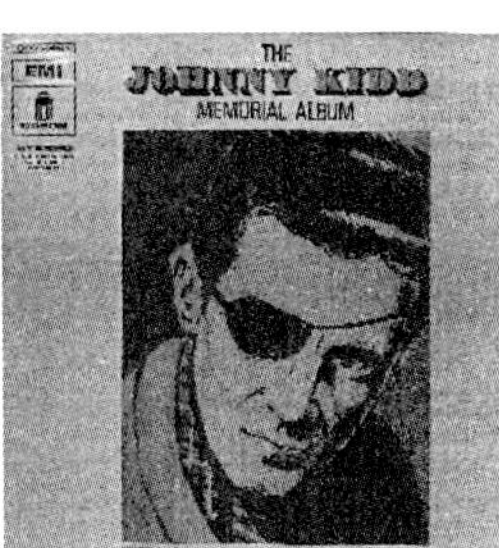

French LP Memorial Album Odeon CO62 04422 1970
The French Buddy Holly Memorial Society commissioned this tribute LP. The compilers were Jacques Grimbot, Serge Dumonteil and George Collange.

French LP Your Cheating Heart French Columbia Pathe Marconi CO62 04731

French LP Johnny Kidd Rocker EMI 2CA154 06653/4 1978
This is a 32 track double album. Featuring a previously unreleased version of Please Don't Bring Me Down.

French EP La Voix De Son Maitre - Shakin' All Over, Shop Around, Restless, Whole Lotta Woman EGF813.

PRIVATELY CUT RECORDINGS

1. Bloody Red Beauty, Shake Rattle and Roll recorded at Wilkinsons Radio Shop in 1957 by members of the Five Nutters. (Still Exists)

2. Freddie Heath on guitar and vocals Regent Sound Studio 1958 title unknown.

3. Wow Wow Beat by Freddie Heath Combo 1958, Radio Music Studios Berwick Street.

4. Always and Ever recorded Berwick Street, The Fool, Some Other Guy Privately Cut.

5. Johnny backing vocals on Pete Newmans demo You Gotta Be Around 1964? (Regent Sound Studio).

6. Johnny updated his ole hits with session musicians including Raye-Du-Val on drums 1966. (Radio Music Studio Berwick Street)

7. Various rehearsals recorded at 20 Manchester Square (EMI House) London W1 by Norman Smith especially with last line-up i.e. Send For That Girl, Please Don't Touch (Indian style with Sitar) 1966.

8. Early run through of Send For That Girl, I'm Only Sleeping on reel-reel home tape recorder, recorded at 74 South Hill Avenue, South Harrow 1966. (Still Exists)

9. We Will Come Together, I Love You, date? on reel-reel home tape recorder.

RECORDING SESSIONS 1959 (E.M.I.)

1. Please Don't Touch 18/4/59, Master Tape TL6501.
Johnny Kidd (vocals), Alan Caddy (lead), Johnny 'Fruit' Gordon (bass), Tony Doherty (rhythm), Mike West - Tom Brown (backing vocals), Don Toy (drums).

2. Growl 18/4/59, Master Tape TL6501.
As above except Ken McKay (drums).

3. Yes Sir, That's My Baby (2), 9/7/59, Master Tape TL10264
As above except (drummer unknown).

4. Steady Date, 2/11/59, Master Tape TL21365.
As above except Bert Weedon (lead), (drummer unknown)

5. Feelin', 2/11/59, Master Tape TL 21365.
Johnny Kidd (vocals), Alan Caddy (lead), Johnny 'Fruit' Gordon (bass), Tony Doherty (rhythm), Mike West - Tom Brown (backing vocals) (drummer unknown).

6. If You Were The Only Girl In The World, 12/11/59, Master Tape TL7810.
Bert Weedon (lead) with Chorus and Orchestra conducted by Ivor Raymonde.

N.B. 5. Pete Newman (Ex Freddie Heath Band)
"Feelin' was an instrumental of mine that Fred liked and re-arranged and put words to."

RECORDING SESSIONS 1960 (E.M.I.)

1. Longin' Lips, 4/1/60, Master Tape TL7810.
Johnny Kidd (vocals), Alan Caddy (lead), Brian Gregg (bass), Clem Cattini (drums), Mike West/Tom Brown (backing vocals).

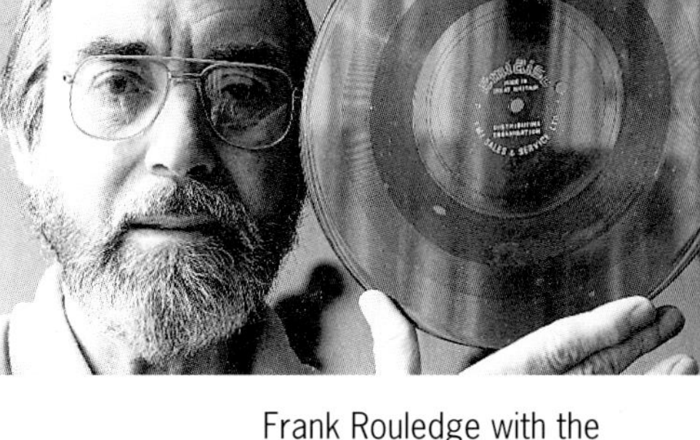

Frank Rouledge with the original acetate of 'Shakin' (© Reed Northern Newspapers)

2. You Got What It Takes, 4/1/60, Master Tape TL7810.
Same line up as above.

3. Shakin' All Over, 13/5/60, Master Tape TL8288.
Johnny Kidd (vocals), Joe Moretti (lead), Alan Caddy (second guitar), Brian Gregg (bass), Clem
Catttini (drums).

4. Yes Sir, That's My Baby, 13/5/60, Master Tape TL10274.
Johnny Kidd (vocals), Alan Caddy (lead), Brian Gregg (bass), Clem Cattini (drums).

5. Restless, 5/9/60, Master Tape TL8288.
Johnny Kidd (vocals), Joe Moretti (lead), Alan Caddy (second guitar), Brian Gregg (bass), Clem Cattini (drums).

6. Magic of Love, 5/9/60, Master Tape TL11341.
Johnny Kidd (vocals), Alan Caddy (lead), Brian Gregg (bass), Clem Cattini (drums).

7. Linda Lu, 6/10/60, Master Tape TL14158.

8. Let's Talk About Us, 6/10/60, Master Tape TL11341.

9. Big Blon' Baby, 6/10/60, Master Tape TL9703.

10. Weep No More, My Baby, 7/10/60, Master Tape TL9703.

Johnny Kidd (vocals), Alan Caddy (lead), Brian Gregg (bass), Clem Cattini (drums).

N.B. Clem Cattini always states that his first session was 'Shakin All Over'.

RECORDING SESSIONS 1961 (E.M.I.)

1. More Of The Same, 31/1/61, Master Tape TL26604.

2. I Just Want To Make Love To You, 31/1/61, Master Tape TL266204.

3. Please Don't Bring Me Down (2), 25/5/61, Master Tape TL26604.

Johnny Kidd (vocals), Alan Caddy (lead), Brian Gregg (bass), Clem Cattini (drums).

4. So What (Crompton-Jones) 17/8/61, Master Tape TL10718.
Line up as above with Thunderclap Jones (piano).

5. Please Don't Bring Me Down, 17/8/61, Master Tape E43371Z.
Johnny Kidd (vocals), Big Jim Sullivan (lead), Alan Caddy (second guitar), Brian Gregg (bass), Clem Cattini (drums).

6. Hurry On Back To Love, 1/12/61, Master Tape E43896A-4T.

7. I Want That, 1/12/61, Master Tape E43896B-4T.
With the Michael Sammes Singers and Orchestra conducted by Michael Sammes. (No Pirates)

RECORDING SESSION 1962 (E.M.I.)

1. I Can Tell, 26/9/62, Master Tape TL14067.
(N.B. Original Black Label single credits Samuel McDaniels)

2. A Shot Of Rhythm n' Blues, 17/10/62, Master Tape Tl2709.

Both songs feature Johnny Kidd (vocals), Mick Green (lead), Johnny Spence (bass), Frank Farley (drums).

RECORDING SESSIONS 1963 (E.M.I.)

1. Some Other Guy, 31/1/63, Master Tape E48828.
Johnny Kidd (vocals), Mick Green (lead), Johnny Spence (bass), Frank Farley (drums).

2. Spanish Armarda (Mick Green) 31/1/63, Demo E48829 Box 1327.

3. Popeye, 31/1/63, Demo E48829 Box 1327.

Both 2 and 3 are instrumentals featuring solo Pirates:
Mick Green (lead), Johnny Spence (bass), Frank Farley (drums).

4. I'll Never Get Over You, 16/5/63, Master Tape TL12709.

5. Then I Got Everything, 16/5/63, Master Tape TL12709.

6. Hungry For Love, 11/10/63, Master Tape TL12709.

7. Ecstasy, 11/10/63, Master Tape TL15512.
Johnny Kidd (vocals), Mick Green (lead), Johnny Spence (bass), Frank Farley (drums).

8. Castin' My Spell (E.A. Johnson) 11/10/63, Master Tape TL25343.

9. My Babe, 11/10/63, Master Tape TL25343.

8 and 9 both solo Pirates featuring Mick Green (lead), Johnny Spence (vocals/bass), Frank Farley (drums).

RECORDING SESSIONS 1964 (E.M.I.)

1. Dr Feelgood, 13/1/64, Master Tape TL14372.

2. Always and Ever, 4/2/64, Master Tape TL14372.
Johnny Kidd (vocals), Mick Green (lead), Johnny Spence (bass), Frank Farley (drums).

(2) Features Alan Wheeler, George Cooper, Mick Green, Johnny Spence, Johnny Irving, Frank Farley on all backing vocals.

3. Whole Lotta Woman, 6/4/64, Master Tape TL26014.

4. Your Cheatin Heart, 6/4/64, Master Tape TL21365.

5. Let's Talk About Us (2), 6/4/64, Master Tape TL52279-2T.

6. A Little Bit Of Soap, 6/4/64, Master Tape E52269Z.
7. The Fool (2), 6/4/64, Master Tape E52270-2T.

8. Oh Boy, 6/4/64, 13/3/64, Master Tape E52269Z.

9. Send Me Some Lovin', 6/4/64, Master Tape E52270-2T.

10. Big Blon' Baby (2), 6/4/64, 7/4/64, Master Tape E52271-2T.

11. Right String But The Wrong Yo Yo, 7/4/64, Master Tape E52271-2T.

12. Shop Around, 7/4/64, Master Tape TL26604.

13. Please Don't Touch (2), 7/4/64, Master Tape E52272Z.

14. I Know, 13/5/64, 20/5/64, Master Tape E52863-2T.

15. Jealous Girl, 14/5/64, Master Tape E52680.
16. Where Are You, 6/4/64, 20/5/64, Master Tape E52905Z.

17. Don't Make The Same Mistake As I Did, 1/10/64, Master Tape E55333.

3-16 All feature Johnny Kidd (vocal), Mick Green (lead), Johnny Spence (bass), Frank Farley (drums), Vic Cooper (keyboards), except 17 Johnny weider (lead).

RECORDING SESSIONS 1965 (E.M.I.)

1. The Birds & The Bees, 5/2/65, 11/2/65, 15/2/65, Master Tape E55333.
Johnny Kidd (vocals), Johnny Weider (lead), Johnny Spence (bass), Frank Farley (drums), Vic Cooper (keyboards) on all 1965 sessions except 5/6??

2. Can't Turn You Loose, 16/2/65, Master Tape E98692Z.
Line up as (1) plus session musicians.

3. Shakin' All Over ('65), 20/4/65, Master Tape E55890 4T.

4. Gotta Travel On, 20/4/65, Master Tape E55890 4T.

5. Bad Case Of Love, 25/5/65, Master Tape TL26604?
6. You Can Have Her, 25/5/65, Master Tape TL26604?

7. I Hate Getting Up In The Morning (2), 10/9/65, Master Tape E57349-4T.

8. This Golden Ring, 10/9/65, Master Tape E57349-4T.

N.B. ? 5 and 6 other sessions on Master Tape TL26604 feature Johnny Kidd, Alan Caddy, Brian Gregg, Clem Cattini dated Jan and May '61.

RECORDING SESSIONS 1966 (E.M.I.)

1. It's Got To Be You, 22/2/66, Master Tape E98692Z.

2. I Hate Getting Up In The Morning, 22/2/66, Master Tape E98692Z.
Johnny Kidd (vocals), No Pirates, Accompaniment directed by Johnny Harris with backing vocals by The Marionettes.

3. Send For That Girl, 23/8/66, Master Tape ?
Johnny Kidd (vocals), Micky Stewart (lead), Nick Simper (bass), Roger Truth (drums), Ray Soaper (keyboards), plus Orchestra arranged and conducted by Harry Robinson.

4. The Fool, 18/8/66, 23/8/66, Master Tape TL26604.
Johnny Kidd (vocals), Micky Stewart (lead), Nick Simper (bass), Roger Truth (drums), Ray Soaper (keyboards).

5. Send For That Girl (2), 6/9/66, Master Tape E61386.
Line-up same as (4).

Other sessions took place at Abbey Road betwen 1959-66 plus many rehearsals at E.M.I. House Manchester Square but with the passing of time line-up details and dates remain undiscovered. Due to the fact that during the late 50's and early 60's there was various charts I have not given chart positions for singles and E.P.'s only sessions and release dates.

(© A. S. Lowes)

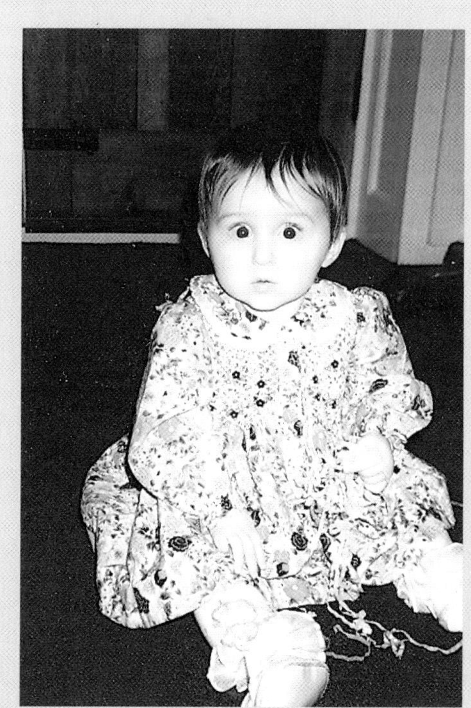

(© Jean Heath Collection)

The Kidd of the Future
Zoe
(born 25/5/94) aged 9 months
Johnny's Grand-Daughter

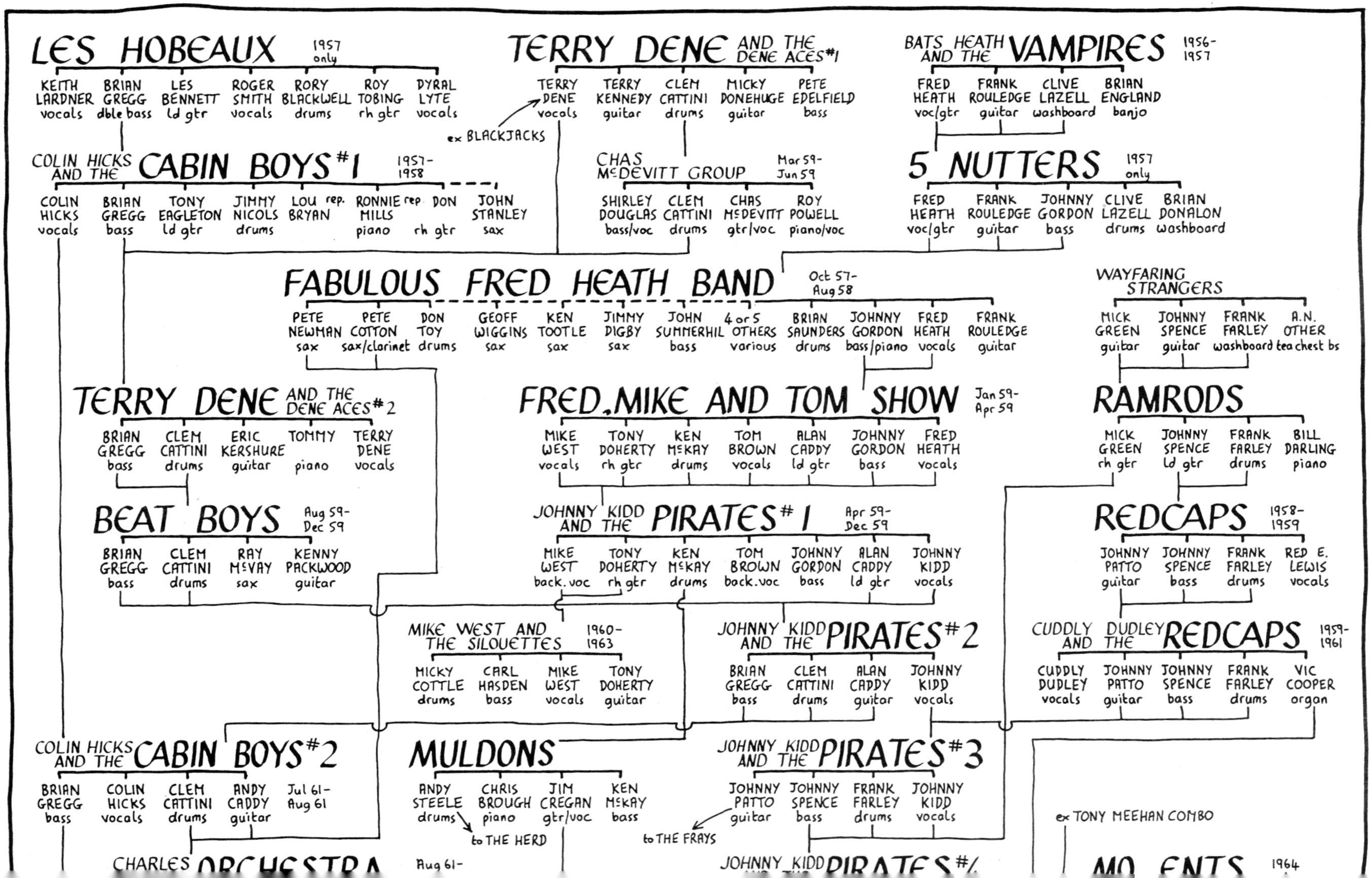

LES HOBEAUX
1957 only
KEITH LARDNER vocals
BRIAN GREGG dble bass
LES BENNETT ld gtr
ROGER SMITH vocals
RORY BLACKWELL drums
ROY TOBING rh gtr
DYRAL LYTE vocals
TERRY DENE AND THE DENE ACES #1
TERRY DENE vocals
ex BLACKJACKS
TERRY KENNEDY guitar
CLEM CATTINI drums
MICKY DONEHUGE guitar
PETE EDELFIELD bass
BATS HEATH AND THE VAMPIRES
1956-1957
FRED HEATH voc/gtr
FRANK ROULEDGE guitar
CLIVE LAZELL washboard
BRIAN ENGLAND banjo
COLIN HICKS AND THE CABIN BOYS #1
1957-1958
COLIN HICKS vocals
BRIAN GREGG bass
TONY EAGLETON ld gtr
JIMMY NICOLS drums
LOU BRYAN
rep.
RONNIE MILLS piano
rep.
DON rh gtr
JOHN STANLEY sax
CHAS McDEVITT GROUP
Mar 59-Jun 59
SHIRLEY DOUGLAS bass/voc
CLEM CATTINI drums
CHAS McDEVITT gtr/voc
ROY POWELL piano/voc
5 NUTTERS
1957 only
FRED HEATH voc/gtr
FRANK ROULEDGE guitar
JOHNNY GORDON bass
CLIVE LAZELL drums
BRIAN DONALON washboard
FABULOUS FRED HEATH BAND
Oct 57-Aug 58
PETE NEWMAN sax
PETE COTTON sax/clarinet
DON TOY drums
GEOFF WIGGINS sax
KEN TOOTLE sax
JIMMY DIGBY sax
JOHN SUMMERHIL bass
4 or 5 OTHERS various
BRIAN SAUNDERS drums
JOHNNY GORDON bass/piano
FRED HEATH vocals
FRANK ROULEDGE guitar
WAYFARING STRANGERS
MICK GREEN guitar
JOHNNY SPENCE guitar
FRANK FARLEY washboard
A.N. OTHER tea chest bs
TERRY DENE AND THE DENE ACES #2
BRIAN GREGG bass
CLEM CATTINI drums
ERIC KERSHURE guitar
TOMMY piano
TERRY DENE vocals
FRED, MIKE AND TOM SHOW
Jan 59-Apr 59
MIKE WEST vocals
TONY DOHERTY rh gtr
KEN McKAY drums
TOM BROWN vocals
ALAN CADDY ld gtr
JOHNNY GORDON bass
FRED HEATH vocals
RAMRODS
MICK GREEN rh gtr
JOHNNY SPENCE ld gtr
FRANK FARLEY drums
BILL DARLING piano
BEAT BOYS
Aug 59-Dec 59
BRIAN GREGG bass
CLEM CATTINI drums
RAY McVAY sax
KENNY PACKWOOD guitar
JOHNNY KIDD AND THE PIRATES #1
Apr 59-Dec 59
MIKE WEST back. voc
TONY DOHERTY rh gtr
KEN McKAY drums
TOM BROWN back. voc
JOHNNY GORDON bass
ALAN CADDY ld gtr
JOHNNY KIDD vocals
REDCAPS
1958-1959
JOHNNY PATTO guitar
JOHNNY SPENCE bass
FRANK FARLEY drums
RED E. LEWIS vocals
MIKE WEST AND THE SILOUETTES
1960-1963
MICKY COTTLE drums
CARL HASDEN bass
MIKE WEST vocals
TONY DOHERTY guitar
JOHNNY KIDD AND THE PIRATES #2
BRIAN GREGG bass
CLEM CATTINI drums
ALAN CADDY guitar
JOHNNY KIDD vocals
CUDDLY DUDLEY AND THE REDCAPS
1959-1961
CUDDLY DUDLEY vocals
JOHNNY PATTO guitar
JOHNNY SPENCE bass
FRANK FARLEY drums
VIC COOPER organ
COLIN HICKS AND THE CABIN BOYS #2
Jul 61-Aug 61
BRIAN GREGG bass
COLIN HICKS vocals
CLEM CATTINI drums
ANDY CADDY guitar
MULDONS
ANDY STEELE drums
to THE HERD
CHRIS BROUGH piano
JIM CREGAN gtr/voc
KEN McKAY bass
JOHNNY KIDD AND THE PIRATES #3
JOHNNY PATTO guitar
to THE FRAYS
JOHNNY SPENCE bass
FRANK FARLEY drums
JOHNNY KIDD vocals
ex TONY MEEHAN COMBO
CHARLES
Aug 61-
JOHNNY KIDD
1964

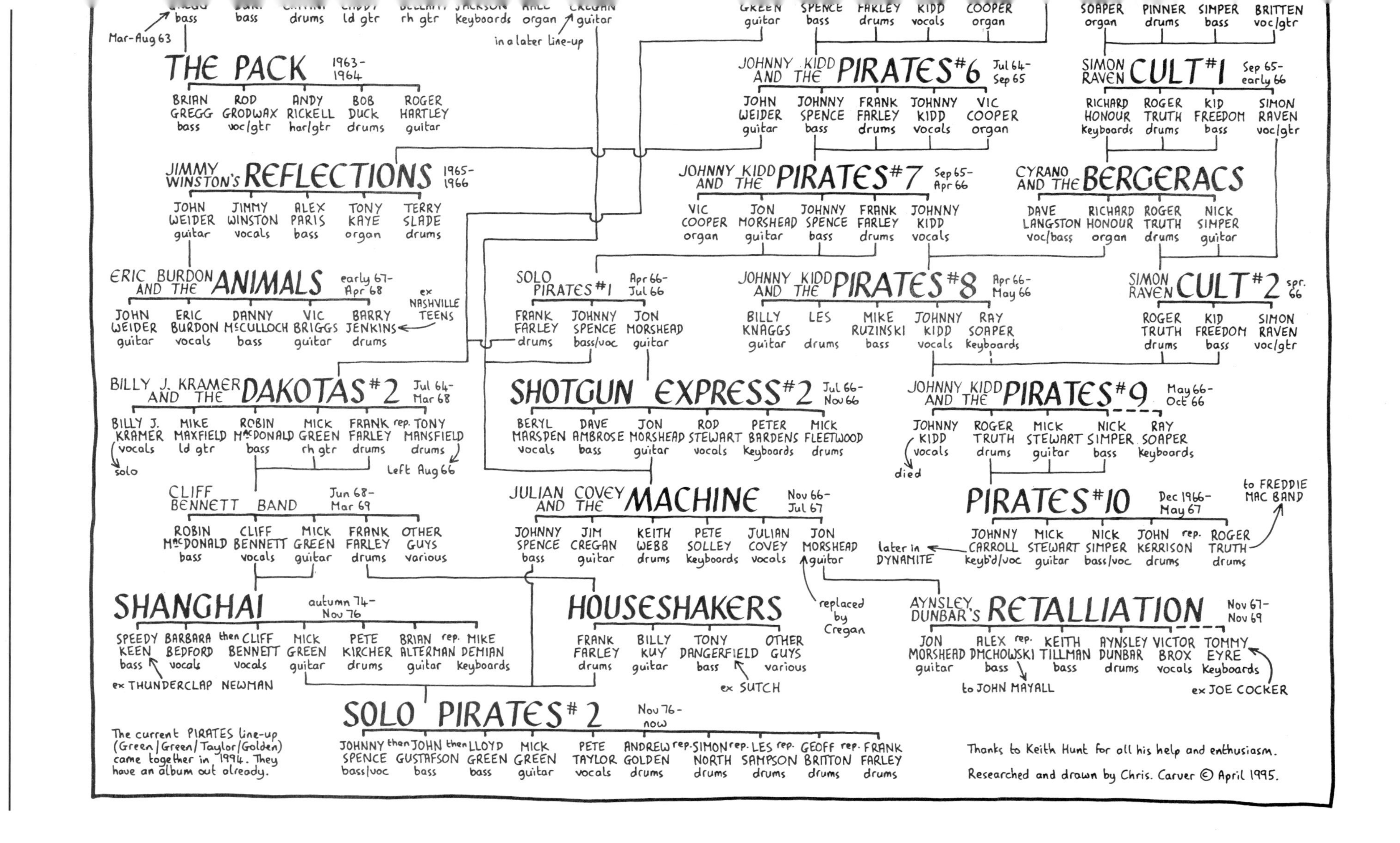
bass
Mar-Aug 63
bass
drums
ld gtr
rh gtr
keyboards
organ
guitar
in a later line-up
THE PACK 1963-1964
BRIAN GREGG bass
ROD GRODWAX voc/gtr
ANDY RICKELL har/gtr
BOB DUCK drums
ROGER HARTLEY guitar
JIMMY WINSTON'S REFLECTIONS 1965-1966
JOHN WEIDER guitar
JIMMY WINSTON vocals
ALEX PARIS bass
TONY KAYE organ
TERRY SLADE drums
ERIC BURDON AND THE ANIMALS early 67-Apr 68
JOHN WEIDER guitar
ERIC BURDON vocals
DANNY McCULLOCH bass
VIC BRIGGS guitar
BARRY JENKINS drums
ex NASHVILLE TEENS
BILLY J. KRAMER AND THE DAKOTAS #2 Jul 64-Mar 68
BILLY J. KRAMER vocals
solo
MIKE MAXFIELD ld gtr
ROBIN McDONALD bass
MICK GREEN rh gtr
FRANK FARLEY drums
rep. TONY MANSFIELD drums
left Aug 66
CLIFF BENNETT BAND Jun 68-Mar 69
ROBIN McDONALD bass
CLIFF BENNETT vocals
MICK GREEN guitar
FRANK FARLEY drums
OTHER GUYS various
SHANGHAI autumn 74-Nov 76
SPEEDY KEEN bass
ex THUNDERCLAP NEWMAN
BARBARA BEDFORD vocals
then CLIFF BENNETT vocals
MICK GREEN guitar
PETE KIRCHER drums
BRIAN ALTERMAN guitar
rep. MIKE DEMIAN keyboards
The current PIRATES line-up (Green/Green/Taylor/Golden) came together in 1994. They have an album out already.
GREEN guitar
SPENCE bass
FARLEY drums
KIDD vocals
COOPER organ
JOHNNY KIDD AND THE PIRATES #6 Jul 64-Sep 65
JOHN WEIDER guitar
JOHNNY SPENCE bass
FRANK FARLEY drums
JOHNNY KIDD vocals
VIC COOPER organ
JOHNNY KIDD AND THE PIRATES #7 Sep 65-Apr 66
VIC COOPER organ
JON MORSHEAD guitar
JOHNNY SPENCE bass
FRANK FARLEY drums
JOHNNY KIDD vocals
SOLO PIRATES #1 Apr 66-Jul 66
FRANK FARLEY drums
JOHNNY SPENCE bass/voc
JON MORSHEAD guitar
JOHNNY KIDD AND THE PIRATES #8 Apr 66-May 66
BILLY KNAGGS guitar
LES drums
MIKE RUZINSKI bass
JOHNNY KIDD vocals
RAY SOAPER keyboards
SHOTGUN EXPRESS #2 Jul 66-Nov 66
BERYL MARSDEN vocals
DAVE AMBROSE bass
JON MORSHEAD guitar
ROD STEWART vocals
PETER BARDENS keyboards
MICK FLEETWOOD drums
JULIAN COVEY AND THE MACHINE Nov 66-Jul 67
JOHNNY SPENCE bass
JIM CREGAN guitar
KEITH WEBB drums
PETE SOLLEY keyboards
JULIAN COVEY vocals
JON MORSHEAD guitar
replaced by Cregan
HOUSESHAKERS
FRANK FARLEY drums
BILLY KUY guitar
TONY DANGERFIELD bass
OTHER GUYS various
ex SUTCH
SOLO PIRATES #2 Nov 76-now
JOHNNY SPENCE bass/voc
then JOHN GUSTAFSON bass
then LLOYD GREEN bass
MICK GREEN guitar
PETE TAYLOR vocals
ANDREW GOLDEN drums
rep. SIMON NORTH drums
rep. LES SAMPSON drums
rep. GEOFF BRITTON drums
rep. FRANK FARLEY drums
SOAPER organ
PINNER drums
SIMPER bass
BRITTEN voc/gtr
SIMON RAVEN CULT #1 Sep 65-early 66
RICHARD HONOUR keyboards
ROGER TRUTH drums
KID FREEDOM bass
SIMON RAVEN voc/gtr
CYRANO AND THE BERGERACS
DAVE LANGSTON voc/bass
RICHARD HONOUR organ
ROGER TRUTH drums
NICK SIMPER guitar
SIMON RAVEN CULT #2 spr. 66
ROGER TRUTH drums
KID FREEDOM bass
SIMON RAVEN voc/gtr
JOHNNY KIDD AND THE PIRATES #9 May 66-Oct 66
JOHNNY KIDD vocals
died
ROGER TRUTH drums
MICK STEWART guitar
NICK SIMPER bass
RAY SOAPER keyboards
PIRATES #10 Dec 1966-May 67
JOHNNY CARROLL keyb'd/voc
later in DYNAMITE
MICK STEWART guitar
NICK SIMPER bass/voc
JOHN KERRISON drums
rep. ROGER TRUTH drums
to FREDDIE MAC BAND
AYNSLEY DUNBAR'S RETALIATION Nov 67-Nov 69
JON MORSHEAD guitar
ALEX DMCHOWSKI bass
to JOHN MAYALL
rep. KEITH TILLMAN bass
AYNSLEY DUNBAR drums
VICTOR BROX vocals
TOMMY EYRE keyboards
ex JOE COCKER
Thanks to Keith Hunt for all his help and enthusiasm.
Researched and drawn by Chris. Carver © April 1995.